SOMETHING ABOUT THE AUTHOR®

Something about
the Author *was named
an "Outstanding
Reference Source,"*
*the highest honor given
by the American
Library Association
Reference and Adult
Services Division.*

ISSN 0276-816X

SOMETHING ABOUT THE AUTHOR®

Facts and Pictures about Authors
and Illustrators of Books for Young People

volume 232

GALE
CENGAGE Learning®

Detroit • New York • San Francisco • New Haven, Conn • Waterville, Maine • London

Something about the Author, Volume 232

Project Editor: Lisa Kumar

Permissions: Leitha Etheridge-Sims

Imaging and Multimedia: Leitha Etheridge-Sims, John Watkins

Composition and Electronic Capture: Amy Darga

Manufacturing: Rhonda Dover

Product Manager: Mary Onorato

For product information and technology assistance, contact us at
Gale Customer Support, 1-800-877-4253.
For permission to use material from this text or product, submit all requests online at **www.cengage.com/permissions**.
Further permissions questions can be emailed to
permissionrequest@cengage.com

Since this page cannot legibly accommodate all copyright notices, the acknowledgments constitute an extension of the copyright notice.

While every effort has been made to ensure the reliability of the information presented in this publication, Gale, a part of Cengage Learning, does not guarantee the accuracy of the data contained herein. Gale accepts no payment for listing; and inclusion in the publication of any organization, agency, institution, publication, service, or individual does not imply endorsement of the editors or publisher. Errors brought to the attention of the publisher and verified to the satisfaction of the publisher will be corrected in future editions.

EDITORIAL DATA PRIVACY POLICY: Does this publication contain information about you as an individual? If so, for more information about our editorial data privacy policies, please see our Privacy Statement at www.gale.cengage.com.

Gale, Cengage Learning
27500 Drake Rd.
Farmington Hills, MI, 48331-3535

LIBRARY OF CONGRESS CATALOG CARD NUMBER 62-52046

ISBN-13: 978-1-4144-6135-9
ISBN-10: 1-4144-6135-6

ISSN 0276-816X

This title is also available as an e-book.
ISBN-13: 978-1-4144-6464-0
ISBN-10: 1-4144-6464-9
Contact your Gale, Cengage Learning sales representative for ordering information.

Printed in Mexico
1 2 3 4 5 6 7 15 14 13 12 11

Contents

Authors in Forthcoming Volumes

Below are some of the authors and illustrators that will be featured in upcoming volumes of *SATA*. These include new entries on the swiftly rising stars of the field, as well as completely revised and updated entries (indicated with *) on some of the most notable and best-loved creators of books for children.

*David Almond ▌ British writer Almond achieved amazing success with his first young-adult novel, *Skellig,* which won several major literary awards, including a Carnegie medal. Other honors have followed for the critically acclaimed books he has written since, including a Michael L. Printz award for *Kit's Wilderness* and a *Boston Globe/Horn Book* award for *The Fire-Eater.* In 2010 Almond accepted the Hans Christian Andersen Award, the highest honor a children's author can receive.

Jessica Bendinger ▌ Bendinger is a screenwriter and director as well as the author of the paranormal novel *The Seven Rays,* which treats teens to a mix of mystery and romance. She is best known for her efforts on *Bring It On,* a hip, sassy cheerleading comedy for which she wrote the screenplay, and *Stick It,* her directorial debut, set in the world of competitive gymnastics.

Monica Brown ▌ Of mixed Hispanic, European, and Jewish ancestry, Brown is a scholar of Latino and multicultural literature as well as the author of a number of entertaining bilingual books for children. Her biographies of noted Hispanic men and women include *My Name Is Celia: The Life of Celia Cruz/Me llamo Celia: La vida de Celia Cruz, My Name Is Gabito: The Life of Gabriel García Márquez/Me llamo Gabito: La vida de Gabriel García Márquez, Pelé, King of Soccer/Pelé, el rey del fútbol,* and *Side by Side: The Story of Dolores Huerta and Cesar Chavez/Lado a lado: La historia de Dolores Huerta y César Chávez.*

*Patrick Carman ▌ Carman's fantasy novels for a middle-grade audience encourage reading while also weaving other media into the mix. While his "Land of Elyon" and "Atherton" books are traditional page-turners, his "Skeleton Key" series incorporates a sequence of Web videos into the narrative. The prolific author has also written several standalone adventures, a mystery novel for adults, as well as the "Elliot's Park" books, which introduce a friendly squirrel and are geared for younger readers. Carman has also contributed to the popular multi-author "39 Clues" mystery series, which focuses on two siblings and their efforts to discover the secret to their family's power.

Leah Cypess ▌ Cypess started work on the manuscript that would grow into her critically praised novel, *Mistwood,* while working her way through law school, and she alternated her time working at a New York City law firm with writing and publishing short fantasy fiction. While completing *Mistwood* she traded her job as an attorney for the challenge of parenting two children. Her ability to multitask has shown success: her companion novel, *Nightspell,* was published only months after *Mistwood* appeared in bookstores.

*Patricia Hermes ▌ In middle-grade and young-adult novels that include *You Shouldn't Have to Say Goodbye, Mama, Let's Dance,* and *Cheat the Moon,* Hermes creates fictional characters who deal with challenges—everything from alcoholic parents and life in foster care to intolerant classmates—while also finding joy and even engaging in a bit of mischief. Her contributions to Scholastic's "My America" series find young people enduring the challenges of various epochs in their nation's history, while her "My Side of the Story" flip-book novels *Salem Witch* and *The Brothers' War* weave together two distinct and contemporary narratives regarding a historic controversy. The author also shows her lighter side in her picture books and the humorous stories in her "Cousins' Club" and "Emily Dilemma" series.

*Sean Qualls ▌ Qualls had an auspicious start to his career in children's-book illustration, earning several awards with only a few publications to his credit. His acrylics-and-mixed-media paintings have continued to earn both honors and praise for their mix of craftsmanship and originality. His work is a highlight of picture books such as Margarita Engle's *The Poet Slave of Cuba: A Biography of Juan Francisco Manzano* and Spike and Tonya Lewis Lee's *Giant Steps to Change the World.*

Kim Vogel Sawyer ▌ Sawyer's fictional characters are inspired by perseverance and a strong Christian faith in novels that include *My Heart Remembers, Waiting for Summer's Return,* and *Courting Miss Amsel* as well as the books in her "Sommerfeld" series. Her stories transport readers to America's heartland and often take place generations in the past, as men, women, and young people confront sometimes conflicting concerns involving their hopes and dreams, their love for others, and their responsibility to do what is right or what is necessary.

Michael Terry ▌ Terry introduces readers to an entertaining storybook character in his self-illustrated picture book *Captain Wag the Pirate Dog,* and its sequels. In addition to his original self-illustrated stories, the British illustrator's images have brought to life tales by such noted children's writers as Vivian French, Ragnhild Scammel, Paul Bright, Dick King-Smith, Sally Grindley, and he has also come to the aid of budding artists by creating the illustrations in his whimsically titled primer *How to Draw Leprechauns in Simple Steps.*

*Terry Windling ▌ Windling has made an enormous impact on the world of fantasy literature as an editor and artist as well as a writer. Best known for editing numerous anthologies of fantasy literature for adults, including the annual *Year's Best Fantasy and Horror* compendiums with Ellen Datlow, she also writes adult novels in addition to authoring and editing works for younger readers. Windling has received a host of honors for her work, including numerous World Fantasy Awards as well as the 2010 Solstice Award from the Science Fiction and Fantasy Writers of America.

Introduction

Something about the Author (*SATA*) is an ongoing reference series that examines the lives and works of authors and illustrators of books for children. *SATA* includes not only well-known writers and artists but also less prominent individuals whose works are just coming to be recognized. This series is often the only readily available information source on emerging authors and illustrators. You'll find *SATA* informative and entertaining, whether you are a student, a librarian, an English teacher, a parent, or simply an adult who enjoys children's literature.

What's Inside *SATA*

SATA provides detailed information about authors and illustrators who span the full time range of children's literature, from early figures like John Newbery and L. Frank Baum to contemporary figures like Judy Blume and Richard Peck. Authors in the series represent primarily English-speaking countries, particularly the United States, Canada, and the United Kingdom. Also included, however, are authors from around the world whose works are available in English translation. The writings represented in *SATA* include those created intentionally for children and young adults as well as those written for a general audience and known to interest younger readers. These writings cover the entire spectrum of children's literature, including picture books, humor, folk and fairy tales, animal stories, mystery and adventure, science fiction and fantasy, historical fiction, poetry and nonsense verse, drama, biography, and nonfiction. Obituaries are also included in many volumes of *SATA* and are intended not only as death notices but also as concise overviews of people's lives and work. Additionally, each edition features newly revised and updated entries for a selection of *SATA* listees who remain of interest to today's readers and who have been active enough to require extensive revisions of their earlier biographies.

Autobiography Feature

Beginning with Volume 103, many volumes of *SATA* feature one or more specially commissioned autobiographical essays. These unique essays, averaging about ten thousand words in length and illustrated with an abundance of personal photos, present an entertaining and informative first-person perspective on the lives and careers of prominent authors and illustrators profiled in *SATA*.

Two Convenient Indexes

In response to suggestions from librarians, *SATA* indexes no longer appear in every volume but are included in alternate (odd-numbered) volumes of the series, beginning with Volume 57.

SATA continues to include two indexes that cumulate with each alternate volume: the Illustrations Index, arranged by the name of the illustrator, gives the number of the volume and page where the illustrator's work appears in the current volume as well as all preceding volumes in the series; the Author Index gives the number of the volume in which a person's biographical sketch, autobiographical essay, or obituary appears in the current volume as well as all preceding volumes in the series.

These indexes also include references to authors and illustrators who appear in *Gale's Yesterday's Authors of Books for Children, Children's Literature Review,* and *Something about the Author Autobiography Series.*

Easy-to-Use Entry Format

Whether you're already familiar with the *SATA* series or just getting acquainted, you will want to be aware of the kind of information that an entry provides. In every *SATA* entry the editors attempt to give as complete a picture of the person's life and work as possible. A typical entry in *SATA* includes the following clearly labeled information sections:

PERSONAL: date and place of birth and death, parents' names and occupations, name of spouse, date of marriage, names of children, educational institutions attended, degrees received, religious and political affiliations, hobbies and other interests.

ADDRESSES: complete home, office, electronic mail, and agent addresses, whenever available.

CAREER: name of employer, position, and dates for each career post; art exhibitions; military service; memberships and offices held in professional and civic organizations.

MEMBER: professional, civic, and other association memberships and any official posts held.

AWARDS, HONORS: literary and professional awards received.

WRITINGS: title-by-title chronological bibliography of books written and/or illustrated, listed by genre when known; lists of other notable publications, such as plays, screenplays, and periodical contributions.

ADAPTATIONS: a list of films, television programs, plays, CD-ROMs, recordings, and other media presentations that have been adapted from the author's work.

WORK IN PROGRESS: description of projects in progress.

SIDELIGHTS: a biographical portrait of the author or illustrator's development, either directly from the biographee—and often written specifically for the *SATA* entry—or gathered from diaries, letters, interviews, or other published sources.

BIOGRAPHICAL AND CRITICAL SOURCES: cites sources quoted in "Sidelights" along with references for further reading.

EXTENSIVE ILLUSTRATIONS: photographs, movie stills, book illustrations, and other interesting visual materials supplement the text.

How a *SATA* Entry Is Compiled

SATA editors examine a wide variety of published sources to gather information for an entry. Biographical and bibliographic sources are consulted, as are book reviews, feature articles, published interviews, and material sometimes obtained from the biographee's family, publishers, agent, or other associates. Whenever possible, the author or illustrator is sent a copy of the entry to check for accuracy and completeness.

Entries that have not been verified by the biographees or their representatives are marked with an asterisk (*).

Contact the Editor

We encourage our readers to examine the entire *SATA* series. Please write and tell us if we can make *SATA* even more helpful to you. Give your comments and suggestions to the editor:

Editor
Something about the Author
Gale, Cengage Learning
27500 Drake Rd.
Farmington Hills MI 48331-3535

Toll-free: 800-877-GALE
Fax: 248-699-8070

Something about the Author Product Advisory Board

The editors of *Something about the Author* are dedicated to maintaining a high standard of excellence by publishing comprehensive, accurate, and highly readable entries on a wide array of writers for children and young adults. In addition to the quality of the content, the editors take pride in the graphic design of the series, which is intended to be orderly yet inviting, allowing readers to utilize the pages of *SATA* easily and with efficiency. Despite the longevity of the *SATA* print series, and the success of its format, we are mindful that the vitality of a literary reference product is dependent on its ability to serve its users over time. As literature, and attitudes about literature, constantly evolve, so do the reference needs of students, teachers, scholars, journalists, researchers, and book club members. To be certain that we continue to keep pace with the expectations of our customers, the editors of *SATA* listen carefully to their comments regarding the value, utility, and quality of the series. Librarians, who have firsthand knowledge of the needs of library users, are a valuable resource for us. The *Something about the Author* Product Advisory Board, made up of school, public, and academic librarians, is a forum to promote focused feedback about *SATA* on a regular basis. The nine-member advisory board includes the following individuals, whom the editors wish to thank for sharing their expertise:

Eva M. Davis
Director,
Canton Public Library,
Canton, Michigan

Joan B. Eisenberg
Lower School Librarian,
Milton Academy,
Milton, Massachusetts

Francisca Goldsmith
Teen Services Librarian,
Berkeley Public Library,
Berkeley, California

Susan Dove Lempke
Children's Services Supervisor,
Niles Public Library District,
Niles, Illinois

Robyn Lupa
Head of Children's Services,
Jefferson County Public Library,
Lakewood, Colorado

Victor L. Schill
Assistant Branch Librarian/Children's Librarian,
Harris County Public Library/Fairbanks Branch,
Houston, Texas

Caryn Sipos
Community Librarian,
Three Creeks Community Library,
Vancouver, Washington

Steven Weiner
Director,
Maynard Public Library,
Maynard, Massachusetts

SOMETHING ABOUT THE AUTHOR

AKBARPOUR, Ahmad 1970-

Personal

Born July 31, 1970, in Lamerd, Fars, Iran. *Education:* Shahid Beheshti University, degree.

Addresses

Home—Shiraz, Iran.

Career

Novelist and author of children's books.

Awards, Honors

Prix Mehregan (France); Iranian National Book Award; Honor Book selection, International Board on Books for Young People (IBBY), 2006, for *Emperatur-e Kalamat;* Outstanding Books for Young People with Disabilities selection, IBBY, 2010, for *Good Night, Commander.*

Writings

Shab Bekheyr Farmandeh!, illustrated by Morteza Zahedi, 2003, translated from the Iranian by Shadi Eskandani and Helen Mixter as *Good Night, Commander,* Groundwood Books (Toronto, Ontario, Canada), 2010.

Also author of novels, poetry, and short fiction for adults as well as children's stories published in Persian, including *Ghatar-e An Shab,* 1998; *Emperatur-e Kalamat,* 2002; and *Ro'yahay-e Jonoubi,* 2005.

Author's works have been translated into French.

Sidelights

Iranian poet-turned-novelist Ahman Akbarpour draws on his Iranian heritage in the stories he writes for younger readers. In the picture book *Good Night, Commander,* he creates an "almost unbearably poignant" story describing the experiences of a young boy during the 1980s Iran-Iraq War, according to a *Publishers Weekly* critic. While Akbarpour's fellow Iranians may well relate to the depictions of war in his compelling story, *Good Night, Commander* also speaks to children in other countries, particularly those who are dealing with emotional loss and disabilities.

Illustrated with sparely tinted, naïf-style line drawings by Morteza Zahedi, *Good Night, Commander* focuses on a young boy who is grieving both the death of his mother and the loss of one of his legs as a result of the bombings in his native Iran. Although the war is now over, the boy's memories of the violence remain, and he views his father's decision to remarry as a betrayal of his dead mother. Alone in his room, the boy gives way to his feelings through play-acting with his toy soldiers, guns, and military vehicles: as a commander, he leads an army forward to conquer the same troops that

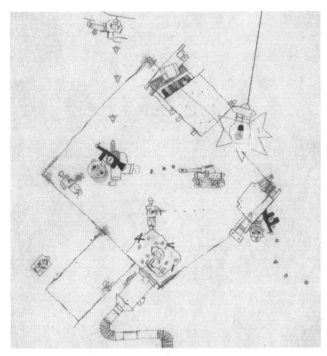

Iranian author Ahmad Akbarpour teams up with artist Morteza Zahedi to present a picture-book viw of the tragic effects of war on childhood in **Good Night, Commander.** (Illustration copyright © 2005 by Morteza Zahedi. Reproduced by permission of Groundwood Books.)

killed his mother and left him disabled. The young commander feels the satisfaction of conquest and a sense that justice has been done until he realizes that the leader of the enemy troops is the mirror image of himself: a sad little boy with one leg.

Akbarpour's "approach lends authenticity to the child's voice," asserted *Canadian Review of Materials* critic Marilynne V. Black, the reviewer adding of *Good Night, Commander* that the book will help children of many ages "understand the impact of wars on children much like themselves—the futility of war and the carnage inflicted by it." In *School Library Journal* Maryann H. Owen described Zahedi's pencil drawings as "unusual and disquieting," adding that *Good Night, Commander* is an "unusual picture book" that will be useful in starting "a discussion of the impact of war on innocent children." The book's "wobbly, childlike sketches reinforce the direct perspective of a child struggling to process horrific events," asserted a *Kirkus Reviews* writer, and in *Booklist* John Peters deemed Akbarpour's "purposeful" tale "an effective springboard for thought and discussion."

Biographical and Critical Sources

PERIODICALS

Booklist, May 1, 2010, John Peters, review of *Good Night, Commander,* p. 86.
Kirkus Reviews, April 15, 2010, review of *Good Night, Commander.*

Publishers Weekly, April 12, 2010, review of *Good Night, Commander,* p. 49.
School Library Journal, May, 2010, Maryann H. Owen, review of *Good Night, Commander,* p. 78.

ONLINE

Ahman Akbarpour Home Page, http://ahmadakbarpoor. blogfa.com (August 15, 2011).
Canadian Review of Materials Online, http://www. umanitoba.ca/cm/ (April 2, 2010), Marilynne V. Black, review of *Good Night, Commander.*
Paper Tigers Web site, http://www.papertigers.org/ (August, 2010), Charlotte Richardson, review of *Good Night, Commander.*

* * *

ALEXANDER, Heather 1967-

Personal

Born 1967. *Education:* Earned college degree.

Addresses

Home—Basking Ridge, NJ.

Career

Writer and editor. Parachute Press, New York, NY, former vice president and editorial director.

Writings

FICTION

Look inside Your Brain (based on the story by Paola Panizon), illustrated by Nicoletta Costa, Grosset & Dunlap (New York, NY), 1991.
Allie Gator's Halloween Hayride, illustrated by Ted Williams, Running Press (Philadelphia, PA), 2006.
All around the Farm, Parachute Press (New York, NY), 2007.
Breakup Blues (novelization), Grosset & Dunlap (New York, NY), 2008.
Allie Gator and the Mixed-up Scarecrow, illustrated by Dave Hill, Running Press Kids (Philadelphia, PA), 2010.
Spider-man and the Movie Mystery, HarperFestival (New York, NY), 2011.

"NEW ADVENTURES OF MARY KATE AND ASHLEY" CHAPTER-BOOK SERIES

The Case of Camp Pom-Pom, HarperEntertainment (New York, NY), 2003.

The Case of the Tattooed Cat, HarperEntertainment (New York, NY), 2003.
The Case of the Easter Egg Race, HarperEntertainment (New York, NY), 2004.
The Case of the Unicorn Mystery, HarperEntertainment (New York, NY), 2005.

"WIZARDS OF WAVERLY PLACE" CHAPTER-BOOK SERIES

(Adaptor) *In Your Face,* Disney Press (New York, NY), 2008.
(Adaptor) *Win or Lose,* Disney Press (New York, NY), 2008.
(Adaptor) *Super Switch,* Disney Press (New York, NY), 2009.
(Adaptor) *Top of the Class,* Disney Press (New York, NY), 2009.
(Adaptor) *All Mixed Up,* Disney Press (New York, NY), 2009.

NONFICTION

(Coauthor) Oksana Baiul, *Oksana: My Own Story,* Random House (New York, NY), 1997.
Big Book of Tractors, Parachute Press (New York, NY), 2007.
Big Book of Construction Machines, Parachute Press (New York, NY), 2009.
A Child's Introduction to the World: Geography, Cultures, and People: From the Grand Canyon to the Great Wall of China, illustrated by Meredith Hamilton, Black Dog & Leventhal (New York, NY), 2010.
A Child's Introduction to Greek Mythology: The Stories of the Gods, Goddesses, Heroes, Monsters, and Other Mythical Creatures, illustrated by Meredith Hamilton, Black Dog & Leventhal (New York, NY), 2011.
Easy Desserts from around the World, Enslow Publishers (Berkeley Heights, NJ), 2011.
Easy Main Dishes from around the World, Enslow Publishers (Berkeley Heights, NJ), 2011.
Easy Snacks from around the World, Enslow Publishers (Berkeley Heights, NJ), 2011.

Biographical and Critical Sources

PERIODICALS

Children's Bookwatch, July, 2010, review of *A Child's Introduction to the World: Geography, Cultures, and People: From the Grand Canyon to the Great Wall of China.*
Kirkus Reviews, April 15, 2010, review of *A Child's Introduction to the World.*
School Library Journal, January, 1992, Denise L. Moll, review of *Look inside Your Brain,* p. 101; May, 1997, review of *Oksana: My Own Story,* p. 142.

ONLINE

Workman Publishing Web site, http://www.workman.com/ (August 15, 2011), "Heather Alexander."*

ALEXANDER, R.C.
(Robert C. Alexander)

Personal

Married; children: one son. *Education:* Earned college degree; pursued Ph.D.

Addresses

Home—FL.

Career

Writer. Worked as a theatre director and in business.

Writings

Unfamiliar Magic, Random House (New York, NY), 2010.

Biographical and Critical Sources

PERIODICALS

School Library Journal, April, 2010, Kathy Kirchoefer, review of *Unfamiliar Magic,* p. 150.
Voice of Youth Advocates, August, 2010, Chris Carlson, review of *Unfamiliar Magic,* p. 260.

ONLINE

R.C. Alexander Home Page, http://unfamiliarmagic.com (August 16, 2011).*

*   *   *

ALEXANDER, Robert C.
See ALEXANDER, R.C.

*   *   *

ALPHIN, Elaine Marie 1955-

Personal

Born October 30, 1955, in San Francisco, CA; daughter of Richard E. (a United Nations procurement officer) and Janice Bonilla; married Arthur B. Alphin (a retired army officer and president and CEO of two companies), May 9, 1982. *Education:* Rice University, B.A., 1977. *Hobbies and other interests:* Puzzles, dinosaurs, theater, needlework, collecting teddy bears and other stuffed animals, raising hamsters.

Addresses

Home—Bozeman, MT; Glenrock, WY; Chamberlain, SD. *Office*—P.O. Box 11423, Bozeman, MT 59719. *E-mail*—ElaineMAlphin@aol.com.

Elaine Marie Alphin (Photograph by Arthur B. Alphin. Reproduced by permission.)

Career

Editor and author. *Rice Thresher,* Houston, TX, writer and department editor, 1974-76; *Houston* (city magazine), feature writer and editor, 1978-79; freelance writer, 1978—; A-Square Company, Cornwall-on-Hudson, NY, Madison, IN, and Bedford, KY, advertising manager and technical service, 1982-93; Hieroglyphics Unlimited, Madison, IN, then Bedford, KY, owner and cross-stitch designer, beginning 1986. Institute of Children's Literature, West Redding, CT, writing instructor, beginning 1992. Speaker at conferences, workshops, and schools.

Member

Author's Guild, Society of Children's Book Writers & Illustrators (Indiana chapter; advisory council member, beginning 1991), Association of American University Women, Psi Iota Xi Philanthropic Sorority (corresponding secretary, 1992-93), Central Indiana Writers' Association, Children's Reading Round Table of Chicago, Bloomington Children's Authors Group.

Awards, Honors

Magazine Merit Award (fiction), Society of Children's Book Writers and Illustrators (SCBWI), 1989, for "A Song in the Dark"; First Prize (fictional detectives), Soda Creek Press, for "Sherlock Holmes"; SCBWI works-in-progress grant, 1989; Recommended Book for Reluctant Readers selection, American Library Association, 1993, for *The Proving Ground;* SCBWI Magazine Merit Award (nonfiction), 1994, for "Cornflower's Test"; Young Readers Award for Best Book (elementary), Virginia State Reading Association, 1995, for *The Ghost Cadet;* Commended selection, Consortium of Latin

American Studies Program, 1996, and New Jersey Garden State Award listee, 1999-2000, both for *A Bear for Miguel;* honorary M.F.A., and International Washington Irving Literary Award for Outstanding Lifetime Achievement in Writing, Indianapolis Christian University, both 2000; Best Children's Books selection, *St. Louis Post-Dispatch,* 2000, Quick Pick for Reluctant Young-Adult Readers selection, YALSA, and Edgar Allan Poe Award for Best Young-Adult Mystery, Mystery Writers of America, both 2001, and Honor Book selection (language arts grades 7-12), Society of School Librarians International, 2002, all for *Counterfeit Son;* Edgar Allan Poe Award nomination, and Children's Fiction Award, Society of Midland Authors, both 2002, and Young Hoosier Award, 2004, all for *Ghost Soldier;* Best Children's Books selection, Bank Street College of Education, 2003, for *Germ Hunter,* 2004, for *I Have Not Yet Begun to Fight; ForeWord* Book of the Year selection, 2005, for *The Perfect Shot;* Carter G. Woodson Book Award, National Council of the Social Studies, 2005, and Honor Book selection, Society of School Librarians International, National Jewish Book Award finalist, Sydney Taylor Notable Book selection, Association of Jewish Libraries, and IPPY Gold Medal for Juvenile-Teen-Young Adult Nonfiction, all 2011, all for *An Unspeakable Crime.*

Writings

The Ghost Cadet, Henry Holt (New York, NY), 1991.
The Proving Ground, Henry Holt (New York, NY), 1992.
101 Bible Puzzles, Standard, 1993.
Rainy Day/Sunny Day/Any Day Activities, Concordia, 1994.
Tournament of Time, Bluegrass Books (Pewee Valley, KY), 1994.
A Bear for Miguel, HarperCollins (New York, NY), 1996.
Vacuum Cleaners, Carolrhoda (Minneapolis, MN), 1997.
Irons, Carolrhoda (Minneapolis, MN), 1998.
Toasters, Carolrhoda (Minneapolis, MN), 1998.
Counterfeit Son, Harcourt (San Diego, CA), 2000.
Creating Characters Kids Will Love, Writer's Digest (Cincinnati, OH), 2000.
Telephones, Carolrhoda (Minneapolis, MN), 2001.
Simon Says, Harcourt (San Diego, CA), 2002.
Davy Crockett, Lerner (Minneapolis, MN), 2002.
Dinosaur Hunter, illustrated by Don Bolognese, HarperCollins (New York, NY), 2003.
Germ Hunter: A Story about Louis Pasteur, illustrated by Elaine Verstraete, Carolrhoda Books (Minneapolis, MN), 2003.
Picture Perfect, Carolrhoda Books (Minneapolis, MN), 2003.
(With husband Arthur B. Alphin) *I Have Not Yet Begun to Fight: A Story about John Paul Jones,* illustrated by Paul Casale, Carolrhoda Books (Minneapolis, MN), 2004.
(With Arthur B. Alphin) *Dwight D. Eisenhower,* Lerner Publications (Minneapolis, MN), 2005.

The Perfect Shot, Carolrhoda Books (Minneapolis, MN), 2006.

An Unspeakable Crime: The Prosecution and Persecution of Leo Frank, Carolrhoda Books (Minneapolis, MN), 2010.

Contributor of stories and articles to periodicals, including *Child Life, Children's Digest, Cricket, Highlights for Children, Hopscotch, On the Line, Primary Treasure,* and *Teen Quest.* Contributor to anthologies, including *The Favorites,* Institute of Children's Literature, 1991; *Writer's Digest Children's Writers & Illustrator's Market,* Writer's Digest, 1992; *Children's Magazine Market,* Institute of Children's Literature, 1993; *Success Stories,* Institute of Children's Literature, 1994; and *But That's Another Story,* Walker, 1996. Contributor to "Power Reading" series, National Reading Styles Institute (Syosset, NY), 2001. Columnist for *Children's Writer* (newsletter), beginning 1993.

Sidelights

In novels such as *The Ghost Cadet, Counterfeit Son,* and *The Perfect Shot,* Elaine Marie Alphin introduces adolescent protagonists who overcome challenges by the power of their imagination. In addition to fiction, Alphin has also turned her talent to nonfiction, producing biographies such as *Germ Hunter: A Story about Louis Pasteur* and *I Have Not Yet Begun to Fight: A Story about John Paul Jones* as well as the compelling *An Unspeakable Crime: The Prosecution and Persecution of Leo Frank,* which focuses on prejudice in early twentieth-century America. "There is often danger, and my heroes must find the courage and conviction to put themselves on the line for what they believe," the author once commented to *SATA.* "I also think that young readers should know more about how exciting history can be, so I often write about mysteries set in the present but rooted in the past, which are complicated by ghosts who can transcend time."

Alphin's love of writing has motivated her throughout her life. "As an only child growing up in San Francisco, I was solitary and introspective," she once recalled. "I loved words and characters, and I loved escaping into a world of the imagination in which I could right all wrongs and change the realities I saw around me. I used to go on long walks with my father on Sunday mornings, and he would tell me stories—funny stories, fractured history, all kinds of stories that made me long to create my own. My parents had an old Royal typewriter with a wide grin and a black-and-red ribbon, and as soon as I taught myself to write I'd bang out stories on it."

Alphin and her family moved to New York State when she was nine years old, and she spent her high-school years in Houston, Texas. She stayed in Houston to earn her degree at Rice University, and there she became involved with a college theater group, wrote for the school newspaper, and completed four novel-length manuscripts, one each year while earning her degree. One of these novels, *Simon Says,* was eventually published and explores the choices teens make regarding whether to live up to the expectations of others or pay the price of nonconformity. Writing for *Booklist,* Frances Bradburn called *Simon Says* "a layered, complex book, full of challenge for thoughtful readers."

Alphin's first published novel, *Ghost Cadet,* is geared for middle-grade readers and finds Benjy unenthusiastic about spending his spring vacation with his older sister and Miss Loetta, the grandmother he has never met. However, when Benjy meets Hugh, the ghost of a Virginia Military Institute cadet, his stay at his grandmother's house becomes more exciting. Now the boy has something important to do: help the ghostly Hugh restore his honor by locating a watch the cadet hid during a U.S. Civil War battle. In the *New York Times* David Haward Bain praised *Ghost Cadet,* writing that, "out of solid research and a clear regard for Virginia's history and heritage, Ms. Alphin has written a fine novel."

Also featuring elements of the supernatural, *Ghost Soldier* again mines the history of the U.S. Civil War. On a visit to a wartime battlefield in North Carolina, Alexander Raskin finds himself accompanied by the ghost of Richeson Francis Chamblee, a Confederate fatality who cannot rest until he finds out whether his family survived Union General George Sherman's notorious "march to the sea." As the preteen investigates the fate of the man's family, he comes to some resolutions about his own troubled home life. Alphin "provides an interesting lesson on how historical research occurs," wrote *Booklist* critic Denise Wilms, while Starr E. Smith described *Ghost Soldier* in *School Library Journal* as "an entertaining blend of paranormal, historical and family themes, with a well-crafted plot that ties up all loose ends in a satisfying conclusion."

In *The Proving Ground* Alphin introduces a ninth grader named Kevin. It has been challenging making new friends every time his U.S. Army-officer dad moves the family, but Kevin finds their latest relocation, to Hadley, Kentucky, particularly difficult for an "Army brat." The townspeople of Hadley have loathed the presence of the army ever since the U.S. government confiscated privately owned land years before. As Kevin learns the reason for one girl's bitterness, he also uncovers a plot to blow up the ammunition proving ground where his father works. Jack Forman, a reviewer for *School Library Journal,* appreciated the "deft mixture of adventure, a romantic undercurrent, local politics, and development of character" in *The Proving Ground,* and a *Publishers Weekly* critic deemed Alphin's novel "a suspenseful, true-to-life coming-of-age story."

Alphin shifts genres, moving from historical novel to psychological thriller in *Counterfeit Son.* Cameron Miller's father is a serial murderer who has kidnaped and killed more than twenty boys. When the man is killed in a shoot-out with police, Cameron decides to claim that he is not his father's son, but rather one of his victims. Masquerading as Neil Lacey, one of the boys his father killed six years ago, Cameron "reunites" with Mr. and Mrs. Lacey and their surviving children, viewing the event as his chance at a normal life with a loving family. Then one of his father's old friends reappears and threatens to ruin everything Cameron has gained. *Counterfeit Son* is "solidly written, fast-paced," and "gripping," asserted Miranda Doyle in a review of the novel for *School Library Journal*. In *Booklist* Todd Morning declared of the same work that "Alphin has done a creditable job" of depicting the psychology of a boy who has suffered horrible abuse and looks for safety in a safe and secure family.

Another father runs afoul of the law in *The Perfect Shot*, but this time the charge is leveled against the neighbor of a high-school basketball star. Brian is in his yard shooting baskets the day his neighbor and best friend Amanda is shot and killed, along with her mom and little brother. The teen is both saddened and amazed when Amanda's father is subsequently arrested for the crime. However, during a classroom project involving research into a real-life murder and miscarriage of justice dating back to 1913, Brian begins to question the man's guilt and wonders whether his sighting of a jogger in the neighborhood on the day of the murder might be relevant to the case. Although his father discourages the teen from going to the police, Brian's class assignment forces him to view his role as a potential witness more seriously. "Alphin scores big with this novel," asserted a *Publishers Weekly* reviewer in appraising *The Perfect Shot,* the critic adding that the teen's gradual "awakening to a sense of personal integrity and responsibility . . . is convincing." A *Kirkus Reviews* writer noted the broad appeal of the novel: "With basketball action, a murder mystery, a compelling story from history, [and] adolescent angst," *The Perfect Shot* should appeal to "most young readers," the critic asserted.

The "compelling story from history" that serves as Brian's class assignment in *The Perfect Shot* is the true-life nineteenth-century crime involving Leo Frank and the murder of Mary Phagan. Highly publicized at the time, the case has since been dramatized in books and film, not only due to the drama of the crime and the resulting trial but also because it led to a miscarriage of justice: the condemned Frank was lynched as a murderer but then shown to be innocent by a witness who came forward too late. When Alphin first discovered the Frank case, she knew "it possessed all the things I feel most passionate about: injustice, extreme political corruption and extreme political integrity, and teenagers poised to either act responsibly or succumb to peer and community pressure," as she noted on her home page. She wrote *The Perfect Shot* as a way of weaving the story into a contemporary novel and allowing the tragedy of Frank's death to inspire her young character. However, as she noted, "the case stayed with me, demanding something more." After in-depth research into

the 1913 murder, which took place in Atlanta, Georgia, she produced the award-winning nonfiction work *An Unspeakable Crime*.

In *An Unspeakable Crime* Alphin uses her storytelling skills in recounting the events surrounding the murder of a young teen and the tragic aftermath that resulted in the establishment of the Anti-Defamation League as well as the re-emergence of the Ku Klux Klan. Her well-illustrated chronicle begins in the spring of 1913, when thirteen-year-old factory worker Mary Phagan disappeared while requesting her pay from Leo Frank, manager of the National Pencil Company. When the girl's body was found near Frank's office, Frank was quickly accused, arrested, and put on trial. Disliked in the Southern community because he was from the North, he was also looked upon with suspicion because of his Jewish faith. Frank was convicted after a show trial, but his death sentence was later commuted by Georgia's governor and this act prompted an angry citizenry to lynch him. Frank was posthumously pardoned in 1986. Alphin's use of a "strictly chronological structure . . . is extremely helpful in understanding both the progression of the case . . . and the impact of anti-

Alphin's stories for younger children include A Bear for Miguel, *a picture book featuring artwork by Joan Sandin.* (Illustration copyright © 1996 by Joan Sandin. Reproduced by permission of HarperCollins Children's Books, a division of HarperCollins Publishers.)

Semitism and resentment toward Northerners" that influenced a Southern populace still nursing anger over the loss of the Confederacy during the U.S. Civil War, according to *School Library Journal* contributor Ann Welton. "Fans of legal thrillers and courtroom dramas will find this outstanding," a *Kirkus Reviews* writer asserted in reviewing *An Unspeakable Crime*, and in *Booklist* Hazel Rochman praised Alphin for her detailed research and her ability to link the Frank case "with the contemporary ongoing struggle by the underprivileged for fair judicial process."

In addition to her books for older readers, Alphin has also entertained younger children with *A Bear for Miguel,* a picture book about a girl in the war-torn El Salvador of the 1980s who trades her teddy bear for butter, cheese, and milk for her family. The parents who barter for her teddy bear want it for their son, Miguel, who has been gravely injured by some of the fighters. The girl is sad to see her toy go at first, but she soon realizes how happy Miguel will be to get it and how much her struggling family will appreciate the extra food. *A Bear for Miguel* was praised as "sensitive and compelling" by Gale W. Sherman, who reviewed it for *School Library Journal. Horn Book* critic Maeve Visser Knoth echoed this praise, commenting of Alphin's tale that "the details of life in war-torn El Salvador are grim yet do not overwhelm this compassionate story."

In addition to her fiction, Alphin has also contributed books to the "Household History" series, which covers the development and mechanics of such common household items as irons, telephones, toasters, and vacuums. "Comprehensive and fascinating," a *Kirkus Reviews* contributor wrote in a review of *Toasters,* while another critic for the same periodical expressed amazement at "how much there is to say about such a humdrum device" as a vacuum cleaner.

"When I talk to kids about writing, I always stress how much *fun* writing is," Alphin once noted. "I can think of no more wonderful way to spend my life than writing." She also admits that writing is sometimes hard work. "As much as my writing is a joy, it is also a business, and I'm as professional as possible in my work schedule. My days are filled with writing and researching. In addition to writing my novels I research a good deal of nonfiction for biography and science articles for magazines like *Cricket* and *Highlights for Children.* I usually work in my office at least eight hours a day, and sometimes longer." Alphin also mentioned that "there are times when I get lost in my writing and hours go by and when it's time for supper I'm stiff and exhausted and utterly drained because I've poured all I had into the writing. Evenings like that we send out for pizza."

Biographical and Critical Sources

BOOKS

Science Fiction and Fantasy Literature, 1975-1991, Gale (Detroit, MI), 1992.

PERIODICALS

Booklist, March 15, 1995, Carolyn Phelan, review of *Tournament of Time,* p. 1327; August, 1996, Carolyn Phelan, review of *A Bear for Miguel,* p. 1910; January 1, 1998, Denia Hester, review of *Vacuum Cleaners,* p. 796; September 15, 2000, Todd Morning, review of *Counterfeit Son,* p. 231; August, 2001, Denise Wilms, review of *Ghost Soldier,* p. 2118; April 15, 2002, Frances Bradburn, review of *Simon Says,* p. 1394; August, 2003, Debbie Carton, review of *Picture Perfect,* p. 1970; September 1, 2003, Carolyn Phelan, review of *Dinosaur Hunter,* p. 127; January 1, 2010, Hazel Rochman, review of *An Unspeakable Crime: The Prosecution and Persecution of Leo Frank,* p. 58.

Horn Book, May-June, 1996, Maeve Visser Knoth, review of *A Bear for Miguel,* pp. 331-332; January-February, 2004, Martha V. Parravano, review of *Dinosaur Hunter,* p. 78.

Kirkus Reviews, November 15, 1992, p. 1437; November, 1, 1997, review of *Vacuum Cleaners,* p. 1640; April 15, 1998, review of *Toasters,* p. 576; April 1, 2002, review of *Simon Says,* p. 486.

New York Times, May 19, 1991, David Haward Bain, review of *The Ghost Cadet;* July 1, 2003, review of *Picture Perfect,* p. 905; September 1, 2003, review of *Dinosaur Hunter;* August 15, 2005, review of *The Perfect Shot;* February 15, 2010, review of *An Unspeakable Crime.*

Kliatt, September, 2005, Jessica Swaim, review of *Simon Says,* p. 17; November, 2005, Janis Flint-Ferguson, review of *The Perfect Shot,* p. 4; January, 2007, Stephanie Squicciarini, review of *Picture Perfect,* p. 20.

Publishers Weekly, November 16, 1992, review of *The Proving Ground,* p. 65; August 28, 2000, review of *Counterfeit Son,* p. 84; May 20, 2002, review of *Simon Says,* p. 68; August 4, 2003, review of *Picture Perfect,* p. 81; November 7, 2005, review of *The Perfect Shot,* p. 75.

School Library Journal, January, 1993, Jack Forman, review of *The Proving Ground,* p. 96; June, 1996, Gale W. Sherman, review of *A Bear for Miguel,* p. 92; July, 1998, Stephanie Hutchinson, reviews of *Toasters* and *Irons,* both p. 101; December, 2000, Miranda Doyle, review of *Counterfeit Son,* p. 138; August, 2001, Starr E. Smith, review of *Ghost Soldier,* p. 175; June, 2002, Vicki Reutter, review of *Simon Says,* p. 130; December, 2002, Anne Chapman Callaghan, review of *Davy Crockett,* p. 114; July, 2003, Donna Cardon, review of *Germ Hunter: A Story about Louis Pasteur,* p. 136; October, 2003, Lynn Evarts, review of *Picture Perfect,* p. 158; December, 2003, Anne Knickerbocker, review of *Dinosaur Hunter,* p. 102; January, 2005, Christine E. Carr, review of *Dwight D. Eisenhower,* p. 101; August, 2005, Blair Christolon, review of *Ghost Soldier,* p. 49; October, 2005, Miranda Doyle, review of *The Perfect Shot,* p. 150; March, 2010, Ann Welton, review of *An Unspeakable Crime,* p. 170.

ONLINE

Elaine Marie Alphin Home Page, http://www.elainemarie
    alphin.com (August 15, 2011).
Elaine Marie Alphin Web Log, http://elainealphin.blogspot.
    com (August 15, 2011).*

*   *   *

ANTHONY, Joëlle

Personal

Born in Portland, OR; married Victor Anthony (a musician). *Education:* B.A. (theatre). *Hobbies and other interests:* Cooking, knitting, reading, walking.

Addresses

Home—Gabriola Island, British Columbia, Canada. *Agent*—Michael Bourret, Dystel & Goderich Literary Management, 1 Union Sq. W., Ste. 904, New York, NY 10003. *E-mail*—restoringharmony10@yahoo.com.

Cover of Joelle Anthony's compelling novel Restoring Harmony, *a teen novel featuring artwork by Hugh Syme.* (Illustration copyright © 2010 by Hugh Syme. Reproduced by permission of G.P. Putnam's Sons, a division of Penguin Young Readers Group, a member of Penguin Group (USA) Inc., 345 Hudson St., New York, NY 10014. All rights reserved.)

Career

Writer. Actor in films, including *Permanent Record,* 1988, *Men of Honor,* 2000, *What the #$*! Do We (K)now!?,* 2004, and *What the Bleep!?: Down the Rabbit Hole,* 2006.

Member

Society of Children's Book Writers and Illustrators.

Writings

Restoring Harmony (novel), Putnam's (New York, NY), 2010.

Contributor to periodicals, including *Society of Children's Book Writers and Illustrators Bulletin.*

Sidelights

A former actress who lives in British Columbia, Canada, Joëlle Anthony is the author of the dystopian novel *Restoring Harmony,* "a suspenseful and highly entertaining read," according to *School Library Journal* critic Jane Henriksen Baird. The idea for *Restoring Harmony* came to Anthony after she read an excerpt from *The Long Emergency,* a 2005 work by James Howard Kunstler that predicted an era of economic, social, and political chaos in the United States that would be driven largely by the depletion of global oil reserves.

Set in 2041, ten years after the "Great Collapse," *Restoring Harmony* focuses on Molly McClure, a sixteen-year-old fiddle player who lives with her family on a small, isolated Canadian island where they grow their own food, rely on solar power for their energy needs, and travel by bicycle and horseback. After learning that her grandmother has fallen seriously ill, Molly undertakes a harsh and dangerous journey to Oregon. There she locates her other grandparents, who are destitute and starving. With help from "Spill," a charismatic young man, Molly begins a neighborhood garden and mothers a pair of orphaned children, although her efforts are threatened by the leaders of a local crime organization. "Molly is smart, plucky, and determined to do what must be done to fulfill her mission," Hillary Crew stated in her *Voice of Youth Advocates* review of *Restoring Harmony,* and a *Publishers Weekly* critic similarly noted that Anthony's "focus is on Molly's toughness and ability to handle and overcome problems." Despite the often bleak subject matter of *Restoring Harmony,* the novel's "tone is hopeful," Cindy Welch remarked in *Booklist,* and Baird deemed *Restoring Harmony* "a surprisingly upbeat and hopeful look at the future."

Biographical and Critical Sources

PERIODICALS

Booklist, May 15, 2010, Cindy Welch, review of *Restoring Harmony,* p. 50.

Publishers Weekly, April 26, 2010, review of *Restoring Harmony,* p. 111.

School Library Journal, August, 2010, Jane Henriksen Baird, review of *Restoring Harmony,* p. 93.

Voice of Youth Advocates, August, 2010, Hillary Crew, review of *Restoring Harmony,* p. 260.

ONLINE

Joëlle Anthony Home Page, http://joelleanthony.com (July 1, 2011).*

B

BARNHOLDT, Lauren 1980(?)-

Personal

Born c. 1980, in Syracuse, NY.

Addresses

Home—Waltham, MA. *Agent*—Alyssa Eisner Henkin, Trident Media Group, 41 Madison Ave., Fl. 36, New York, NY 10010; ahenkin@tridentmediagroup.com. *E-mail*—lauren@laurenbarnholdt.com.

Career

Writer. Formerly worked for Firebrand Literary Agency; teacher of online writing courses.

Awards, Honors

Books for the Teen Age selection, New York Public Library, and Popular Paperbacks for Young Adults designation, American Library Association, both 2007, both for *Two-way Street.*

Writings

Reality Chick, Simon Pulse (New York, NY), 2006.
(Editor) *Fab Girls Guide to Sticky Situations,* Discovery Girls (San Jose, CA), 2007.
The Secret Identity of Devon Delaney, Aladdin Mix (New York, NY), 2007.
Two-way Street, Simon Pulse (New York, NY), 2007.
Four Truths and a Lie, Aladdin (New York, NY), 2008.
Devon Delaney Should Totally Know Better, Aladdin (New York, NY), 2009.
Aces Up, Delacorte Press (New York, NY), 2010.
Hailey Twitch Is Not a Snitch, illustrated by Suzanne Beaky, Sourcebooks Jabberwocky (Naperville, IL), 2010.
Hailey Twitch and the Great Teacher Switch, illustrated by Suzanne Beaky, Sourcebooks Jabberwocky (Naperville, IL), 2010.

One Night That Changes Everything, Simon Pulse (New York, NY), 2010.
Rules for Secret Keeping, Aladdin (New York, NY), 2010.
Watch Me, Simon Pulse (New York, NY), 2010.
Hailey Twitch and the Campground Itch, illustrated by Suzanne Beaky, Sourcebooks Jabberwocky (Naperville, IL), 2010.
Sometimes It Happens, Simon Pulse (New York, NY), 2011.

Contributor to periodicals, including *Elements* and *Girls' Life.*

Sidelights

Massachusetts-based writer Lauren Barnholdt is the author of more than a dozen books, including novels for young adults and preteens and chapter books for apprentice readers. In addition to her fantasy series featuring the whimsically named second grader Hailey Twitch, Barnholdt entertains older readers with novels such as *Reality Chick, Two-way Street, One Night That Changes Everything,* and *Watch Me.* Illustrated by Suzanne Beaky, *Hailey Twitch Is Not a Switch* features an "engaging narration" and "serves as a solid selection for transitioning readers," according to a *Kirkus Reviews* writer.

Barnholdt's debut young-adult title, *Reality Chick,* focuses on Ally Cavanaugh, a college freshman who agrees to appear on *In the House,* a reality television show that documents her first year on campus, warts and all. Reviewing the novel in *School Library Journal,* Leah Krippner noted that *Reality Chick* "is simply mind candy—but it is delicious."

In *Two-way Street* a college-bound teenager reluctantly embarks on a cross-country journey with her ex-boyfriend. After spending months planning a trip from Florida to Boston to attend college orientation together, Jordan suddenly dumps Courtney, claiming that he met another girl through the Internet. Although Courtney and Jordan are no longer a couple, they must prepare for the three-day drive after Courtney's parents refuse to buy her a last-minute plane ticket so she can travel solo. Along the way, Courtney discovers the real reason Jordan ended their relationship, and this knowledge has dramatic repercussions for her entire family. According to *Kliatt* reviewer Holley Wiseman, *Two-way Street* gains effectiveness through its dual narratives by Jordan and Courtney, resulting in "a timeless tale of love, misperceptions, and faith."

A high-school junior learns to face her greatest fears in *One Night That Changes Everything*. When Eliza loses her private notebook, which contains lists of everything she is afraid of doing, it falls into the hands of Tyler, a schoolmate who threatens to post its contents online unless Eliza does as he commands. With her parents gone for the weekend, Eliza agrees to the deal, and she spends a wild night engaged in the very behaviors that cause her so much trepidation, including posing for a bikini photo and kissing a guy in a nightclub. *One Night That Changes Everything* opens a "lighthearted window into contemporary teen life," Ragan O'Malley commented in her review for *School Library Journal.*

In *Aces Up* a high-school senior gets more than she bargained for when she joins a secretive group of card sharks. Needing money to attend prestigious Wellesley College after her father loses his job, Shannon Card uses a fake ID to land a waitressing gig at a local casino. There she meets the enigmatic Cole, who invites Shannon to join Aces Up, a network of young, talented poker players. Shannon's gambling now begins to take a toll on her grades and her relationships, and she grows concerned when Cole unveils a suspicious plan to take down a high-stakes poker tournament. "Shannon is a quirky and earnest overachiever," wrote Erin Carrillo in her *School Library Journal* review of Barnholdt's novel.

Lauren Barnholdt's entertaining middle-grade novel Hailey Twitch Is Not a Snitch *features artwork by Suzanne Beaky.* (Sourcebooks Jabberwocky, 2010. Illustration copyright © 2010 by Suzanne Beaky. Reproduced by permission of Sourcebooks, Inc.)

A work for middle graders, *Rules for Secret Keeping* concerns a successful young entrepreneur whose business—divulging secrets for those who wish to remain anonymous—faces competition from a new classmate. Sherry Rampey, writing in *School Library Journal,* remarked that Barnholdt's novel "will be a hit with the audience." Secrets are also at the heart of *The Secret Identity of Devon Delaney,* "a quick-paced, believable story of modern teens," as Wiseman reported. While spending the summer with her grandmother, mousy Devon concocts a fanciful persona to impress Lexi, a new friend. When Lexi transfers to Devon's school, however, Devon begins spinning even more complicated yarns to keep Lexi from discovering the truth behind her stories. In *Booklist,* Gillian Engberg noted that "readers just entering adolescence will easily connect with the drama of friendships and first romances," and *School Library Journal* reviewer Amelia Jenkins praised the "fast pace, simple dialogue, and vivid visual descriptions" in Barnholdt's tale.

Biographical and Critical Sources

PERIODICALS

Booklist, August, 2007, Gillian Engberg, review of *The Secret Identity of Devon Delaney,* p. 78; July 1, 2010, Julie Cummins, review of *Hailey Twitch Is Not a Snitch,* p. 60.

Bulletin of the Center for Children's Books, October, 2010, Elizabeth Bush, review of *Aces Up,* p. 62; January, 2011, Karen Coats, review of *Rules for Secret Keeping,* p. 226.

Kirkus Reviews, May, 2010, review of *Hailey Twitch Is Not a Snitch.*

Kliatt, May, 2007, Holley Wiseman, review of *The Secret Identity of Devon Delaney,* p. 22; September, 2007, Holley Wiseman, review of *Two-way Street,* p. 20.

Publishers Weekly, July 5, 2010, review of *One Night That Changes Everything,* p. 45.

School Library Journal, September, 2006, Leah Krippner, review of *Reality Chick,* p. 200; August, 2007, Amelia Jenkins, review of *The Secret Identity of Devon Delaney,* p. 109; October, 2007, Shannon Seglin, review of *Two-way Street,* p. 143; October, 2010, Ragan O'Malley, review of *One Night That Changes Everything,* p. 106; January, 2011, Sherry Rampey, review of *Rules for Secret Keeping,* p. 99; February, 2011, Erin Carrillo, review of *Aces Up,* p. 101.

ONLINE

Lauren Barnholdt Home Page, http://laurenbarnholdt.com (July 15, 2011).

Simon & Schuster Web site, http://www.simonandschuster.com/ (July 15, 2011), "Author Revealed: Lauren Barnholdt."*

BASS, L.G.
See GERINGER, Laura

* * *

BENIOFF, Carol

Personal

Born in San Francisco, CA; partner's name Heinz. *Education:* Studied painting with Ronald Chase; attended California College of Arts and Crafts; studied printmaking at Massachusetts College of Art.

Addresses

Home—Berkeley, CA. *E-mail*—carol@carolbenioff.com.

Career

Artist and illustrator. Worked as an artists' model, Boston, MA, beginning 1972; Great American T-Shirt Company, San Francisco, CA, cofounder, 1975-78; Info-World, San Francisco, graphic production artist, beginning mid-1980s. Teaches workshops on mixed-media printmaking and digital art and printing. *Exhibitions:* Work shown at galleries and museums, including Pacific Art League, Palo Alto, CA; Pro Arts, Oakland, CA; Triton Museum, Santa Clara, CA; Stanwood Gallery, San Francisco; Estampería Quiteña, Quito, Ecuador, 2003; Santa Rosa Junior College, Santa Rosa, CA, 2004; San Francisco Museum of Modern Art Artists Gallery, 2005; Kala Art Institute, Berkeley, CA, 2006; Mercury 20 Gallery, Oakland, 2006; and Addison Street Windows Gallery, Berkeley, 2008.

Member

Society of Children's Book Writers and Illustrators.

Awards, Honors

Award of Excellence for Illustration, *Communication Arts,* 1995; James D. Phelan Award in Printmaking, 1995; Kala Art Institute printmaking fellowship, 1996.

Illustrator

Lyn Manuel, *The Christmas Thingamajig,* Dutton Children's Books (New York, NY), 2002.

Steven L. Layne, *Preacher's Night before Christmas,* Pelican (Gretna, LA), 2006.

Sarah Marwil Lamstein, *Big Night for Salamanders,* Boyds Mills Press (Honesdale, PA), 2010.

Contributor to books, including *The Painter Eight Wow Book* and *Painter XI Wow,* for Peachpit Press, 2007 and 2010 respectively. Contributor to periodicals, including *Atlantic Monthly, Parenting, Time,* and *Utne Reader.*

Sidelights

A respected artist whose work combines traditional drawing and printmaking techniques with digital imagery, Carol Benioff also creates illustrations for chil-

Sarah Marwil Lamstein's picture book Big Night for Salamanders *comes to life in paintings by Carol Benioff.* (Illustration copyright © 2010 by Carol Benioff. Reproduced by permission of Boyds Mills Press, Inc.)

dren's books, among them Lyn Manuel's *The Christmas Thingamajig* and Sarah Marwil Lamstein's *Big Night for Salamanders.* Benioff's art, which has appeared in such publications as *Time* and *Utne Reader,* is marked by "her ability to nourish an illustration with intangible, affecting, emotional content," in the words of *Print* contributor Carol Stevens.

In *The Christmas Thingamajig* Manuel offers a poignant tale about a youngster who, still grieving the recent death of her grandmother, approaches the upcoming holiday season with reluctance. Chloe especially misses Grandma's homemade ornaments, called "thingamajigs," and the special dance they both shared after decorating the tree. With help from her widowed grandfather, the girl learns to honor the woman's memory by creating a new set of rituals. Linda Israelson, writing in *School Library Journal,* noted that the book's "artwork is pleasant and nicely complements the story," and a *Kirkus Reviews* critic remarked of *The Christmas Thingamajig* that Benioff's "jewel-toned paintings of the present contrast with sepia-toned illustrations that recall fond memories of earlier days with Grandma."

A young boy serves as a crossing guard for a host of amphibians in *Big Night for Salamanders.* On a warm spring night, Evan joins his parents in their effort to warn motorists about the annual migration of the spotted salamanders from their winter burrows across the road to a vernal pool, their mating ground. In *School Library Journal,* Kathleen Kelly MacMillan observed that "Benioff's gouache illustrations" for Lamstein's story "impart a sense of wonder," while in *Booklist* Carolyn Phelan concluded of *Big Night for Salamanders* that the artist's images "add color and drama to this informative picture book."

Biographical and Critical Sources

PERIODICALS

Booklist, September 15, 2002, Shelley Townsend-Hudson, review of *The Christmas Thingamajig,* p. 246; February 15, 2010, Carolyn Phelan, review of *Big Night for Salamanders,* p. 88.
Kirkus Reviews, November 1, 2002, review of *The Christmas Thingamajig,* p. 1621; January 15, 2010, review of *Big Night for Salamanders.*
Print, November-December, 1998, Carol Stevens, "Memory and Illusion" (profile of Benioff), p. 48.
Publishers Weekly, September 23, 2002, Shelley Townsend-Hudson, review of *The Christmas Thingamajig,* p. 37.
School Library Journal, October, 2002, Linda Israelson, review of *The Christmas Thingamajig,* p. 61; March, 2010, Kathleen Kelly MacMillan, review of *Big Night for Salamanders,* p. 124.

ONLINE

Carol Benioff Home Page, http://www.carolbenioff.com (July 1, 2011).

Pelican Publishing Web site, http://pelicanpub.com/ (July 1, 2011), "Carol Benioff."

* * *

BERGER, Carin

Personal

Married; children: one daughter. *Education:* Earned college degree (graphic design).

Addresses

Office—533 W. 112th St., No. 4C, New York, NY 10025. *E-mail*—carin@carinberger.com.

Career

Graphic designer and author/illustrator of children's books. Pentagram (design studio), London, England, former graphic designer; freelance graphic artist and illustrator. Presenter at schools. *Exhibitions:* Work included in Society of Illustrators Original Art Show, 2008, 2009, 2010, 2011.

Awards, Honors

Best Illustrated Children's Book selection, Bank Street College of Education, and Chicago Public Library Best of the Best designation, both 2004, both for *Not So True Stories and Unreasonable Rhymes;* Founder's Award, Society of Illustrators, 2006; New York Public Library One Hundred Titles for Reading and Sharing inclusion, 2006, Scandiuzzi Children's Book Award, Seattle Public Library, 2007, and Best of Show award, *3 x 3* magazine Children's Book Show, all for *Behold the Bold Umbrellaphant, and Other Poems* by Jack Prelutsky; *New York Times* Best Illustrated Children's Books selection, and Best Children's Book selection, Bank Street College of Education, both 2008, both for *The Little Yellow Leaf.*

Writings

SELF-ILLUSTRATED

Not So True Stories and Unreasonable Rhymes, Chronicle Books (San Francisco, CA), 2004.
All Mixed Up, Chronicle Books (San Francisco, CA), 2006.
The Little Yellow Leaf, Greenwillow Books (New York, NY), 2008.
OK Go, Greenwillow Books (New York, NY), 2009.
Forever Friends, Greenwillow Books (New York, NY), 2010.
A Perfect Day, Greenwillow Books (New York, NY), 2011.

ILLUSTRATOR

Jack Prelutsky, *Behold the Bold Umbrellaphant, and Other Poems,* Greenwillow Books (New York, NY) 2006.

Bobbi Katz, *Trailblazers: Poems of Exploration,* Greenwillow Books (New York, NY), 2007.

Jan Peck and David Davis, *The Green Mother Goose: Saving the World One Rhyme at a Time,* Sterling (New York, NY), 2011.

Jack Prelutsky, *Stardines,* Greenwillow Books (New York, NY) 2012.

Contributor to periodicals, including trade publications *CA, Print, How,* and *3x3.*

Sidelights

"Channeling Hieronymus Bosch, but with a smile," is how a *Kirkus Reviews* contributor described the work of author and illustrator Carin Berger. Crafted from sought-after scraps torn from mail-order catalogues, newspapers, and other paper ephemera and containing interesting colors, textures, or typography, Berger's playful and vintage-inspired art has been paired with original texts in highly praised picture books that include *Not So True Stories and Unreasonable Rhymes, OK Go,* and *Forever Friends.*

Raised in upstate New York, Berger developed a love for bookbinding and illustration as a young reader. She studied graphic design in college, minoring in illustration, and then worked in a British design firm before returning to the United States and beginning her career as

Carin Berger's stylized collage art is a highlight of her original picture book **The Little Yellow Leaf.** (Illustration copyright © 2008 by Carin Berger. Reproduced by permission of HarperCollins Children's Books, a division of HarperCollins Publishers.)

a freelance graphic artist and illustrator. Although she is best known to young children through her book illustrations, Berger also designs book jackets for adult novels, although this work has been increasingly eclipsed by picture-book projects.

Berger wrote the nonsense poems that eventually became her first picture book, *Not So True Stories and Unreasonable Rhymes,* while coaxing her infant daughter to sleep. Reviewing the work, a *Publishers Weekly* critic noted that the author/illustrator "exert[s] an immediate pull" on readers due to her use of "intricate" cut-paper-collage images featuring elongated shapes and dramatic contrasts. "The imagination at work here marks this author-artist as one to watch," the critic added.

Although Berger focused on painting in college and her early design work, working on *Not so True Stories and Unreasonable Rhymes* prompted her to return to her artistic roots. "As a kid, I always enjoyed making art out of found objects and I also often did collage," she noted in an interview for *Aqua Velvet* online. "When I started playing around with sample illustrations for my first book, I assumed that I would make paintings," she added. However, a period spend without access to painting supplies inspired Berger to reconnect with her childhood scavenger. "There was a big stack of old magazines and catalogs in the house that we were staying in. Then, my friend gave me a box of beautiful, dusty, history-filled ephemera, decades worth of letters and bills from the turn of the [twentieth] century. There was no turning back!"

In creating her images, Berger begins with a small-scale pencil sketch, which she then enlarges to size for use as a guide. Each figure in her collage art is crafted separately and then incorporated with other figures and background elements and glued in place. "My materials are really pedestrian," she noted in her *Aqua Velvet* interview: "The perfectly sharp pair of scissors, an X-Acto knife and tons of blades, and simple white glue. And a treasure trove of ephemera."

Each of Berger's picture books reflects her sense of whimsy and originality. An interactive picture book with spiral-bound pages cut into three segments, *All Mixed Up* allows readers to combine tops and bottoms of various characters along with a text caption in hundreds of humorous variations. Both *The Little Yellow Leaf* and *Forever Friends* contain gentle stories that share simple truths: in the first, a yellow leaf refuses to follow its companions and flutter to the ground before it is ready, while in the second a small wild bunny and a blue bird become fast friends even when the changing seasons force them to spend time apart. Berger's story in *The Little Yellow Leaf* "has a modestly elegant beauty . . . that makes it a delight to read aloud," asserted a *Kirkus Reviews* writer, while in *Booklist* Abby Nolan cited the book's "inventive collage-based illustrations." With its season-shifting color scheme, "the effect [in

Forever Friends] is enchanting," proclaimed *School Library Journal* contributor Donna Atmur, and a *Kirkus Reviews* writer deemed the same picture book by Berger to be "sophisticated, sensitive, and accessible." Noting the artist's "superb, stylized" collage images with their "graceful curves and airy compositions," *Booklist* contributor Kristen McKulski predicted that *Forever Friends* "will give young children much to ponder."

Berger promotes an ecological consciousness in *OK Go,* which pairs a "simple environmental message" with "clever, innovative illustrations," according to *School Library Journal* reviewer Barbara Elleman. Supplementing her characteristic paper collages with buttons, scraps of fabric, and other objects, she shows how the desire for increasingly complex and powerful motorized vehicles can harm wild places and cause the skies to fill with ominous gray clouds. Her "visual commentary on the fast pace of contemporary society . . . is powerful in its simplicity," asserted a *Kirkus Reviews* writer, and McKulski dubbed *OK Go* a "playful take on going green." In reviewing the picture book for the *New York Times Book Review,* Rich Cohen compared Berger's illustration style to that of modernist Spanish painter Joan Miró and a *Publishers Weekly* critic predicted that "the detailed scenes and wackily endearing characters" in *OK Go* "invite poring over."

As an illustrator, Berger has seen her work paired with poetry by notable children's writer Jack Prelutsky. In a review of the collaboration resulting in *Behold the Bold Umbrellaphant, and Other Poems,* Donna Cardon dubbed the work "whimsical" in her *School Library Journal* review. The critic added that the illustrator's mixed-media collage art "create[s] a rich visual treat well suited to the poetry." "Berger's . . . inventive, textured collages add up to a visual treat," concluded a *Publishers Weekly* critic of the same volume, calling *Behold the Bold Umbrellaphant, and Other Poems* kid-friendly and "fantastically silly." Prelusky's work has been brought to life by some of the most talented illustrators working in contemporary children's books, according to J. Patrick Lewis, the critic concluding in the *New York Times Book Review* that "Berger's cut paper and collage art complements" Prelutsky's "galloping zaniness."

Biographical and Critical Sources

PERIODICALS

Booklist, September 1, 2006, Gillian Engberg, review of *Behold the Bold Umbrellaphant, and Other Poems,* p. 123; November 1, 2009, Abby Nolan, review of *The Little Yellow Leaf,* p. 48; June 1, 2009, Kristen McKulski, review of *OK Go,* p. 76; March 1, 2010, Kristen McKulski, review of *Forever Friends,* p. 77.
Bulletin of the Center for Children's Books, November, 2006, Deborah Stevenson, review of *Behold the Bold Umbrellaphant, and Other Poems,* p. 141.

Horn Book, November-December, 2006, Susan Dove Lempke, review of *Behold the Bold Umbrellaphant, and Other Poems,* p. 730; March-April, 2010, Joanna Rudge Long, review of *Forever Friends,* p. 43.

Kirkus Reviews, March 15, 2004, review of *Not So True Stories and Unreasonable Rhymes,* p. 266; September 15, 2006, review of *Behold the Bold Umbrellaphant, and Other Poems,* p. 964; August 1, 2008, review of *The Little Yellow Leaf;* April 15, 2009, review of *OK Go;* February 15, 2010, review of *Forever Friends.*

New York Times Book Review, February 11, 2007, J. Patrick Lewis, review of *Behold the Bold Umbrellaphant, and Other Poems,* p. 17; November 9, 2008, David Barringer, review of *The Little Yellow Leaf,* p. 38; November 8, 2009, Rich Cohen, review of *OK Go,* p. 24; July 18, 2010, Jim McMullan, review of *Forever Friends,* p. 14.

Publishers Weekly, March 29, 2004, review of *Not so True Stories and Unreasonable Rhymes,* p. 63; August 28, 2006, review of *Behold the Bold Umbrellaphant, and Other Poems,* p. 52; March 16, 2009, review of *OK Go,* p. 60.

School Library Journal, June, 2004, Kathleen Whalin, review of *Not So True Stories and Unreasonable Rhymes,* p. 123; October, 2006, Donna Cardon, review of *Behold the Bold Umbrellaphant, and Other Poems,* p. 142; July, 2007, Lee Bock, review of *Trailblazers: Poems of Exploration,* p. 117; October, 2008, Susan Scheps, review of *The Little Yellow Leaf,* p. 101; April, 2009, Barbara Elleman, review of *OK Go,* p. 100; March, 2010, Donna Atmur, review of *Forever Friends,* p. 114.

ONLINE

Aqua Velvet Web Log, http://aqua-velvet.com/ (January 25, 2010), interview with Berger.

Carin Berger Home Page, http://www.carinberger.com (July 25, 2011).

Carin Berger Web log, http://www.carinberger.blogspot.com (July 25, 2011).

ISpot Web site, http://www.theispot.com/ (December 15, 2007), "Carin Berger."*

*   *   *

BLOOM, Suzanne 1950-

Personal

Born 1950; married; children: two sons. *Education:* Cooper Union, B.F.A.

Addresses

Home—McDonough, NY.

Career

Children's writer and illustrator. Former toymaker.

Awards, Honors

100 Titles for Reading and Sharing selection, New York Public Library, 2005, Time of Wonder Honor Book selection, and Notable Children's Books designation and Theodor Seuss Geisel Award Honor Book, both American Library Association, all 2006, and Pennsylvania One Book selection, 2007, all for *A Splendid Friend, Indeed;* books included on several children's choice lists.

Writings

SELF-ILLUSTRATED

We Keep a Pig in the Parlor, C.N. Potter (New York, NY), 1988.

A Family for Jamie: An Adoption Story, C.N. Potter (New York, NY), 1991.

The Bus for Us, Boyds Mills Press (Honesdale, PA), 2001.

Piggy Monday: A Tale about Manners, Albert Whitman (Morton Grove, IL), 2001.

No Place for a Pig, Boyds Mills Press (Honesdale, PA), 2004.

A Splendid Friend, Indeed, Boyds Mills Press (Honesdale, PA), 2005.

Treasure, Boyds Mills Press (Honesdale, PA), 2007.

A Mighty Fine Time Machine, Boyds Mills Press (Honesdale, PA), 2009.

What about Bear?, Boyds Mills Press (Honesdale, PA), 2010.

ILLUSTRATOR

Eve Bunting, *Girls: A to Z,* Boyds Mills Press (Honesdale, PA), 2002.

Eve Bunting, *My Special Day at Third Street School,* Boyds Mills Press (Honesdale, PA), 2004.

Pat Brisson, *Melissa Parkington's Beautiful, Beautiful Hair,* Boyds Mills Press (Honesdale, PA), 2006.

Sidelights

Suzanne Bloom is an award-winning author and illustrator of children's books, among them *The Bus for Us, No Place for a Pig,* and *A Splendid Friend, Indeed.* "When I'm writing or drawing," Bloom stated on her home page, "I feel like a detective, searching for clues or a chef concocting a tasty treat. Each project offers a delicious new challenge."

In *The Bus for Us* Bloom tells the story of big brother Gus, who must keep explaining to his little sister that each vehicle that passes is not their school bus. While it is clearly the excited young girl's first day of school, readers soon suspect that she is also gently teasing her older brother. While her text relates this simple vignette, Bloom's illustrations add more levels to the story, such as a runaway turtle that is switching the children's

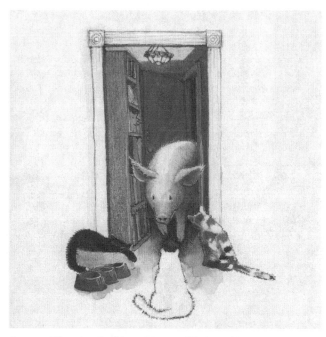

Suzanne Bloom's colorful art brings to life her whimsical story in the picture book **No Place for a Pig.** (Illustration copyright © 2003 by Suzanne Bloom. Reproduced by permission of Boyd Mills Press.)

school lunches. "Though the bright watercolors spread against crisp white backgrounds are eyecatching," according to Thomas Pitchford in *School Library Journal,* readers will really be drawn in by the "repetitive chorus" of the girl's questionings. Ilene Cooper predicted in her *Booklist* review of *The Bus for Us* that young readers will "really enjoy" Bloom's "watercolor art, alive with hijinks and humor."

Piggy Monday: A Tale about Manners features a classroom of children who are so poorly behaved that they start transforming into pigs. Fortunately, adopting proper manners will allow them to shed their piggy ears and curlicue tails and become children again. "The charming illustrations of pigs will draw young children to this moralistic but enjoyable bit of fun," wrote Kathy Broderick in a *Booklist* review of *Piggy Monday,* while a *Kirkus Reviews* contributor praised the author/ illustrator's ability to relate "a needed theme with enough wit to make it palatable." According to *School Library Journal* critic Doris Gebel, Bloom's "comical, cartoon-style illustrations . . . add to the fun of the humorous, rhymed, if somewhat didactic text."

A woman with a passion for collecting anything featuring pigs wins a real porker for a pet in *No Place for a Pig.* Although she loves her new four-legged housemate, Serena the pig, Ms. Taffy is worried that her small apartment is not big enough for the growing piglet. She contemplates a move to the country until her neighbors get together and transform a small, adjacent outdoor lot into a garden where Serena can live. "The busy, colorful illustrations are heavy on amusing detail," wrote Catherine Threadgill in *School Library Journal,* the critic dubbing Serena "a pig with personality." Apprais-

ing Bloom's illustrations in her *Booklist* review, Louise Brueggemann noted that their "bright, vividly colored settings . . . capture the warmth and joy of the community."

In *A Splendid Friend, Indeed*—named as a Theodor Seuss Geisel Award Honor Book—Goose and Bear are best friends. Sometimes Goose gets on Bear's nerves, however. Just when Bear thinks he has had enough, he sees how much Goose appreciates their friendship and remembers that he cares for Goose as well. "A more perfect union between giggle-inducing but reassuring images and a text of very few words is hard to conjure," wrote a *Kirkus Reviews* contributor. As Cooper noted in *Booklist,* Bloom gets "maximum effect with minimum words, in part because of Goose's energetic dialogue," while *School Library Journal* critic Shawn Brommer recommended *A Splendid Friend, Indeed* as "an ideal book for storytimes about friendship and sharing."

Goose and Bear return in *Treasure,* a tale that centers on a colossal misunderstanding. As Bear prepares for a leisurely game of Tic-Tac-Toe, impulsive Goose spots the "X" his friend has drawn in the middle square and begins a frantic search for buried loot. When Goose realizes that his efforts are in vain, Bear calms his frus-

Bloom continues to entertain young readers and their parents with her mix of story and art in **A Splendid Friend, Indeed.** (Boyds Mills Press, 2005. Illustration copyright © 2005 by Suzanne Bloom. Reproduced by permission of Boyds Mills Press.)

trated pal with a simple reminder about the value of friendship. *What about Bear?* finds the two friends joined by Little Fox, who disrupts their delicate harmony by initiating games that make it impossible for the larger animal to participate. "Bloom's proficiency in depicting characterization with kinesics is humorously on display again," Kate McClelland observed in her *School Library Journal* review of *Treasure*, while in *Booklist* Randall Enos remarked that Bloom's "simple text" in *What about Bear?* "is perfect for beginning readers and complements the glowing pastels." In each of her books featuring Bear and Goose, Bloom "artfully uses body language rather than text . . . to crank up the emotional intensity," according to a *Kirkus Reviews* writer.

A Mighty Fine Time Machine, another tale of friendship written and illustrated by Bloom, follows the adventures of Samantha the anteater, Grant the aardvark, and Antoine the armadillo. With a wagon-load of books in tow, Samantha learns that Grant and Antoine have traded some precious goodies for a "time machine," which appears to be nothing more than an oversized packing crate. Despite her objections to the deal, the anteater helps her friends decorate their contraption and witnesses their disappointment when it fails to launch. Although Grant and Antoine lose interest in the project, Samantha finds a clever use for the box that incorporates her love of literature. "The gouache and colored-pencil illustrations of the gadgets and gizmos attached to the crate add humor," *School Library Journal* reviewer Martha Simpson remarked. *A Mighty Fine Time Machine* also drew praise from *Booklist* critic Shauna Yusko, who suggested that readers "who have ever created anything out of a box will identify with the trio's ingenuity."

In addition to her self-illustrated books, Bloom has also contributed art to stories by other writers. In *Melissa Parkington's Beautiful, Beautiful Hair,* by Pat Brisson, young Melissa would prefer to be recognized for her accomplishments instead of her long, shiny locks. Although she attempts to set a school basketball record, develops her artistic skills, and donates time to helping others, Melissa finds what she seeks when she spots a sign in a beauty salon window asking for donations to create children's wigs. "Brisson's clear and heartening story is balanced by Bloom's mixed-media, deeply colored gauche/pencil/crayon paintings," noted a contributor in *Kirkus Reviews*. Reviewing *Melissa Parkington's Beautiful, Beautiful Hair* for *School Library Journal,* Rebecca Sheridan noted that the artist's "fluid lines and saturated hues" for the picture book "depict a cast of diverse characters and colorful settings."

Biographical and Critical Sources

PERIODICALS

Booklist, March 15, 2001, Ilene Cooper, review of *The Bus for Us,* p. 1400; August, 2001, Kathy Broderick,

review of *Piggy Monday: A Tale about Manners,* p. 2127; January 1, 2994, Louise Brueggmann, review of *No Place for a Pig,* p. 872; February 15, 2005, Ilene Cooper, review of *A Splendid Friend, Indeed,* p. 1082; May 1, 2009, Shauna Yusko, review of *A Mighty Fine Time Machine,* p. 87; March 15, 2010, Randall Enos, review of *What about Bear?,* p. 50.

Childhood Education, winter, 2003, Sue Grossman, review of *No Place for a Pig,* p. 90; spring, 2007, Merritt M. Arnold, review of *A Splendid Friend, Indeed,* p. 178.

Kirkus Reviews, September 15, 2001, review of *Piggy Monday,* p. 1353; February 15, 2005, review of *A Splendid Friend, Indeed,* p. 226; September 15, 2006, review of *Melissa Parkington's Beautiful, Beautiful Hair,* p. 947; February 15, 2009, review of *A Mighty Fine Time Machine;* February 15, 2010, review of *What about Bear?*

Publishers Weekly, November 10, 2003, review of *No Place for a Pig,* p. 61; February 9, 2004, review of *My Special Day at Third Street School,* p. 81.

School Library Journal, June, 2001, Thomas Pitchford, review of *The Bus for Us,* p. 102; January, 2002, review of *Piggy Monday,* p. 95; November, 2003, Catherine Threadgill, review of *No Place for a Pig,* p. 88; May, 2005, Shawn Brommer, review of *A Splendid Friend, Indeed,* p. 77; November, 2006, Rebecca Sheridan, review of *Melissa Parkington's Beautiful, Beautiful Hair,* p. 84; February, 2008, Kate McClelland, review of *Treasure,* p. 83; March, 2009, Martha Simpson, review of *A Mighty Fine Time Machine,* p. 106; June, 2010, Julie Roach, review of *What about Bear?,* p. 65.

ONLINE

Suzanne Bloom Home Page, http://www.suzannebloom. com (July 1, 2011).*

*   *   *

BLOSS, Josie 1981-

Personal

Born 1981, in MI. *Education:* University of Michigan, B.S. (political science). *Hobbies and other interests:* Watching television, karaoke, marching-band music.

Addresses

Home—Bloomington, IN.

Career

Writer. Formerly worked in law offices.

Writings

Band Geek Love, Flux (Woodbury, MN), 2008.
Band Geeked Out, Flux (Woodbury, MN), 2009.
Albatross, Flux (Woodbury, MN), 2010.
Faking Faith, Flux (Woodbury, MN), 2011.

Sidelights

During college, Josie Bloss gave no sigh that she would one day focus on writing for young adults. Majoring in political science at the University of Michigan, Bloss also performed in the marching band and had her eye on law school. The writing that she did was for the school paper, the *Michigan Daily.* A job at a law office after graduation eventually prompted Bloss to revisit her career plans, to the benefit of teen fiction fans. In addition to *Band Geek Love* and its sequel, *Band Geeked Out,* which draw on her experience as a dedicated high-school trumpet player, Bloss has also written the well-received teen novels *Albatross* and *Faking Faith,* the latter in which a lonely seventeen year old creates the fictional "Faith" in order to build an online relationship with a group of fundamentalist Christian teens who are making comfortingly old-fashioned life choices.

When readers meet Ellie Snow in *Band Geek Love,* she has started senior year at Winslow High and is now trumpet section leader in the school's marching band.

Cover of Josie Bloss's young-adult novel Albatross, *in which a young woman's new boyfriend proves to be as problematic as her father.* (Flux, 2010. Book cover photographs copyright © 2010 by Stockbyte and Brand X Pictures. Reproduced by permission of Llewellyn Publications.)

In addition to pushing her fellow trumpeters toward perfection, Ellie is also practicing for her solo performance at the homecoming game. Then, at band practice, she finds herself face to face with newly moved-to-town sophomore Connor Higgins, who happens to be: a) extremely good looking; and b) a trumpet player. While both teens feel an attraction, Ellie knows that dating an underclassman will only spark gossip. She returns in *Band Geeked Out,* as her acceptance into a prestigious east-coast women's college comes with a caveat: the school has no marching band. Commending Bloss's choice of an unusual marching-band setting in *Band Geek Love, Kliatt* reviewer Amanda MacGregor added that while Ellie is a difficult and often unlikable character, "her behavior and attitude come off as refreshingly real and honest" and her relationship with the ever-patient Connor "is interesting to watch unfold."

In *Albatross* Bloss focuses on another high-school senior embarking on a relationship, but for Tess the dynamics are complex. Recently relocated from Chicago to western Michigan in the wake of her parents' divorce, Tess is resentful of her entire situation: the divorce, the move, and the loss of her friends. When she meets Micah, she ignores the rumors that abound about him: that he is handsome but nobody to rely on as boyfriend material. Attractive in a dark, brooding way, Micah impresses her with his insights and keeps her off balance with his mercurial moods. As their relationship deepens, Tess is drawn increasingly into her new friend's world, and then she realizes that Micah reminds her of her über-controlling father. Reviewing *Albatross* for *Publishers Weekly,* a contributor noted that, despite the story's melodramatic theme, Bloss's "descriptions of lust and envy are honest and captivating," while in *School Library Journal* Leah Krippner dubbed the book "a startlingly realistic portrayal of emotionally abusive relationships." Watching the evolution of Tess's relationship "will wrench hearts," asserted a *Kirkus Reviews* writer, the critic adding that *Albatross* may correct the perceptions of "girls who believe in the [possibility of a] swept-off-her-feet romance."

Biographical and Critical Sources

PERIODICALS

Kirkus Reviews, January 1, 2010, review of *Albatross.*
Kliatt, July, 2008, Amanda MacGregor, review of *Band Geek Love,* p. 22.
Publishers Weekly, February 1, 2010, review of *Albatross,* p. 51.
School Library Journal, March, 2010, Leah Krippner, review of *Albatross,* p. 152.

ONLINE

Josie Bloss Home Page, http://josiebloss.com (May 9, 2011).*

BOTTNER, Barbara 1943-

Personal

Born May 25, 1943, in New York, NY; daughter of Irving (a business executive) and Elaine Bottner; married Gerald Kruglik, 1988. *Education:* Attended Boston University, 1961-62, and École des Beaux Arts, 1963-64; University of Wisconsin—Madison, B.S., 1965; University of California, Santa Barbara, M.A., 1966; studied animation at School of Visual Arts. *Hobbies and other interests:* Dancing, travel, politics, Buddhism.

Addresses

Home—Los Angeles, CA. *E-mail*—bhb1@sbcglobal.net.

Career

Writer, illustrator, producer, actor, and educator. Formerly taught kindergarten; set designer for off-Broadway theater; Café La Mama, New York, NY, actor in touring productions in United States and Europe; producer of short animated films; Parsons School of Design, New York, NY, instructor, beginning 1973; instructor at Oris Art Institute of Los Angeles County and New School for Social Research, c. 1990; staff writer for television series *Nickelodeon*, 1992. Director of short animated films, including *Goat in a Boat* and *Later That Night.* Mentor for WriteGirl (nonprofit), Los Angeles. *Exhibitions:* Work has been represented in film festivals in London, England; Melbourne, Victoria, Australia; Ottawa, Ontario, Canada; and New York, NY.

Member

Writers Guild of America, Author's Guild.

Awards, Honors

Best Film for Television award, International Animation Festival (Annecy, France), 1973, for *Goat in a Boat;* Children's Choice citation, International Reading Association/Children's Book Council (IRA/CBC), 1980, for *Mean Maxine;* Distinguished Teaching Award, New School for Social Research (now New School University), 1990; Cine Golden Eagle, Council for International Nontheatrical Events, for animated film *Later That Night;* Bank Street College of Education Honor citation, and *School Library Journal* Best Books designation, both 2005, both for *Wallace's Lists;* Best Children's Books of the Year selection, Bank Street College of Education, and Best of the Best selection, Chicago Public Library, both 2010, and Bill Martin, Jr., Picture Book Award nomination, Kansas Reading Association, Teacher's Choice and Children's Choice selections, IRA/CBC, all 2011, all for *Miss Brooks Loves Books! (and I Don't);* several other Notable Book and Children's Choice selections.

Writings

(Self-illustrated) *What Would You Do with a Giant?,* Putnam (New York, NY), 1972.

Barbara Bottner (Reproduced by permission.)

(Self-illustrated) *Fun House,* Prentice-Hall (Englewood Cliffs, NJ), 1975.

Eek, a Monster, Macmillan (New York, NY), 1975.

The Box, Macmillan (New York, NY), 1975.

What Grandma Did on Her Birthday, Macmillan (New York, NY), 1975.

(Self-illustrated) *Doing the Toldedo,* Four Winds Press (New York, NY), 1977.

Big Boss! Little Boss!, Pantheon (New York, NY), 1978.

Jungle Day! Delacorte (New York, NY), 1978.

(Self-illustrated) *There Was Nobody There,* Macmillan (New York, NY), 1978.

Messy, Delacorte (New York, NY), 1979.

(Self-illustrated) *Dumb Old Casey Is a Fat Tree,* Harper (New York, NY), 1979.

(Self-illustrated) *Myra,* Macmillan (New York, NY), 1979.

(Self-illustrated) *Horrible Hannah,* illustrated by Joan Drescher, Crown (New York, NY), 1980.

(Self-illustrated) *Mean Maxine,* Pantheon (New York, NY), 1980.

(Self-illustrated) *The World's Greatest Expert on Absolutely Everything . . . Is Crying,* Harper (New York, NY), 1985.

Nothing in Common (young-adult novel), Harper (New York, NY), 1986.

Zoo Song, illustrated by Lynn Munsinger, Scholastic (New York, NY), 1987.

Let Me Tell You Everything: Memoirs of a Lovesick Intellectual (young-adult novel), Harper (New York, NY), 1989.

Bootsie Barker Bites, illustrated by Peggy Rathmann, Putnam (New York, NY), 1992.

Hurricane Music, illustrated by Paul Yalowitz, Putnam (New York, NY), 1995.

Nana Hannah's Piano, illustrated by Diana Cain Bluthenthal, Putnam (New York, NY), 1996.

Bootsie Barker, Ballerina, illustrated by G. Brian Karas, HarperCollins (New York, NY), 1997.

Two Messy Friends, Scholastic (New York, NY), 1998.

Marsha Makes Me Sick, illustrated by Denise Brunkus, Golden Books (New York, NY), 1998.

Marsha Is Only a Flower, illustrated by Denise Brunkus, Golden Books (New York, NY), 2000.

(With husband, Gerald Kruglik) *It's Not Marsha's Birthday,* illustrated by Denise Brunkus, Golden Books (New York, NY), 2001.

Be Brown!, illustrated by Barry Gott, Grosset & Dunlap (New York, NY), 2002.

Charlene Loves to Make Noise, illustrated by Alex Stadler, Running Press (Philadelphia, PA), 2002.

The Scaredy Cats, illustrated by Victoria Chess, Simon & Schuster (New York, NY), 2003.

Wallace's Lists, illustrated by Olof Landström, Katherine Tegen Books (New York, NY), 2004.

Rosa's Room, illustrated by Beth Spiegel, Peachtree Publishers (Atlanta, GA), 2004.

(With Gerald Kruglik; and illustrator) *Pish and Posh,* HarperCollins (New York, NY), 2005.

(With Gerald Kruglik; and illustrator) *Pish and Posh Wish for Fairy Wings,* HarperCollins (New York, NY), 2005.

(Self-illustrated) *Miss Mabel Is Able,* Knopf (New York, NY), 2007.

Raymond and Nelda, illustrated by Nancy Hayashi, Peachtree Publishers (Atlanta, GA), 2007.

You Have to Be Nice to Someone on Their Birthday, illustrated by Tatjana Mai-Wyss, Putnam (New York, NY), 2007.

Miss Brooks Loves Books! (and I Don't), illustrated by Michael Emberley, Knopf (New York, NY), 2010.

Writer for television series *Shelley Duvall's Bedtime Stories* and *Winnie the Pooh,* both for Disney Channel; author of *Mrs. Piggle Wiggle* (television program), Showtime. Contributor to periodicals, including *Los Angeles Times Book Review;* contributor of short fiction to *Cosmopolitan* and *Playgirl.* Contributing editor, *LA Weekly, Lion and the Unicorn,* and *Miami Herald.* Contributor of illustrations to periodicals, including *New York Times, Viva,* and *Ms.;* contributor of cartoons to *Viva, Penthouse,* and the *New York Times* op-ed page.

Bottner's work has been translated into French and Swedish.

Adaptations

Myra was adapted as an animated film, Churchill Films, 1980; *Wallace's Lists* was adapted as an animated film, Weston Woods.

Sidelights

An accomplished writer and illustrator, Barbara Bottner is the author of such popular children's books as *Bootsie Barker Bites, Wallace's Lists,* and *Miss Brooks Loves Books! (and I Don't),* all which feature stories that pair humorous narratives and endearing characters. "I am drawn to work that respects that children have integrity, deep feelings, and need to be mirrored and validated," Bottner remarked in a *Seven Impossible Things before Breakfast* online interview. In addition to her work as a

writer, Bottner is also an acclaimed writing instructor who has worked with such individuals as Lane Smith, April Halprin Wayland, and Bruce Degen.

As a child, Bottner grew up dreaming of becoming an artist, a dancer, and a story teller. After studying painting in Paris, France, she studied acting and toured for two years both in the United States and Europe. Bottner became a substitute teacher to supplement her acting wages, and after a year in the classroom, she decided to establish a career in children's book illustration. Encouraged by her editors, she also tried her hand at writing, her self-illustrated debut, *What Would You Do with a Giant?,* was published in 1972.

In her young-adult novel *Nothing in Common,* Bottner chronicles the lives of Melissa Warren, a wealthy teenager, and Sara Gregori, the daughter of Melissa's maid. Mrs. Grigori had a motherly relationship with both girls, and following her death Melissa and Sara each attempt to circumvent their grief in different ways. *Let Me Tell You Everything: Memoirs of a Lovesick Intellectual* introduces Brogan Arthur, a high-school senior who is passionate about books, politics, and the world of ideas. Brogan's feminist ideals are confused, however, by her infatuation with a handsome social-studies teacher. Hazel Rochman commented in *Booklist* that in *Let Me Tell You Everything* Bottner's "witty voice is nicely controlled as she mocks feminist rhetoric, yet at the same time affirms her commitment."

Bootsie Barker Bites is one of several books in which Bottner features an unusual heroine. The dreadful

Diana Cain Bluthenthal creates the humorous picture-book art for Bottner's whimsical story in **Nana Hannah's Piano.** (G.P. Putnam's Sons, 1996. Illustration copyright © 1996 by Diana Cain Bluthenthal. Reproduced by permission of G.P. Putnam's Sons, a division of Penguin Young Readers Group, a member of Penguin Group (USA) Inc., 345 Hudson St., New York, NY 10014. All rights reserved. In the British Commonwealth by RLR Associates for Barbara Bottner.)

The cartoon art of Olof Landström is a feature of Bottner's humorous mouse-centered story in **Wallace's Lists.** (Illustration copyright © 2004 by Olof Landström. Reproduced by permission of HarperCollins Children's Books, a division of HarperCollins Publishers.)

Bootsie Barker appears to be a sweet girl, but when the adults disappear she becomes thoroughly cruel. Bootsie terrorizes the story's narrator, a younger girl who is forced to play with Bootsie while their mothers visit with one another. A *Kirkus Reviews* contributor called *Bootsie Barker Bites* "an entertaining, insightful glimpse into a child's real world," while Ann A. Flowers concluded in *Horn Book:* "The satisfaction of seeing a bully get her comeuppance is guaranteed to make a young reader's heart sing." Bootsie returns in *Bootsie Barker, Ballerina.*

The comical *Hurricane Music* showcases another side of Bottner's humor. After discovering a clarinet in her basement, Aunt Margaret finds herself unable to afford music lessons and opts to "study the sounds of life" instead. *Booklist* reviewer Mary Harris Veeder noted that "any child who's ever tried to master an instrument will identify with [Aunt Margaret's] vigorous glee." As a *Kirkus Reviews* critic remarked, in *Hurricane Music* "Bottner makes her playful, syncopated text tongue-in-cheek from start to finish."

Another Bottner story with musical undertones is *Nana Hannah's Piano,* which puts a spin on the time-tested story about a boy who would rather play baseball than practice the piano. A week spent with Nana Hannah while recovering from a sprained ankle changes the boy's attitude, however. A *Kirkus Reviews* critic praised *Nana Hannah's Piano,* commenting: "Sharing, caring and a patch of common ground—Bottner knows the ingredients, and fashions them into a minor ode to encouragement."

Bottner touches on the subject of fear in *The Scaredy Cats,* which introduces a feline family whose members are easily made afraid of things. Mother and Father Cat are afraid to drive because they fear that the car will go too fast; they do not open their mail because they are afraid of being disappointed; and they are afraid to let Baby Scaredy wear her new dress because they fear she will stain it. *The Scaredy Cats* presents "a funny and revealing look at our fears," according to a *Kirkus Reviews* critic. Kathleen Kelly MacMillan, writing in *School Library Journal,* noted of Bottner's stylistic approach that her "serious tone is a perfect counterpoint to the increasing ridiculousness of the Scaredy Cats' fears."

Bottner depicts a familiar childhood experience in *Rosa's Room*. After moving to a new house, Rosa notices how large and empty her bedroom looks. Even after she begins to unpack her belongings and decorate her walls, Rosa stills feels that something is missing. When she gazes out her window and spots a neighbor girl. She suddenly realizes what she needs to bring her room to life. Noting that many authors have addressed the theme of a family move, *School Library Journal* critic Linda Staskus remarked that "few describe taking a space and making it one's own in such a positive and creative manner." In *Booklist*, Connie Fletcher described *Rosa's Room* as an "optimistic, encouraging book that will help make a strange and scary situation less so." In *You Have to Be Nice to Someone on Their Birthday*, young Rosemary's plans for her special day take a depressing turn when her mother forgets to make her favorite breakfast, she gets in trouble at school, and her troublesome cousins arrive for a visit. Bottner's story garnered praise from a *Kirkus Reviews* contributor, who called it a "subtle tale about feelings and friendships."

A misunderstanding between friends is at the heart of *Raymond and Nelda*, a tale that offers "a healthy dose of sincerity, pure and simple," according to a critic in *Kirkus Reviews*. Raymond the squirrel and Nelda the rabbit share an enjoyment of singing and dancing. When Nelda stumbles and falls while attempting a twirl, Raymond laughs at his companion, hurting her feelings and causing a rift between the two. Although Raymond and Nelda grow lonely without one another, neither will apologize until their mail carrier devises a clever solution to the problem. "The intense feelings are elemental, and the scenarios are part of every preschoolers' world," observed Hazel Rochman in her *Booklist* review of *Raymond and Nelda*.

A stubborn youngster meets her match in *Miss Brooks Loves Books! (and I Don't)*, a work illustrated by Michael Emberley. In Bottner's story a sardonic first grader bristles at the unbridled enthusiasm of Miss Brooks, her school librarian, until the student discovers a book that suits her ogre-ish disposition: William Steig's *Shrek!* "Bottner's deadpan humor and delicious prose combine with Emberley's droll caricatures to create a story sure to please those who celebrate books," commented *School Library Journal* reviewer Wendy Lukehart, and a critic in *Kirkus Reviews* similarly noted that the illustrator brings Bottner's "charmingly quirky characters perfectly to life." In the words of a *Publishers Weekly* contributor, *Miss Brooks Loves Books! (and I Don't)* "should persuade hard-to-please children that the perfect book for them is out there."

Wallace's Lists is one of several comic collaborations between Bottner and her husband, Gerald Kruglik. Focusing on the disadvantages of detailed planning, the book introduces Wallace, a mouse who starts each day of his orderly life by checking his to-do lists. Wallace's life is thrown asunder when he meets a new neighbor, Albert the mouse, who approaches life in a more impetuous way. Under Albert's influence, Wallace gradually gives up his systematic approach to life and learns to appreciate the value of spontaneity. Critics applauded Bottner's story, remarking on the author's humor and ability to engage readers. Lauralyn Persson, writing in *School Library Journal*, reviewed the title and noted: "The writing is memorable . . . and the authors provide just the right amount of details," making "this picture book . . . a winner." Similarly a *Publishers Weekly* reviewer stated of the book that *Wallace's Lists* "goes on the recommended list."

Bottner and Kruglik have also collaborated on *Pish and Posh*, the first of several stories that follow the adventures of two friends. When they discover a handbook for fairies at their front door, no-nonsense Pish wants nothing to do with the volume while the curious Posh decides to try her hand at magic, with predictably wacky results. In a sequel, *Pish and Posh Wish for Fairy Wings*, the protagonists seek advice from the Monster under the Bed with regard to helping them make wiser wishes that will help them earn their fairy wings. Bottner's "expressive" illustrations "provide extra help for those readers who are better at identifying words than comprehending them," according to *Horn Book* contributor Betty Carter.

Bottner notes that one of the most enjoyable aspects of her job is visiting schools to meet readers. "I love children for their frankness," she remarked in her *Seven Impossible Things before Breakfast* interview. "When I visit schools, there is always some young child who will give me their unadulterated opinion on my books or tell me who they really love. They are more interesting to me than my die-hard fans. I love that children are bold and outspoken, so when I'm with them it strengthens my voice—it is a reminder of how fierce kids can be. They live in childhood; writers only visit."

Biographical and Critical Sources

PERIODICALS

Booklist, July, 1989, Hazel Rochman, review of *Let Me Tell You Everything: Memoirs of a Lovesick Intellectual* p. 1891; June 1, 1995, Mary Harris Veeder, review of *Hurricane Music*, p. 1782; April 1, 2004, Connie Fletcher, review of *Rosa's Room*, p. 1368; December 1, 2006, Hazel Rochman, review of *Pish and Posh Wish for Fairy Wings*, p. 51; March 1, 2007, Hazel Rochman, review of *Raymond and Nelda*, p. 87; March 1, 2010, Hazel Rochman, review of *Miss Brooks Loves Books! (and I Don't)*, p. 78.

Horn Book, March-April, 1993, Ann A. Flowers, review of *Bootsie Barker Bites*, pp. 193-194; November-December, 2006, Betty Carter, review of *Pish and Posh Wish for Fairy Wings*, p. 705; May-June, 2010, Susan Dove Lempke, review of *Miss Brooks Loves Books! (and I Don't)*, p. 62.

Kirkus Reviews, May 15, 1989, review of Let Me Tell You Everything, p. 760; September, 1, 1992, review of *Bootsie Barker Bites,* p. 1126; August 1, 1996, review of *Nana Hannah's Piano,* p. 1147; April 1, 1997, review of *Bootsie Barker Ballerina,* p. 549; December 15, 2001, review of *Be Brown!,* p. 1754; March 15, 2003, review of *The Scaredy Cats,* p. 76; March 1, 2004, review of *Rosa's Room,* p. 219; October 1, 2006, review of *Pish and Posh Wish for Fairy Wings,* p. 1010; January 15, 2007, review of *You Have to be Nice to Someone on their Birthday,* p. 70; February 15, 2007, review of *Raymond and Nelda;* February 15, 2010, review of *Miss Brooks Loves Books! (and I Don't).*

Publishers Weekly, December 21, 1984, review of *The World's Greatest Expert on Absolutely Everything . . . Is Crying,* p. 87; August 28, 1987, review of *Zoo Song,* p. 78; March 1, 2004, review of *Rosa's Room,* p. 68; June 7, 2004, review of *Wallace's Lists,* p. 49; February 8, 2010, review of *Miss Brooks Loves Books! (and I Don't),* p. 50.

School Library Journal, November, 1986, Kathleen D. Wahlin, review of *Nothing in Common,* p. 97; February, 1993, Heide Piehler, review of *Bootsie Barker Bites,* p. 69; May, 1995, Virginia Opocensky, review of *Hurricane Music,* pp. 81-82; April, 2003, Kathleen Kelly MacMillan, review of *The Scaredy Cats,* p. 116; May, 2004, Linda Staskus, review of *Rosa's Room,* p. 102; June, 2004, Lauralyn Persson, review of *Wallace's Lists,* p. 96; August, 2007, Maryann H. Owen, review of *Raymond and Nelda,* p. 77; February, 2010, Wendy Lukehart, review of *Miss Brooks Loves Books! (and I Don't),* p. 76.

ONLINE

Barbara Bottner Home Page, http://www.barbarabottnerbooks.com (July 1, 2011).

Penguin Books Web site, http://us.penguingroup.com/ (July 1, 2011), "Barbara Bottner."

Seven Impossible Things before Breakfast Web log, http://blaine.org/sevenimpossiblethings/ (December 21, 2010), interview with Bottner.

Teaching Authors Web log, http://www.teachingauthors.com/ (August 13, 2010), April Halprin Wayland, interview with Bottner.*

* * *

BOYLE, Bob
(Robert Boyle, II)

Personal

Born in NJ; married. *Education:* B.F.A.

Addresses

Home—Pasadena, CA. *Agent*—Jen Rofe, Andrea Brown Literary Agency, jennifer@andreabrownlit.com. *E-mail*—wubbzybob@gmail.com.

Career

Author/illustrator and television producer. Creator and writer for television series, including *Yin! Yang! Yo!* and *Wow! Wow! Wubbzy!* Producer of television series *The Fairly OddParents* and *Danny Phantom.* Presenter at schools.

Awards, Honors

Emmy Award for production design, for *Wow! Wow! Wubbzy.*

Writings

Hugo and the Really, Really, Really Long String, Random House (New York, NY), 2010.

Adaptations

Characters from Boyle's television series *Wow! Wow! Wubbzy!* have been adapted for many picture books by Scholastic, including *Everybody Loves Wubbzy* and *A Little Help from My Friends.*

Sidelights

Beginning his career in animation working for Nickelodeon, Bob Boyle has won over legions of young television fans as the creator of the *Wow! Wow! Wubbzy!* cartoon program, featuring an upbeat yellow character. Boyle's other television credits include creating and producing the television program *Yin! Yang! Yo!* for Disney as well as working on *The Fairly OddParents, Garfield and Friends,* and *The Jimmy Timmy Power Hour.* His instantly recognizable cartoon style features gently geometric shapes drawn with thick black lines and filled with bright colors; he credits the idea for the initial Wubbzy storyline to his young niece. Despite his success as an animator, Boyle always dreamed of creating picture books, and he achieved this goal in 2010 with the publication of *Hugo and the Really, Really, Really Long String.*

Captured in Boyle's engaging animation-style cartoon art, *Hugo and the Really, Really, Really Long String* introduces a smiling purple character who lives with his dog, Biscuit, on a hill. When a red string appears outside their door, Hugo and Biscuit follow it to its source, picking up a menagerie of new friends along the way. The rhyming text in Boyle's story moves along with a "pacing [that] is able," according to a *Publishers Weekly* contributor, and the author/illustrator "scatters his artwork with amusing details." In *School Library Journal* Lisa Glasscock viewed Boyle's picture-book debut with favor, dubbing *Hugo and the Really, Really, Really Long String* "a smart standalone picture book with lovable, fun characters."

Biographical and Critical Sources

PERIODICALS

Kirkus Reviews, March 1, 2010, review of *Hugo and the Really, Really, Really Long String.*
Publishers Weekly, February 22, 2010, review of *Hugo and the Really, Really, Really Long String,* p. 64.
School Library Journal, February, 2010, Lisa Glasscock, review of *Hugo and the Really, Really, Really Long String,* p. 76.

ONLINE

Animation World Network Web site, http://www.awn.com/ (November 10, 2006), John Cawley, interview with Boyle.
Bob Boyle Web Log, http://bobboyle.blogspot.com (July 25, 2011).

*   *   *

BOYLE, Robert, II
See BOYLE, Bob

*   *   *

BRIMNER, Larry Dane 1949-

Personal

Born November 5, 1949, in St. Petersburg, FL; son of George Frederick (a military officer) and Evelyn A. Brimner (a homemaker). *Education:* San Diego State University, B.A. (literature), 1971, M.A. (writing), 1981. *Hobbies and other interests:* Reading, working out at the gym, riding mountain bikes, cooking.

Addresses

Home—San Diego, CA. *E-mail*—ldb@brimner.com.

Career

Writer. Central Union High School, El Centro, CA, writing teacher, 1974-84; San Diego State University, San Diego, CA, lecturer, 1984-91; freelance writer, 1985—. Instructor at Highlights Foundation Writers Workshop. Has also worked as a waiter, interior designer, and house builder.

Member

International Reading Association, Authors' Guild, Society of Children's Book Writers and Illustrators, National Council of Teachers of English, California Association of Teachers of English, Southern California Council on Literature for Children and Young People, Sierra Club, AmFar.

Awards, Honors

Children's Choice Award, International Reading Association, 1988, for *BMX Freestyle* and *Snowboarding,* 2000, for *The Official M & M's Brand Book of the Millennium;* Pick of the List designation, American Booksellers Association, 1988, for *Country Bear's Good Neighbor;* Best Children's Science Book listee, *Science Books and Films,* 1991, for *Animals That Hibernate;* Notable Trade Book in the Field of Social Studies designation, National Council of Social Studies/Children's Book Council, 1992, for *A Migrant Family;* Oppenheim Gold Medal for Best Book, and San Diego Books Award, both 2002, Great Lakes' Great Books Honor Book selection, 2004, and Arkansas Diamond Award, 2005, all for *The Littlest Wolf;* Jane Addams Children's Book Award, Norman A. Sugarman Children's Biography Award, Books for the Teen Age selection, New York Public Library, and Best Children's Books of the Year selection, Bank Street College of Education, all 2008, all for *We Are One;* Gold Award, National Parenting Publications Awards, Best of the Best listee, Chicago Public Library, Best Children's Books of the Year selection, Bank Street College of Education, Orbis Pictus Honor Book selection, National Council of Teachers of English, and Jane Addams Honor Book selection, all 2011, all for *Birmingham Sunday.*

Writings

FOR CHILDREN

Country Bear's Good Neighbor, Orchard Books (London, England), 1988.
Cory Coleman, Grade 2, Henry Holt (New York, NY), 1990.
Country Bear's Surprise, Orchard Books (London, England), 1991.
A Migrant Family, Lerner Publishing (Minneapolis, MN), 1992.
Max and Felix, Boyds Mills Press (Honesdale, PA), 1993.
Elliot Fry's Goodbye, illustrated by Eugenie Fernandes, Boyds Mills Press (Honesdale, PA), 1994.
Voices from the Camps: Internment of Japanese Americans during World War II, F. Watts (New York, NY), 1994.
Merry Christmas, Old Armadillo, illustrated by Dominic Catalano, Boyds Mills Press (Honesdale, PA), 1995.
If Dogs Had Wings, illustrated by Chris L. Demarest, Boyds Mills Press (Honesdale, PA), 1996.
Skiing, Children's Press (New York, NY), 1997.
How Many Ants?, illustrated by Joan Cottle, Children's Press (New York, NY), 1997.
The Harvest Fair, illustrated by Steve Henry, Children's Press (New York, NY), 1997.
The Cool Hot Day, illustrated by Steve Henry, Children's Press (New York, NY), 1997.
E-mail, Children's Press (New York, NY), 1997, revised edition, 2000.
The World Wide Web, Children's Press (New York, NY), 1997, revised edition, 2000.

Praying Mantises, Children's Press (New York, NY), 1999.

The Official M & M's Brand Book of the Millennium, illustrated by Karen Pellaton, Charlesbridge (Watertown, MA), 1999.

Flies, Children's Press (New York, NY), 1999.

Cat on Wheels, illustrated by Mary Peterson, Boyds Mills Press (Honesdale, PA), 2000.

Caving: Exploring Limestone Caves, F. Watts (New York, NY), 2001.

The Littlest Wolf, illustrated by José Aruego and Ariane Dewey, HarperCollins (New York, NY), 2002.

Everybody's Best Friend, illustrated by Christine Tripp, Children's Press (New York, NY), 2002.

Trash Trouble, illustrated by Christine Tripp, Children's Press (New York, NY), 2003.

The New Kid, illustrated by Christine Tripp, Children's Press (New York, NY), 2003.

Subway: The Story of Tunnels, Tubes, and Tracks, illustrated by Neil Waldman, Boyds Mills Press (Honesdale, PA), 2004.

We Are One: The Story of Bayard Rustin, Calkins Creek (Honesdale, PA), 2007.

Birmingham Sunday, Calkins Creek (Honesdale, PA), 2010.

Trick or Treat, Old Armadillo, illustrated by Dominic Catalano, Boyds Mills Press (Honesdale, PA), 2010.

Sophie in Love, illustrated by Sue Porter, Mathew Price (Dallas, TX), 2011.

"FIRST BOOKS" SERIES

BMX Freestyle, F. Watts (New York, NY), 1987.

Karate, F. Watts (New York, NY), 1988.

Footbagging, F. Watts (New York, NY), 1988.

Snowboarding, F. Watts (New York, NY), 1989.

Animals That Hibernate, F. Watts (New York, NY), 1991.

Unusual Friendships . . ., F. Watts (New York, NY), 1993.

Rolling . . . In-line!, F. Watts (New York, NY), 1994.

Mountain Biking, F. Watts (New York, NY), 1997.

Rock Climbing, F. Watts (New York, NY), 1997.

Surfing, F. Watts (New York, NY), 1997.

Mountains, Children's Press (New York, NY), 2000.

"TRUE BOOKS" SERIES

Polar Mammals, Children's Press (New York, NY), 1996.

Figure Skating, Children's Press (New York, NY), 1997.

Bobsledding and the Luge, Children's Press (New York, NY), 1997.

Speed Skating, Children's Press (New York, NY), 1997.

The Winter Olympics, Children's Press (New York, NY), 1997.

Earth, Children's Press (New York, NY), 1998.

Mars, Children's Press (New York, NY), 1998.

Mercury, Children's Press (New York, NY), 1998.

Venus, Children's Press (New York, NY), 1998.

Bees, Children's Press (New York, NY), 1999.

Butterflies and Moths, Children's Press (New York, NY), 1999.

Cockroaches, Children's Press (New York, NY), 1999.

Jupiter, Children's Press (New York, NY), 1999.

Neptune, Children's Press (New York, NY), 1999.

Pluto, Children's Press (New York, NY), 1999.

Saturn, Children's Press (New York, NY), 1999.

Uranus, Children's Press (New York, NY), 1999.

Caves, Children's Press (New York, NY), 2000.

Geysers, Children's Press (New York, NY), 2000.

Glaciers, Children's Press (New York, NY), 2000.

Valleys and Canyons, Children's Press (New York, NY), 2000.

"ROOKIE READERS" SERIES

Firehouse Sal, illustrated by Ethel Gold, Children's Press (New York, NY), 1996.

Aggie and Will, illustrated by Rebecca McKillip Thornburgh, Children's Press (New York, NY), 1998.

Dinosaurs Dance, illustrated by Patrick Girouard, Children's Press (New York, NY), 1998.

Lightning Liz, illustrated by Brian Floca, Children's Press (New York, NY), 1998.

Nana's Hog, illustrated by Susan Miller, Children's Press (New York, NY), 1998.

What Good Is a Tree?, illustrated by Leo Landry, Children's Press (New York, NY), 1998.

Cowboy Up!, illustrated by Susan Miller, Children's Press (New York, NY), 1999.

Raindrops, illustrated by David J. Brooks, Children's Press (New York, NY), 1999.

Cats!, illustrated by Tom Payne, Children's Press (New York, NY), 2000.

Gatitos!, illustrated by Tom Payne, Children's Press (New York, NY), 2000.

The Long Way Home, illustrated by Terry Sirrell, Children's Press (New York, NY), 2000.

Here Comes Trouble, illustrated by Pablo Torrecilla, Children's Press (New York, NY), 2001.

Nana's Fiddle, illustrated by Susan Miller, Children's Press (New York, NY), 2002.

A Bit Is a Bite, illustrated by Erin Eitter Kono, Children's Press (New York, NY), 2007.

Monkey Math, illustrated by Joe Kulka, Children's Press (New York, NY), 2007.

Quiet Wyatt, illustrated by Rusty Fletcher, Children's Press (New York, NY), 2007.

Silent Kay and the Dragon, illustrated by Bob McMahon, Children's Press (New York, NY), 2007.

Slower than a Slug, illustrated by Deborah Zemke, Children's Press (New York, NY), 2007.

"CORNERSTONES OF FREEDOM" SERIES

The Names Project, Children's Press (New York, NY), 1999.

Angel Island, Children's Press (New York, NY), 2001.

"TALL TALES" SERIES

(Reteller) *Calamity Jane,* illustrated by Judy DuFour Love, Compass Point Books (Minneapolis, MN), 2004.

(Reteller) *Casey Jones,* illustrated by Drew Rose, Compass Point Books (Minneapolis, MN), 2004.

(Reteller) *Davy Crockett,* Compass Point Books (Minneapolis, MN), 2004.

(Reteller) *Molly Pitcher,* illustrated by Patrick Girouard, Compass Point Books (Minneapolis, MN), 2004.

(Reteller) *Captain Stormalong,* illustrated by Chi Chung, Compass Point Books (Minneapolis, MN), 2004.

"ROOKIE CHOICES" SERIES; ILLUSTRATED BY CHRISTINE TRIPP

The Big Beautiful Brown Box, Children's Press (New York, NY), 2001.

The Big Tree Ball Game, Children's Press (New York, NY), 2001.

The Messy Lot, Children's Press (New York, NY), 2001.

Money Trouble, Children's Press (New York, NY), 2001.

The Noodle Game, Children's Press (New York, NY), 2001.

The Sparkle Thing, Children's Press (New York, NY), 2001.

The Pet Show, Children's Press (New York, NY), 2002.

Unsinkable!, Children's Press (New York, NY), 2002.

A Flag for All, Children's Press (New York, NY), 2002.

The Birthday Flowers, Children's Press (New York, NY), 2002.

The Promise, Children's Press (New York, NY), 2002.

School Rules, Children's Press (New York, NY), 2002.

The Sidewalk Patrol, Children's Press (New York, NY), 2002.

The Cool Cats, Children's Press (New York, NY), 2003.

Summer Fun, Children's Press (New York, NY), 2003.

"MAGIC DOOR TO READING" SERIES

Spring Sail, illustrated by R.W. Alley, Child's World (Chanhassen, MN), 2005.

Max's Math Machine, illustrated by Robert Squier, Child's World (Chanhassen, MN), 2006.

Bigger and Smaller, illustrated by Patrick Girouard, Child's World (Chanhassen, MN), 2006.

Elwood's Bath, illustrated by Teri Weidner, Child's World (Chanhassen, MN), 2006.

In the Fall, illustrated by R.W. Alley, Child's World (Chanhassen, MN), 2006.

Loud Larry, illustrated by JoAnn Adinolfi, Child's World (Chanhassen, MN), 2006.

One Summery Day, illustrated by R.W. Alley, Child's World (Chanhassen, MN), 2006.

Rumble Bus, illustrated by Ronnie Rooney, Child's World (Chanhassen, MN), 2006.

Sammy's Something Sweet, illustrated by Kathleen Petelinsek, Child's World (Chanhassen, MN), 2006.

A Shake and a Shiver, illustrated by JoAnn Adinolfi, Child's World (Chanhassen, MN), 2006.

Twelve Plump Cookies, illustrated by Sharon Holm, Child's World (Chanhassen, MN), 2006.

Winter Blanket, illustrated by R.W. Alley, Child's World (Chanhassen, MN), 2006.

"AMERICAN HEROES" SERIES

Booker T. Washington: Getting into the Schoolhouse, Marshall Cavendish Benchmark (New York, NY), 2009.

Chief Crazy Horse: Following a Vision, Marshall Cavendish Benchmark (New York, NY), 2009.

Pocahontas: Bridging Two Worlds, Marshall Cavendish Benchmark (New York, NY), 2009.

OTHER

(Editor) *Being Different: Lambda Youths Speak Out,* F. Watts (New York, NY), 1995.

(Editor) *Letters to Our Children: Lesbian and Gay Adults Speak to the New Generation,* F. Watts (New York, NY), 1997.

Sidelights

Larry Dane Brimner is the author of more than one hundred books for children and young adults, including such award-winning titles as *A Migrant Family, We Are One: The Story of Bayard Rustin,* and *Birmingham Sunday.* Born in St. Petersburg, Florida, Brimner was raised in Kodiak Island, Alaska, where his parents began reading him to at a very young age. Introduced to some of the greatest literary giants, including Mark Twain, Ernest Hemingway, and F. Scott Fitzgerald, he was able to read simple sentences by age four and blossomed into an avid bookworm. In addition to reading all the children's books in his family's library, Brimner eventually began creating his own stories. After attended elementary and high school in Alaska, he moved to California where he published several poems while pursuing his B.A. in literature at San Diego State University. After graduating, Brimner began a teaching career that lasted for twenty years before he left to start his prolific writing career.

Brimner's childhood in Alaska inspired his interests in sports, nature, and fiction. "Ever since I was a small child growing up on Kodiak Island, with no television and only sporadic radio reception, I have enjoyed reading and listening to stories," he once recalled to *SATA.* "My early experience in Alaska must also explain why I'm happiest in a snowy environment, surrounded by nature, and why winter is my favorite season of the year." "*Animals That Hibernate* and *Unusual Friendships* are both about nature," the author added, "and *Cory Coleman, Grade 2* features a 'winter' sport—ice skating, something I've been doing almost since I started to walk."

Several of Brimner's books introduce young people to sports and provide guides for learning more about them. In *BMX Freestyle,* for example, he discusses motocross biking and includes chapters on the history of the sport, safety tips, trick techniques, selecting equipment, and directions for building a ramp. Connie Tyrrell Burns, reviewing this book for *School Library Journal,* described *BMX Freestyle* as "well done."

Karate provides descriptions of various martial-arts styles and moves and discusses their development. A reviewer for *Booklist* predicted that readers interested in the martial arts "will be well served by Brimner's introduction" here. *Footbagging,* another sports book by Brimner, explains the background, benefits, and how-tos of footbagging, or hacky-sack, a sport involving the kicking of a small ball or "bag." According to *Young Adults/Children's Reviews,* Brimner's instructions are "clear and encouraging." Reviewing *Snowboarding,* which follows the format of Brimner's other sports books, Ann G. Brouse concluded in *School Library Journal* that "the clarity and thoroughness of this introduction is sure to satisfy the merely curious and serious snowboarding beginners." All of Brimner's sport books are enhanced by bibliographies and/or addresses of sport organizations and associations.

Animals That Hibernate reflects Brimner's enthusiasm for natural subjects. Here the author illuminates the behavior of animals that sleep (lightly or deeply) through the winter as they store food, prepare a den, and, finally, go to sleep. Although the majority of the book is devoted to mammals, animals included range from woodchucks to birds to reptiles. In *School Library Journal* Diane Nunn explained that the "uncluttered format" of *Animals That Hibernate* incorporates "frequent subheadings [that] make the information accessible" and a bibliography, glossary, and index are helpful auxiliaries to the text. In *Subway: The Story of Tunnels, Tubes, and Tracks* Brimner explores the history of underground transportation systems in New York City and London, England, focusing on construction techniques as well as individuals such as Alfred Ely Beach, who designed a railway to run beneath Broadway. Here the author "offers a solid overview of why subways developed," Gillian Engberg noted in *School Library Journal.*

In *We Are One,* Brimner examines the life of civil rights activist Bayard Rustin, a trusted advisor to Martin Luther King, Jr. Rustin, who adhered to the teachings of Mahatma Gandhi, practiced nonviolent methods of civil disobedience. Once arrested for refusing to give up his seat on a segregated bus, he convinced U.S. President Franklin D. Roosevelt to sign key legislation outlawing racial discrimination in the national defense industry and helped organize the 1963 March on Washington for Jobs and Freedom, where King delivered his famous "I Have a Dream" speech. A contributor in *Kirkus Reviews* applauded the "effective mix of major historical events and small, telling anecdotes" in *We Are One,* and Marcia Kochel reported in *School Library Journal* that Brimner "adeptly places Rustin in the larger context of the Jim Crow era and the Civil Rights Movement."

Issues of race are also the subject of *Birmingham Sunday,* a Jane Addams Honor Book selection. On September 15, 1963, a bomb hurled from a moving car destroyed the Sixteenth Street Baptist Church in Birmingham, Alabama, killing four African-American girls attending services there and igniting an outbreak of violence in which two more black youngsters lost their lives. Brimner sets this incident within the context of the civil rights era, discussing such topics as Jim Crow laws, the origin of the National Association for the Advancement of Colored People, and the landmark U.S. Supreme Court ruling *Brown vs. Board of Education* that was handed down in 1954. Using FBI reports and court transcripts, he also chronicles the decades-long investigation into the crime that resulted in the conviction of two men. A *Kirkus Reviews* critic described *Birmingham Sunday* as a "standout book for its thorough research," while Margaret Auguste observed in *School Library Journal* that Brimner "successfully blends the facts of the event with the intense emotions of the period in order to bring it to life."

Moving to older readers, in *Letters to Our Children: Lesbian and Gay Adults Speak to the New Generation* Brimner compiles essays and letters that offer advice and support for gay and lesbian youth. The essays were written by a range of writers; one was penned by an openly gay politician, while another was written by the archbishop of the Ecumenical Catholic Church. Additional contributions came from attorneys, college professors, school teachers, and professional writers. Brimner's common theme is to support teens struggling with their identity as homosexuals, and the book is meant to encourage young adults to love themselves regardless of their sexual orientation. Debbie Carton reviewed the anthology for *Booklist* and described the work as a "warm and supportive collection" that offers a compassionate voice from gay and lesbian adults.

Country Bear's Good Neighbor, Brimner's first work of fiction for children, was described by a *Publishers Weekly* contributor as "a sweet debut." In this story, Country Bear borrows ingredient after ingredient from his neighbor in order to bake a cake. Just when his neighbor, a little girl, decides that Bear has borrowed enough, he brings the baked cake to her house to share. Brimner includes the recipe for "Country Bear's Good Neighbor Cake." According to Anna Biagioni Hart, writing for *School Library Journal,* the "unpretentious and kind" book will be enjoyed by preschoolers and kindergartners. In another "Country Bear" book, *Country Bear's Surprise,* Country Bear fears that the little girl and her friends have forgotten his birthday and are interested only in the private club they have created. Just as Country Bear decides to run away, the little girl surprises him with a birthday party. A recipe for surprise cookies is included with this story, which Kay Weisman, writing for *Booklist,* called a "charmer." *Max and Felix* is also targeted at a young audience. In this work, two frogs capture their comic experiences—ranging from fishing to telling spooky stores—with a camera. According to Marge Loch-Wouters in *School Library Journal,* children will "enjoy spending time" with these frogs.

Cory Coleman, Grade 2 tells the story of a boy who invites his class to the ice-skating rink for his birthday

***Larry Dane Brimner takes readers back to the civil rights era and the violence inflicted on black churches in his nonfiction book* Birmingham Sunday.** (Calkins Creek, 2010. Photograph of destroyed church in Birmingham, Alabama by AP Photo.)

party. Although he does not want to invite a boy named Delphinius, who he calls "Dumbphinius," his mother insists that the entire class attend the party. Delphinius does come to the party and attempts to spoil it by knocking children down. Although Cory manages to humiliate Delphinius, the two ultimately become friends. Laura Culberg, reviewing the book for *School Library Journal,* wrote that the novel's resolution is "predictable" yet "believable."

Brimmner's humorous story about a young boy's attempt to run away from home unfolds in *Elliot Fry's Good-Bye,* which *Booklist* contributor Annie Ayres called "a story that most young children will identify with and find reassuring." Throughout the day Elliott is scolded for his missteps: his mother reprimands him for

tracking mud into the house, his father tells him he is being too loud, and his sister tattles to his parents when he jumps on the bed. Elliot's tolerance is truly tested when he is informed that he will be sharing his room with visiting Uncle Abe. When Elliot decides to leave home, his parents begin offering tools to assist in his departure, including snacks and a suitcase. The boy packs his bag and makes a short trip around the block before returning home to his wise and loving parents.

Brimner addresses young readers dealing with sibling rivalry in *The Littlest Wolf.* In his story, Little Wolf does not measure up to his older brothers and sisters: he does not run as fast as his siblings, he does not roll in a straight line as they do, and he is no match when it comes to his pouncing abilities. Finally, Little Wolf is set at ease by his father, who reminds the young pup of his uniqueness. Deborah Stevens, writing in the *Bulletin of the Center for Children's Books*, noted that Brimner's "text is reassuring and enjoyably humorous," while a *Publishers Weekly* critic commended the book for its ability to "give fledgling young ones a boost of confidence." According to a contributor in *Kirkus Reviews*, in *The Littlest Wolf* "Brimner has written a wonderful and reassuring read-aloud, full of comfort, rhythm, and repetition."

Biographical and Critical Sources

PERIODICALS

Booklist, May 15, 1988, review of *Karate*, pp. 1605-1606; February 15, 1991, Kay Weisman, review of *Country Bear's Surprise*, pp. 1199-1201; March 1, 1994, Annie Ayres, review of *Elliot Fry's Good-Bye*, p. 1267; September 15, 1997, Debbie Carton, review of *Letters to Our Children: Lesbian and Gay Adults Speak to a New Generation*, p. 218; October 15, 2004, Gillian Engberg, Gillian. review of *Subway: The Story of Tunnels, Tubes, and Tracks*, p. 400; September 1, 2007, Hazel Rochman, review of *We Are One: The Story of Bayard Rustin*, p. 112; February 1, 2010, Hazel Rochman, review of *Birmingham Sunday*, p. 56.

Bulletin of the Center for Children's Books, July-August, 2002, Deborah Stevenson, review of *The Littlest Wolf*, p. 395.

Kirkus Reviews, January 15, 1988, review of *Footbagging*, pp. 120-121; March 15, 2002, review of *The Littlest Wolf*, p. 406; October 1, 2004, review of *Subway*, p. 957; September 1, 2007, review of *We Are One*; February 15, 2010, review of *Birmingham Sunday*.

New York Times Book Review, January 17, 1993, Henry Mayer, review of *A Migrant Family*.

Publishers Weekly, May 13, 1988, review of *Country Bear's Good Neighbor*, p. 272; December 6, 1993, review of *Elliot Fry's Good-Bye*, p. 73; March 11, 2002, review of *The Littlest Wolf*, p. 71.

School Library Journal, September, 1987, Connie Tyrell, review of *BMX Freestyle*, p. 186; December, 1989, Anne G. Brouse, review of *Snowboarding*, p. 106; November, 1990, Laura Culberg, review of *Cory Coleman, Grade 2*; October, 1988, Anna Biagioni Hart, review of *Country Bear's Good Neighbor*, p. 115; March, 1993, Marge Loch-Wouters, review of *Max and Felix*, p. 171; July, 1991, Diane Nunne, review of *Animals That Hibernate*, p. 77; May, 2002, Bina Williams, review of *The Littlest Wolf*, p. 105; July, 2004, Rita Soltan, review of *Captain Stormalong*, p. 91; March, 2005, Ellen Loughran, review of *Subway*, p. 191; November, 2005, Melinda Piehler, reviews of *In the Fall, One Summery Day, Spring Sail*, and *Winter Blanket*, p. 83; December, 2005, Laura Scott, reviews of *Loud Larry, Max's Math Machine, Sammy's Something Sweet*, and *Twelve Plump Cookies*, all p. 101; January, 2007, Colleen D. Bocka, review of *Monkey Math*, p. 88; November, 2007, Marcia Kochel, review

of *We Are One*, p. 142; March, 2009, Tracy H. Chrenka, reviews of *Booker T. Washington: Getting into the Schoolhouse, Chief Crazy Horse: Following a Vision*, and *Pocahontas: Bridging Two Worlds*, all p. 132; April, 2010, Margaret Auguste, review of *Birmingham Sunday*, p. 174; October, 2010, Susan E. Murray, review of *Trick or Treat, Old Armadillo*, p. 81.

ONLINE

Boyds Mills Press Web site, http://www.boydsmillspress.com/ (April 10, 2006), "Larry Dane Brimner."

Larry Dane Brimner Home Page, http://www.brimner.com (July 1, 2011).*

* * *

BROWN, Alan
See BROWN, Alan James

* * *

BROWN, Alan James 1947-
(Alan Brown)

Personal

Born 1947, in England; married Berlie Doherty (a writer). *Education:* College degree. *Hobbies and other interests:* Tennis, walking.

Addresses

Home—Derbyshire, England. *Agent*—Caroline Walsh, David Higham Associates, 5-8 Lower John St., Golden Square, London W1F 9HA, England, dha@davidhigham.co.uk *E-mail*—hushwing@windhover.free-online.co.uk.

Career

Educator and author of books for children. Formerly worked as a technical writer; Sheffield Hallam University, former teacher of writing for children in master's program. Speaker at schools and libraries.

Awards, Honors

Environmental Award shortlist, Wilderness Society of Australia, 2002, for *Turtle's Song*.

Writings

PICTURE BOOKS; AS ALAN BROWN, EXCEPT WHERE NOTED

The Windhover, illustrated by Christian Birmingham, Harcourt (New York, NY), 1997.

Old Hushwing, illustrated by Angelo Rinaldi, Collins Children's (London, England), 1998.

Nikki and the Rocking Horse, illustrated by Peter Utton, Collins Children's (London, England), 1998.

Humbugs, illustrated by Adrian Reynolds, Hodder Children's (London, England), 1998.

The Dreaming Tree, illustrated by Claire Fletcher, Collins Children's (London, England), 2000.

Hoot and Holler, illustrated by Rimantas Rolia, Hutchinson (London, England), 2001.

I Am a Dog, illustrated by Jonathan Alan, Red Fox (London, England), 2002.

Turtle's Song, illustrated by Kim Michelle Toft, University of Queensland Press (Brisbane, Queensland, Australia), 2002.

(As Alan Brown; with Stephen Elboz and Kate Ruttle) *Billy the Hero,* illustrated by Chris Mould, Oxford University Press (Oxford, England), 2006.

Love-a-Duck, illustrated by Francesca Chessa, Holiday House (New York, NY), 2010.

NOVELS; AS ALAN BROWN

A Dog of My Own, illustrated by Rob Hefferan, Hodder Children's (London, England), 1997.

Sword and Sorcery, Hodder Children's (London, England), 1997.

The Incredible Journey of Walter Rat, Hodder Children's (London, England), 1999.

King of the Dark Tower, illustrated by Peter Melnyczuk, Hodder Children's (London, England), 1999.

The Tolpuddle Boy, Hodder Children's (London, England), 2002.

Michael and the Monkey King, Lulu.com, 2008.

OTHER

(As Alan Brown) *The Smallpox Slayer: One Man's Fight against a Deadly Disease,* Hodder Children's (London, England), 2001.

Also author, as Alan Brown, of *Dead Good: Tales from a Cemetery,* illustrated by Caroline Firenz, Friends of the General Cemetery (Sheffield, England). Contributor to books, including *Handbook of Creative Writing,* edited by Steve Earnshaw, Edinburgh University Press.

Biographical and Critical Sources

PERIODICALS

Booklist, November 1, 1997, Shelley Townsend-Hudson, review of *The Windhover,* p. 478; November 1, 2001, Kathy Broderick, review of *Hoot and Holler,* p. 481.

Kirkus Reviews, March 1, 2010, review of *Love-a-Duck.*

School Librarian, winter, 2010, Jackie Oates, review of *The Tolpuddle Boy,* p. 250.

School Library Journal, October, 2001, Jane Marino, review of *Hoot and Holler,* p. 106; July, 2010, Maryann H. Owen, review of *Love-a-Duck,* p. 56.

ONLINE

Alan James Brown Home Page, http://www.alanjames brown.com (June 12, 2011).*

*   *   *

BROWN, Rod 1961-

Personal

Born 1961, in Columbia, SC; married; wife's name Cathy.

Addresses

Home—Washington, DC. *E-mail*—rodbrown1961@ gmail.com.

Career

Artist and illustrator. Fine-art painter, beginning 1989; also worked as a graphic designer. *Exhibitions:* Work exhibited at museums and galleries, including Charles Sumner School Museum, Washington, DC, 1991; B'nai B'rith Klutznick National Jewish Museum, Washington, DC, 1991; Schomburg Center for Research in Black Culture, New York, NY, 1993, 2000; Project Understanding, Ventura, CA, 1994; W.K. Kellogg Foundation, Battle Creek, MI, 1994; Avery Research Center, Charleston, SC, 1995; National Geographic Society, Washington, DC, 2002; British Empire & Commonwealth Museum, Bristol, England, 2007; and Potteries Museum & Art Gallery, Stoke-on-Trent, England, 2007. *Military service:* Served in U.S. Army.

Awards, Honors

Best Book for Young Adults designation, American Library Association, and Notable Children's Trade Book in the Field of Social Studies selection, National Council for the Social Studies/Children's Book Council, both 1998, both for *From Slave Ship to Freedom Road* by Julius Lester.

Illustrator

Julius Lester, *From Slave Ship to Freedom Road,* Dial Books (New York, NY), 1998.

Ntozake Shange, *We Troubled the Waters* (poems), Amistad/Collins (New York, NY), 2009.

Ntozake Shange, *Freedom's A-calling Me,* Amistad/Collins (New York, NY), 2012.

Rod Brown (Photograph by Robert Cannon. Reproduced by permission.)

Contributor of illustrations to books, including *Jubilee: The Emergence of African-American Culture,* by Howard Dodson, National Geographic Society; and *Making Thinking Visible,* Jossey-Bass.

Books featuring Brown's work have been translated into several languages, including Korean and Japanese.

Sidelights

An accomplished artist, Rod Brown focuses on the African-American experience in his highly praised oil paintings, some of which have appeared in children's books such as Julius Lester's award-winning *From Slave Ship to Freedom Road.* "I have focused my attention on teaching communities around the country about African American culture and history, and the power of the human spirit," the artist noted on his home page. Brown's evocative paintings have appeared in academic books such as Howard Dodson's *Jubilee: The Emergence of African-American Culture,* and they reached a far different audience when they were featured on the popular television sitcom *Fresh Prince of Bel Air.*

In *From Slave Ship to Freedom Road* Lester explores the slave trade in the Americas, presenting the reader with probing questions designed to elicit visceral reactions. More than twenty of Brown's paintings are included in the work, all drawn from his celebrated ex-

hibition "From Slavery to Freedom." "Many of the scenes so artfully portrayed are those depicting suffering, from the dreaded Middle Passage to field labor," Shirley Wilson noted in her *School Library Journal* review of *From Slave Ship to Freedom Road.* "Brown's paintings provide the cohesive narrative line and have a stunning power of their own," observed a *Publishers Weekly* critic, the reviewer adding that these images "provide[d] the inspiration for Lester's . . . strong and searing text."

Brown also provided the artwork for *We Troubled the Waters* and *Freedom's A-calling Me,* two collections of poems by Ntozake Shange that offer a stark and honest look at the struggle for civil rights in the United States. In one painting for *We Troubled the Waters,* Brown's depiction of a pleasant, sunny day "gives way to the unspeakable reality of Jim Crow in the form of a faceless body that tarnishes the tranquil scene," as Margaret Auguste wrote in *School Library Journal.* Praising Shange's verse in the same book for its "malleable voice," a *Publishers Weekly* critic added that Brown's "iconic, earth-toned paintings add even more dimension" to the poems, and Hazel Rochman maintained in *Booklist* that the "powerful poetry and art" in *We Troubled the Waters* "confront the brutality and hatred that had to be overcome."

Its ability to capture history has made Brown's artwork a useful tool for teachers as far away as the Netherlands, where children have critically studied and discussed images in *From Slave Ship to Freedom Road.* The artist himself has also traveled abroad in the service of sharing the African-American story: In 2010, Brown and his wife were invited guests of President Abdoulaye Wade of Senegal, and joined a 200-member

Brown's picture-book projects include creating the art for Ntozake Shange's poetry collection **We Troubled the Waters.** (Illustration copyright © 2009 by Rod Brown. Reproduced by permission of HarperCollins Children's Books, a division of HarperCollins Publishers.)

Brown's illustrations include evocative pictures from the African-American past, such as his portrait "Tibby." (Courtesy of Rod Brown.)

U.S. delegation in speaking on African-American culture and how it can benefit the African Diaspora.

Biographical and Critical Sources

PERIODICALS

Booklist, February 15, 1998, Hazel Rochman, review of *From Slave Ship to Freedom Road,* p. 1009; October 1, 2009, Hazel Rochman, review of *We Troubled the Waters,* p. 43.

Bulletin of the Center for Children's Books, February, 1998, review of *From Slave Ship to Freedom Road,* p. 212.

Kirkus Reviews, October 15, 2009, review of *We Troubled the Waters.*

Publishers Weekly, December 1, 1997, review of *From Slave Ship to Freedom Road,* p. 54; November 23, 2009, review of *We Troubled the Waters,* p. 56.

School Library Journal, February, 1998, Shirley Wilson, review of *From Slave Ship to Freedom Road,* p. 119; December, 2009, Margaret Auguste, review of *We Troubled the Waters,* p. 142.

Voice of Youth Advocates, February, 1999, review of *From Slave Ship to Freedom Road,* p. 412.

Washington Post, December 13, 1993, Eric Brace, "A Painter Enslaved by History: Rod Brown's Harrowing Lessons."

ONLINE

Rod Brown Home Page, http://rodbrownsartcollection.com (July 1, 2011).

*   *   *

BUSCEMA, Stephanie

Personal

Born in NY; married; husband's name Rob. *Education:* School of Visual Arts, B.F.A. (illustration). *Hobbies and other interests:* Collecting mid-twentieth-century vintage objects, monster movies, baking, sewing, photography.

Addresses

Home—Brooklyn, NY. *Agent*—Shannon Associates, 333 W. 57th St., Ste. 809, New York, NY 10019. *E-mail*—sbuscema@gmail.com.

Career

Illustrator and cartoonist, beginning 1998. Graphic artist. *Exhibitions:* Work included in exhibitions at Gallery 1988, Venice and Melrose, CA.

Member

Society of Illustrators, New York (artist member).

Illustrator

Debbie Levy, *Maybe I'll Sleep in the Bathtub Tonight, and Other Funny Bedtime Poems,* Sterling Pub. (New York, NY), 2010.

Peggy Archer, *Name That Dog!: Puppy Poems from A to Z,* Dial Books for Young Readers (New York, NY), 2010.

Creator, with Marsha and Candis Cooke, of cross-platform Web comic "Teenage Satan!"

Sidelights

Inspired by the work of her grandfather, noted Marvel comics illustrator John Buscema, Stephanie Buscema learned the technique of brush-style inking as a girl and she continues this tradition as a sequential artist in her own right. In addition to her work as a graphic artist and cartoonist—she is cocreator of the original Web comic "Teenage Satan!"—Buscema treats younger readers to her imaginative visual style as illustrator of the picture books *Maybe I'll Sleep in the Bathtub Tonight, and Other Funny Bedtime Poems* by Debbie Levy and Peggy Archer's equally humorous *Name That Dog!: Puppy Poems from A to Z.* Praising the latter book as "ebullient," a *Publishers Weekly* contributor acknowledged Buscema's success at maintaining her family's artistic tradition by remarking that her colorful illustrations "have a retro style reminiscent of early Disney cartoons."

While working as an inker on the Marvel superhero comics created by her grandfather, Buscema gained an appreciation for the quality of line that could be created by cartooning using a fine paintbrush rather than a nibbed or technical drawing pen. While studying for her B.F.A. in illustration at New York City's School of Vi-

Stephanie Buscema's illustration projects include creating art for Peggy Archer's **Name That Dog!: Puppy Poems from A to Z.** (Illustration copyright © 2010 by Stephanie Buscema. Reproduced by permission of Dial Books for Young Readers, a division of Penguin Young Readers Group, a member of Penguin Group (USA) Inc., 345 Hudson St., New York, NY 10014. All rights reserved.)

sual Arts, she added the use of gouache to her creative repertoire and continued to hone to traditional media rather than the digitized approaches used by most of her peers. Buscema's work as a book illustrator has meshed with other graphic projects, including illustrations and designs for comics and book publishers as well as to corporations.

Reviewing *Maybe I'll Sleep in the Bathtub Tonight, and Other Funny Bedtime Poems,* which contains twenty poems by Levy, *School Library Journal* critic Julie Roach cited Buscema's "bright, busy gouache illustrations" for their "retro feel." A *Publishers Weekly* reviewer shared a similar perception, writing that the "slightly modern edge" of the book's art helps make the work "a fun, hip take on traditional bedtime books."

A run up the alphabet is marked by dogs of all sorts in Archer's *Name That Dog!,* and the twenty-six poems in this collection introduce "dogs whose monikers generally stem from their looks, behavior traits, or personalities," according to Roach. "Young pup fanciers might enjoy both Buscema's retro-style art and the names that describe the dogs," predicted a *Kirkus Reviews* writer of *Name That Dog!,* and in *Booklist* Kara Dean noted that the "energetic, stylized illustrations" accompanying each animal in Archer's "rogues gallery of pooches" "encourage viewers to giggle over" their favorite canine.

Biographical and Critical Sources

PERIODICALS

Booklist, March 1, 2010, Hazel Rochman, review of *Maybe I'll Sleep in the Bathtub Tonight, and Other Funny Bedtime Poems,* p. 75; April 1, 2010, Kara Dean, review of *Name That Dog!: Puppy Poems from A to Z,* p. 43.

Kirkus Reviews, March 1, 2010, review of *Name That Dog!*

Publishers Weekly, February 8, 2010, review of *Maybe I'll Sleep in the Bathtub Tonight, and Other Funny Bedtime Poems,* p. 48; April 26, 2010, review of *Name That Dog!,* p. 110.

School Library Journal, April, 2010, Julie Roach, review of *Maybe I'll Sleep in the Bathtub Tonight, and Other Funny Bedtime Poems,* p. 147; May, 2010, Julie Roach, review of *Name That Dog!,* p. 95.

ONLINE

Stephanie Buscema Home Page, http://www.stephanie buscema.com (July 25, 2011).

Stephanie Buscema Web log, http://stephaniebuscema. blogspot.com/ (July 25, 2011).*

C

CASSIDY, Kay

Personal
Married. *Education:* Bachelor's degree; M.B.A. *Hobbies and other interests:* Tennis, yoga, reading, movies, NFL football, NASCAR, spending time with family.

Addresses
Home—Midwestern U.S.

Career
Writer. Formerly worked in business as a professional trainer. Creator of The Great Scavenger Hunt Contest (online reading program), 2009. Presenter at schools; motivational speaker.

Member
Mensa.

Writings

The Cinderella Society, Egmont USA (New York, NY), 2010.

Sidelights
Novelist Kay Cassidy often surprises people when she explains that she was a college cheerleader and bookworm before earning her M.B.A. and working as a motivational speaker. Cassidy's first teen novel, *The Cinderella Society,* is brimming with the upbeat, can-do spirit that reflects its author's accomplishments. In addition to writing, Cassidy has also created The Great Scavenger Hunt Contest, a reading program geared for middle-grade and teen readers that uses entertaining trivia challenges—ten questions per book—to inspire readers to scour the pages of hundreds of age-appropriate stories. "As a YA author and proud owner of a well-worn library card, I wanted to give something back to all the librarians whose book recommendations helped me grow as a writer and fed my imagination over the years," Cassidy explained to online interviewer Cynthia Leitich Smith in discussing the program. The Great Scavenger Hunt Contest "offers year-round free programming that will keep readers coming back to the library for more."

In *The Cinderella Society* readers meet sixteen-year-old Jess Parker as she winds up her sophomore year of high school. Although she has excelled at being a cheerleader, Jess feels cut off from her classmates, so she is surprised when she receives an invitation to join the Cinderella Society. This secret group—whose members call themselves the Cindys and who are among the nicest girls in Jess's school—has banded together to undermine the rumor mills, disses, and other machinations of the meaner girls, the aptly named Wickeds. At first Jess enjoys her new friends' enthusiasm for makeovers, closet clean-outs, and other confidence-building activities, and these aid her in winning the attention of her current crush. However, she soon realizes that there is a responsibility to being a Cindy as well: protecting the regular students (the Reggies) against harms caused by the evil but popular Wickeds. It is a battle that has been ongoing among teens for centuries and one that the Wickeds are intent upon winning. Noting the story's obvious appeal to teens "who dream of being accepted within their own schools," Laura Amos added in *School Library Journal* that *The Cinderella Society* benefits from "characters [that] are multidimensional" and a storyline that "is well paced." "Jess's up-and-down romance is interesting to follow," asserted a *Kirkus Reviews* writer in reviewing Cassidy's high-school fantasy.

Discussing the things that inspire her stories, Cassidy noted on her home page that ideas come from "everything and nothing. Sometimes I'll see a commercial that gives me an idea for a character, sometimes I'll have a dream I actually remember that I think would make a fun story idea. Even fortune cookies are fair game! I've learned to tune into what's going on around me and pick up ideas in the oddest of places. For me, that's part of the fun of writing."

Cover of Kay Cassidy's upbeat young-adult novel The Cinderella Society. (Egmont USA, 2010. Book cover photograph by Image Source. Reproduced by permission of Egmont USA.)

Biographical and Critical Sources

PERIODICALS

Bulletin of the Center for Children's Books, May, 2010, Karen Coats, review of *The Cinderella Society,* p. 374.

Kirkus Reviews, March 1, 2010, review of *The Cinderella Society.*

Publishers Weekly, March 29, 2010, review of *The Cinderella Society,* p. 60.

School Library Journal, April, 2010, Laura Amos, review of *The Cinderella Society,* p. 152.

Voice of Youth Advocates, February, 2011, Shari Fesko, review of "The Great Scavenger Hunt," p. 540.

ONLINE

Cynsations Web log, http://cynthialeitichsmith.blogspot.com/ (April 30, 2009), Cynthia Leitich Smith, interview with Cassidy.

Kay Cassidy Home Page, http://www.kaycassidy.com (August 9, 2011).*

CÓRDOVA, Amy

Personal

Born in WI; partner of Dan Enger; children: Esau, Jess. *Education:* Attended college.

Addresses

Office—P.O. Box 3043, Taos, NM 87571. *E-mail*—amycordova.art@gmail.com.

Career

Artist, author, and educator. Artist-in-residence in NM, CA, OK, NE, TX, and MN; designer of art curriculum and programs. Teacher at personal-creativity workshops. *Exhibitions:* Work exhibited in numerous museums and galleries throughout the United States, including at Florida Gulf Coast Art Center, 1989; Carolyn Ruff Gallery, Minneapolis, MN, 1996; Milicent Rogers Musem, Taos; and Juanita Harvey Museum, Wichita Falls, TX; and in "Latino Folk Tales: Cuentos Populares—Art by Latino Artists" (traveling exhibition), 2011-15. Works included in private and corporate collections throughout the United States and Europe.

Awards, Honors

Folk Art Award, National Endowment for the Arts; Pura Belpré Illustrator Award Honor Book citation, American Library Association, 2009, for *What Can You Do with a Rebozo?* by Carmen Tafollo; Wisconsin Library Association Illustrators Award, 2009, for *Namaste!* by Diana Cohn; Américas Award Commended Title, and Pura Belpré Illustrator Award Honor Book citation, both 2011, both for *Fiesta Babies* by Tafolla.

Writings

SELF-ILLUSTRATED

Abuelita's Heart, Simon & Schuster Books for Young Readers (New York, NY), 1997.

Talking Eagle and the Lady of Roses: The Story of Juan Diego and Our Lady of Guadalupe, afterword by Eugene Gollogly, SteinerBooks (Great Barrington, MA), 2010.

ILLUSTRATOR

Roy Owen, *My Night Forest,* Four Winds Press (New York, NY), 1994.

Rudolfo Anaya, *My Land Sings: Stories from the Rio Grande,* Morrow Junior Books (New York, NY), 1999.

Linda Boyden, *The Blue Roses,* Lee & Low Books (New York, NY), 2002.

Diana Cohn, *Dream Carver,* Chronicle Books (San Francisco, CA), 2002.

Rudolfo Anaya, *The Santero's Miracle: A Bilingual Story,* Spanish translation by Enrique Lamadrid, University of New Mexico Press (Albuquerque, NM), 2004.

Rudolfo Anaya, *The First Tortilla: A Bilingual Story,* Spanish translation by Enrique R. Lamadrid, University of New Mexico Press (Albuquerque, NM), 2007.

Carmen Tafolla, *What Can You Do with a Rebozo?,* Tricycle Press (Berkeley, CA), 2008.

Enrique R. Lamardrid and Juan Estevan Arellano, translators and retellers, *Juan the Bear and the Water of Life/La acequia de Juan del Oso,* University of New Mexico Press (Albuquerque, NM), 2008.

Rudolfo Anaya, *Juan and the Jackalope: A Children's Book in Verse,* University of New Mexico Press (Albuquerque, NM), 2009.

Diana Cohn, *Namaste!,* afterword by Ang Rita Sherpa, SteinerBooks (Great Barrington, MA), 2009.

Carmen Tafolla, *Fiesta Babies,* Tricycle Press (Berkeley, CA), 2010.

Enrique LaMadrid, *Amadito and the Horo Children,* University of New Mexico Press (Albuquerque, NM), 2011.

Rudolfo Anaya, *La Llorona: The Crying Woman,* Spanish translation by Enrique R. Lamadrid, University of New Mexico Press (Albuquerque, NM), 2011.

Diana Cohn, *Roses for Isabella,* SteinerBooks (Great Barrington, MA), 2012.

Contributor of illustrations to educational publications, including *National Geographic Educational.*

Sidelights

A respected artist and educator, Amy Córdova creates artwork for numerous picture books, among them stories by such authors as Rudolfo Anaya, Diana Cohn, and Carmen Tafolla, as well as writing and illustrating original stories of her own. Córdova has earned recognition for her vivid, brightly colored painting style. Her focus is on pedagogy of place and those who inhabit different landscapes. Among her honors are two Pura Belpré Illustrator Award Honor Book citations for *What Can You Do with a Rebozo?* and *Fiesta Babies,* both featuring a text by Tafolla.

Born in Wisconsin, Córdova made her literary debut in 1994 when her illustrations brought to life Roy Owen's story in *My Night Forest,* a bedtime tale in which a child imagines how the world appears to a variety of different animals. The artist "infuses the tale with vibrant, Hispanic folk imagery," a *Publishers Weekly* reviewer noted of the book. In *Abuelita's Heart,* her first original story, Córdova explores the warm, loving relationship between a girl and her grandmother, who teaches the youngster about the connection between the natural and supernatural worlds. "The story's mystical mood is juxtaposed with strong, primitive-style paintings," as Ilene Cooper remarked in her *Booklist* review of *Abuelita's Heart.*

For *The Blue Roses,* a picture book by Linda Boyden, a young Native American girl mourns the loss of her beloved grandfather, with whom she shared a love of gardening. "Córdova's pleasant childlike pictures" offer readers the opportunity to "see Rosalie's grief as well as her growth, both physical and emotional," Lauren

Peterson explained in her *Booklist* review of *The Blue Roses,* and Kathy Piehl wrote in *School Library Journal* that the illustrations "have a static quality that reinforces the reflective tone of the text." Cohn's *Dream Carver* was inspired by the life of Manuel Jiménez, a renowned woodcarver from Oaxaca, Mexico. According to *Booklist* critic Julie Cummins, "Córdova's intensely colored acrylic illustrations" for this book "do justice to the vibrant Mexican art form," and a contributor in *Publishers Weekly* asserted that she "animates the compositions with big, bold shapes and electric, saturated colors."

Namaste!, another work by Cohn, centers on the daily activities of Nima, a young Nepalese girl. In the words of *School Library Journal* critic Monika Schroeder, "the vibrant folk-art illustrations showing the details of Nima's life . . . support the simple story perfectly." Enrique R. Lamardrid and Juan Estevan Arellano offer a retelling from New Mexican folklore in *Juan the Bear and the Water of Life/La acequia de Juan del Oso.* "Córdova's bold colors and brushstrokes evoke the rustic folk-art styles of the Southwest," Mary Landrum noted in her *School Library Journal* review of this work.

In *The First Tortilla: A Bilingual Story* Anaya recounts a Mexican legend about a child's efforts to help her village during a horrible drought. Córdova's illustrations "lend a traditional feel to the setting while maintaining the tale's mystical elements," according to Susan E. Murray in her review of the picture-book retelling for *School Library Journal.* Tafolla examines a traditional Mexican garment in *What Can You Do with a Rebozo?,* and Mary Elam applauded the "rich bands of jewel-toned acrylics" that the illustrator weaves throughout this tale. Celebrations are the focus of Tafolla's *Fiesta Babies,* described as a "Latino rhyming romp" by a contributor in *Kirkus Reviews.* Landrum offered praise for Córdova's artwork here, remarking that her "bold acrylic colors and brisk brushstrokes capture the fiesta's energy and [the] good cheer" of Tafolla's engaging text.

Biographical and Critical Sources

PERIODICALS

Booklist, August, 1997, Ilene Cooper, review of *Abuelita's Heart,* p. 1905; May 15, 2002, Lauren Peterson, review of *The Blue Roses,* p. 1600; June 1, 2002, Julie Cummins, review of *Dream Carver,* p. 1721; February 15, 2010, Ilene Cooper, review of *Fiesta Babies,* p. 80.

Kirkus Reviews, April 1, 2002, review of *The Blue Roses,* p. 486; June 1, 2002, review of *Dream Carver,* p. 802; January 15, 2010, review of *Fiesta Babies.*

Publishers Weekly, October 3, 1994, review of *My Night Forest,* p. 67; April 29, 2002, review of *Dream Carver,* p. 70.

School Library Journal, June, 2002, Kathy Piehl, review of *The Blue Roses,* p. 88; July, 2002, Ann Welton, review of *Dream Carver,* p. 86; July, 2007, Susan E.

Murray, review of *The First Tortilla: A Bilingual Story,* p. 66; January, 2008, Mary Elam, review of *What Can You Do with a Rebozo?,* p. 98; February, 2009, Mary Landrum, review of *Juan the Bear and the Water of Life/La acequia de Juan del Oso,* p. 93; November, 2009, Monika Schroeder, review of *Namaste!,* p. 74; March, 2010, Mary Landrum, review of *Fiesta Babies,* p. 134.

Taos News, May 17, 2007, "Local Color: Amy Córdova's Heart," p. TE16.

ONLINE

Amy Córdova Home Page, http://www.amycordova.com (July 15, 2011).

Santero's Miracle Web site, http://santeros.nmsu.edu/ (July 15, 2011), "Amy Córdova."

Tweed Museum of Art Web site, http://tweedmuseum.org/ (July 15, 2011), "Amy Córdova."

*   *   *

CRANE, Carol 1933-

Personal

Born 1933, in MI; married; husband's name Conrad; has children.

Addresses

Home—Holly Springs, NC. *E-mail*—ccranelit@aol.com.

Carol Crane's **P Is for Palmetto** *pairs the A-to Z sights and sounds of South Carolina with twenty-six paintings by Mary Whyte.* (Illustration copyright © 2002 by Gale, a part of Cengage Learning, Inc. Reproduced by permission: www.cengage.com/permissions.)

Crane's nostalgic-themed story is paired with evocative illustrations by Gary Palmer in **The Handkerchief Quilt.** (Sleeping Bear Press, 2010. Illustration copyright © 2010 by Gale, a part of Cengage Learning. Reproduced by permission: www.cengage.com/permissions.)

Career

Educational consultant, lecturer, book reviewer, and author. Owner of bookstore in Flint, MI. Founder of "Bed, Breakfast & Books" (summer institute for teachers and media specialists).

Member

International Reading Association, National Council of Teachers of English, Michigan Reading Association, Florida Reading Association.

Awards, Honors

S Is for Sunshine selected to represent Florida at National Book Festival, 2005.

Writings

S Is for Sunshine: A Florida Alphabet, illustrated by Michael Glenn Monroe, Sleeping Bear Press (Chelsea, MI), 2000.

L Is for Lone Star: A Texas Alphabet, illustrated by Alan Stacy, Sleeping Bear Press (Chelsea, MI), 2001.

Sunny Numbers: A Florida Counting Book, illustrated by Jane Monroe Donovan, Sleeping Bear Press (Chelsea, MI), 2001.

L Is for Last Frontier: An Alaska Alphabet, illustrated by Michael Glenn Monroe, Sleeping Bear Press (Chelsea, MI), 2002.

P Is for Palmetto: A South Carolina Alphabet, illustrated by Mary Whyte, Sleeping Bear Press (Chelsea, MI), 2002.

P Is for Peach: A Georgia Alphabet, illustrated by Mark Braught, Sleeping Bear Press (Chelsea, MI), 2002.

P Is for Pilgrim: A Thanksgiving Alphabet, illustrated by Helle Urban, Sleeping Bear Press (Chelsea, MI), 2003.

Round Up: A Texas Number Book, illustrated by Alan Stacy, Sleeping Bear Press (Chelsea, MI), 2003.

T Is for Tar Heel: A North Carolina Alphabet, illustrated by Gary Palmer, Sleeping Bear Press (Chelsea, MI), 2003.

Y Is for Yellowhammer: An Alabama Alphabet, illustrated by Ted Burn, Sleeping Bear Press (Chelsea, MI), 2003.

F Is for First State: A Delaware Alphabet, illustrated by Elizabeth Traynor, Sleeping Bear Press (Chelsea, MI), 2004.

Wright Numbers: A North Carolina Number Book, illustrated by Gary Palmer, Sleeping Bear Press (Chelsea, MI), 2005.

D Is for Dancing Dragon: A China Alphabet, illustrated by Zong-Zhou Wang, Sleeping Bear Press (Chelsea, MI), 2006.

Net Numbers: A South Carolina Number Book, illustrated by Gary Palmer, Sleeping Bear Press (Chelsea, MI), 2006.

A Peck of Peaches: A Georgia Number Book, illustrated by Mark Braught, Sleeping Bear Press (Chelsea, MI), 2007.

Little Florida, illustrated by Michael Glenn Monroe, Sleeping Bear Press (Ann Arbor, MI), 2010.

Little Texas, illustrated by Michael Glenn Monroe, Sleeping Bear Press (Ann Arbor, MI), 2010.

The Handkerchief Quilt, illustrated by Gary Palmer, Sleeping Bear Press (Ann Arbor, MI), 2010.

The Christmas Tree Ship, illustrated by Chris Ellison, Sleeping Bear Press (Ann Arbor, MI), 2011.

Little South Carolina, illustrated by Jeannie Brett, Sleeping Bear Press (Ann Arbor, MI), 2011.

Little North Carolina, Sleeping Bear Press (Ann Arbor, MI), 2011.

Sidelights

A recognized authority on children's literature, Carol Crane has written more than twenty work for young readers, among them *T Is for Tar Heel: A North Carolina Alphabet,* *A Peck of Peaches: A Georgia Number Book,* and *The Handkerchief Quilt.* A former bookstore owner, Crane lectures and conducts seminars across the country, and she is also the founder of "Bed, Breakfast & Books," a popular summer reading program for teachers, librarians, and media specialists.

While speaking at the University of Michigan in 1998, Crane was approached by an editor from Sleeping Bear Press who asked her to help the company with a new series of books that used the alphabet to teach youngsters about the fifty states. Two years later, Crane's debut title, *S Is for Sunshine: A Florida Alphabet,* was released; illustrated by Michael Glenn Monroe, that work was selected to represent the State of Florida at the 2005 National Book Festival. Crane has gone on to produce a variety of abecedarian works, such as *P Is for Pilgrim: A Thanksgiving Alphabet* and *D Is for Dancing Dragon: A China Alphabet,* the latter a "fascinating glimpse into Chinese culture," according to *School Library Journal* reviewer Julie R. Ranelli.

Set in the 1950s, Crane's *The Handkerchief Quilt* is based on a true incident from her mother's life. The work concerns Miss Anderson, a beloved schoolteacher who devises a clever way to raise funds for new books

Ted Burn creates the light-filled paintings that capture the charm of Crane's alphabet-focused picture book **Y Is for Yellowhammer.** (Sleeping Bear Press, 2003. Illustration Copyright © 2003 Gale, a part of Cengage Learning, Inc. Reproduced by permission: www.cengage.com/permissions.)

and supplies for her students after a classroom water pipe bursts, causing extensive damage. Sara Polace described *The Handkerchief Quilt* as a "heartwarming tale" in her *School Library Journal* review, noting that Crane's story "will resonate with readers today."

Biographical and Critical Sources

PERIODICALS

Kirkus Reviews, March 1, 2010, review of *The Handkerchief Quilt.*

Publishers Weekly, September 22, 2003, review of *P Is for Pilgrim: A Thanksgiving Alphabet,* p. 66.

School Library Journal, January, 2004, Donna Cardon, review of *P Is for Pilgrim,* p. 112; March, 2007, Julie R. Ranelli, review of *D Is for Dancing Dragon: A China Alphabet,* p. 194; September, 2010, Sarah Polace, review of *The Handkerchief Quilt,* p. 120.

ONLINE

Carol Crane Home Page, http://www.carolcrane.org (July 1, 2011).

*   *   *

CUMMINGS, Phil 1957-

Personal

Born December 22, 1957, in Port Broughton, South Australia, Australia; son of Cyril Gordon (a carpenter and builder) and Rachel Henrietta (a homemaker) Cummings; married Susan Chalmers (a teacher), February 1, 1987; children: Benjamin David, Alyssa Claire. *Education:* Salisbury College of Advanced Education, degree (education). *Hobbies and other interests:* Listening to music, playing guitar, sports, reading, "playing with my kids."

Addresses

Home—Hillbank, South Australia, Australia. *Office*—P.O. Box 84, Para Hills, South Australia 5096, Australia.

Career

Writer and educator. Education Department of South Australia, teacher, 1979-2000; full-time writer, beginning 2000.

Writings

Goodness Gracious!, illustrated by Craig Smith, Omnibus (Norwood, South Australia, Australia), 1992.

Phil Cummings (Reproduced by permission.)

Tully and Claws, illustrated by Rob Mancini, Random House (Milsons Point, New South Wales, Australia), 1994.

Marty and Mei-Ling, illustrated by Craig Smith, Random House (Milsons Point, New South Wales, Australia), 1995.

Monster, Monster, Big and Hairy, illustrated by Marina McAllan, Macmillan Education Australia (South Melbourne, Victoria, Australia), 1995.

Surfing the Mudgiewallop Pool, illustrated by Mark Payne, Macmillan Education Australia (South Melbourne, Victoria, Australia), 1996.

Sid and the Slimeballs, illustrated by Stephen Axelson, Heinemann (Port Melbourne, Victoria, Australia), 1996.

African Animal Crackers, illustrated by Cameron Scott, Rigby Heinemann (Port Melbourne, Victoria, Australia), 1996.

Angel (novel), Random House Australia (Milsons Point, New South Wales, Australia), 1997.

The Great Jimbo James, illustrated by David Cox, Omnibus (Norwood, South Australia, Australia), 1997.

Lavinia Lavarr, illustrated by Terry Denton, Lothian (Port Melbourne, Victoria, Australia), 2000.

Eggs for Breakfast, Pearson Education (South Melbourne, Victoria, Australia), 2000.

Breakaway (novel), Random House Australia (Milsons Point, New South Wales, Australia), 2000.

The Rented House (novel for younger readers), Random House Australia (Milsons Point, New South Wales, Australia), 2000.

On the Run (novel for younger readers), Random House Australia (Milsons Point, New South Wales, Australia), 2001.

Spike, illustrated by David Cox, Omnibus/Ashton (Norwood, South Australia, Australia), 2001.

Tearaway, Random House Australia (Milsons Point, New South Wales, Australia), 2002.

The Tobbley Twins, illustrated by Anna Pignataro, Lothian Books (South Melbourne, Victoria, Australia), 2002.

Big Al, illustrated by Don Hatcher, Omnibus (Norwood, South Australia, Australia), 2003.

Danny Allen Was Here, illustrated by David Cox, Pan Macmillan Australia (Sydney, New South Wales, Australia), 2007.

The Stargazers, illustrated by Leanne Argent, Era Publications (Flinders Park, South Australia, Australia), 2007.

Riding the Waves, Era Publications (Flinders Park, South Australia, Australia), 2007.

Take It Easy, Danny Allen, illustrated by David Cox, Pan Macmillan Australia (Sydney, New South Wales, Australia), 2007.

Sophie Spy: The Case of the Missing Beagle, illustrated by Deborah Baldassi, Era Publications (Flinders Park, South Australia, Australia), 2007.

The Wild Whirlpool, illustrated by Simon Scales, Era Publications (Flinders Park, South Australia, Australia), 2007.

Writing and Recording Rock, Era Publications (Flinders Park, South Australia, Australia), 2008.

Boom Bah!, illustrated by Nina Rycroft, Working Title Press (Kingswood, South Australia, Australia), 2008, Kane Miller Books (Tulsa, OK), 2010.

Little Twitching, illustrated by R.P. Cooper, Windy Hollow Books (Kew East, Victoria, Australia), 2008.

(Reteller) *The Thick, Fat Pancake,* illustrated by Leanne Argent, Era Publications (Flinders Park, South Australia, Australia), 2009.

Wang Want and Funi, illustrated by Shane Devries, Imagination Ventures (Kent Town, South Australia, Australia), 2009.

Chook Shed Snake, illustrated by Greg Holfeld, Omnibus (Malvern, South Australia, Australia), 2009.

Wilbur: English, Amharic, Chinese, Arabic, and French/ Wilbur: English, Burmese, Somali, Tamil, and Farsi/ Wilbur: English, Dinka, Hindi, Khmer, and Nuer, illustrated by Amanda Graham, Big Book Club (Norwood, South Australia, Australia), 2010.

All Together Now, illustrated by Cassandra Allen, Omnibus (Malvern, South Australia, Australia), 2010.

Also author of *Midge Mum and the Neighbours* and *Find My Friends,* both published in Australia.

Sidelights

Trained as a teacher, Australian author Phil Cummings is known for his rhyming picture books and beginning readers. He wrote his first story while attending teacher college, and the experience convinced Cummings that writing for children is hardly as simple as it looks. His picture books include *Goodness Gracious!, Midge, Mum, and the Neighbours, The Tobbley Twins,* and *Boom Bah!,* while *The Great Jimbo James, Sid and the Slimeballs,* and *Grandma's Pictures of the Past* feature engaging, high-interest stories that help build confidence in budding readers. *Wilbur,* a beginning readers illustrated by Amanda Graham, has perhaps earned Cummings his largest and most diverse audience: published in three versions with parallel multilingual texts, it has been translated into twelve languages.

While most of Cummings' books are published in Australia, his first picture book, 1989's *Goodness Gracious!,* caught the attention of American readers when it was released in the United States with illustrations by Craig Smith. The story revolves around a red-headed, pig-tailed girl who romps with such fanciful creatures as a witch, a pirate, and a wild baboon. "It's the words that will hold them," asserted Hazel Rochman in *Booklist,* while a *Publishers Weekly* critic predicted that "children are likely to enjoy [Cummings'] . . . silly rhymes." "The word play is imaginative and appealing," claimed Lauralyn Persson in a *School Library Journal* review. Over the course of this rhyming tale, different body parts are highlighted, making it a "delightfully creative expansion of a truly childlike activity," according to a *Kirkus Reviews* critic.

Featuring artwork by Nina Rycroft, *Boom Bah!* is a cumulative story that begins with a single mouse who makes a tiny "ting" by hitting a silver spoon against a china cup. From there, a cat, hen, chicks, a goat, and several other animals join in on the music making, forming a rag-tag parade across the book's pages. "Rycroft's . . . pencil and watercolor illustrations are as exuberant as Cummings' bouncy rhyming text," asserted Kitty Flynn in her *Horn Book* review of *Boom Bah!,* and a *Kirkus Reviews* critic suggested that pre-readers will easily follow the book's "simple text and catch the rhythm." "The infectious joy of spontaneous music making comes through loud and clear," concluded a *Publishers Weekly* critic in a review of *Boom Bah!,* and in *School Library Journal* Lauralyn Persson recommended Cummings' story as "a natural fit for toddler programs."

In addition to stories for younger children, Cummings has also written juvenile novels featuring boy protagonists. *Angel* deals with the topic of a dead brother who visits his sibling at night in the form of an angel, while *A Piece of Mind* explores peer-group pressure. Other novels for middle graders include *A Rented House, Tearaway,* and *Breakaway.* Used to following his pack of friends on their trouble-making pranks, Matt, the young protagonist of *A Piece of Mind,* worries when he begins hearing voices in his head urging him on to more dangerous stunts. Writing in *Magpies,* Cecile Grumelart praised *A Piece of Mind* for its verisimilitude, predicting that Cummings' story will appeal to boys seven to nine years old, particularly those interested in in-line roller skating.

Cummings once told *SATA:* "I love to write. It's great to come up with something that entertains others, particularly 'little' others. Writing books for young children presents numerous rewards for me. Giving them language to play with, use and expand upon, is fuel for my creativity. Creating characters, settings, and images and moulding them like clay is also exciting.

"I am the youngest of a family of eight children. I grew up in the dusty town of Peterborough in the mid-North of the state of South Australia. In my most recent works, it is the experiences from those wonderfully adventurous years that I am now calling upon as I write. And, you know, I don't think there are going to be enough years in my life to record them *all* in print, but I'm going to give a real good try."

Biographical and Critical Sources

PERIODICALS

Booklist, January 16, 1992, Hazel Rochman, review of *Goodness Gracious!,* p. 950.
Horn Book, May-June, 2010, Kitty Flynn, review of *Boom Bah!,* p. 66.
Kirkus Reviews, January 15, 1992, review of *Goodness Gracious!,* p. 113.
Magpies, September, 1999, Cecile Grumelart, review of *A Piece of Mind,* p. 34.
Publishers Weekly, March 30, 1992, review of *Goodness Gracious!,* p. 104; February 1, 2010, review of *Boom Bah!,* p. 46.
Resource Links, April, 2002, Elaine Rospad, review of *The Great Jimbo James,* p. 25.
School Library Journal, July, 1992, Lauralyn Persson, review of *Goodness Gracious!,* p. 57; May, 2010, Lauralyn Persson, review of *Boom Bah!,* p. 80.

ONLINE

Phil Cummings Home Page, http://www.philcummings. com (August 15, 2011).*

*   *   *

CUMMINGS, Troy

Personal

Born in Cunot, IN; married; wife a college professor; children: one daughter. *Education:* DePauw University, degree, 1996.

Addresses

Home—Greencastle, IN. *Agent*—Herman Agency, 350 Central Park W., New York, NY 10025. *E-mail*—troy@ trox5.com.

Career

Illustrator, graphic designer, animator, and author. *Times of Northwest Indiana,* Munster, illustrator and designer, 1996; *Chicago Tribune,* Chicago, IL, Web designer, 1996-2000; FreeZone (Web site), illustrator, 1999-2000; freelance illustrator and designer, 2000—.

Writings

(Self-illustrated) *The Eensy Weensy Spider Freaks Out! (Big Time!),* Random House (New York, NY), 2010.

ILLUSTRATOR

Liz Palika, *The Ultimate Dog Treat Cookbook: Homemade Goodies for Man's Best Friend,* Howell Book House (Hoboken, NJ), 2005.
Kenn Nesbit, *More Bears!,* Sourcebooks Jabberwocky (Naperville, IL), 2010.

Contributor to periodicals, including *New York Daily News* and *Indy Men.*

Sidelights

In his self-illustrated story for *The Eensy Weensy Spider Freaks Out! (Big Time!),* Indiana native Troy Cummings offers a modern take on an old favorite, focusing on the aftermath of the title character's unfortunate waterspout incident. Cummings began drawing at a very young age and created his own comics as an elementary school student; he later served as a cartoonist for his high school and college newspapers. He also showed a talent for graphic design, recalling on his home page: "Pretty soon I was designing newspaper pages, laying out posters, and editing photos almost every day. I even learned what 'kerning' was. This led to internships and jobs at a bunch of newspapers and Web sites, which in turn led to my becoming a full-time illustrator. Slashwriter."

The Eensy Weensy Spider Freaks Out! (Big Time!) concerns the titular arachnid's emotional response to being washed off the downspout during a rainstorm. Vowing to stay on solid ground, the frightened spider suffers even greater embarrassment when news of her spill hits the Internet. With encouragement from ladybug friend Polly, Eensy finds the strength to confront her fears and begin climbing again. A *Publishers Weekly* reviewer applauded the story's mix of "humorous illustrations and clever text," and *Booklist* contributor Shelle Rosenfeld noted that Cummings' use of "varying perspectives add to the fun." In the words of a *Kirkus Reviews* critic, *The Eensy Weensy Spider Freaks Out! (Big Time!)* "not only models problem-solving but how to be a good friend as well."

Cummings has also created the artwork for *More Bears!,* a humorous, offbeat children's story by Kenn Nesbit in which an anonymous narrator, frustrated by his audience's constant interruptions, tries to comply with their demands to add an ever-increasing number of furry creatures to his tale. "In Nickelodeon-ready cartoons, Cummings brings the idiosyncratic, one-of-a-kind bears to life," a contributor in *Publishers Weekly* observed, and Susan E. Murray remarked in her *School Library Journal* review that the artist's "smooth, digitally rendered artwork does the job admirably."

Biographical and Critical Sources

PERIODICALS

Booklist, April 1, 2010, Shelle Rosenfeld, review of *The Eensy Weensy Spider Freaks Out! (Big Time!),* p. 46.

Kirkus Reviews, April 15, 2010, review of *The Eensy Weensy Spider Freaks Out! (Big Time!).*

Publishers Weekly, April 26, 2010, review of *The Eensy Weensy Spider Freaks Out! (Big Time!),* p. 105; October 18, 2010, review of *More Bears!,* p. 42.

School Library Journal, April, 2010, Kathleen Kelly MacMillan, review of *The Eensy Weensy Spider Freaks Out! (Big Time!),* p. 122; January, 2011, Susan E. Murray, review of *More Bears!,* p. 81.

ONLINE

Herman Agency Web site, http://www.hermanagencyinc.com/ (July 1, 2011), "Troy Cummings."

Random House Web site, http://www.randomhouse.com/ (July 1, 2011), "Author Spotlight: Troy Cummings."

Troy Cummings Home Page, http://www.trox5.com (July 1, 2011).

Troy Cummings Web log, http://troycummings.tumblr.com (July 1, 2011).*

D-E

DEWDNEY, Anna

Personal

Daughter of a doctor and Winifred Luhrmann (an author); children: two daughters. *Hobbies and other interests:* Running, walking, puttering.

Addresses

Home—Putney, VT. *E-mail*—annadewdney@gmail.com.

Career

Author, illustrator, and educator. Formerly worked as a waitress, furniture salesperson, daycare provider, teacher, and mail carrier. Presenter at schools, libraries, and conferences.

Member

Society of Children's Book Writers and Illustrators, Western Massachusetts Illustrators Guild.

Writings

SELF-ILLUSTRATED

Llama, Llama Red Pajama, Viking (New York, NY), 2005.
Grumpy Gloria, Viking (New York, NY), 2006.
Llama, Llama Mad at Mama, Viking (New York, NY), 2007.
Nobunny's Perfect, Viking (New York, NY), 2008.
Llama Llama Misses Mama, Viking (New York, NY), 2009.
Llama Llama Holiday Drama, Viking (New York, NY), 2010.
Roly Poly Pangolin, Viking (New York, NY), 2010.

ILLUSTRATOR

Dian Curtis Regan, *The Peppermint Race,* Holt (New York, NY), 1994.

Matt Christopher, *All-Star Fever: A Peach Street Mudders Story,* Little Brown (Boston, MA), 1995, reprinted, Norwood House Press (Chicago, IL), 2010.
Matt Christopher, *Shadow over Second: A Peach Street Mudders Story,* Little Brown (Boston, MA), 1996, reprinted, Norwood House Press (Chicago, IL), 2010.
Jake Wolf, *What You Do Is Easy, What I Do Is Hard,* Greenwillow (New York, NY), 1996.
Dorothy McKerns, *The Kid's Guide to Good Grammar: What You Need to Know about Punctuation, Sentence Structure, Spelling, and More,* Lowell House (Los Angeles, CA), 1998.
Harriet Heath, *Using Your Values to Raise Your Child to Be an Adult You Admire,* Parenting Press (Seattle, WA), 2000.

Sidelights

A teacher, artist, and author, Anna Dewdney began her career in children's literature by illustrating chapter books and is best known for creating a series of self-illustrated picture books featuring Baby Llama. A toddler stand-in who explores his ever-enlarging world with a combination of trepidation and excitement, Baby Llama stars in *Llama, Llama Red Pajama, Llama, Llama Mad at Mama, Llama Llama Misses Mama,* and *Llama Llama Holiday Drama.* Dewdney's first illustration project, creating artwork for Jake Wolf's *What You Do Is Easy, What I Do Is Hard,* was praised for "watercolor, gouache and pencil pictures" that "favor the delicate and sweet," according to a *Publishers Weekly* contributor. Along with her children's books, she has also created artwork for the parenting book *Using Your Values to Raise Your Child to Be an Adult You Admire.*

"Persistence is key," Dewdney noted in discussing her path to becoming an author on her home page. In fact, she held fast to her dream of becoming a published writer for two decades, although her illustrations began appearing in books in the early 1990s. Things changed for Dewdney when her first self-illustrated picture book, *Llama, Llama Red Pajama,* was published in 2005 and became a hit with the toddler set.

In *Llama, Llama Red Pajama* Dewdney's titular hero becomes agitated when his mother does not appear quickly with his bedtime glass of water. He worries and whimpers until finally she arrives to reassure him that she is always nearby. "Dewdney gives a wonderfully fresh twist to a familiar nighttime ritual with an adorable bug-eyed baby llama," wrote Julie Cummins in *Booklist*. In her *School Library Journal* review of *Llama, Llama Red Pajama*, Corrina Austin noted that the artist's "large, boldly colored pictures have a grand and sweeping quality," and a *Kirkus Review* contributor described Dewdney's story as "uproariously funny" and a soon-to-be "comical classic" that will be "oft-requested at bedtime."

Baby Llama returns in *Llama, Llama Mad at Mama, Llama Llama Misses Mama,* and *Llama Llama Holiday Drama,* all which find the adventurous young camelid following the path of a typical young child. In *Llama, Llama Mad at Mama*, for example, Baby Llama and his mother are shopping when she pulls him away from all of the fun displays, makes him try on clothing he does not like, and will not let him play with toys. After the inevitable tantrum, Mama reassures the child that they will be done soon; she invites him to help push the cart so they can finish faster and then go get ice cream. "Snappy rhythm, pleasing rhyme and large-scale art . . . make this an involving read-aloud," wrote a *Publishers Weekly* contributor. Jayne Damron, writing in *School Library Journal*, predicted that "children will giggle at Dewdney's rhythmic rhymes," and a *Kirkus Reviews* critic deemed *Lllama, Llama Mad at Mama* "a perfect choice for preschool read-alouds."

More adventures are in store for Baby Llama in *Llama Llama Misses Mama,* as the first day of school means the first day away from Mama. The pre-holiday hustle and bustle overwhelms the excitable llama in *Llama Llama Holiday Drama,* as Christmas Eve histrionics require some gentle words from a loving mother. "Emotionally realistic storytelling, a bouncing rhythm, skilled rhyming, and expressive paintings in bright colors"

Anna Dewdney illustrates an original warmhearted bedtime tale in her picture book **Llama Llama Red Pajama.** (Illustration copyright © 2005 by Anna Dewdney. Reproduced by permission of Viking Children's Books, a division of Penguin Young Readers Group, a member of Penguin Group (USA) Inc., 345 Hudson St., New York, NY 10014. All rights reserved.)

characterize the third book in Dewdney's engaging "Baby Llama" series, stated Heidi Estrin in *School Library Journal,* and Mara Alpert noted that "llama fans and newcomers alike will be charmed," noted Mara Alpert in her *School Library Journal* review of *Llama Llama Holiday Drama.* Reviewing the same book, Jennifer M. Brabander asserted in *Horn Book* that "Dewdney's illustrations convey the hectic atmosphere" of the holidays while also leaving readers with the message that "a quick snuggle is always a good idea."

A toddler's task is often one of testing boundaries, and several of Dewdney's books illustrate these efforts. In *Grumpy Gloria* readers meet a pouting bulldog whose grumpiness is the result of worries that it has been replaced by its owner's new doll, and a trio of young bunnies exhibits a range of good and bad behaviors in *Nobunny's Perfect.* The book's "large illustrations done in rich, bright colors are great for viewing at a distance," noted Kirsten Cutler in her *School Library Journal* review of *Grumpy Gloria,* and a *Kirkus Reviews* contributor maintained of the same book that Dewdney's bulldog heroine "has personality to spare." Paired with her "straightforward" rhyming text, the artist's colorful illustrations for *Nobunny's Perfect* "effectively . . . convey . . . the bunnies' changing emotions," according to *School Library Journal* contributor Lynn K. Vanca. This "whimsical primer of good manners for little ones is bound to elicit giggles," wrote a *Kirkus Reviews* writer of the same book, and a *Publishers Weekly* critic recommended *Nobunny's Perfect* for its "age-appropriate" message "that feelings are both a cause and an effect of individual behavior."

Readers meet an endangered resident of Southeast Asia, Africa, and China in Dewdney's *Roly Poly Pangolin,* which features an author's note about the rare creatures. The only mammal to be covered in scales, long-tailed and toothless pangolins live in trees, are nocturnal, can roll themselves up into a ball to escape from predators, spray like a skunk, and have a tongue as long as an anteater. In Dewdney's characteristic rhyming text, she describes a young pangolin that is terribly shy, so shy in fact that an unexpected sound or anything new prompts it to roll up into a tight, scaley ball. Paired with her gentle story, her "expressive close-up illustrations aptly portray Roly Poly's feelings of insecurity and happiness," according to *School Library Journal* contributor Martha Simpson. "Dewdney again taps into common toddler insecurities," wrote a *Publishers Weekly* contributor in reviewing *Roly Poly Pangolin,* "and her "artwork readily transmits her protagonist's emotions." The proceeds from *Roly Poly Pangolin* went to fund research on pangolins at Vietnam's Cuc Phuong National Park.

Discussing her drawing process on her home page, Dewdney explained: "People ask me how I come up with the faces that I draw. I answer that they are self-portraits. I make a lot of funny faces, anyway, just going about my day, but when I draw, I usually make the face of the character as I draw."

A formerly fussed-over family dog worries that it has lost its special place in Dewdney's humorous **Grumpy Gloria.** (Illustration copyright © 2006 by Anna Dewdney. Reproduced by permission of Viking Children's Books, a division of Penguin Young Readers Group, a member of Penguin Group (USA) Inc., 345 Hudson St., New York, NY 10014. All rights reserved.)

Biographical and Critical Sources

PERIODICALS

Booklist, November 15, 1994, Hazel Rochman, review of *The Peppermint Race,* p. 603; December 15, 1996, April Judge, review of *What You Do Is Easy, What I Do Is Hard,* p. 734; April 1, 2005, Julie Cummins, review of *Llama, Llama Red Pajama,* p. 1365; January 1, 2008, Abby Nolan, review of *Nobunny's Perfect,* p. 95; February 1, 2010, Julie Cummins, review of *Roly Poly Pangolin,* p. 51.

Horn Book, November-December, 2010, Jennifer M. Brabander, review of *Llama Llama Holiday Drama,* p. 61.

Kirkus Reviews, May 1, 2005, review of *Llama, Llama Red Pajama,* p. 537; September 1, 2006, review of *Grumpy Gloria,* p. 902; August 1, 2007, review of *Llama, Llama Mad at Mama;* December 1, 2007, review of *Nobunny's Perfect;* February 15, 2010, review of *Roly Poly Pangolin.*

Library Journal, December, 1999, Elizabeth Caulfield Felt, review of *Using Your Values to Raise Your Child to Be an Adult You Admire,* p. 174.

Publishers Weekly, October 21, 1996, review of *What You Do Is Easy, What I Do Is Hard,* p. 82; October 9, 2006, review of *Grumpy Gloria,* p. 54; July 16, 2007, review of *Llama, Llama Mad at Mama,* p. 162; December 3, 2007, review of *Nobunny's Perfect,* p. 69; February 22, 2010, review of *Roly Poly Pangolin,* p. 63.

Dewdney introduces readers to a very unusual Asian animal in her self-illustrated picture book **Roly Poly Pangolin.** (Illustration copyright © 2010 by Anna Dewdney. Reproduced by permission of Viking Children's Books, a division of Penguin Young Readers Group, a member of Penguin Group (USA) Inc., 345 Hudson St., New York, NY 10014. All rights reserved.)

School Library Journal, April, 2005, Corrina Austin, review of *Llama, Llama Red Pajama,* p. 96; September, 2006, Kirsten Cutler, review of *Grumpy Gloria,* p. 165; September, 2007, Jayne Damron, review of *Llama, Llama Mad at Mama,* p. 162; August, 2008, Lynn K. Vanca, review of *Nobunny's Perfect,* p. 86; June, 2009, Heidi Estrin, review of *Llama Llama Misses Mama,* p. 82; February, 2010, Martha Simpson, review of *Roly Poly Pangolin,* p. 80; October, 2010, Mara Alpert, review of *Llama Llama Holiday Drama,* p. 70.

ONLINE

Anna Dewdney Home Page, http://www.annadewdney.com (July 25, 2011).
Western Massachusetts Illustrators Guild Web site, http://www.wmig.org/ (October 22, 2007), "Anna Dewdney."*

*   *   *

ELLIS, Helen

Personal

Born in AL; married (husband a managing editor). *Education:* B.A.; New York University, M.A. (fiction writing).

Addresses

Home—New York, NY. *Agent*—Susanna Einstein, LJK Literary Management, 133 W. 25th St., Ste 8W, New York, NY 10001; susanna@ljkliterary.com.

Career

Writer.

Awards, Honors

Los Angeles Times Best Book nomination, and Southern Critics Circle Best Book of the Year nomination, both for *Eating the Cheshire Cat.*

Writings

NOVELS

Eating the Cheshire Cat (for adults), Scribner (New York, NY), 2000.
What Curiosity Kills (first book in "The Turning" series), Sourcebooks (New York, NY), 2010.

Adaptations

Eating the Cheshire Cat was optioned for film.

Sidelights

Helen Ellis draws on her experiences growing up in the American South in her first novel, *Eating the Cheshire Cat.* Described as "dark and, surprisingly, often humorous" by *Library Journal* contributor Nancy Pearl, the book takes place in Tuscaloosa, Alabama, Ellis's home town. Sarina, Nicole, and Bitty are educated in their mother's culture of competitive social climbing, backstabbing, and cultivating personal beauty as a means of getting what one wants from others. Although *Eating the Cheshire Cat* focuses on adolescents, Ellis views her subject from a mature adult perspective. She writes specifically for a teen readership in her second novel, *What Curiosity Kills,* which is the first book in her planned series called "The Turning."

"The Turning" refers to a genetic abnormality that manifests itself from age sixteen to twenty-one and occasionally transforms those with the condition transform into something feline. Mary Richards is a foster child who, born in Alabama, has found a secure home with a loving and upscale family living in New York's Upper East Side. Her discovery that she has this abnormality comes as something of a shock. Mary's craving for odd foods, her fainting spells and purring, the sudden impulse to chase mice, and her odd growths of fur-like hair are not shared by the other teens she knows, and she is afraid to confide her concerns to either her foster parents or her teachers at prestigious Purser-Lilley Academy. She eventually learns that there are others like her, other teens who wander the streets of Manhattan at night, in their catlike form. One of them is Nick, a boy who she has been crushing on for months. While her relationship with Nick grows stronger, Mary recognizes that there is a dark side to being one of the city's cat people: age-old grudges have sparked a war between two factions—domestics and strays—and it may be her destiny to help determine the outcome. Citing the "fantastical premise" in *What Curiosity Kills,* Gillian Engberg added in *Booklist* that Ellis's story features a mix of "contemporary realism and fantasy, romance, humor, and adrenaline-charged action [that] is sure to hook an eager teen audience." A *Publishers Weekly* critic dubbed the novel's structure "impressive," adding that the author's "original and consistent world-building . . . bodes well for later books in the . . . series."

"I'm a bit of a Luddite," Ellis admitted to *National Examiner* online interviewer Lori Calabrese: "No cell phone, no ATM card. Never had them, never will." Although she enjoys cultivating a mid-1980s lifestyle, she has embraced the Internet, and shares her "old-fashioned ways" on her home page, which is full of quirky short videos ranging from instructions on using a rotary phone to the intriguingly titled "Write What You Know: Cats Are Not Amused by Kittens."

Biographical and Critical Sources

PERIODICALS

Booklist, May 15, 2010, Gillian Engberg, review of *What Curiosity Kills,* p. 51.
Library Journal, October 1, 1999, Nancy Pearl, review of *Eating the Cheshire Cat,* p. 132; June 15, 2000, review of *Eating the Cheshire Cat,* p. 148.

Cover of Helen Ellis's novel **What Curiosity Kills,** *the first book in her* **"The Turning"** *series.* (Sourcebooks Fire, 2010. Book cover photographs by Lukasz Laska/iStockphoto.com; Veni/iStockphoto.com; Terraxplorer/iStockphoto.com. Reproduced by permission of Sourcebooks, Inc.)

Publishers Weekly, October 18, 1999, review of *Eating the Cheshire Cat,* p. 69; May 3, 2010, review of *What Curiosity Kills,* p. 54.

ONLINE

Helen Ellis Home Page, http://www.helenelliswrites.com (August 12, 2011).
National Examiner Online, http://www.examiner.com/ (May 6, 2010), Lori Calabrese, interview with Ellis.*

*   *   *

EMBERLEY, Michael 1960-

Personal

Born June 2, 1960, in Boston, MA; son of Edward R. (an artist and writer) and Barbara (a writer and craftsperson) Emberley. *Education:* Attended Rhode Island School of Design, 1979-80, and California College of Arts and Crafts, 1981-82. *Hobbies and other interests:* Bicycle racing, mountain biking, cycling, bicycle riding.

Addresses

Home—San Diego, CA.

Career

Writer and illustrator, 1980—.

Writings

SELF-ILLUSTRATED

Dinosaurs!: A Drawing Book, Little, Brown (Boston, MA), 1980.

The Sports Equipment Book, Little, Brown (Boston, MA), 1982.

More Dinosaurs! and Other Prehistoric Beasts: A Drawing Book, Little, Brown (Boston, MA), 1983.

Ruby, Little, Brown, 1990.

The Present, Little, Brown (Boston, MA), 1991.

Welcome Back, Sun, Little, Brown (Boston, MA), 1993.

Ruby and the Sniffs, Little, Brown (Boston, MA), 2004.

ILLUSTRATOR

Zachary Judd, *Roller Coaster Ride,* Silver Burdett & Ginn (Morristown, NJ), 1992.

Robert L. May, *Rudolph's Second Christmas,* Applewood Books, 1992.

Robert L. May, *Rudolph the Red-nosed Reindeer,* Applewood Books, 1994.

Robie H. Harris, *It's Perfectly Normal: Changing Bodies, Sex, and Sexual Health,* Candlewick Press (Cambridge, MA), 1994, third edition, 2009.

Robie H. Harris, *Happy Birth Day!,* Candlewick Press (Cambridge, MA), 1996.

Robie H. Harris, *It's So Amazing! A Book about Eggs, Sperm, Birth, Babies, and Families,* Candlewick Press (Cambridge, MA), 1999.

Robie H. Harris, *Hi, New Baby!,* Candlewick Press (Cambridge, MA), 2000.

Mary Ann Hoberman, *You Read to Me, I'll Read to You: Very Short Stories to Read Together,* Little, Brown (Boston, MA), 2001.

Robie H. Harris, *Hello Benny!,* Margaret K. McElderry Books (New York, NY), 2002.

Robie H. Harris, *Go! Go! Maria!: What It's like to Be One,* Margaret K. McElderry Books (New York, NY), 2003.

Mary Ann Hoberman, *You Read to Me, I'll Read to You: Very Short Fairy Tales to Read Together,* Little, Brown (Boston, MA), 2004.

Robie H. Harris, *Sweet Jasmine, Nice Jackson: What It's like to Be Two—and to Be Twins!,* Margaret K. McElderry Books (New York, NY), 2004.

Robie H. Harris, *David Dinosaur-rrr!: What It's like to Be Three,* Margaret K. McElderry Books (New York, NY), 2005.

Mary Ann Hoberman, *You Read to Me, I'll Read to You: Very Short Mother Goose Tales to Read Together,* Little, Brown (New York, NY), 2005.

Robie H. Harris, *It's Not the Stork!: A Book about Girls, Boys, Babies, Bodies, Families, and Friends,* Margaret K. McElderry Books (New York, NY), 2006.

Mary Ann Hoberman, *You Read to Me, I'll Read to You: Very Scary Stories to Read Together,* Little, Brown (New York, NY), 2007.

Robie H. Harris, *Maybe a Bear Ate It!,* Orchard Books (New York, NY), 2007.

Sally Lloyd-Jones, *The Ultimate Guide to Grandmas and Grandpas!,* HarperCollins (New York, NY), 2008.

Robie H. Harris, *Mail Harry to the Moon!,* Little, Brown (New York, NY), 2008.

Barbara Bottner, *Miss Brooks Loves Books (and I Don't),* Alfred A. Knopf (New York, NY), 2010.

Mary Ann Hoberman, *You Read to Me, I'll Read to You: Very Short Fables to Read Together,* Little, Brown (New York, NY), 2010.

Robie H. Harris, *What's in There?: A Book about before You Were Born,* Candlewick Press (Cambridge, MA), 2010.

Barbara Bottner, *An Annoying ABC,* Alfred A. Knopf (New York, NY), 2011.

Sidelights

The son of author and illustrator Ed Emberley and the brother of illustrator Barbara Emberley, Michael Emberley retains strong memories from his childhood of rowing to the ocean with friends and riding his bicycle along the narrow winding road of his Massachusetts hometown. After graduating from high school, he began working with his father, an established children's book author and illustrator. With his father's encouragement, Emberley eventually developed a unique illustration style and generated ideas for children's books of his own. His original self-illustrated works include *Dinosaurs!: A Drawing Book, Ruby,* and *Welcome Back, Sun,* and they often draw upon classic children's literature. Emberley has also teamed up with a number of authors to illustrate their stories, among them frequent collaborator Robie H. Harris, with whom he has created a number of picture books. In a review of the collaborative *Maybe a Bear Ate It!, Booklist* contributor Stephanie Zvirin observed that Emberley "obviously knows how toddlers move and react": In each of his engaging cartoons, "every calibrated movement and feeling blasts out across the page." With art that is "unexpectedly irresistible, not to mention moving," *Maybe a Bear Ate It!* is likely to "become a very special book" for its readers, according to a *Kirkus Reviews* writer.

In his picture-book debut, *Dinosaurs!,* Emberley focuses on ten well-known dinosaurs and presents children with simple instructions on how they can be drawn. Although comparisons with the work of Ed Emberley inevitably found the younger illustrator less the master of his craft, a *Publishers Weekly* reviewer deemed the

Michael Emberley is best known for his collaborations with author Robie H. Harris, among them **It's Not the Stork!** (Illustration copyright © 2006 by Michael Emberley. Reproduced by permission of Candlewick Press, Somerville, MA.)

book "amusing and instructive" and *School Library Journal* critic Lynn S. Hunter called the drawings of Emberly *fils* "more complex" than those of his father. *More Dinosaurs! And Other Prehistoric Beasts: A Drawing Book,* a sequel to *Dinosaurs!,* was also generally well received by reviewers, W.A. Handley predicting in a *School Library Journal* review that "budding artists will love this one."

Emberley turns to storytelling with *Ruby,* a version of the Little Red Riding Hood folktale in which a mouse is asked by her mother to take a bag of triple-cheese pies to her sick grandmother. To get there, Ruby must travel through a dangerous city, and along the way she encounters a con-artist reptile and a far-too-friendly cat, both of whom she manages to outwit. A *New York Times Book Review* critic praised Emberley's text and illustrations as "very clever." Although a *Publishers Weekly* critic feared only "readers on the older end of the intended age spectrum" will appreciate Emberley's "somewhat sophisticated humor," Martha Topol asserted

Emberley and Harris continue their preschool-focused family silliness in the picture book **Mail Harry to the Moon!** (Little, Brown & Company, 2008. Illustration copyright © 2008 by Michael Emberley. Reproduced by permission of Hachette Book Group.)

in *School Library Journal* that "this Red Riding Hood variation has enough plot twists and innovation to keep readers involved and interested."

Readers meet up again with Emberley's engaging rodent heroine in *Ruby and the Sniffs,* a new take on the story of the Three Bears. Here Ruby hears some strange noises coming from the vacant apartment upstairs. When she decides to investigate (against the orders of strict babysitter, Mrs. Mastiff), the mouse discovers that, rather than the burglars she expected, the apartment is actually home to some rather unusual new neighbors. Young readers "will . . . enjoy the street-smart Ruby" as well as Emberley's "very funny cartoon vignettes," wrote a *Kirkus Reviews* writer, while in *Booklist* Linda Perkins called *Ruby and the Sniffs* a "delightful mix of mild tension and side-splitting humor" and "a worthy sequel for Ruby's fans." "Story and illustrations work wonderfully together to create a hilarious romp that will keep older children laughing and re-reading," concluded Marianne Saccardi in her *School Library Journal* review.

In *The Present,* set in Denmark, Uncle Arne buys a pocket knife as a gift for his nephew's birthday, but he likes it so much that he decides to keep it himself. He then buys an old bicycle and fixes it up to give to his nephew, but then realizes he must learn how to ride it in order to deliver it. Many reviewers praised Emberley's cinematic technique, which comically shows Uncle Arne learning to ride a bicycle; others noted that the author gives an adult figure concerns that a child can understand. Although a *Publishers Weekly* writer described *The Present* as "droll but somewhat wordy," the book's "gentle, homey watercolors are particularly winning." Ann A. Flowers was more enthusiastic in *Horn Book,* noting that Emberley's "homey, busy illustrations . . . are just right for the affectionate story."

Also set in Scandinavia, *Welcome Back, Sun* takes place during the long winter when the sun is never seen. The story centers on a little girl who convinces her family to follow the steps of an ancient legend and climb the highest mountain, there to find the sun and show it the way home. Along the way, the girl and her family meet their neighbors, who are also intent on ushering in the spring after a long gray winter. *Welcome Back, Sun* was warmly received by critics who, like a *Publishers Weekly* contributor, found it "both an enlightening glimpse of another culture and a lyrical, heartwarming story." *School Library Journal* reviewer Linda Davis singled out Emberley's drawings for special praise, writing that the author/illustrator "captures the feel of both the cold, gray 'murky time' and the brilliant, clear sunshine" in "captivating artwork" that ably expresses the warmth of the family relationships.

In his collaborations with Harris, Emberley creates art for nonfiction books on sexuality and physical development. In *It's Perfectly Normal: Changing Bodies, Sex, and Sexual Health,* a book intended for middle-grade readers, Harris recounts the facts of life, from intercourse, conception, and birth to topics such as the onset of puberty, birth control, AIDS, and sexual abuse. In his artwork, Emberley creates interesting dual narrators in a bird and a bee that play straight man/funny man with comments, asides, and questions. For many reviewers, this approach to teaching sexuality to young people was deemed remarkably successful. "It is the best book I have seen regarding the physical changes that puberty brings," averred Tim Moses in *Boston Book Review.* "Besides being warm and unaffected," Stephanie Zvirin wrote in *Booklist,* Emberley's illustrations for *It's Perfectly Normal* "are eyepoppers—especially in a book for this age group."

Part of Emberley and Harris's philosophy, as expressed in the title of *It's Perfectly Normal,* is that, as strange and occasionally embarrassing as sexuality may seem during the onset of puberty, it is perfectly normal. However, *It's Perfectly Normal* was viewed by some as a controversial purchase for public libraries, and Emberley's illustrations depicting human nudes in a wide variety of shapes, sizes, and colors as well as a boy masturbating, intercourse between two people, and a girl examining her genitalia in the mirror also inspired consternation. Reviewers concurred, however, that the book's effectiveness lies in its ability to convey lots of important information in a way intended to relax, reassure, and entertain children. "The book will serve as a useful tool in the sex education curriculum," contended Nancy Vasilakis in her *Horn Book* appraisal of *It's Perfectly Normal.*

In *It's So Amazing! A Book about Eggs, Sperm, Birth, Babies, and Families,* Emberley and Harris provide a look at human sexuality similar in a format similar to their *It's Perfectly Normal,* but for a younger, elementary-grade audience. The result is "an equally outstanding book," contended Amy Brandt in *Booklist.* As in the earlier book, Emberley's illustrations run the gamut from humorous cartoons to straightforward graphic illustrations of the human body and reproductive system. The bird and the bee are also back to provide comic relief, ask questions, and reinforce and define important concepts. According to a *Publishers Weekly* critic, the collaborators successfully convey a wealth of important information "with candor and humor, neatly distilling various aspects of sex, reproduction and love."

Similar in focus but with an even younger audience in mind, *It's Not the Stork!: A Book about Girls, Boys, Babies, Bodies, Families, and Friends* also focuses openly on body parts and sexuality, under the entertaining guidance of Bird and Bee. "Emberley's affectionate, mood-lightening cartoons keep things approachable," wrote *Booklist* reviewer Jennifer Mattson, the critic adding that "Harris's respectful writing targets children's natural curiosity" with clarity. *It's Not the Stork!* "will be accessible to its intended audience, comforting in its

Emberley's cartoon art is a highlight of Mary Ann Hoberman's picture book You Read to Me, I'll Read to You: Very Short Stories to Read Together. (Little, Brown & Company, 2001. Illustration copyright © 2001 by Michael Emberley. Reproduced by permission of Little, Brown & Company.)

clarity and directness, and useful to a wide range of readers," asserted Martha Topol, reviewing the book for *School Library Journal*.

Other collaborations between Emberley and Harris comprise their "Growing up Stories." In *Happy Birth Day!* they couch facts about birth in a story about the first day of life for a newborn infant. "All the milestones of a baby's first day are lovingly chronicled," noted a reviewer for *Publishers Weekly*. Turning to stories, *Mail Harry to the Moon!* depicts a new baby's arrival from the point of view of his older sibling. Calling Emberley and Harris "old hands at striking the right balance between comic Sturm und Drang and genuine poignancy," a *Publishers Weekly* contributor added that the "considerable talents" of author and illutrator transform *Mail Harry to the Moon!* from a "familiar tale" into one that readers will find "fresh and funny."

In *Hello Benny! What It's Like to Be a Baby* Emberley and Harris treat readers to another sequel to *Happy Birth Day!* by following the newborn through the first twelve months of life, as he grows and changes. "Emberley's large-scale artwork, rendered in watercolor, pastel, and ink, brims with warmth," wrote Ilene Cooper in a review of *Hello Benny!*, while a *Publishers Weekly* contributor noted that the illustrator "infuses his artwork with a spontaneity and humor" and "does a terrific job of depicting Benny's evolving physiognomy from newborn to toddler."

Emberley has also illustrated several stories for well-known writer Barbara Bottner, among them *Miss Brooks Loves Books (and I Don't)* and *An Annoying ABC*. In

Miss Brooks Loves Books (and I Don't) a school librarian engages her first-grade charges through her dramatic changes of costume as well as her creative presentation of picture-book stories. As narrated by a girl who finds Miss Brooks a tad overly enthusiastic, "Bottner's deadpan humor and delicious prose combine with Emberley's droll caricatures to create a story sure to please those who celebrate books," according to *School Library Journal* contributor Wendy Lukehart. Emberley's "cartoon-style illustrations extend the comedy in images of the expressive girl and her librarian," asserted *Booklist* critic Hazel Rochman, while a *Publishers Weekly* contributor wrote that the artist's "slice-of-life cartooning is funny, empathetic, and of-the-moment."

Working with the other members of his creative family, Emberley has also collaborated on *Three: An Emberley Family Sketch Book,* in which Michael, Ed, and Barbara Emberley each contribute stories, poems, drawings, and other tidbits that play on the theme of three-ness. Michael Emberley's contribution showcases his several styles of illustration, including pen-and-ink, watercolor, pastel, and crayon artwork, offering stories and poems to go with each. "Children will be intrigued by this big book of fun, which celebrates togetherness and individuality all in one family," predicted Kathleen Squires in *Booklist*.

Other creative collaborations include working with writer Mary Ann Hoberman to produce the story collection *You Read to Me, I'll Read to You: Very Short Stories to Read Together* and its sequels. "Felicitous rhyming, clear page design, and well-sequenced pictures all work together to make [*You Read to Me, I'll Read to You: Very Short Mother Goose Stories to Read Together*] . . . a two-on-a-tuffet treat," according to *Horn Book* contributor Roger Sutton, while *Booklist* critic Diane Foote praised *You Read to Me, I'll Read to You: Very Short Fables to Read Together* a "winning" combination of engaging verse and Emberley's "lively spot illustrations."

Biographical and Critical Sources

PERIODICALS

Booklist, March 15, 1980, Barbara Elleman, review of *Dinosaurs!: A Drawing Book,* p. 1055; September 15, 1994, review of *It's Perfectly Normal: Changing Bodies, Sex, and Sexual Health,* p. 133; May 1, 1996, Stephanie Zvirin, review of *Happy Birth Day!,* p. 1502; August, 1998, Kathleen Squires, review of *Three: An Emberley Family Sketch Book,* p. 1993; January 1, 2000, Amy Brandt, review of *It's So Amazing!,* p. 912; October 15, 2002, Ilene Cooper, review of *Hello Benny!,* p. 407; August, 2004, Linda Perkins, review of *Ruby and the Sniffs,* p. 1942; June 1, 2006, Jennifer Mattson, review of *It's Not the Stork!: A Book about Girls, Boys, Babies, Bodies, Families, and Friends,* p. 74; December 15, 2007, Stephanie Zvirin, review of *Maybe a Bear Ate It!*, p. 46; March 1, 2010, Hazel Rochman, review of *Miss Brooks Loves Books! (and I Don't)*, p. 78; January 1, 2011, Diane Foote, review of *You Read to Me, I'll Read to You: Very Short Fables to Read Together*, p. 84.

Bulletin of the Center for Children's Books, October, 1993, Roger Sutton, review of *Welcome Back, Sun*, pp. 42-43.

Horn Book, September-October, 1991, Ann A. Flowers, review of *The Present*, p. 582; March-April, 1995, Nancy Vasilakis, review of *It's Perfectly Normal*, p. 214; November-December, 2002, Lauren Adams, review of *Hello Benny!*, p. 776; July-August, 2005, Roger Sutton, review of *You Read to Me, I'll Read to You: Very Short Mother Goose Tales to Read Together*, p. 450; September-October, 2006, Christine M. Heppermann, review of *It's Not the Stork!*, p. 605; May-June, 2010, Susan Dove Lempke, review of *Miss Brooks Loves Books! (and I Don't)*, p. 62; January-February, 2011, Roger Sutton, review of *You Read to Me, I'll Read to You: Very Short Fables to Read Together*, p. 106.

Kirkus Reviews, May 1, 1980, review of *Dinosaurs!*, p. 576; September 15, 2002, review of *Hello Benny!*, p. 1391; May 15, 2004, review of *Ruby and the Sniffs*, p. 491; June 15, 2005, review of *You Read to Me, I'll Read to You: Very Short Mother Goose Tales to Read Together*, p. 684; July 15, 2006, review of *It's Not the Stork!*, p. 722; December 1, 2007, review of *Maybe a Bear Ate It!*; April 1, 2008, review of *The Ultimate Guide to Grandmas and Grandpas!*; May 1, 2008, review of *Mail Harry to the Moon!*

New York Times Book Review, March 10, 1991, review of *Ruby*, p. 29.

Publishers Weekly, January 25, 1980, review of *Dinosaurs!*, p. 341; October 12, 1990, review of *Ruby*, pp. 62-63; May 31, 1991, review of *The Present*, p. 75; September 13, 1993, review of *Welcome Back, Sun*, p. 130; June 17, 1996, review of *Happy Birth Day!*, p. 63; December 20, 1999, review of *It's So Amazing!*, p. 80; July 15, 2002, review of *Hello Benny!*, p. 72; November 12, 2007, review of *Maybe a Bear Ate It!*, p. 54; April 18, 2008, review of *Mail Harry to the Moon!*, p. 137; February 8, 2010, review of *Miss Brooks Loves Books!*, p. 50.

School Library Journal, May, 1980, Lynn S. Hunter, review of *Dinosaurs!*, p. 54; February, 1984, W.A. Handley, review of *More Dinosaurs! and Other Prehistoric Beasts: A Drawing Book*, pp. 68-69; October, 1990, Martha Topol, review of *Ruby*, p. 90; September, 1991, p. 232; January, 1994, Lisa Dennis, review of *Welcome Back, Sun*, p. 88; July, 2003, Joyce Adams Burner, review of *It's So Amazing!*, p. 78; May, 2004, Shelley B. Sutherland, review of *You Read to Me, I'll Read to You: Very Short Mother Goose Tales to Read Together*, p. 132; June, 2004, Marianne Saccardi, review of *Ruby and the Sniffs*, p. 108; September, 2006, Martha Topol, review of *It's Not the Stork!*, p. 193; January, 2008, Judith Constantinides, review of *Maybe a Bear Ate It!*, p. 88; June, 2008, Jayne Damron, review of *Mail Harry to the Moon!*, p. 104; July, 2008, Jane Marino, review of *The Ultimate Guide to Grandmas and Grandpas!*, p. 77; February, 2010, Wendy Lukehart, review of *Miss Brooks Loves Books (and I Don't)*, p. 76.

ONLINE

Michael Emberley Home Page, http://www.michaelemberley.com (August 12, 2011).*

F-G

FALLS, Kat
(Kathleen Moynihan Falls)

Personal

Born in MD; married Robert Falls (a theatre director); children: three. *Education:* Rensselaer Polytechnic Institute, bachelor's degree; Northwestern University, M.F.A. (screenwriting).

Addresses

Home—Evanston, IL. *Agent*—Adams Literary, New York, NY; info@adamsliterary.com. *E-mail*—katfalls77@gmail.com.

Career

Educator and writer. Northwestern University, Evanston, IL, instructor in screenwriting on graduate level.

Member

Writers' Guild.

Awards, Honors

Best Books selection, Bank Street College of Education, and named to Sunshine State Young Reader's Award Master List, both 2011, both for *Dark Life.*

Writings

Dark Life, Scholastic Press (New York, NY), 2010.
Rip Tide, Scholastic Press (New York, NY), 2011.

Adaptations

Dark Life was adapted for audiobook, narrated by Keith Nobbs, Scholastic Audiobooks, 2010; and as a film produced by the Gotham Group/Disney. *Rip Tide* was optioned for film by Disney, 2011.

Sidelights

In the fictional future Kat Falls depicts in her novels *Dark Life* and *Rip Tide,* a period of global warming has caused Earth's seas to rise, reducing the amount of habitable land and motivating some humans to move into underwater communities. The teens in Falls' stories—fifteen-year-old, ocean-dwelling Ty and "Topsider" friend Gemma—have adventures that were inspired by the author's own son, who enjoys books that feature strangely tentacled sea creatures, brave pioneers traveling West by wagon train, and popular comic-book superheroes the X-men. "Because I wanted to write science fiction and not fantasy, I didn't want to stray too far from the possible," Falls noted on her home page. "Therefore I tried to base all the technology . . . on some prediction or theory posed by an engineer, scientist or architect. In some cases, the science has been developed but is still in the experimental stages. For example, liquid breathing is used to help premature babies and coma patients who are in respiratory distress, but it's a long way from being something people use for scuba diving."

When readers first meet Ty in the pages of *Dark Life,* his family has left the problems on Earth's surface and now homestead on the ocean floor. Much like pioneer families of the early nineteenth-century American West, they live an isolated existence in a small community of likeminded individualists and must defend themselves against a band of roaming undersea outlaws known as the Seablite Gang. It is clear to Ty that these outlaws have an unusual ability to live underwater. When he teams up with Gemma, an orphaned teen from above ground who has traveled into the ocean to search for her brother, he determines to locate the gang's base camp and discover their secret. Along the way, he uncovers secret medical discoveries, exotic creatures, and a superpower of his own. Writing in *Booklist,* Cindy Welch noted that the "exotic setting and . . . likable characters" in *Dark Life* "will keep readers turning the pages," and *School Library Journal* critic Leah J. Sparks predicted that the "budding romance between Ty and

Cover of Kat Falls' suspenseful teen novel Dark Life, *featuring artwork by Christopher Stengel.* (Scholastic, 2010. Book cover art and design copyright © 2010 by Christopher Stengel. Reproduced by permission of Scholastic, Inc.)

Gemma" will be as popular with teens as the author's "marvelous, imaginative depictions of life on the ocean floor." A *Publishers Weekly* writer concluded of Falls' "action-packed aquatic adventure" that "there's no denying the nifty premise, solid characterization, and tense moments that contribute to a cinematic reading experience."

In *Rip Tide* Ty and Gemma's adventures continue. While bringing the family's seaweed crop to market, Ty discovers a town that appears to have been recently abandoned, its residents laying, murdered, nearby. After his mother and father are captured by the Surfs, a band whose members live underwater, the teen and Gemma ask the aid of the Seablite Gang in tracking them down. With sea creatures bearing down, and his parents still in danger, the teen is also aided by the gang in uncovering the facts behind the mystery. "Atmospheric and tense, [and] built around an expertly used post apocalyptic-meets-Wild West setting, this story's a whole lot of fun," concluded a *Publishers Weekly* critic. "Throughout, Falls displays an undeniable gift for long-range plotting," asserted *Voice of Youth Advocates* contributor Mark Flowers, the critic adding that in *Rip Tide* the au-

thor "expertly weav[es] pieces of a growing mystery into an action-filled story . . . culminating in another twistily satisfying ending.

Biographical and Critical Sources

PERIODICALS

Booklist, May 15, 2010, Cindy Welch, review of *Dark Life,* p. 46.
Chicago Tribune, March 15, 2009, Louis R. Carlozo, interview with Falls.
Kirkus Reviews, June 15, 2011, review of *Rip Tide.*
Publishers Weekly, April 5, 2010, review of *Dark Life,* p. 60; June 6, 2011, review of *Rip Tide,* p. 42.
School Library Journal, June, 2010, Leah J. Sparks, review of *Dark Life,* p. 100; November, 2010, Tricia Melgaard, review of *Dark Life,* p. 57.
Voice of Youth Advocates, April, 2010, Jonathan Basye, review of *Dark Life,* p. 68; August, 2011, Mark Flowers, review of *Rip Tide,* p. 287.

ONLINE

Adams Literary Web site, http://www.adamsliterar.com/ (August 12, 2011), "Kat Falls."
Kat Falls Home Page, http://katfalls.com (August 12, 2011).*

*   *   *

FALLS, Kathleen Moynihan
See FALLS, Kat

*   *   *

FRIEDEN, Sarajo

Personal
Born in CA; children: one son.

Addresses
Home—Los Angeles, CA. *Agent*—Lilla Rogers Studio, MA, info@lillarogers.com. *E-mail*—info@sarajofrieden.com.

Career
Artist, illustrator, and designer. *Exhibitions:* Work has been exhibited in group and solo shows at galleries in Los Angeles and San Diego, CA; New York, NY; NC; MN; Rome, Venice, and Naples, Italy; and Australia.

Awards, Honors
Awards from Society of Illustrators New York and Society of Illustrators Los Angeles.

Writings

(And illustrator) *The Care and Feeding of Fish: A Story with Pictures,* Houghton Mifflin (Boston, MA), 1996.

(Illustrator) Lisa Railsback, *Noonie's Masterpiece,* Chronicle Books (San Francisco, CA), 2010.

Work included in anthology *Drawn In: A Peek into the Inspiring Sketchbooks of 44 Fine Artists, Illustrators, Graphic Designers, and Cartoonists,* edited by Julia Rothman, Quarry Books, 2011. Contributor to periodicals, including *Boston Globe, National Geographic, New Yorker, Time, Travel & Leisure,* and *Village Voice.* Artwork has been selected for publication in trade periodicals *American Illustration, Communication Arts,* and *3x3.*

Sidelights

California-based artist and graphic designer Sarajo Frieden creates images inspired by influences ranging from Japanese woodblock prints and East Indian textiles to remembered images that evoke her family's Hungarian heritage. "A host of disparate vocabularies from the worlds of fine, folk and decorative art, including Persian miniatures, Shaker trance drawings, Japanese ukiyo-e, and my Hungarian great aunt's embroidery, can be found wandering through my images," Frieden explained on her home page. "Using open ended narratives, folk tales, abstraction and the juxtaposition of discordant images, I try to give form to the human experience as I see it." In addition to her fine art and her designs for textiles and other consumer products, Frieden has created the original picture book *The Care and Feeding of Fish: A Story with Pictures,* as well as illustrating *Noonie's Masterpiece,* a chapter book by Lisa Railsback that focuses on blossoming creativity. Loosely rendered in what *Booklist* contributor Carolyn Phelan described as "a 1960s-retro look," her "ink-and-watercolor illustrations float through the book like the dreamy thoughts of an aspiring young artist," according to D. Maria LaRocco in her *School Library Journal* appraisal of *Noonie's Masterpiece.*

In *The Care and Feeding of Fish* Frieden introduces Loulou, who leads a lackluster life until a well-traveled aunt sends Harold the fish her way. Following the detailed instructions for Harold's care, Loulou soon has a human-sized fish confidante on her hands, as well as a companion during her everyday activities. As Harold grows in size, he also grows in ambition, and by book's end he has left to follow his dreams, with another fish taking his place in Loulou's quiet life. Noting that Frieden's story can be read on several levels, Ilene Cooper predicted in *Booklist* that adults will enjoy the "sophisticated sly [verbal] wink" in the narrative while smaller children will appreciate its silliness. A *Publishers Weekly* critic described *The Care and Feeding of Fish* as a "whimsical debut" that channels the creative work of New York artist/illustrator Maira Kalman, adding that Frieden's "wordplay and flamboyant, action-filled paintings" reflect her "bold imagination and a fondness for puns."

Biographical and Critical Sources

PERIODICALS

Booklist, November 15, 1996, Ilene Cooper, review of *The Care and Feeding of Fish: A Story with Pictures,* p. 593; May 1, 2010, Carolyn Phelan, review of *Noonie's Masterpiece,* p. 87.
Bulletin of the Center for Children's Books, October, 1996, review of *The Care and Feeding of Fish,* p. 58.
Communication Arts, July, 2005, "Sarajo Frieden," pp. 160-61.
Kirkus Reviews, March 1, 2010, review of *Noonie's Masterpiece.*
Publishers Weekly, August 5, 1996, review of *The Care and Feeding of Fish,* p. 442; April 19, 2010, review of *Noonie's Masterpiece,* p. 53.
School Library Journal, October, 1996, Karen James, review of *The Care and Feeding of Fish,* p. 94; July, 2010, D. Maria LaRocco, review of *Noonie's Masterpiece,* p. 95.

ONLINE

Sarajo Frieden Home Page, http://www.sarajofrieden.com (June 12, 2011).
Sarajo Frieden Web Log, http://sarajofrieden.blogspot.com (June 12, 2011).*

*   *   *

GERINGER, Laura
(L.G. Bass)

Personal

Married; husband a clinical psychologist; children: Ethan, Adam. *Education:* Degrees from Barnard College and Yale University. *Hobbies and other interests:* Martial arts.

Addresses

Home—New York, NY.

Career

Editor and author of children's books. Formerly worked as an art teacher and journalist; HarperCollins, New York, NY, editor, 1980-91, head of Laura Geringer Books imprint, 1991-2008. First Book, Washington, DC, member of national advisory board.

Awards, Honors

Notable Children's Books designation, American Library Association (ALA), for *A Three-Hat Day;* Best Books for Young Adults designation, ALA, 2005, for *Sign of the Qin.*

Writings

Seven True Bear Stories, illustrated by Carol Maisto, Hastings House (New York, NY), 1979.

A Three-Hat Day, illustrated by Arnold Lobel, Harper & Row (New York, NY), 1985.

Molly's New Washing Machine, illustrated by Petra Mathers, Harper & Row (New York, NY), 1986.

Silverpoint (young-adult novel), HarperCollins (New York, NY), 1991.

Look out, Look out, It's Coming!, illustrated by Sue Truesdell, HarperCollins (New York, NY), 1992.

Yours 'til the Ice Cracks: A Book of Valentines, illustrated by Andrea Baruffi, HarperCollins (New York, NY), 1992.

(Adaptor) *The Seven Ravens,* illustrated by Edward S. Gazsi, HarperCollins (New York, NY), 1994.

(Adaptor) *The Pomegranate Seeds: A Classic Greek Myth,* illustrated by Leonid Gore, Houghton Mifflin (Boston, MA), 1995.

The Stubborn Pumpkin, illustrated by Holly Berry, Scholastic (New York, NY), 1999.

(As L.G. Bass) *Sign of the Qin,* Hyperion Books for Children (New York, NY), 2004.

There Was a Little Gnome, illustrated by Bagram Ibatoulline, Atheneum Books for Young Readers (New York, NY), 2009.

Boom Boom Go Away!, illustrated by Bagram Ibatoulline, Atheneum Books for Young Readers (New York, NY), 2010.

Author of introduction to *Up All Night: A Short Story Collection,* Laura Geringer Books/HarperTeen (New York, NY), 2008.

"MYTH MEN, GUARDIANS OF THE LEGEND" SERIES

Perseus: The Boy with Super Powers, illustrated by Peter Bollinger, Scholastic (New York, NY), 1996.

Hercules: The Strong Man, illustrated by Peter Bollinger, Scholastic (New York, NY), 1996.

Ulysses: The Soldier King, illustrated by Peter Bollinger, Scholastic (New York, NY), 1996.

Andromeda: The Flying Warrior Princess, illustrated by Peter Bollinger, Scholastic (New York, NY), 1996.

Iole: The Girl with Super Powers, illustrated by Peter Bollinger, Scholastic (New York, NY), 1997.

Castor and Pollux: The Fighting Twins, illustrated by Peter Bollinger, Scholastic (New York, NY), 1997.

Theseus: The Hero of the Maze, illustrated by Peter Bollinger, Scholastic (New York, NY), 1997.

Atalanta: The Wild Girl, illustrated by Peter Bollinger, Scholastic (New York, NY), 1997.

Sidelights

A former children's book editor whose publishing imprint produced titles by such noted authors as William Joyce, Laura Numeroff, and Richard Egielski, Laura Geringer has written more than twenty works for young

readers, among them the picture books *The Seven Ravens* and *Boom Boom Go Away!* and the award-winning fantasy novel *Sign of the Qin,* the last published under the pen name L.G. Bass. Geringer spent almost three decades working for HarperCollins in New York City, and she began her writing career in the late 1970s. As a writer, she also produced several picture-book retellings of Greek and Roman myths in her "Myth Men" series, which includes *Theseus: The Hero of the Maze* and *Andromeda: The Flying Warrior Princess.*

In *The Seven Ravens* Geringer retells a Brothers Grimm fairytale. Her story follows a young girl as she goes in search of her seven older brothers who, years earlier, were transformed into ravens by their father's angry, unthinking curse. On her journey the girl carries her brothers' shirts, which are embroidered with the sun, moon, and stars. She meets three wondrous characters who represent those same celestial bodies, and they act as guides, directing her to Glass Mountain, where her siblings now reside. Once there, the girl uses her embroidered shirts to help her brothers regain their human

Writing under her pseudonym L.G. Bass, Laura Geringer treats teens to a futuristic fantasy in **Sign of the Oin,** *featuring artwork by Tim Zulewski.* (Disney-Hyperion Books, 2004. Illustration by Tim Zulewski; Chinese calligraphy by Jiaxuan Zhang. Reproduced by permission of Disney-Hyperion, an imprint of Disney Book Group LLC. All rights reserved.)

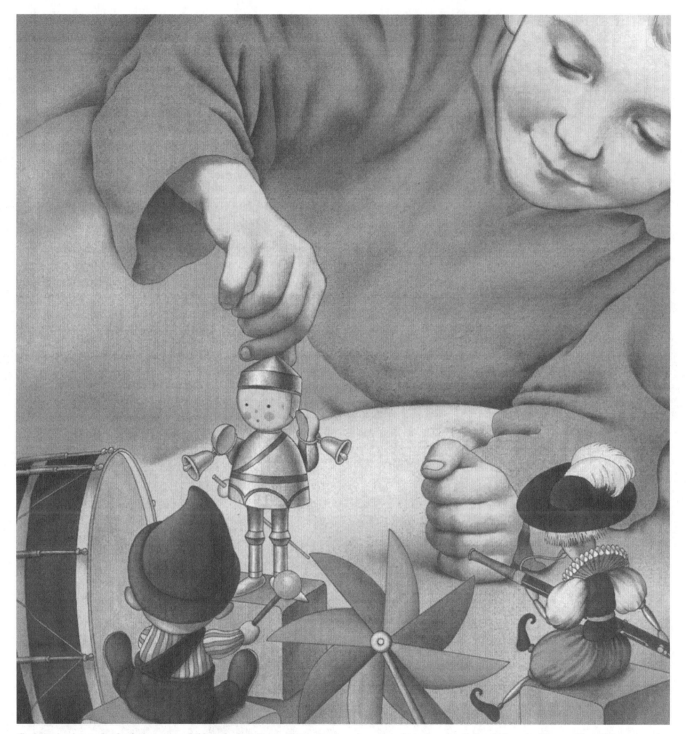

Geringer's picture books for younger children include Boom Boom Go Away!, *a story featuring detailed paintings by Bagram Ibatoulline.* (Atheneum Books for Young Readers, 2010. Illustration copyright © 2010 by Bagram Ibatoulline. Reproduced by permission of Atheneum Books for Young Readers, an imprint of Simon & Schuster Publishing Division.)

form. "Geringer concentrates on the girl and her thoughts, thus strengthening the bond between young readers and the protagonist," Wendy Lukehart noted in her *School Library Journal* review of *The Seven Ravens.* "The language is spare yet elegant," wrote Kay Weisman in *Booklist,* while a *Publishers Weekly* critic maintained that Geringer's "poetic, immediate style" enriches a "deeply satisfying adaptation [that] honors the Grimm tradition."

Geringer retells the tale of Demeter and Persephone in *The Pomegranate Seeds: A Classic Greek Myth,* an adaptation of a story published in 1853 in Nathaniel Hawthorne's *Tanglewood Tales for Boys and Girls.* She depicts Demeter, the Greek goddess of the harvest, as a hard-working mother whose headstrong daughter, Persephone, is abducted by her uncle, Hades, and taken to his dark realm beneath the earth. Although she knows that tasting any food underground will doom her to spend the rest of her life in the underworld, Persephone is tricked into eating three pomegranate seeds. Even after her rescue by Hermes, the young woman must suffer the consequences of her action, spending three months of every year with Hades. According to a *Publishers Weekly* contributor, in *The Pomegranate Seeds* Geringer "captures the timeless, bittersweet atmosphere of the ancient tale."

A bedtime story, *Boom Boom Go Away!* is based on Geringer's son's experiences in a Dalcroze class, where musical concepts are taught through physical activities. When his mother suggests that he prepare for sleep, a toy gnome refuses to quiet down, preferring to bang away on his drum. The gnome is soon joined in protest by his compatriots, including a gong-playing elf and a bassoon-loving prince, all who add to the cacophony until their owner, a young boy, grows tired. A reviewer in *Publishers Weekly* observed of *Boom Boom Go Away!* that "the story's energetic action exploits readers' after-dinner punchiness," and Marianne Saccardi remarked in *School Library Journal* that the "rhythmical text has an appealing cadence and a catchy refrain." Andrew Medlar, writing in *Booklist,* recommended *Boom Boom Go Away!* as "timeless and colorful fun for the eyes and ears" of the picture-book set.

In her young-adult novel *Sign of the Qin* Geringer takes readers through two starkly contrasting worlds: the lavish world inside a royal Chinese palace and the impoverished world of the slums stretching beyond the palace gates. Drawing from both traditional Chinese epics of the Song dynasty and twentieth-century kung fu films, Geringer creates a world of glittering heroes and evil villains in her story about a cold-hearted emperor who forces his young wife into exile after she gives birth to a child with a tainted birthmark, the outlaw sign of the Qin. The empress then meets a monk who trains her in the martial arts, also sharing in the raising of her son, Prince Zong. As Zong grows to manhood, he fights the assassins sent to kill him and eventually joins with a trio of brothers who involve him in an effort to save the world from a demonic threat. Reviewing *Sign of the Qin,* a *Publishers Weekly* critic wrote that "fantasy readers looking for a break from conventional swords and sorcery will likely become enthralled."

Biographical and Critical Sources

PERIODICALS

Booklist, February 1, 1996, Kay Weisman, review of *The Seven Ravens,* p. 45; February 1, 1996, Kay Weisman, review of *The Pomegranate Seeds: A Classic Greek Myth,* p. 934; April 15, 2004, Jennifer Mattson, review of *Sign of the Qin,* p. 1451; December 15, 2009, Andrew Medlar, review of *Boom Boom Go Away!,* p. 43.

Kirkus Reviews, April 1, 2004, review of *Sign of the Qin,* p. 324; February 15, 2010, review of *Boom Boom Go Away!*

Publishers Weekly, July 25, 1994, review of *The Seven Ravens,* p. 55; November 13, 1995, review of *The Pomegranate Seeds,* p. 61; March 29, 2004, review of *Sign of the Qin,* p. 63; January 18, 2010, review of *Boom Boom Go Away!,* p. 45.

School Library Journal, December, 1994, Wendy Lukehart, review of *The Seven Ravens,* p. 98; April, 2004, John Peters, review of *Sign of the Qin,* p. 148; January, 2010, Marianne Saccardi, review of *Boom Boom Go Away!,* p. 74.

Voice of Youth Advocates, June, 2004, Meredith Jenson-Benjamin, review of *Sign of the Qin,* p. 139; April, 2005, review of *Sign of the Qin,* p. 10.

ONLINE

Hyperion Books for Children Web site, http://www.hyperionbooksforchildren.com/ (March 28, 2005), interview with Geringer (L.G. Bass).*

*   *   *

GRAVETT, Emily 1972(?)-

Personal

Born c. 1972, in Brighton, England; partner's name Mik; children: Oleander (daughter). *Education:* Brighton University, B.F.A. (illustration), 2001.

Addresses

Home—Brighton, England.

Career

Author and illustrator.

Awards, Honors

Kate Greenaway Medal for illustration, and Nestlé Award Bronze Medal, both 2006, and Macmillan Illustrator's Prize, all for *Wolves;* Kate Greenaway Medal for illustration, 2008, for *Little Mouse's Big Book of Fears.*

Writings

SELF-ILLUSTRATED

Wolves, Macmillan (London, England), 2005, Simon & Schuster Books for Young Readers (New York, NY), 2006.

Orange Pear Apple Bear, Macmillan (London, England), 2006, Simon & Schuster Books for Young Readers (New York, NY), 2007.

Meerkat Mail, Macmillan (London, England), 2006, Simon & Schuster Books for Young Readers (New York, NY), 2007.

Emily Gravett's Big Book of Fears, Macmillan (London, England), 2007, published as *Little Mouse's Big Book of Fears,* 2007, Simon & Schuster Books for Young Readers (New York, NY), 2008.

Monkey and Me, Simon & Schuster Books for Young Readers (New York, NY), 2008.

Spells, Macmillan Children's (London, England), 2008, Simon & Schuster Books for Young Readers (New York, NY), 2009.

The Odd Egg, Macmillan Children's (London, England), 2008, Simon & Schuster Books for Young Readers (New York, NY), 2009.

Dogs, Macmillan Children's (London, England), 2009, Simon & Schuster Books for Young Readers (New York, NY), 2010.

The Rabbit Problem, Macmillan Children's (London, England), 2009, Simon & Schuster Books for Young Readers (New York, NY), 2010.

(With Julia Donaldson) *Cave Baby,* Macmillan (London, England), 2010.

Blue Chameleon, Simon & Schuster (New York, NY), 2011.

Wolf Won't Bite!, Macmillan (London, England), 2011, Simon & Schuster Books for Young Readers (New York, NY), 2012.

Sidelights

British artist Emily Gravett became a book illustrator and author while raising her young daughter and her first two books were actually adaptations of projects she had completed during college. Heralded by *School Library Journal* contributor Kirsten Cutler as an "imaginative, cleverly designed story" that is paired with "eloquent multimedia illustrations," *Wolves* stands both as Gravett's award-winning debut and the cornerstone of a career that has become known for innovation. Further kudos have come the artist's way through her work on such original self-illustrated stories as *The Odd Egg, Blue Chameleon, The Rabbit Problem, Wolf Won't Bite!,* and *Cave Baby,* the last a collaboration with popular children's author Julia Donaldson.

Featuring two different endings, *Wolves* follows Rabbit as he visits the local library to find a book about wolves. While walking back home with his nose in his book, long-eared Rabbit finds more between the covers than he bargained for when a bushy wolf tail and sharp wolf claws start to poke out from the pages. Soon a big, bad wolf makes its appearance, brought to life in charcoal drawings that artfully reflect the creature's scruffy wildness. In his review for *Booklist,* Michael Cart commented on the sophistication of Gravett's concept, dubbing *Wolves* a "postmodern picture book" and a "sly celebration of libraries and reading." A *Kirkus Reviews* contributor expressed the consensus among several critics, proclaiming the book to be "brilliant fun," while in the *New York Times Book Review* J.D. Biersdorfer com-

mended the author/illustrator's innovative approach: using "an eye-catching collage of hand-drawn sketches and photography" to create "a modern trompe l'oeil effect—complete with 3-D shadows and playful shifts in scale and perspective," according to the critic. *Wolves* earned Gravett her first Kate Greenaway medal for illustration; she would earn a second such honor for her picture book *Little Mouse's Big Book of Fears.*

Also based on a project completed during Gravett's college studies, *Orange Pear Apple Bear* restricts its text to five words (including the four on the book's cover). Each page of the work features a different combination of these nouns, some of which double as adjectives in the accompanying illustrations. Gravett's illustrations for *Orange Pear Apple Bear* "have a fresh spontaneity yet reflect careful deliberation," observed *Horn Book* writer Nell Beram, and in *School Library Journal* Maryann H. Owen concluded that the "softly hued watercolor illustrations loosely outlined in black pen and ink are delightful." A "deliciously playful romp" that stars a large, "genial bear" in its spare watercolor illustrations, *Orange Pear Apple Bear* unfolds as "a masterpiece of superbly controlled pacing," according to a *Kirkus Reviews* writer.

In *Meerkat Mail* Gravett serves up another unique picture-book experience. Here readers meet Sunny, an adventure-seeking meerkat, as the young mongoose decides to leave his home as part of a large, busy family living in the Kalahari Desert and visit several enclaves of cousins. As readers learn through Sunny's postcards and letters home, the hospitality of the Marsh Mongoose is overshadowed by its damp abode, and the Malagasy Mongoose is far too much of a night owl to become Sunny's long-term friend. Ultimately, Sunny's overly hot and overcrowded desert home begins to seem very attractive. "Along with humor and suspense, [Gravett] . . . folds snippets of natural history into the tale," wrote a *Kirkus Reviews* writer, and in *Publishers Weekly* a critic noted that *Meerkat Mail* effectively "conveys not just how a landscape looks, but also how its lighting and climate feels to a very small mammal."

A fearful young rodent is the star of *Little Mouse's Big Book of Fears,* which finds the bewhiskered creature determined to deal with a number of phobias by expressing his feelings in drawing and writing. An interactive book featuring liftable flaps, die-cut holes, and fold outs, *Little Mouse's Big Book of Fears* is an "ingenious worrier's guide to phobias," according to London *Sunday Times* contributor Nicolette Jones, while Meg Smith cited the combination of Gravett's "spare text and delightful illustrations" in her *School Library Journal* review.

Other picture books written and illustrated by Gravett include *Monkey and Me,* a story of an imaginative little girl and her beloved toy monkey, and *Dogs,* which Daniel Kraus recommended in *Booklist* as "a wonderfully warmhearted ode to four-legged friends." *Blue*

Chameleon focuses on a lonely amphibian who attempts to find his soul mate among a succession of unusual but slightly chameleon-like objects. "As always, Gravett's art charms," asserted a *Publishers Weekly* contributor in reviewing this picture book; her colored-pencil drawings in *Blue Chameleon* "repay attention as readers spot similarities to and differences from the things the chameleon mimics."

Biographical and Critical Sources

PERIODICALS

Booklist, December 1, 2006, Michael Cart, review of *Wolves,* p. 52; June 1, 2007, Julie Cummins, review of *Orange Pear Apple Bear,* p. 84; December 1, 2008, Janice Del Negro, review of *Little Mouse's Big Book of Fears,* p. 56; January 1, 2009, Julie Cummins, review of *The Odd Egg,* p. 92; March 15, 2010, Daniel Kraus, review of *Dogs,* p. 46.

Bookseller, October 7, 2005, "Nestlé Shortlist Revealed," p. 10; April 7, 2006, Katie Hawthorne, review of *Orange Pear Apple Bear,* p. 13.

Daily Mail, August 6, 2010, Sally Morris, review of *Cave Baby,* p. 62.

Guardian (London, England), May 19, 2007, Julia Eccleshare, review of *Monkey and Me,* p. 20; March 22, 2008, Julia Eccleshare, review of *The Odd Egg,* p. 22; June 28, 2008, Joanna Carey, "With Thanks to My Daughter's Pet Rats . . . ," p. 14; July 31, 2010, Julia Eccleshare, review of *Cave Baby,* p. 12.

Herald (Glasgow, Scotland), February 3, 2007, Sara Valentin, "It Turns Out Words Can Be Fun Too," p. 13.

Horn Book, July-August, 2007, Nell Beram, review of *Orange Pear Apple Bear,* p. 377; January-February, 2009, Rebecca E. Schaffner, review of *Little Mouse's Big Book of Fears,* p. 78; January-February, 2009, Christine M. Heppermann, review of *The Odd Egg,* p. 79; January-February, 2011, Robin L. Smith, review of *The Rabbit Problem,* p. 78.

Kirkus Reviews, July 1, 2006, review of *Wolves,* p. 678; April 15, 2007, review of *Orange Pear Apple Bear;* September 1, 2007, review of *Meerkat Mail;* August 1, 2008, review of *Little Mouse's Big Book of Fears;* December 1, 2008, review of *The Odd Egg;* September 1, 2009, review of *Spells;* February 15, 2010, review of *Dogs.*

New York Times Book Review, September 10, 2006, J.D. Biersdorfer, review of *Wolves,* p. 19; November 9, 2008, Daniel Handler, review of *Little Mouse's Big Book of Frears,* p. 19; October 11, 2009, Lawrence Downes, review of *Spells,* p. 23; November 8, 2009, Sherie Posesorski, review of *The Odd Egg,* p. 23.

Publishers Weekly, March 19, 2007, review of *Orange Pear Apple Bear,* p. 62; September 17, 2007, review of *Meerkat Mail,* p. 53; October 27, 2008, review of *The Odd Egg,* p. 53; October 12, 2009, review of *Spells,* p. 49; January 25, 2010, review of *Dogs,* p. 116; October 18, 2010, review of *The Rabbit Problem,* p. 48; January 31, 2011, review of *Blue Chameleon,* p. 46.

School Librarian, winter, 2010, Chris Brown, review of *Cave Baby,* p. 217.

School Library Journal, August, 2006, Kirsten Cutler, review of *Wolves,* p. 87; August, 2006, Rick Margolis, "Like a Rolling Stone" (profile), p. 31; April, 2007, Maryann H. Owen, review of *Orange Pear Apple Bear,* p. 106; January, 2009, Susan Weitz, review of *The Odd Egg,* p. 76; October, 2009, Wendy Lukehart, review of *Spells,* p. 92; March, 2010, Kathleen Finn, review of *Dogs,* p. 119; December, 2010, Wendy Lukehart, review of *The Rabbit Problem,* p. 82.

Sunday Times (London, England), August 5, 2007, Nicolette Jones, review of *Little Mouse's Big Book of Fears,* p. 47; July 27, 2008, Nicolette Jones, review of *Spells,* p. 48; July 25, 2010, Nicolete Jones, review of *Cave Baby,* p. 50; January 30, 2011, Nicolette Jones, review of *Wolf Won't Bite,* p. 53.

Times, August 30, 2008, Amanda Craig, review of *Spells,* p. 15; May 29, 2010, Amanda Craig, review of *Blue Chameleon,* p. 12; February 19, 2011, Amanda Craig, review of *Wolf Won't Bite!,* p. 12.

ONLINE

Emily Gravett Home Page, http://www.emilygravett.com (August 11, 2011).*

H

HALE, Stephanie 1973-

Personal

Born March 23, 1973, in IL; married; children: two sons. *Education:* Southern Illinois University at Carbondale, degree.

Addresses

Home—IL. *Agent*—Jenny Bent, The Bent Agency, 204 Park Place, No. 2, Brooklyn, NY 11238; jenny@ thebentagency.com. *E-mail*—Stephanie@stephaniehale. com.

Career

Writer. Worked variously in customer service and as a bartender. Presenter at schools.

Member

Romance Writers of America, Society of Children's Book Writers and Illustrators.

Writings

The Alpha Bet, Flux (Woodbury, MN), 2010.

"ASPEN BROOKS" YOUNG-ADULT NOVEL SERIES

Revenge of the Homecoming Queen, Berkley Jam (New York, NY), 2007.
Twisted Sisters, Berkley Jam (New York, NY), 2008.
Spring Breakup, Berkley Jam (New York, NY), 2009.

Sidelights

"Like most people when I finally went to work for real I didn't have a clue what I truly wanted to do," Stephanie Hale noted on her home page, reflecting on her evolution as a young-adult novelist. "I spent more hours than I care to remember trapped in a cubicle working various customer service jobs," she recalled. Fortunately, Hale's long-held interest in writing combined with a memory from high school, and her first novel, *Revenge of the Homecoming Queen,* was born. Together with two sequels, *Twisted Sisters* and *Spring Breakup, Revenge of the Homecoming Queen* comprises Hale's "Aspen Brooks" series; she has also produced a standalone novel, *The Alpha Bet.*

Series star Aspen Brooks is one of the most popular girls in her high school, and she is fittingly dating popular football quarterback Lucas Riley. It is no surprise, therefore, that Aspen assumes that she will be named Homecoming Queen of her school. Unfortunately, her vision of riding in the parade wearing the prized tiara alongside Lucas are dashed when a group of mischievous fellow students secretly campaign to award the homecoming titles to scruffy and unfashionable Angel Ives and geeky Rand Bachrach. Things go from devastating to creepy when an equally humiliated Angel begins to exact her revenge, starting a girl vs. girl war that quickly escalates while an unexpected romance blooms.

Fortunately, Aspen is accepted into a popular sorority—the Zetas—when she arrives at college in *Twisted Sisters,* but the mysterious disappearance of sorority sister Mitzi and unwanted attention from her boyfriend's lovestruck roommate quickly lead events down the road to disaster. Midterm exams lead to a few weeks of vacation in *Spring Breakup,* but as Hale's title suggests, spring break is not an energizing reprieve for Aspen when a trip to Las Vegas involves her and her boyfriend in the disappearance of yet another popular and pretty coed.

Cover of Stephanie Hale's young-adult novel **The Alpha Bet,** *in which a naive college freshman whose efforts to rush a sorority begin to overwhelm her life.* (Flux, 2010. Book cover photographs copyright © 2009 by Thomas Northcut/Lifesize/Getty Images; Image Source/Punchstock. Reproduced by permission of Llewellyn Publications.)

Grace Kelly Cook, the central character in Hale's *The Alpha Bet*, is sixteen, super smart, and looking forward to changing her image from geeky to gorgeous when she arrives at McMillan College. Finally away from her overcontrolling mom, Grace decides to rush a sorority in order to ride the fast track to popularity. When she finds herself in the crosshairs of a crotchety fellow student who is determined to ruin Grace's chances at joining the Alphas, the clever teen turns to fiction and crafts a past that qualifies her for legacy status. While going through the sorority's initiation ritual—performing an A-to-Z list of challenges—Grace must keep one step ahead of the truth while also starting a new romance and reconsidering her top priority as popularity over principles. Reviewing *The Alpha Bet*, a *Kirkus Reviews* writer dubbed it a "sunny story" that treats readers to a "sweet romance," while Debbie Carton wrote in *Booklist* that the novel's "cute moments" make it a "quick and light read" geared for chick-lit fans. Grace is "a likeable protagonist who learns to recognize the value of

friendship, sisterhood, and being herself," concluded a *Publishers Weekly* critic in appraising Hale's "satisfying" teen novel.

Biographical and Critical Sources

PERIODICALS

Booklist, April 1, 2010, Debbie Carton, review of *The Alpha Bet,* p. 32.
Herald & Review (Decatur, IL), October 24, 2008, Theresa Churchill, "Young-Adult Fiction Author Shares Her Story."
Kirkus Reviews, March 1, 2010, review of *The Alpha Bet.*
Publishers Weekly, April 19, 2010, review of *The Alpha Bet,* p. 55.
School Library Journal, May, 2010, Lynn Rashid, review of *The Alpha Bet,* p. 114.
Voice of Youth Advocates, June, 2008, Heather Pittman, review of *Twisted Sisters,* p. 142.

ONLINE

Class of 2k7 Web site, http://classof2k7.com/ (August 15, 2011), "Stephanie Hale."
Stephanie Hale Home Page, http://www.stephaniehale.com (August 15, 2011).*

*   *   *

HATHORN, Libby 1943-

Personal

Full name, Elizabeth Helen Hathorn; surname is pronounced "hay-thorn"; born September 26, 1943, in Newcastle, New South Wales, Australia; married John Hathorn (died, 1998); children: Lisa, Keiran. *Education:*

Addresses

Home—Australia. *Agent*—Fran Moore, Curtis Brown, Level 1/ 2 Boundary St., Paddington 2021 Australia; fax: 612-93616161.

Career

Writer and educator. Teacher and librarian in schools in Sydney, New South Wales, Australia, 1965-81; worked as a deputy principal, 1977; consultant and senior education officer for government adult-education programs, 1981-86; full-time writer, 1987—. Writer-in-residence at University of Technology, Sydney, 1990, Woollahra Library, 1992, and Edith Cowan University, 1992. Consultant to Dorothea Mackellar National Poetry Competition/Festival for children; speaker for student, teacher, and parent groups. Australia Day Amabassador, beginning 1992.

Libby Hathorn (Courtesy of Libby Hathorn.)

Awards, Honors

Highly commended designation, Children's Book Council of Australia (CBCA), 1982, for *The Tram to Bondi Beach*; Children's Book of the Year Award shortlist, and New South Wales Premier's Literary awards, both 1986, both for *Paolo's Secret*; CBCA Honour Award, 1987, Kids Own Australian Literary Award (KOALA) shortlist, 1988, and Young Australians Best Book Award (YABBA) shortlist, 1989 and 1990, all for *All about Anna;* Literature Board of the Australia Council fellowships, 1987, 1988; CBCA Honour Award, 1988, for *Looking out for Sampson;* Children's Book of the Year Award shortlist, 1990, for *The Extraordinary Magics of Emma McDade;* Society of Women Writers honors, 1990, for the body of her work during 1987-89; Honour Book of the Year for Older Readers selection, CBCA, 1990, and American Library Association Best Book for Young Adults citation, and Canberra's Own Outstanding List shortlist, both 1991, all for *Thunderwith;* CBCA Notable Book citation, 1991, for both *So Who Needs Lotto?* and *Jezza Says;* New South Wales Children's Week Medal for literature, 1992; Kate Greenaway Award, 1995, for *Way Home;* Australian Violence Prevention Certificate Award, 1995, for both *Feral Kid* and *Way Home;* Parent's Choice Award, and Society of Women Writers (New South Wales, Australia) award, both for *Way Home;* Society of Women Writers award, 1995, for *Feral Kid* and *The Climb,* 1997, for *Rift,* 2001,

for *Grandma's Shoes,* and 2003, for *The River;* CBCA Notable Book citations, 1993, 1996, 1997, 2003; White Raven citation, Bologna Children's Book Fair, 2001, for *The Gift;* best adaptation citation, Australian Writers' Guild, 2001, for libretto of *Grandma's Shoes;* Australian Interactive Media Industry Award for Best New Children's Product, 2003, for *Weirdstop 2003;* Prime Minister's Centenary Medal, 2003; Society of Women Writers Biennial Book Award, 2009, for *Georgiana: Woman of Flowers,* and commended book selection, 2009, for *Letters to a Princess,* and 2010, for *Fire Song;* Prime Minister's Literary Award highly commended selection, 2010, for *Fire Song;* Woollahra Library Word Festival Poetry Prize, 2010, for *Vietnam Reflections.*

Writings

FOR CHILDREN AND YOUNG ADULTS

(Under name Elizabeth Hathorn, with John Hathorn) *Go Lightly: Creative Writing through Poetry,* illustrated by Joan Saint, Boden (Sydney, New South Wales, Australia), 1974.

Talks with My Skateboard (poetry), Australian Broadcasting Corp., 1991.

(Editor) *The Blue Dress* (stories), Heinemann (Melbourne, Victoria, Australia), 1991.

Help for Young Writers (nonfiction), Nelson (Melbourne, Victoria, Australia), 1991.

Good to Read (textbook), Nelson (Melbourne, Victoria, Australia), 1991.

Who? (stories), Heinemann (Melbourne, Victoria, Australia), 1992.

There and Back (poetry), Macmillan/McGraw Hill (Santa Rosa, CA), 1993.

Heard Singing (poetry anthology), Out of India Press, 1998.

(Author of libretto) *Grandma's Shoes* (children's opera; based on her picture book; also see below), music by Grahame Koehne, produced in Sydney, New South Wales, Australia, 2000.

(Author of libretto) *Sky Sash So Blue* (children's opera; based on her picture book; also see below), music by Phillip Ratlifee, produced in Fairfield, AL, 2004.

(With J. Andrew Johnstone) *The Tram to Bondi Beach* (play; based on her picture book; also see below), Bondi Beach (Bondi Junction, New South Wales, Australia), 2006.

(Compiler) *The ABC Book of Australian Poetry: A Treasury of Poems for Young People,* illustrated by Cassandra Allen, ABC (Sydney, New South Wales, Australia), 2010.

Vietnam Reflections (poetry), illustrated by Leon Coward, Pax (Woollahra, New South Wales, Australia), 2010.

Also writer and producer for interactive storytelling CD-ROM series including *Weirdstop 2003, Coolstop 2004,* and *Wonderstop 2005.*

PICTURE BOOKS

Stephen's Tree, illustrated by Sandra Laroche, Methuen (Sydney, New South Wales, Australia), 1979.

Lachlan's Walk, illustrated by Sandra Laroche, Heinemann (London, England), 1980.

The Tram to Bondi Beach, illustrated by Julie Vivas, Collins (London, England), 1981, Kane/Miller (Brooklyn, NY), 1989.

Freya's Fantastic Surprise, illustrated by Sharon Thompson, Scholastic (New York, NY), 1988.

Stuntumble Monday, illustrated by Melissa Web, Collins Dove (Australia), 1989.

The Garden of the World, illustrated by Tricia Oktober, Margaret Hamilton Books (Australia), 1989.

Way Home, illustrated by Greg Rogers, Crown (New York, NY), 1993.

The Surprise Box, illustrated by Priscilla Cutter, SRA School Group (Santa Rosa, CA), 1994.

Looking for Felix, illustrated by Ned Culio, SRA School Group (Santa Rosa, CA), 1994.

Grandma's Shoes, illustrated by Elivia Savadier, Little, Brown (Boston, MA), 1994, illustrated by Caroline Magerl, Hodder (Sydney, New South Wales, Australia), 2000.

The Wonder Thing, illustrated by Peter Gouldthorpe, Penguin (Camberwell, Victoria, Australia), 1995.

Sky Sash So Blue, illustrated by Benny Andrews, Simon & Schuster (New York, NY), 1998.

Magical Ride, Hodder Headline (Sydney, New South Wales, Australia), 1999.

The Gift, illustrated by Greg Rogers, Random House (New York, NY), 2000.

The River, Curriculum Corporation (Shanghai, China), 2001.

The Wishing Cupboard, Lothian (South Melbourne, Victoria, Australia), 2002.

Over the Moon, illustrated Caroline Magerl, Lothian (South Melbourne, Victoria, Australia), 2003.

The Great Big Animal Ask, illustrated Anna Pignato, Lothian (South Melbourne, Victoria, Australia), 2004.

Zahara's Rose, illustrated by Doris Unger, IP Kids (Carindale, Queensland, Australia), 2009.

I Love You Book, illustrated by Heath McKenzie, IP Kids (Carindale, Queensland, Australia), 2011.

NOVELS FOR CHILDREN

Paolo's Secret, illustrated by Lorraine Hannay, Heinemann (London, England), 1985.

Friends and Secrets, Hodder Headline (Sydney, New South Wales, Australia), 1985.

All about Anna, Heinemann (London, England), 1986.

Looking out for Sampson, Oxford University Press (Oxford, England), 1987.

The Extraordinary Magics of Emma McDade, illustrated by Maya, Oxford University Press (New York, NY), 1989.

Jezza Says, illustrated by Donna Rawlins, Angus & Robertson (Melbourne, Victoria, Australia), 1990.

So Who Needs Lotto? illustrated by Simon Kneebone, Penguin (Camberwell, Victoria, Australia), 1990.

The Lenski Kids and Dracula, Penguin (Camberwell, Victoria, Australia), 1992.

Love Me Tender, Oxford University Press (New York, NY), 1992, published as *Juke-box Jive,* Hodder (Sydney, New South Wales, Australia), 1996.

What a Star, HarperCollins (New York, NY), 1994.

A Face in the Water, illustrated by Uma Krishnaswamy, Goodbooks (Australia), 2000.

Okra-Acacia: The Story of the Wattle Pattern Plate, Curriculum Corporation (Shanghai, China), 2001.

Caravan Kids, illustrated by Julie Connor, National Museum of Australia (Canberra, Australian Capital Territory, Australia), 2006.

NOVELS FOR YOUNG ADULTS

Thunderwith, Heinemann (Melbourne, Victoria, Australia), 1989, Little, Brown (Boston, MA), 1991.

Valley under the Rock, Reed Heinemann (Melbourne, Victoria, Australia), 1993.

Feral Kid, Hodder & Stoughton (Sydney, New South Wales, Australia), 1994.

The Climb, Penguin (Camberwell, Victoria, Australia), 1996.

Chrysalis (sequel to *Thunderwith*), Reed (Melbourne, Victoria, Australia), 1997.

Rift, Hodder Headline (Sydney, New South Wales, Australia), 1998.

(With Gary Crew) *Dear Venny, Dear Saffron,* Lothian (Sydney, New South Wales, Australia), 1999.

The Painter, Hodder Headline (Sydney, New South Wales, Australia), 2001.

Volcano Boy (verse novel), Lothian (South Melbourne, Victoria, Australia), 2002.

Letters to a Princess, ABC (Sydney, New South Wales, Australia), 2007.

Georgiana: Woman of Flowers, Hachette Livre (Sydney, New South Wales, Australia), 2008.

Fire Song, ABC (Sydney, New South Wales, Australia), 2009.

"GHOSTOP" SERIES; NOVELS FOR YOUNG ADULTS

Double Sorrow, Hodder Headline (Sydney, New South Wales, Australia), 1999.

Twice the Ring of Fire, Hodder Headline (Sydney, New South Wales, Australia), 1999.

For Love to Conquer All, Hodder Headline (Sydney, New South Wales, Australia), 1999.

FOR ADULTS

(With G. Bates) *Half-Time: Perspectives on Mid-life,* Fontana Collins (Australia), 1987.

Better Strangers (stories), Millennium Books, 1989.

Damascus, a Rooming House (libretto), produced in Sydney, New South Wales, Australia, 1990.

The Maroubra Cycle: A Journey around Childhood (performance poetry), University of Technology, Sydney, New South Wales, Australia, 1990.

(And director) *The Blue Dress Suite* (music theater piece), produced in Melbourne, Victoria, Australia, 1991.

(With Margaret Wild) *Move Ahead with Street Sense* (teaching and learning package), 2001.

Author of "On Course!: Today's English for Young Writers" series, Macmillan, and "Help for Young Writers" series, Nelson.

Author's works were translated into Danish, Dutch, French, German, Greek, Italian, Korean, Norwegian, Portuguese, and Swedish.

Adaptations

Thunderwith was produced as the *Hallmark Hall of Fame* television movie *The Echo of Thunder; Songs with My Skateboard* was adapted for music by Stephen Lalor.

Sidelights

Libby Hathorn is an Australian writer who produces poetry, picture books, plays, novels, short stories, and nonfiction for children, young adults, and adults. Best known in the United States for her critically acclaimed novel *Thunderwith,* Hathorn has created works ranging from serious stories of troubled youth to lighthearted, fast-paced comedies. She writes of strong female char-

acters in her novels for junior readers, such as the protagonists in *All about Anna* and *The Extraordinary Magics of Emma McDade;* and of lonely, misunderstood teenagers in young-adult novels such as *Feral Kid, Love Me Tender,* and *Valley under the Rock.* As Maurice Saxby noted in the *St. James Guide to Children's Writers,* "In her novels for teenagers especially, Hathorn exposes, with compassion, sensitivity, and poetry the universal and ongoing struggle of humanity to heal hurts, establish meaningful relationships, and to learn to accept one's self—and ultimately—those who have wronged us."

Hathorn decided to become a writer at an early age, although she started her career as a teacher and librarian. Her first book for children, *Stephen's Tree,* was published in 1979. "Hathorn knows exactly how today's children think and feel," observed Saxby in *The Proof of the Puddin': Australian Children's Literature, 1970-1990.* "She has an uncanny ear for the speech nuances of the classroom, playground and home. . . . [She] is always able to penetrate the facade of her characters and with skill and subtlety reveal what they are really like inside."

Hathorn followed *Stephen's Tree* with two picture books: *Lachlan's Walk* and *The Tram to Bondi Beach. The Tram to Bondi Beach* tells the story of Keiran, a nine-year-old boy who longs for a job selling newspapers to passengers on the trams traveling through Sydney. Keiran wants to be like Saxon, an older boy who is an experienced newspaper seller. Reviewers commented on the nostalgic quality of the story, which is set in the 1930s. Marianne Pilla, writing in *School Library Journal,* complimented the "smooth" narrative and "vivid" passages in *The Tram to Bondi Beach. Times Literary Supplement* contributor Ann Martin called it "a simple but appealing tale," and Karen Jameyson wrote in *Horn Book* that Hathorn's book for younger children "will undoubtedly hold readers' interest."

Sky Sash So Blue tells the story of a young slave, Susannah, who is willing to give up her one bit of ornament—her sky-blue sash—to ensure that her sister has a lovely wedding dress. A writer for *Children's Book Review Service* called this book a "lovely story of hardship, perseverance and love," while reviewer Carol Ann Wilson pointed out in *School Library Journal* that Hathorn employs an article of clothing, as she did in *Grandma's Shoes,* "to symbolize the indomitable spirit of family." Wilson concluded that "Susannah's narrative makes human and accessible the poignant struggles of a people, a family, and one little girl." Hathorn collaborated with American composer Phillip Ratliffe to adapt *Sky Sash So Blue* as a children's opera, which was produced at Miles College in Birmingham, Alabama in 2004 and 2005.

All about Anna, her first novel, details the comic adventures of Lizzie, the narrator, and siblings Harriet and Christopher as well as her energetic, imaginative cousin,

Anna. Like *All about Anna, Looking out for Sampson* touches on family themes. Bronwyn wishes that her younger brother, Sampson, were older so that she could have a friend instead of someone to babysit. When Cheryl and her mother come to stay with Bronwyn's family, Bronwyn's situation worsens. A disagreeable girl, Cheryl hints that Bronwyn's parents must care more about Sampson, since they give the toddler so much attention. After Sampson is lost briefly at the beach, however, Cheryl and Bronwyn reconcile and Bronwyn's parents express their appreciation of her.

Among Hathorn's other books for beginning readers is *The Extraordinary Magics of Emma McDade.* The story describes the adventures of the title character, whose superhuman powers include incredible strength, the ability to call thousands of birds by whistling, and control over the weather. Another of Hathorn's books geared toward beginning readers is *Freya's Fantastic Surprise,* which was published in the United States as well as in Australia. In it Miriam tells the class at news time that her parents bought her a tent, a surprise that Freya attempts to top by making up fantastic stories that her classmates realize are false. Freya eventually has a real surprise to share, however, when her mother announces that Freya will soon have a new sister. Louise L. Sherman noted in her review of the book for *School Library Journal* that "Freya's concern about impressing her classmates . . . is on target." In a *Horn Book* review, Elizabeth S. Watson called *Freya's Fantastic Surprise* "a winner" and commented that "the text and pictures combine to produce a tale that proves truth is best."

Hathorn began writing for young adults after receiving an Australia Council grant in 1987. Published in 1989, her young-adult novel *Thunderwith* is the story of fourteen-year-old Lara, who begins living with the father she barely knows after her mother dies of cancer. Lara's new home is in the remote Wallingat Forest in New South Wales, Australia. Although Lara's relationship with her father develops smoothly, he is often away on business and Lara's stepmother is openly antagonistic towards her. Lonely and grief-stricken, Lara finds solace in her bond with a mysterious dog that appears during a storm. She names the dog Thunderwith and keeps its existence a secret; she only tells the aboriginal storyteller she has befriended at school. Eventually, Lara realizes that Thunderwith has filled the space that her mother's death created, enabling her to come to terms with her loss. Lara is also able to slowly win over her stepmother and to adjust to her new home and family life.

Thunderwith garnered praise as a sensitive and realistic young-adult novel, a *Publishers Weekly* reviewer commenting that "Hathorn deftly injects a sense of wonderment into this intense, very real story." According to *Horn Book* contributor Watson, the author possesses "a believable plot featuring a shattering climax and a satisfyingly realistic resolution." Robert Strang, writing in

the *Bulletin of the Center for Children's Books,* commended Hathorn's "especially expert weaving of story and setting" in *Thunderwith,* while *Magpies* contributor Jameyson wrote that Hathorn's "control over her complex subject is admirable; her insight into character sure and true; her ear for dialogue keen." Jameyson added of *Thunderwith* that its "nimble detour from the usual route will leave readers surprised, even breathless."

Hathorn's other novels include *Love Me Tender* and a comic work for junior readers, *The Lenski Kids and Dracula.* In the former, Alan and his sister and brothers are abandoned by their mother and sent to live with various relatives. Alan is taken in by his bossy, unsmiling Aunt Jessie, and the story chronicles his internal struggle regarding his desire to see his mother again. Reviewing the book, which was more-recently published as *Juke-box Jive, School Librarian* critic Mary Hoffman commented that "this could so easily have been just a collection of cliches." "What raises it," the critic added, "is Libby Hathorn's honesty about Alan's feelings for his mother and his aching realization that the family will never all live together again."

In several books Hathorn has combined her interest in young people with her concerns about the environment, poverty, and homelessness. Both her picture book *Way Home* and her novel *Feral Kid* focus on homeless young people, while an abandoned adolescent figures in her novel, *Rift.* Here readers meet Vaughan Jasper Roberts, a boy who is stuck with his grandmother in an isolated coastal town when his parents take off. "At times ponderous and confusing, this is a complex novel in which Hathorn explores human fragility and courage, manipulation and madness and the comfort of habit and ritual," noted Jane Connolly in a *Magpies* review of *Rift.*

Hathorn has also teamed up with noted writer Gary Crew to produce an epistolary novel between two teenagers in *Dear Venny, Dear Saffron,* and has experimented with online storytelling on her home page, adapting the *Ghostop* novels from that format. She is also a passionate lover of poetry, and along with writing and compiling her own poetry for children and adults, she has edited the poetry anthology *The ABC Book of Australian Poetry,* which contains many "gems" according to Jill Rowbotham of the *Australian.* Hathorn is also actively involved in Pier Poetry, a series of events and launches for Australian poets. As reported in the *Northern Rivers Echo,* Hathorn told an Australian Poetry Day audience: "Poetry helps make you smart. . . . If you don't share poetry with your kids you're walking past the best."

Biographical and Critical Sources

BOOKS

Hathorn, Libby, *Talks with My Skateboard,* Australian Broadcasting Corp., 1991.

St. James Guide to Children's Writers, 5th edition, edited by Sara Pendergast and Tom Pendergast, St. James Press (Detroit, MI), 1999, pp. 482-483.

Saxby, Maurice, *The Proof of the Puddin': Australian Children's Literature, 1970-1990,* Ashton Scholastic, 1993, pp. 219-221.

PERIODICALS

Australian, June 26, 2010, Jill Rowbotham, "Kids' Lit," p. 20.

Bulletin of the Center for Children's Books, April, 1991, Robert Strang, review of *Thunderwith,* p. 194.

Children's Book Review Service, August, 1998, review of *Sky Sash So Blue,* pp. 164-165.

Horn Book, March-April, 1989, Elizabeth S. Watson, review of *Freya's Fantastic Surprise,* p. 199; July, 1989, Karen Jameyson, review of *The Tram to Bondi Beach,* p. 474; July, 1991, Elizabeth S. Watson, review of *Thunderwith,* p. 462.

Magpies, March, 1990, Karen Jameyson, review of *Thunderwith,* p. 4; July, 1998, Jane Connolly, review of *Rift,* p. 38; November, 1999, p. 38; November, 1999, Annette Dale Meiklejohn, "Know the Author: Libby Hathorn," pp. 10-13.

Northern Rivers Echo (Lismore, Australia), January 28, 2010, "A Day for the Best to Shine," p. 9.

Publishers Weekly, May 17, 1991, review of *Thunderwith,* p. 65.

Richmond River Express Examiner (Casino, Australia), February 3, 2010, "Australiana on Display for the Big Day," p. 8.

School Librarian, August, 1996, Mary Hoffman, review of *Juke-box Jive,* p. 105.

School Library Journal, July, 1989, Marianne Pilla, review of *The Tram to Bondi Beach,* p. 66; August, 1989, Louise L. Sherman, review of *Freya's Fantastic Surprise,* p. 120; June, 1998, Carol Ann Wilson, review of *Sky Sash So Blue,* p. 108.

Times Literary Supplement, July 23, 1982, Ann Martin, "Encouraging the Excellent," p. 792.

ONLINE

Libby Hathorn Web Log, http://www.libby-hathorn. blogspot.com (June 7, 2011).

Libby Hathorn Home Page, http://www.libbyhathorn.com (June 7, 2011).

Autobiography Feature

Libby Hathorn

L ibby Hathorn contributed the following autobio-graphical essay to *SATA:*

I wish I could say I was born abroad, in far off Africa or deep in Papua New Guinea, and it was my exotic, isolated childhood that fed my imagination so that I was destined to be a writer. Or that I was raised on a remote, sprawling cattle station in the outback of Australia, where books and radio were my only friends. But no! Mine was a suburban childhood, busy with two sisters and a brother for company, spent in Sydney, Australia. And this is where I have spent most of my life, despite traveling widely as an adult, and is a place that has had its significance in all my writing life.

In fact, I was born in the city of Newcastle, some two hours north of Sydney, where my father had been posted for two years during the Second World War. However, most of my early childhood was in the eastern suburbs of Sydney, at Maroubra where we lived, a little too far from Maroubra Beach; and my adolescence was spent at Tamarama, a more picturesque suburb. Our house, in a tiny but verdant valley park, was a stone's throw from the small (and later to become highly fashionable), treacherous, and yet quite lovely city beach. We could look out the kitchen window and see the breakers of the Pacific Ocean crash onto the fine yellow sand of Tamarama Beach any time of day, and I remember going to sleep strangely calmed by the rhythm and roar of that surf. And we could take the walk along rugged cliffs to the much loved expanse of nearby Bondi Beach. One of my early books, *The Tram to Bondi Beach,* celebrates this beach, albeit as it was way back in the 1930s. Even now I don't like to be inland, to be too far from the edge that's been part and parcel of my whole life.

And yet how I longed for Europe and England during my adolescent years, a desire fed by the books and movies I'd seen and that perpetuated the idea that "real life" was elsewhere. I was to discover much later certain riches were to be discovered "in my own backyard," so to speak, when I began writing stories. In fact, I'd written poetry since my early childhood, completing a rhyming alphabet when I was in second grade—a first remembered "publication" because of the praise my grandmother, in particular, gave it. I'd read every book I could lay my hands on in our house, many of them with English backgrounds, and many way beyond my years, so that I felt I knew England, country

Young Libby, ready for Sunday school, c. 1950s. (Courtesy of Libby Hathorn.)

and city, as if it were my place. But at the same time, I was listening to many a story by different members of our large, extended family, set firmly in an Aussie setting.

Despite a lack of romantic origins, my childhood was rich—tilled with the busy-ness of being part of a largeish family of four children and countless aunts and uncles, some of whom came and went. It wasn't without its trials of course—a small house, too many people, and certain tensions between family members at times—but it was a household that shared stories and poetry and valued books, all the stuff of feeding the imagination. From our parents, who—especially my mother—quoted long tracts of poetry, to a father fond of recounting gritty tales of his country boyhood, to an uncle who was a fabulist, to a grandmother who read poetry aloud, our childhood was immersed and flavoured by story and poem.

Another grandmother lived in the Blue Mountains, running tearooms there, and this was a marvelous contrast to city living. Megalong Valley was the setting for many of my early "rapturous" nature poems. To wake to the smell of the eucalypt with overtones of last night's open fire, to hear the raucous song of the kookaburra and other native birds, and to look out onto the green and more green and rugged, yellow brown steep cliffs lit by morning sun . . . no wonder my sisters and I delighted in our holidays there.

It was a life to which books and story were intrinsic. Our father, a young detective at the time, told bedtime stories of his boyhood whenever he was home from work on time to do so, but also—and maybe even more importantly for me—he was fond of reading from our old grey-covered, much loved *A Treasury of Verse*. In those days kids went to bed early, with the ritual of being dosed with something called Fry's Emulsion which, we were told—though we didn't believe a word of it—" was good for your system," whatever that meant. The poetry did far more good than the ghastly tasting medicine. Who would not thrill to strange, entrancing, yet incomprehensible to a small child, words like Coleridge's?

> In Xanadu did Kubla Khan
> A stately pleasure-dome decree

Or the opening lines of the famous Australian ballad by Henry Kendall,

> By channels of coolness the echoes are calling,
> And down the dim gorges I hear the creek falling

My father's readings booked no interruption and we listened intently. We would shed a tear sometimes for the dog that drowned in *The Ballad of the Drover*, hugely enjoyed his more light-hearted reading of a poem such as *The Jackdaw of Rheims*, and wondered at the mysterious story of *Abou Ben Adhem*. But we never spoke a word when he gave forth those heartfelt readings.

I think my love affair with words began right there, if it didn't with mother's recitation, word perfect, of "The Slip-rails and the Spur." And of course, her singing—the truly melancholy rendition of "Come to Me My Melancholy Baby" or the more light-hearted "Little Mister Baggy Britches" when our baby brother was a bit fractious. I loved this quiet time in our house, but best of all I loved to hear the poetry that seemed so natural to her and so important to my dad. Something was "lit up" so that the words seemed alive and singing and powerful or playful, like the surf of Maroubra Beach or Bondi that beat out a rhythm that dramatically pounded in my bones and in my blood. Even a disliked teacher, primly reading the famous Australian ballad by Banjo Patterson, "The Man from Snowy River" (later to become a movie), had its own inexorable charm. It all lay in the poetry itself! The power of words to evoke images, to make music and to make you feel so many emotions just by their saying, the way it did, was extraordinary to me. And still is. Also extraordinary is the particular cadence and "truth" a good poem seems to hold in some magical way.

During my lifetime—as a child of the forties and an adolescent of the fifties and sixties—I was lucky to see Australian children's literature come into full flower. In fact, the seventies and eighties, as our publishing houses began publishing local voices, was a time described as the "Golden Age" of Australian children's literature by critic and revered elder in the field, Maurie Saxby. My library teacher at Maroubra Junction Girl's School in Sydney in the early 1950s would never have dreamed of such a thing, while tidying those shelves of largely English adventure stories such as Enid Blyton's Famous Five. Classics like *Black Beauty, Anne of Green Gables,* and *The Secret Garden* rubbed spines with only a few Australian children's texts, among them such memorable names as Patricia Wrightson, Joan Phipson, and Nan Chauncy.

But it was really the well-worn "Billabong" series by Mary Grant Bruce and the equally well-worn work of Ethel Turner's that I read over and over, attracted by serial narratives in an Australian setting. Television was something that had happened in America and had no bearing on our lives yet, so the characters of those books peopled our childhood. Reading was all-important and we could simply never have enough books. To this day I have several books on my bedside table and always travel "heavy," taking old friends that I might need near me along with a clutch of new to some far-off city or country town that may not sport a bookshop.

But harking back, we lived in a small, two-bedroom house in Maroubra during my early childhood, a family of four children: Margaret, Elizabeth, Suzanne, and Stephen. Everything was done at the old oak kitchen table, from homework to ironing to shelling peas. It wasn't until my older sister Margi went to high school that my mother bought us our first desk, which was to be communally owned, of course, and which fitted miraculously in the verandah sleep-out my sister and I shared. To me, it was luxury to have a place set apart specially for writing, not to mention the added pleasure of a set of drawers in the desk to be filled just with the accoutrements of writing. I loved touching the packet of envelopes, the writing pads (loose sheets of paper were a rarity), the floral stationery set I had been lucky enough to get for Christmas, and the HB pencils and opening the special spotted black-and-white case that housed my precious Conway Stewart fountain pen and matching propelling pencil.

When we reached high school, each of us children was given a "good" pen-and-pencil set and instructed that it had been expensive to purchase and was expected to last through all our high-school days. My father owned a treasured maroon and silver Parker pen and I don't remember ever seeing him with another writing implement. We never shared pens, as we understood it could damage the unique way the user had shaped the nib. But I remember practising his distinctive signature and wishing I could use his fine pen to replicate the downstroke. "Light on the upstroke and heavy on the downstroke," our teachers endlessly instructed us, endeavouring for each and every child to achieve a "copperplate" writing style.

We were all readers in that house, though I was the only writer. That is, the only child who crept away to write her own stories or poems, finding a private though darkish space behind the big tapestry lounge chair in the lounge room, in our busy and noisy household.

In infants school, we were supplied readers, each child with the same one. I'd wrestled in Grade 1 with the boredom of Fay and Don, walking down English-style streets in English-type clothes and living in smart English-type bungalows with never a gum tree in sight. However, my Grade 2 reader remains in mind as a pleasurable compilation of poems and stories, well thumbed and well loved. Dramatic stories about girls like Grace Darling, whose daring rescue of shipwrecked souls intrigued me, especially the idea that a girl could ride a horse into the surf and save people! And then the poems that were read aloud and "performed" in what was known as Verse Speaking—a lesson I found thrilling. Fragments of verse, and the particular intonation of my Grade 2 teacher Miss Hinder, have stayed with me a lifetime. "I shall lie in the reeds and hoooowl for your green glass beads, I love them so . . . give them me," and so on.

The readers were exhausted after a term and yet we were obliged to re-read around the class on a regular basis. And often the teacher requested we keep to the place, "finger on the word please" of the poor stumbling child selected to read aloud.

The introduction at home to Australian storybooks such as *Blinky Bill* and *Snugglepot and Cuddlepie* and the beloved Gumnutland host of characters was significant. Books that speak to children about the place they themselves know well, as Dorothy Wall and May Gibbs did for me as young child, must have a lasting impression and a lifelong significance. Here among Peter Rabbit and friends, Pooh Bear and friends, and a host of Disney characters in far-flung settings, which were loved too, were stories of our own land, our bush, our city, our animals, and our flora, very much our place.

I distinctly remember the thrill of pleasure at May Gibbs' gentle and environmentally friendly Gumnutland stories, coupled with her charming Australian artwork of our own bottle brush and gum trees and bush creatures. British books and British influence were still so strong in the 1950s, though things were slowly beginning to change in that regard. The arts were reflecting this change, our burgeoning literature at the forefront in the naming (and thus the possessing) of things in our own landscape. This was a gradual process of relinquishing Britain and Europe as the centre of our world and recognising our own country as an entity in itself, with Asian countries as our closest neighbours.

Having said that, much later in the 1990s it was still not easy to have children's books with an Asian theme published. I'd made plans to write a series I'd called "Asiastory"—six stories set in various Asian countries close to home—as a kind of interesting challenge. But it was to be more difficult than I'd imagined. The first one, a picture storybook set in Vietnam, *The Wishing Cupboard,* which was the first published story to go online in Australia, took six or seven years to find a publisher. And it was only in 1999 that I had my book *The River,* which is set in China, launched in Shanghai through an educational publishing house, Curriculum Corporation. I've had four of these Asian-themed stories published to date, and am currently determinedly working on a Korean story.

*

In high school, we were steeped in English literature—from John Donne to the Romantics, our Shakespeare texts studied thoroughly over a whole year, so thoroughly that we could quote whole tracts. There was not much modem poetry taught at school so I had to find that elsewhere. It was years later that I would discover the charms of other cultures. Translations of Spanish poets Lorca and Pablo Neruda, American poets like William Carlos Williams, Monica Dickens, and Hugh Langston, and Welsh poet Dylan Thomas, to mention a few.

Teachers had an enormous impact on my life right through my schooling. The shy and beautiful Miss Miller (Grade 1), who, incidentally, I remember to this day never returned the book on China that my German grandfather gave the family and I proudly took to school, a beautiful book with the unusual treat of coloured pictures. The ample and warm Mrs. Tanner (Grade 3), who always delayed to chat and laugh when my handsome father called to pick us up from school (a really unusual event) and who relentlessly encouraged the use of "good words." A memorable lesson was writing the words "got" and "said" on a piece of paper, going into the school garden which the kids attended to in Nature Study lessons, and burying the words. "You can think of a better one to use in your compositions, girls!"

Then there was the principal, the chaotic Miss Swain (Grade 6), who loved to see the whole school march from assembly—where we saluted the flag and swore allegiance to the king of England and later the Queen—to military style music like "Colonel Bogey's March." She was generally a good-natured teacher despite having the dual role of running the whole school. But she made what she called "a terrible mistake" that we kids all paid for.

Every week we had to write a tightly structured, two-page composition: opening paragraph, two more paragraphs using adverbial or adjectival phrases that were listed on the blackboard, and a closing paragraph that "tied off" all ends neatly. One memorable day, when she obviously hadn't had time to prepare the "strait-jacket," we were told: "Today girls, you may write an adventure story!" It was music to our ears. She did not mention any length at all, let alone an adverbial phrase.

Forty-five twelve-year-old girls, well schooled on Enid Blyton and her "Famous Five" adventure books and Ethel Turner's heart-rending *Seven Little Australians,* went to town. It was a black afternoon when our work was handed back to the class with cold and disapproving comments for each and every one of us.

At least half of us, wild with freedom, had written six or eight or even ten pages of story! She told us she refused to read beyond page three of any of them, that they were generally poor, undisciplined, and imitative—well, yes! But then followed a diatribe when poor, hapless, overweight, unpopular, super-bright classmate Judith Meakin was made to stand up and explain why her "disgusting" story had featured something as horrific as murder. And not just one; this vile child had included three murders on board a launch in Sydney Harbour. She laboured the girl's inappropriate subject matter in a rage of disapproval so humiliating that I'd have been reduced to tears, But Judith stood there, clutching the desk red-faced and, I'm certain, not understanding what all the fuss was about.

It seems laughable in this day and age of violence and death depicted on film and television, including the news of the day, that a child writing a murder story

Libby (center), with her sisters Suzanne (left) and Margaret. (Courtesy of Libby Hathorn.)

could be so castigated. But the 1950s were the days before television in Australia, and straightlaced was the way you would describe suburban Maroubra. In any case, there was censorship about what books were allowed into the country (for example, D.H. Lawrence's *Lady Chatterly's Lover* could be read only by university professors even in my adolescence) and the press of the day could not refer directly to things such as a pregnancy. Poor Judith had no doubt read a diet of cheap thrillers and, in reflecting them in her own way, took the full fury of our teacher's annoyance at the outpourings of frustrated writers. I remember thinking then that Judith had been daring and that there was surely a power in a story that could make an adult so mad!

Endorsements for budding writers must have been important. I was in Year 4 when I received my first award, a purplish certificate from a large department store, Farmer's, that for some mysterious reason encouraged young Sydney writers. I believe I still have that certificate. But it was not for certificates I wrote the poems and stories that seemed to come from some mysterious source, poured out into precious exercise books where every page was covered, paper being in short supply and thus prized.

In the incredible paper affluence of my adulthood it's almost unimaginable to think how paper and pencils and pens were such prized possessions. It was a luxury to have a Woolworth's Jumbo-sized writing pad. Single sheets such as our fax and computer paper were simply not available.

I knew more of British history at ten, twelve, fourteen years of age than I did of Australian history. Aboriginal history was for the most part shamefully ignored or, what little there was, often quite inaccurately presented. This was all to change dramatically when I reached college. But I must say I'm grateful to this day for that rich literary background afforded by our schools, which set up a continual love affair with writers of the stature of William Shakespeare and the Romantic poets, to mention but a few.

My sisters and I haunted libraries like the one in Maroubra with the unlikely and agreeable name of Quandong, where one paid, say, a shilling to borrow two books for a week. Later we traveled by bus a few suburbs away to the Randwick Public Library to take out our precious one book each. I was ten or eleven before Maroubra had a public library in the guise of the Mobile Library—a wondrous caravan of books that traveled some of the library-less suburbs of our area, hooking into the powerline to light up its intriguing interior and the eager knot of readers—and thus herald the demise of private libraries.

The brightness of some of those childhood memories may be somewhat enhanced by time, but images of us just being around books and readers are especially clear.

Lying on the beds during long sunny afternoons totally immersed in Mary Grant Bruce's "Billabong" series, my big sister, head in a book, occasionally making a comment about the outback world and the characters we knew and loved. "I think I have a bit of crush on Wally," she might say.

"Well, I think I'm in love with Jim and I want to be Norah," I'd reflect.

"But they're brother and sister!" she'd tell me, usually having the last word.

I know as a big sister to Suzanne, three years my junior, I'd often read aloud to her. She always attests to my improving her reading comprehension, as I'd read some of our school-set novels (not my choice of fiction) such as *Black Arrow* or *The Hill,* and then each three pages or so I'd quiz her on what I'd read. "You really have to listen!" I'd threaten, "or I won't read to you anymore." Thus improving her concentration.

I love that idea of sharing other worlds and I believe that the act of reading allows us to share the dream. We can enter into another's thoughts and another's world as if it were our own.

It's strange how certain memories of a less-happy kind remain imprinted. There was a procession of pets who had a great impact on the family. Though we longed to own a dog and my little sister Suzanne arrived home occasionally with a stray, we had cats and kittens! A series of cats were called, variously, Tiddles if male or Skinny Minny if female. There was no commercially prepared petfood at the time, and the pets always ate the scraps from the family table and were generally more on the lean side compared to the cats I've owned since the advent of tinned petfood. With the birth of several batches of kittens, we ran out of willing recipients. Vets were not plentiful and the drowning of kittens was not unusual in our street, and was by far more merciful than dumping those hapless kittens in back lanes. But somehow neither of our parents could bring themselves to do the deed when we'd done our best but had clearly run out of prospective owners.

My mother's brother, Uncle Allen, was called to do the job. Not a particularly aggressive or bold man, he must nonetheless have had the requisite skills for kitten-drowning. It was done on the back step where all the children gathered and I remember watching with a certain amount of fear mixed with an awful curiosity. We knew it was inevitable the kittens must go or became strays, uncared for, but how could you actually kill something that was alive and soft and warm? The dark, the cluster of children, the metal bucket, the tiny squirming still blind soft little creatures, Uncle Allen grim but resolute. The hapless mother, Skinny Minny, being cuddled somewhere else, the thought of death in the air, the realization of utter powerlessness. That's a vivid memory for me.

Another stark memory was being locked in. This was a holiday with my older sister Margaret, on a farm on the Nepean River at the foot of the Blue Mountains, where boy cousins were good company for most of the time. It was a dairy farm and magical to us city girls. I didn't realize the grind of 200 cows having to be milked morning and night and the effort this must have cost my uncle and his older son. We loved to come here as the days were long and filled with fun. We learned boys' sports, bows and arrows, the wonder of an air rifle and the game of mice trapping in a recently ploughed field. Then there was riding a tractor to the Nepean River and discovering the wonder of the fact that potatoes didn't grow on bushes but were grown under the ground.

The milking sheds were fascinating and to be visited most afternoons. The cows were always docile, there was a certain exciting smell, milky in the shed and overlain with the cow manure in the yard, the sound of the milking machines sucking away at so many cows' teats—probably thirty cows milked at a time. There was the added wonder of the separation room, and then the cold room, where huge metal milk drums were stored, waiting for pickup. Bruce, my cousin, was a good-natured boy, a year or so older, but he seized the opportunity one afternoon as we two visited the cold room to experience the shiveriness once again, to heave closed the thick metal door and leave us not only shivering in the cold, but marooned in the terror of utter darkness.

Screams were to no avail it seemed, and the few minutes we were incarcerated there seared some memory of terror forever. When he gleefully opened the door and we emerged, I was changed. I was shaking and couldn't speak and remained so, despite the sun on my arms and that comforting ordinary odour of cow manure, for some time. Once again it was the notion of facing death and knowing you were powerless. And worse still, not brave. Not in the least brave. Ever since then, I have felt a kind of panic at the idea of being closed in, and like at least a sliver of light at night when asleep.

*

My first year in high school I made a very special friend in Pat, who had laughing eyes, a mop of black curly hair, and an outrageous sense of humour, She also just happened to live not far around the corner from my house in Maroubra—a wonderful accident of fate. Some fifty years later we are still friends and still discussing some of the same issues about the arts, despite both having brought up our families separately. Ten years ago I tried to set down something of the preciousness of this relationship in my poem "Childhood Friend" from *Maroubra Cycle*. (*Maroubra Cycle* has been set to music by composer Stephen Lalor and performed under the direction of Paul Weingott at UTS as a musical when I was writer in residence there.)

> You were farewelling me, I saw you there
> Standing by the gate
> And heard your laughter

As a young teacher, 1965. (Courtesy of Libby Hathorn.)

Down the midnight road
And thought
A poem is there in you
Standing, laughing
Talking, delaying, beside
The darkened paling fence
So reminiscent of our childhood. . . .
Where we plotted our bright futures,
—"Childhood Friend"

Pat was "artistic" and dreamed of becoming a painter and our conversations over the adolescent years were always of the arts: debates, musings as we fledgling artists tested our own theories in painting and writing in a world not much interested in two Maroubra lasses and their dreams. Pat illustrated my first picture storybook *Kyo,* which was the story of a much-loved dog of my mother's. Kyo, who gained this name from the New South Wales country town Kyogle, was a wonderful black-and-white terrier my mother swore could smile—at her, of course. Kyo was picked up by the RSPCA when she wandered off one day from Tamarama Beach; we never saw her again. My mother was inconsolable and in fact never had another dog, so Pat and I wrote a story about Kyo's wandering with a very happy ending. She was found! It wasn't even published but I have the original artwork to this day among my treasures.

I attended Teachers' College after an unsuccessful stint as a laboratory assistant in the Medical School at the University of Sydney. Two lecturers at Balmain Teachers' College—as it was then called before becoming part of UTS (University of Technology)—greatly influenced my writing: Ray Cattell who moved to the University of New South Wales as I arrived) and the principal, a tall, forbidding-looking gentleman, Mr. Greenhalgh. It was the English lecturer at Balmain who introduced me to Ray Cattell after my poem won the College Poetry Prize. Ray in turn introduced me to the works of W.B. Yeats when I unwittingly cautioned him to "tread softly" on his criticisms of my own poetry. "Tread softly for you tread on my dreams," he quoted immediately and there began a love affair with works of Yeats. Visits to his home gave timely insight to my passionate but sometimes rambling first poetry, and he insisting I could make poetry my life's work. If only I didn't have to earn a living, I thought, though poetry I knew even then would remain central to my life and inform all my writing.

The other lecturer, the principal of the college, also stands out in my mind, impressing me with his far-too-short series of lectures on philosophy and imploring us, the young students about to embark on our teaching lives, not to "walk through the fields with our gloves on" referring to a famous poem whose name eludes me. I remember buying Will Durant's *The Story of Philosophy* and a whole world opening up to me.

This was intensified by the advent of a soulful and totally engaging person in my life. It's true he was a man, several years older and much more sophisticated than I, but this seemed incredibly attractive to me in itself. With him I could discuss poetry and philosophy and many an evening we sat in the rose garden in Hyde Park; he was too poor to take me to dinner and I was but a poor college student. I listened to the wisdom of John C. It didn't occur to me that when we did go out to the movies or even to coffee that it was I who paid, and it was only years later that I understood why John became attracted to a woman closer to his age who had a smart apartment and a high-paying job. Still, I never regretted his flair for romance and his rather Oscar Wildish take on life.

My school friend Pat and I had discussed classical music but were introduced to the joys of ownership through a friend's dad who'd joined something called The World Record Club. *Brahms' Hungarian Dances* was the first 45rpm classical record that I ever purchased. Dad was mad about *The Student Prince*, as we all were, and I played it along with Beethoven symphonies. Later came admiration for Bach—I even purchased a small harmonium from a friend, Wendy's dad, who worked at the music shop Paling's, so I could learn to play Bach's "Toccata and Fugue."

Saturday mornings the three girls were expected to do the housework, which consisted of vacuuming the house, scrubbing, polishing, and—as custom had it in summertime—give the whole house a good spray of Mortein Plus, which had just come onto the market with a bright red, large, pump flyspray. Our work was made lighter by the stereogram, a large polished wood affair with a lid that was raised to reveal the turntable, a side compartment for 33's and another for 78's and the smaller 45's. We'd put on the long playing 33's (LPs) of which our parents had such delights as *Oklahoma, Carousel, South Pacific,* and *Showboat*. A favourite was an LP called *The Merry Widow,* considered classical music.

This didn't mean I wasn't in love with Elvis Presley or didn't dance to the new rock and roll and later favour the magical Beatles! My novel *Love Me Tender* reflects this time through the eyes of a young boy, Alan.

Round the corner at Pat's house, her mother had secured a real treasure of an LP, sent all the way from England, of Emlyn Williams reading Charles Dickens. Though I'd read *A Tale of Two Cities,* I was delighted by excerpts from *Pickwick Papers* and *Oliver Twist* read aloud to us as we gathered in the lounge room around the precious record player to listen before the advent of television in Australia of course.

The bookcase in the small lounge room of our house at Maroubra was cram-packed. My parents had sets of books alongside the novels, encyclopedias, and dictionary (Webster's), a huge tome. Sets of science and philosophy (The Living Thoughts Library: of Thoreau, Descartes, Spinoza, etc.) alongside *Readers' Digest* series books and World War II books. These I remember were large and clothbound with firm spines: *Soldiering On,* Army, Navy, and Air Force accounts of the returned men anxious to somehow tell something of their disquieting stories.

Arthur Mees' *Book of Everlasting Things* seems such a quaint idea in a world of computers with knowledge at your fingertips. But it was a much loved tome, a book of wonder, despite its rather smudgy black and white photographs of sights such as the pyramids, or the Amazon River.

An aunt of mine was housekeeper for a very well-off family in nearby Dover Heights and this was rather fortunate for us. The Rusten girls were readers, and we only imagined their life, as we never met them. But in a way I thought we had, for their names were often inscribed in the books that came our way. The Rustens gave our aunt the entire set of "Billabong" books by Mary Grant Bruce, doled out on birthdays and Christmases to eager recipients; twelve or fourteen of them that were published in Great Britain by Ward Lock. Some rather trashy love stories such as *Broken Wings* by F.J. Thwaites found their way onto our shelves, made all the more meaningful because of the fact that our mother admitted she had once or twice gone out with him when she was a young woman.

Shy the Platypus by Lesley Reece was another treasure. I was to later meet Lesley at the Fremantle Children's Literary Centre in 1997, and to learn that as a young journalist he'd actually interviewed James Joyce in Paris.

My story *The Day TV Came* was published by the Museum of Contemporary Art when it opened to an exhibition celebrating the coming of television to Australia in the 1950s; though fictional, it tried to capture some of the wonder of film on tap in one's own house. Our television, like our record player, was a substantial piece of furniture—two wooden doors in a cabinet with fake gold handles, opening to reveal a screen below which giant knobs conveyed us to worlds beyond our world, albeit in black and white. When our family bought a television in 1959, we were transfixed by any and every program. Sunday nights were family occasions when we gathered for a TV dinner generally, toasted tomato and cheese on specially designed TV plates, either made in a waffle iron or in our Dad's new-fangled griller. Bought from a door-to-door salesman, the Spaceship, so named for its shape, could grill anything to a crisp, from sausages to sandwiches. One of the features of Sunday evening viewing was *Disney World* and eating toasted "samos" as our Dad called them, toasted to perfection on the Spaceship. Or during the week watching exciting American shows like *77 Sunset Strip, The Fugitive, Maverick, I Love Lucy,* and *Father Knows Best.* There were very few Australian shows. *Homicide,* the first cop show, comes to mind as well as a copycat Saturday afternoon *Bandstand* where you could watch people your own age rock and rolling—and even get a ticket to go out to Gore Hill and become part of the audience that was filmed! If you were brave enough.

*

As a young woman I began writing poetry, hesitatingly at first given the models of such accomplishment I'd had. I was drawn to write about what I knew, events and landscapes and people and all the strange yet somehow "ordinary" miracles that Walt Whitman so cleverly describes in his poem of that name. Poetry writing was a major pastime but I began keeping notebooks, fragments of conversation, dreams, reflections. I remember a line of poetry I wrote when I was eighteen years old that said though I, too, longed for Europe, I wanted to know my own country and that henceforth I was "stepping out into Australian times."

In a lustful search for a diversity of texts after my school years and whilst at college, I began consciously exploring Australian literature, particularly poetry: the work of Judith Wright, David Campbell, John Shaw Neilsen, and Chrisopher Brennan. I still keep a raggedy copy of that very first *Penguin Anthology of Australian Verse* that introduced to me to the wealth of Australian voices. Later at college I began to explore more contemporary voices: the likes of Les Murray, Gwen Harwood, Elizabeth Riddell, and Peter Porter. The wonderful old bookshop on Pitt Street in Sydney, Angus & Robertson's with its polished linoleum-covered basement where poetry and plays resided, became a place of miraculous discoveries. As did the magical little Rowe Street with its first coffee shops and book shops and records imported from overseas for which you'd have to save to buy.

Translations by Arthur Waley and Ezra Pound of Chinese poetry, and that extreme jewel of verse, the Japanese haiku, were discovered in Rome Street. This largesse, along with the newly translated novels of European authors such as Gide and Mann, Camus, and a whole range of Russian novels from Tolstoy to Chekov and Dostoyovsky.

My head was hardly ever out of a book and it was a wonder I graduated from college at all. When I did, I was to discover the real joys of teaching and must say that my first year at Bankstown Primary School was a year of wonders. Despite the rigours of the timetable imposed then (thirty minutes for this and twenty-five for that, and woe betide you if you didn't teach the said subject at the said hour) I found I could encourage poetry writing with my nine year olds—forty-five of them in a room designed to take up to fifty pupils! This was 1964 and classes were large.

I remember distinctly the exciting drives to Bankstown Primary School (a long train and bus ride from my home at Tamarama Beach) with my new friend Wendy Stites. She was a young teacher at Bankstown Infants who was lucky enough to own a car, a VW Beetle, with whom I shared petrol money and long conversations. We talked of life and love at length being young women at the time, alongside the joys of art and poetry, and how we could influence the kids we taught. She was later to marry Australian filmmaker Peter Weir and devote all her creative passion to design and wardrobe for movies.

At this time I was going out with a young medical student, Ron Gray, of Polish parentage (his mother had promptly changed their name on arrival as a migrant to Australia), who shared this love of the arts and especially of poetry, and gave into my hands some treasure tomes from his own bookcase. I still have the poetical works of Rainer Maria Rilke he parted with somewhat reluctantly, because I'd told him the book was not to be had in any Sydney bookshop and *La Dolce Vita* at Savoy, Lido, or the Paris Theatre, where at interval there was the luxury of buying Italian coffee, were part and parcel of the discovery of "other times." Ron was an extraordinarily clever fellow academically, but I remember his frustration at not being able to paint or write poetry and sometime a flash of annoyance when I'd produce some writing about a place we'd visited together—the fir forest where we'd camped or the Blue Mountains where we'd taken long bracing walks. He was a loving person to me and I am glad to have had such a strong and tender relationship over three or four years of growing-up time. But it was through him I realised that understanding and loving poetry or fiction was not enough, that there was another dimension that has nothing to do with the will, and that perhaps in some miraculous and inexplicable way, writing had chosen me!

I broke my medical student's heart when after four years and with our inevitable marriage in sight, I met John Hathorn, a teacher seven years my senior, dashing, romantic, and persuasive. But there was grief for me too, in that break, as I felt Ron was part of my most formative years and intoxicated though I was with John's energy and excitement, there were moments of real longing to see Ron again.

My own writing in that time consisted of largely unpublished poetry. I remember the thrill of first acceptance in *The Poetry Journal,* then managed by poet Grace Perry, of my first poem. This coincided with meeting John, my husband to be, at the school I'd been transferred to, Bellevue Hill Primary School. In those first heady days of our relationship I expressed my desire to be a writer—and a published writer at that!—and explained that it was central to my life. After we were

Engaged to John Hathorn, 1966. (Courtesy of Libby Hathorn.)

married in 1968, John Hathorn, being a practical soul, suggested that I begin my foray into publishing by writing textbooks. We worked together on the first little books for infants and then I decided I'd write up all the marvelous work the children were capable of in poetry, and *Go Lightly,* my first substantial book, was published. As I was not fully confident to "go it alone," John was actually listed as co-author. He had, after all, I reasoned, trialed all the poetry techniques written up in the book.

The birth of my children—daughter Lisa in 1970 and then Keiran in 1973—changed our lives once again. I could not think about writing, especially children's books, in the same way. Bringing up children enlivens your perceptions and memories of your own childhood, feeding the fires.

The seventies saw a new confidence in the arts that we all responded to. We'd left behind to some extent the "outback image" that had been promulgated through books and movies, and began to record our urban and indeed our multicultural experiences as wave after wave

of migrants settled into the cities, impacting on the Australian way of life. It seemed to young artists unburdened by the weight of a long European history that we were free to go in any direction. But Australian children were still largely invisible in the body of literature available to them and I think myself lucky to have been writing at the time that publishers acknowledged that "gap."

I had been a classroom teacher but moved into the role of librarian in the primary school where I worked now at Drummoyne, a significant move on my part. Librarianship suited my addiction to books and story and gave me an up-to-the-minute overview of what children were reading. I was very much aware that we needed books about our place, the city as well as the country. I read hundreds of books and was delighted by some Australian novels by Colin Thiele and Ivan Southall and early Australian picture storybooks like Lydia Pender's *Barnaby's Rocket,* and the Aboriginal tales *The Rainbow Serpent* by Dick Roughsey.

Looking back, there were two particular writers I discovered in well-stacked shelves who I think deeply influenced my own writing. A series of readers by the English writer Leila Berg that told hilarious stories of working-class kids and their parents, opened my eyes to the way ordinary folk could be written about and also to the fact that ordinary folk were not really well represented in Australian children's literature. And then the work of the Dutch writer Meindert de Jong with his wonderful novel, *Journey from Peppermint Street,* and for younger readers *Nobody Plays with a Cabbage.* These were sensitive stories written in spare and beautiful prose and they truly inspired me. I also noticed at this time some very "cool" paperbacks books for struggling readers by a certain Paul Jennings that were being very well borrowed from the library. Paul was to become a legend in his own lifetime with a series of hilarious novels some years later.

*

It all happened at a party, whose I don't recall, but I was introduced to a young man who worked for an English publishing company, Methuen, who had an office in Sydney. And yes, he'd talk to the children's editor there about a book I was writing.

Stephen's Tree was my first picture storybook. It was set at my brother's then garden market in Waverley, a veritable rainforest of ferns and trees and Australian plants right in the heart of the suburbs. I was thrilled to have a work of fiction underway but I had to debate long and hard with Methuen about having a gum tree central to the story. They strongly advised a beech, ash, or elm so the work would sell better in England! It was important for me to have the gum tree but it was equally important to be published.

My first children's book editor, the gentle but resolute Liz Fulton, must have argued well, for a gum tree it was! The book was launched at our local Waverley Library by Peter Weir, who'd already begun to make his name with his first movie, *Picnic at Hanging Rock,* and all Sandra Laroche's delicate depictions of gum trees and kids were exhibited. The book attracted much media attention not only because it was about an Australian tree but also because *Stephen's Tree* was a publishing experiment. The publisher, responsive to our multicultural society of largely Greek and Italian migrants, published *Stephen's Tree* in dual-text versions, both Greek and Italian! This experiment was repeated with *Lachlan's Walk.* Though the books sold well in the English version, the dual language was not a great seller and, sad to say, the idea of dual texts was canned!

This connection to Waverley Library for my first-ever book launch was auspicious. Sandra illustrated my next children's picture storybook *Lachlan's Walk,* set at Watson's Bay and based on a true story about my sister's son Lachlan wandering away from home towards a dangerous cliffside park. It too, was launched at Waverley Library by cartoonist Bruce Petty. And it was to be there at the library that I became aware of the outstand-

ing work of illustrator Julie Vivas through enthusiastic children's librarian, Roniet Myerthal. Julie had an exhibition of her watercolours and after I'd seen her work, Roniet arranged a meeting where I invited Julie to illustrate my next book, *The Tram to Bondi Beach,* to be set in the 1930s, the time of paperboys and trams in Sydney. Julie assured me that her art was not suitable for children's literature, but I thought differently and asked to show some of her work to my Methuen publishers, who immediately agreed with me that she would make a fine partner for the text. Julie had a tough time of it family-wise the year she undertook her superb illustrations for the story, her first picture book, for her husband was away in Spain and she had two small children to look after. We visited the Loftus, the Tram Museum south of Sydney, to get reference photographs because by that time, in 1980s, trams had disappeared from the Sydney streets. Here the children Ana and Kate, along with my children Lisa and Keiran, acted as models for paperboys and passengers. *The Tram to Bondi Beach,* launched by Maurie Saxby, was highly commended by the Children's Book Council of Australia, and Julie's new career was begun. The then NSW Film and Television group wanted to make a movie of *Tram* with its setting in the Depression in Bondi. I wrote the first filmscript filled with hope about the possibility of Julie's marvellous artwork and my story, but it was to be one of those many movie projects that only "almost" came off.

During this time in the seventies with two children and a teacher-librarian career, I was fortunate on the home front to have the help of a wonderful woman my mother's age who came to help for three weeks and stayed instead over a period of twenty years. Without Paddy's help, her organisation of household matters, her sense of humour, and her winning ways with little children, I could not have given such time to my own writing. She became a treasured family member at our house and, though elderly now, is still interested to hear every scrap of information about our children, Lisa and Keiran.

Back in the eighties, as my own children were growing older—though it's true I'm forever interested in picture storybooks—I began to write "chapter books," or what we called junior novels, for young readers. *All about Anna,* which recalled my Maroubra childhood and was where I consciously placed a girl as an adventurous main character, won honours in the CBA awards. This was followed by a fantasy, *The Extraordinary Magics of Emma McDade,* the first of my short novels to be translated into Korean, and was similarly shortlisted for awards. *Paolo's Secret* was written to portray the loneliness of some children in the school yard when limited by language. As a teacher-librarian at an inner-city school I was very much aware of this situation for shy children who found the prospect of the playground daunting. But the novel that was to change my life in the late eighties, and indeed take me all the way to Hollywood, was written for young-adult readers and was strongly inspired by the bushland setting of the central coast of New South Wales.

Thunderwith was written in 1988 on my brother's farm in the Wallingat Forest, which is north of Sydney. This is the story of the loss and alienation of a young girl, Lara, as she comes to terms not only with the death of a beloved mother, but with a dad she barely remembers and a hostile new stepmother. Its setting is uniquely Australian and when my agents, Curtis Brown, offered it for publication, in 1988, the $10,000 advance paid by the publisher Heinneman was then considered the largest ever given in Australia for a children's book.

Immediately there were offers for movie options from three Australian companies and it was finally optioned to Southern Star Xanadu. Sandra Levy (currently the head of the Australian Broadcasting Company) was the producer of Xanadu then, and I would have been more than happy to work with her as she had such a sensitivity to the story. But there was to be a lull in movie-making, which meant it was difficult to get finances together. In the meantime, *Thunderwith* the novel travelled well into Europe, being bought in Holland and Denmark, Sweden, and Great Britain, and then was also published in the United States and serialized in India. It

The author's children, Christmas, 1979: (front) Lisa and (back, right) Keiran, with their friend Isabelle. (Courtesy of Libby Hathorn.)

went into reprint several times in its first year, picking up honours in the CBA awards, too. But it was the offer by Hallmark Hall of Fame in the United States in the late nineties to adapt it as a television movie—and to have me as the writer—that was the most exciting news for this story. Several meetings in Hollywood with producer Dick Welsh indicated that they wanted me to write a treatment for the movie placing Gladwyn, the mother, central to the story. This was because their demographic was largely adult females, they told me, and for family viewing. Armed with some how-to-write-movies guidebooks back home, I took off to Seal Rocks and the Wallingat and began the arduous task of writing a movie script to please my producers. Later, American writers were brought on to finish the script and though I was disappointed, I knew I'd reached a time when I simply couldn't make any more changes and still feel it was my story.

Simon Wincer, as director, had chosen Victoria, his home state, rather than NSW where the story is actually set. My husband John, who had become ill with leukemia, had been under heavy treatment and though in remission had little energy at this time. He encouraged me to take our daughter Lisa and visit the set. It was amazing to go on the set at Mt. Beauty in Victoria to see a whole property changed, roads built, a farmhouse and outhouses constructed, palms planted to create a plantation, a dam built, to mention just a few of the wonders that happened. Judy Davis played a marvelous Gladwyn and was nominated for an Emmy for her performance in *The Echo of Thunder,* as it was called. Lauren Hewitt made a strong Lara and Emily Browning (later starring in *Lemony Snicket*) made her film debut as an engaging young Opal. *Thunderwith* today is still one of my best-selling novels and is a set text in many schools across Australia.

*

In the mid-nineties John had retired from school and we traveled widely, including living in a loft in Mulberry Street in New York City, whilst I made better contact with my then agent Laura Blake at Curtis Brown. During that time I met Little, Brown editor Maria Modugno, who had taken both *Thunderwith* and *Grandma's Shoes,* and later Simon & Schuster's Virginia Duncan who had taken *Sky Sash So Blue.* Virginia, moving to Greenwillow, was to hand over to Stephanie Owens Lurie but told me in a farewell letter that *Sky Sash* was the best children's story she'd ever worked on! Stephanie was incredibly enthused and put Benny Andrews' wonderful artwork for the cover of *Sky Sash* on their Simon & Schuster catalogue. Whilst in New York City I also visited the office of the legendary Margaret McElderry who told me how she'd enjoyed reading *Thunderwith.* It was a great visit, at the end of which came the American offers for the movie of *Thunderwith.*

Another book that had a huge impact was my picture storybook *Way Home.* It was inspired by the sight of a

Writing **Thunderwith** *in the Wallingat Forest, 1998.* (Courtesy of Libby Hathorn.)

boy in the underground in London who was begging at the bottom of the giant escalators. He seemed incredibly young to be there alone. I boarded the train and began thinking of my own children safe and sound in a Midland farmhouse, and wrote a poem about a boy called Shane that was to become the basis of the text of *Way Home*. Mark McLeod, who was a publisher with Random House then, loved the text and magically brought the illustrator Greg Rogers and me together. We traversed the streets of Sydney taking photographs as source material and then Greg returned to Brisbane, where he worked over his amazing artwork that was to win the much-coveted Kate Greenaway Medal in the United Kingdom.

That it was an Australian artist illustrating and Australian text has always amazed and pleased me. It also won a Parents' Choice in America. Praise for the book in Britain and the United States, where it was also published, was high. Luminaries such as Jeremy Briggs and Anthony Browne had positive things to say about it, and after meeting Anthony at an Australian conference, he invited me to send a text I might think suitable for his work. The reviews for *Way Home* in Australia were not generally good, and it garnered no honours here in any award. But the book has remained in print ever since and is a set text in many schools. The theatre

company Barking Gecko produced a play I'd written based on the book with music by a composer Stephen Lalor, whom I'd worked with over the years and who has set much of my children's poetry to music. It remains one of my favourites. At the same time, taken up with the reports I was reading on homeless kids around the world, and surprised at the number in Australia, I wrote *Feral Kid*. This is a young-adult novel about an older boy who is homeless, and it was to be optioned by Hallmark Hall of Fame, as well.

On our travels, John and I lived in Holland for a few months in a wonderful apartment on the Prinsengracht found by my Dutch publishers at Ploegsma. There we met the delightful Nanny Brinkman, at this time still the head of the company, and her husband Paul, who gave us much of his time in showing us Holland. Nanny had taken my novels *Thunderwith* and *Feral Kid* and later *The Climb*. Their own house on the Kaisergracht, a huge former merchant's home, was a wonder to us with its ample, beautifully furnished rooms and its rooftop garden with views of Amsterdam all around.

I was inspired at the Vincent Van Gogh Museum in Amsterdam to write my novel *The Painter,* based on the imagined life of an adolescent would-be painter, Bernard, who meets Vincent in Aries and whose life is changed by this encounter. Every morning I'd get on the tram to the museum whilst John hunted antiques and, in the library there, undertake he delightful task of reading Vincent's letters, and then viewing letters that the offspring of his models had written and so on. John and I felt we could have stayed in Amsterdam forever, I had previously signed a six-book contract with publishers Hodder Headline in Australia, and my novels were in the hands of a wonderful children's publisher, Belinda Bolliger. I still consult with Belinda on all my work and trust her judgment particularly when it comes to editing.

Picture storybook texts are the closest thing to poetry for me and I'll always want to write them. But it is a pretty amazing thing when they move from picture storybook to opera. *Grandma's Shoes,* which was published in Great Britain and the United States and has been published twice in Australia with two different artists (one of Belinda's choice), was to become the first children's opera performed in Australia in the new millennium. This is the story of a young girl's search for her grandmother, wearing her precious shoes, and deals with the loss of a beloved family member in a consoling way. There is even an air of triumph for the little girl as she pledges to take up her grandma's storytelling skills.

Not only did I approach Opera Australia with the story text and the idea for an opera, but through my editor at Oxford University Press, Rita Scharf, I had an auspicious meeting with Kim Carpenter, director of Theatre of Image. Kim loved the text and encouraged me to write the libretto. He introduced me to Graeme Koehne, an Adelaide composer whose work is known world wide. We gained support from Opera Australia by way of musicians and singers, rehearsal spaces, and advertising. *Grandma's Shoes* had a Kim Carpenter setting of a giant book out of which stepped all the characters, and his puppets and backdrop of animations made it a truly wonderful performance. It played to full houses and later I was thrilled to receive an award from the AWGIE (Australian Writers Guild) for this libretto. And later to receive a Prime Minister's Millennium Award for 2000.

Opera is expensive and difficult to mount, so it was with some delight in 2003 that I received an invitation from Alabama to have my text for my picture storybook *Sky Sash So Blue*—published in the States by Simon & Schuster in 1998—used as libretto. This picture storybook, embellished so lovingly by the artwork of Benny Andrews, is a celebration of freedom; it was inspired by reading Toni Morrison's powerful novel *Beloved* and is set in the same period of slavery in the Deep South. The invitation was from a music lecturer at Miles, an

The author with her husband, John, in Monet's garden, Giverny, 1996. (Courtesy of Libby Hathorn.)

With authors David Malouf and Gillian Mears, Chennai, India, 1997. (Courtesy of Libby Hathorn.)

all-black college in Birmingham. Alabama. Phillip Rat-liffe had plans for a children's opera using the text already written in verse.

We undertook a long correspondence by e-mail and eventually Philip announced that not only had he almost completed the opera but that he'd secured the funds for its performance in November, 2004. The visit, which enabled me to see the rehearsals and the calibre of opera singers and chamber orchestra, was an exciting

one, for it was my first experience of the south. But I must admit that on first hearing Philip's startling atonal music I wondered how young people—some as young as Grade 2—would respond. However, a group of teachers using Maxine Green's music, of the Lincoln Centre reputation, as an inspirational aesthetic education model had fully prepared their students.

So on the day of performance, around 700 African-American students enjoyed the opera with its sparse set and accomplished singers and the use of a long, trailing sky sash of deep blue. In 2005, I had more correspondence from Phillip, to indicate that *Sky Sash So Blue* would be performed again, this time made possible by the Cultural Alliance and the Division of Humanities at Miles College, with in-kind donations from the Birmingham Museum of Art, UAB, Midfield Schools, and the Alabama School of Fine Arts. Miracles do happen!

*

I have been fortunate over the years in invitations to speak in other countries and often am asked if this is the stuff of inspiration. If it's true that settings do have a huge impact, you never know whether you are going to be found by a story no matter how dramatic or how different the landscape. My initial visit to Papua New Guinea was to launch the first ever PNG Children's Book Fair in 1994. After a tour of some of the schools in Port Moresby, accompanied by an Australian journalist who lived there, I was taken to various island schools and was touched by the enthusiasm with which a writer was greeted in schools that often lacked libraries and were even sometimes short of notepaper. On the volcanic island of Rabaul, viewing the terrifying outcome of the 1993 eruption and talking to the locals, I was inspired for my verse novel *Volcano Boy,* though it wasn't to be written until many years later. The following year, 1995, I was invited to run a writing course on the marvelous island of Madang in Papua New Guinea, and had my first experience of snorkeling in a truly tropical place. I couldn't wait for my workshops to be over, to run helter skelter to my cabin, change into swimming gear, and spend hours in the water, in a world that was dramatically lovely, strange, and inspirational. At home, my son, who had undertaken a SCUBA diving course, had enthused about the underwater world being a great subject for a novel. And it was strange that after a cult leader in California had enticed a group of his followers, some of them quite young, to commit suicide together, and I'd seen a video of his "explanation" to them, that all these things came together in the novel *Rift.*

An author tour organized by the Australia Council in 1997 took revered Australian writer David Malouf and Gillian Mears and me to India for a marvelous three

Libby Hathorn with her son, Kieran, and daughter, Lisa (holding baby Ruby Rose), Dorrigo, New South Wales, 2004. (Courtesy of Libby Hathorn.)

weeks. Visiting bookshops and universities, we had speaking engagements in New Delhi, Bangalore, Madras (now Chennai), and Bombay (now Mumbai). We were met by writers in each of these places and had two each of our own books launched there by Senator Alston, the then minister for the arts. The impact of India on the tourist has been attested to many times. Suffice to say we were enthralled by the diversity, delighted by our hosts, upset by the poverty that was so apparent, and yet charmed by the generosity of those we met. However, we were so programmed as to never get to see the Taj Mahal, something I'd always dreamt of visiting, and where I was sure a story would be lurking. One fortunate connection I'd made was with a printer at an ashram at Pondicherry that was famous for the quality of the paper it produced. To and fro communication indicated they'd do a limited edition of a book of my poems on specially chosen paper of a generous thickness, with petal impressed endpapers and a handmade binding in Hablik cloth.

Invited to speak at the prestigious IBBY (International Board of Books for Young People) Conference, which was to be held in New Delhi, India, I returned the next year in 1998, this time with my friend Pat and my two sisters Margaret and Suzanne, who had heard my enthusiastic descriptions of this exotic culture. This time, after IBBY, I determined to make the journey to Agra as well as to the equally famed Lake Palace. India simply seduced us as we moved from place to place, dazzled by all we saw and especially but the Taj Mahal, which was all and more than I'd expected.

I'd met a charming publisher at IBBY and was invited to present my text set at the Taj Mahal to her small, brave children's publishing house, Tulika Books, just getting underway in Chennai. *A Face in the Water* is a timeslip story that takes an historic view of the building of the Taj and stars the daughter of the emperor Shah Jahan and two present-day Australian kids. It was illustrated by a young Indian artist, Uma Krishnaswamy, and published in India in 2000.

We visited Pondicherry and the ashram where *Heard Singing* was to be printed on hand-made paper. Australian paper-cutting artist Brigitte Stoddard's delicate work in Australian wildflowers graced this limited edition. Brigitte eventually illustrated my junior novel, *Okra and Acacia: The Story of the Wattle Pattern Plate,* based on the Chinese legend "The Story of the Willow Patter Plate," which was published by Hodder Headline. A wonderful hand-sewn, hessian wrapped bundle of poetry books eventually arrived in Sydney from India and it gave me a great deal of pleasure to have seen the whole process and to know that I had been able to influence the look and feel of *Heard Singing.* Gifts were made of the book, some were sold and it remains a favourite book on my own shelves.

My husband John died in 1998 when the leukemia he'd contracted in 1996 re-occurred. He had been fighting it for two years and his bravery in the face of a bone marrow transplant was amazing, though so difficult to witness, even though he remained positive in the face of all his trials. I've tried to write a book about our last overseas journey together in 1997 between his treatments, where we lived for a short time in a magical chateau in Normandy, John collecting antiques whilst I wrote a filmscript; but somehow that book is still unfinished.

There have been some big life changes in that time both at home and in my work. Both my children are with partners and in fact I'm a grandmother to a baby girl, Ruby Rose (inspiration for storybooks of course). My son Keiran's work in information technology has inspired me to work on interactive stories. Our small company has released two CD-ROM's thus far. The first one, *Weirdstop,* which comprises stories of the weird variety for ten-to fourteen-year-olds, immediately won the Australian Interactive Media Industry Award for Best New Children's Product in 2003. *Coolstop,* which links sport and literacy, was launched by an Olympic medallist in late 2004, and we're currently working on a game and story for younger readers we've called *Wonderstop,* which is environmental in approach. A whole new world of writing and producing has opened up.

This does not mean that I'm not writing story books. My historical novel *Georgiana* is still underway, as is a new picture storybook; whilst last year saw the launch of children's picture storybook *The Great Big Animal Ask* by film producer Rebel Penfold Russell. I'm also working on a poetry Web site, which is a long-overdue project with notes for parents and teachers as to how to "turn kids on to poetry!" You see, poetry has rewarded me in every possible way. Writer Shirley Hazzard has attested that poetry changes things. And there's no doubt in my mind that those early poetry sessions with our parents, the reading and the reciting; and always having poetry books to hand, has illuminated my world and taking on poetry as a significant companion has been the greatest influence on my writing, and indeed on all of my life.

*

Hathorn contributed the following update to her autobiographical essay in 2011:

Taking up where I left off some seven years ago with my writing is quite a good exercise, as I measure my life not so much in "coffee spoons" as in publications. And it is useful if not fascinating to see trends even in your own work. Poetry, which has been such an influence on my life—both family life and "writerly" life, if these can be separated—still remains a huge focus. And it is interesting to me when reviewing my work to date that poetry is very much coming to the fore again. A recent appointment as member of the advisory committee for Australian poetry and as poetry ambassador for the Society of Women Writers of New South Wales, as well

The ABC Book of Australian Poetry, *compiled by Hathorn.* (Courtesy of HarperCollins.)

as the bringing together of my upcoming poetry book *Collecting Evidence,* has made me all the more aware of the importance of encouraging poetry whenever and wherever I can. Perhaps this is because of a spate of new writing on my part (poetry for adult readers that is) and actually taking part and giving poetry readings from time to time. And also for the years taken in putting together ninety or so poems for *The ABC Book of Australian Poetry: A Treasury of Poems for Young People.* I am working with a prestigious museum here, the Powerhouse Discovery Centre, in coupling some of these poems with objects in the museum (perhaps a double decker bus, perhaps a shard of early Australian poetry or old photos) and helping students tease out poetry, modelling on some of the poets in the collection. I have also been working with Generation One, a body set up to try to generate change for Aboriginal youth through school and other programs. In the meantime novels continue to be written.

Georgiana: Woman of Flowers was launched in Western Australia at the Georgiana Molloy Anglican School. It was wonderful to travel to with Lesley Reece, director of the Fremantle Children's Literature Centre, dine with the headmaster and his wife, and waken to a launch day begun with an Aboriginal smoking ceremony. The

novel, which is set in Augusta in colonial times in Australia, tells the story of young Georgiana, who married new settler and ex-army officer Captain Jack Molloy and took up a land grant in a place hitherto unsettled by Europeans in Western Australia. I was struck by her bravery: the fact she gave birth to seven children far from her own family and friends, lost her only son down a well in the garden, dealt with isolation loneliness and frightening situations, and yet saw the beauty of this adopted place in the form of wildflowers. This remarkable woman went on to collect Australian wildflowers and send them in perfect condition (sometimes with the help of pepper in the absence of any other preservative) in boxes of tanbark to an awaiting and curious England, where one Captain Mangles distributed them to Kew Gardens and Europe. And yet Georgiana went largely unsung, really, until now. The Kangaroo Paw, Western Australia's state flower, was named after Mangles and not Molloy! I studied her letters in the Batty Library in Perth and actually handled the diary (wearing white gloves of course), a scuffed red leather and quite small book that contained fragments of her life. Lists of Aboriginal words and their translations (some of the settlers believed the original inhabitants did not talk!), livestock descriptions, planting and farm business, all in her own flowing hand.

I was so engrossed in Georgiana's history that I wrote a play based on *Georgiana: Woman of Flowers,* which was put on at the National Institute of Drama Parade Theatre for a short season with the help of Randwick Council. I've sent the play script to the Georgiana Molloy School of course! The book won the Biennial Society of Women Writers Prize in 2009 and garnered good reviews.

In my personal life, there was the much awaited birth of my second granddaughter, Isabel Harriet, in 2006, but what followed quelled our joy. This little one was ill and hospitalized for most of the first part of her life. It is a miracle indeed to see her flourishing and much in love with my latest picture storybook, *I Love You Book,* which is dedicated in part to her, as well as to two other granddaughters: Ruby, who is now seven, and little Harriet, not yet one. Having grandchildren around one certainly gives fresh insight into those precious early years and is inspiration for writing more picture storybooks.

And novels still keep coming. In 2007, *Letters to a Princess* was published in the tenth anniversary of the death of Princess Diana of Wales. I'd written something heartfelt on the night and following day after she died that became a slender novel and offered it for publication, though it was not really ready. Some years later a publisher remembered this book, which had been relegated to a deep drawer somewhere in my house, and asked me to review the manuscript. I did, rewriting a much-longer novel. After *Letters to a Princess* was published, I took courage and sent it to her sons Prince William and Prince Harry, given that it showed Princess

Diana in a good light as a great influence for my protagonist. Imagine my delight when I received a letter from Buckingham Palace saying the princes had indeed enjoyed the book and thanking me for writing it!

The blurb from *Letters to a Princess* indicates it is a young girl's journey, one much affected by the life and death of Princess Diana. In the main character's own words:

My name is Diana Moore and I'm the kind of girl who doesn't stand out from the crowd. Average height. Average curly brown hair. The only thing not average about me is that I seem to land in trouble on a regular basis. My mum died suddenly a year ago and I don't get on with my stepfather. Among other things, he keeps telling me I have an eating disorder! As for his loudmouth son, Marcus, I won't even go there . . . if it weren't for Babs, Zoe and my letters to Princess Diana, I'd have lost it by now.

In 2009 I saw the expansion of an arts program I'd begun some years earlier, which is based on poetry and art in the community. The idea for the Hundred Views Project, which has its home at www.100views.com.au, was triggered by the work of Japanese artist Hokusai and his major work, *One Hundred Views of Mt Fuji,* first published in Japan in the 1830s. The publication came into my hands in a bookshop in 1995 and was inspirational for me as a writer. At the same time, I was aware of the task Chilean poet Pablo Neruda had set for himself: to write one hundred love poems for his beloved. The discipline of conceiving a hundred ideas or images on one subject, to find an "inner meaning," as Hokusai put it, had great appeal. I thought I'd like to experiment with the idea, but wondered how it might apply to children themselves attempting do the same thing.

I wanted to provide workshops for teachers to help their children achieve the Hundred Views of their community "icon." This is through poetry and art in the first instance, using technology to showcase their offerings and then working toward a celebration of the community in the form of a festival. I came to conclude that the best place to test the idea was with students and their teachers in a school, in a living experiment. I decided it should be a public school to begin with, as it needed to be a schoolwide endeavour. I had to find a school principal sympathetic to the idea of using the Hundred Views concept, combining the arts and reaching out to its community. Bondi Beach Public School had such a principal in Ms. Maria Hardy, and Bondi Beach was indeed iconic as a place to celebrate one hundred times over. Since then several other schools have taken part: Bronte Public, Maroubra Junction, Randwick Public, Emanuel School, and Claremont College worked on several art projects through Randwick Council, using my Hundred Views inspiration. And there is more to come with several other schools asking to become part of this program.

Zahara's Rose, a picture storybook—in fact a chapter picture storybook—was published in 2009. This manuscript was another inspired largely by nature and the garden, and in particular the rose. I love tracking the journeys of plants and decided on a child's-eye view of the story of the rose finding its way to Babylon. And why not have it brought to the wonderfully described Hanging Gardens of Babylon built by Nebuchadnezzar for his homesick bride Amyritis? All imagined but all perfectly acceptable.

I realised I must have some sort of a fascination for the Seven Wonders of the Ancient World, for of course I've already written *A Face in the Water,* which is a story set at the Taj Mahal. *Zahara's Rose,* set in the Hanging Gardens of Babylon, was launched, quite fittingly, close to home in Centennial Parklands, where several schools from the area gathered their children to sing and dance and act out the story set so many thousands of years ago.

The ABC Book of Australian Poetry: A Treasury of Poems for Young People was launched at the Children's Book Council of Australia New South Wales Conference in 2010 by Margaret Hamilton. It was morning tea, and so the hotel lobby where the launch took place was filled with librarians and teachers. I was somewhat taken aback when Margaret chose to do a kind of "This-is-your-life, Libby Hathorn," but delighted too. Secretly, even more delighted that, through my favourite folk, school librarians and teachers, the book would find its way into many a student and teacher's hand. Here's the Foreword as an indication of what I am trying to do with poetry.

My wish for *The ABC Book of Australian Poetry: A Treasury of Poems for Young People* was to compile a rich collection of Australian poetry, peppered with old favourites alongside works of contemporary poets, which would offer readers pleasure and renewed appreciation of our Australian culture and land.

I have been concerned that works of certain classic Australian poets may be slipping out of sight, while the fine works of poets of our time may never be heard or read by young people. This anthology gave me the opportunity to invigorate classic works and highlight contemporary Australian voices, using the metaphor of the river of life for each section, and reflecting so aptly the phases of history.

I hope that this collection stirs something in the heart and mind of the young and old alike, so that poems will be shared, read aloud, even sung, for the sheer pleasure of their particular Australian poetic voice and identity.

There soon followed a slim volume of my poems, *Vietnam Reflections,* and the birth of Pax Press. Many years ago when I was writer in residence at the University of Technology—Sydney on the Kuring-gai campus, I was researching the Vietnam war for part of a novel I was writing (*Valley under the Rock*). I was stopped in my tracks by several photographs that jumped out as striking examples of the sorrow and waste of war. I made myself study them in depth. The novel was put aside as I wrote a series of poems attached to each horrifying photograph. The Australian War Memorial expressed interest in the poems, but only poetry in book form. So Pax Press was born. Below is a poem which was translated into Vietnamese and published by PEN in 2010.

> Photograph 4: *Nui Dat Australian Task Force Headquarters*
> The young woman
> being led away for interrogation
> with her heart-shaped face
> and sweep of dark hair,
> looks like an old school friend.
> What would they do to her?
> how would they make her,
> Captive as she is in that place
> that is her country,
> captive, say what it is they
> want to hear her say?
> The young man beside her
> except for the glaze
> in his young soldier eyes,
> who holds her arm so lightly,
> could be leading her somewhere,
> kindly.
> It's permissible to think,
> in some other time, soon,
> could be bending to embrace
> the girl with the heart-shaped face,
> familiar like a school friend.
> But something is shining in his eyes,
> Anticipation, victory, duty,
> and in hers,
> and there is something terrible
> not of their doing
> between them.

My novel *Fire Song* is set in rather a favourite part of the world for me and a landscape of many a holiday of childhood. My grandmother ran the tearooms down deep in Megalong Valley in the Blue Mountains, and this is where my love affair with the Australian bush and with these strange and alluring mountains began. Started on a plane flying from Tokyo to Vancouver, the story of *Fire Song* was one which told itself. Mid-air I was seized by the idea of a young girl—twelve or thirteen years of age—in a situation where she is opposing a mother she loves and fears. Ingrid is trying to seek help, or somehow resolve the situation herself, with a maturity beyond her years. Or is it? Her mother wants to burn her grandmother's old house down so as to gain the insurance, but Ingrid knows this is wrong in every way. It begs the question for me: at what stage do children actually become adults and take the initiative?

For five weeks in 2010, on a writers' retreat in Buenos Aires with novelist Sue Woolfe and her husband, playwright Gordon Graham, I took it upon myself to write

the treatment for *Fire Song*, as I have never stopped seeing it as a movie. In between exploring the delights of Buenos Aires and taking tango lessons, I completed the treatment, so the first step is taken. One of the wonderful side trips we took was to Chile and to the house of Pablo Neruda at Isla Negra. We walked through that eccentric and wonderful house and stood by one of Neruda's desks—several are littered throughout the house—where he penned so many of those vital and appealing poems. The visit was nothing short of inspiring for this writer. An article followed on this most satisfactory experience, and it was published in the Australian journal *Good Reading* in April of 2010.

The idea for *I Love You Book*—was born in Papua New Guinea some years ago. On a book tour there and making my way through the highlands to the town of Goroka, I was asked to address a boys' school, where some 500 boys were in an assembly. I was happy to talk stories with them, but was surprised and pleased when the principal told me that a group of mothers from the school had prepared a play and wanted to perform it for me. Imagine how I felt as they acted out their story of what books had done for them, opened windows to the whole world in a way I could scarcely begin to imagine, for these women had only just learned to read! They called their play *I Love You Book,* and then and there I knew that one day, I would write a book extolling the virtues of books and the power of literacy. With the staggering pace of technology and the swift way in which e-books are finding their place, I wanted to pay homage to the paper book in its unique sensory qualities, and not just the pleasure of the senses, but even the pleasure of the weight and shape of a pa-

I Love You Book, *Hathorn's 2011 picture book* (Courtesy of HarperCollins.)

Hathorn at the launch of Australia Poetry Ltd., 2011. (Courtesy of Libby Hathorn.)

per book in your hands. Excited as I am that many of my books are also e-books now, and that e-books themselves are proliferating, I see the paper book surviving side by side, with perhaps fewer paper books being published, but, I hope, with the quality of them improving.

I Love You Book is a picture book in verse that is lit up by Heath Mackenzie's lively artwork, showing two kids in all the kinds of adventurous places reading takes you. It has been launched in both Brisbane and Sydney, with kids attending one launch dressed up as favourite book characters. Both launches had spirited discussions about reading from books or the screen. I don't see this as an either-or book, and I made sure Heath showed a TV and computer in the house of the children on their book adventure. In fact, I am putting out some ghost stories as e-books-only at this time, but I really wanted and needed to write about the delights of paperbound books and focus on those enduring good qualities.

> I love you book
> I love your papery smell
> The picture that you show me
> The stories that you tell.

I continue to measure my life in those publications that are still in progress. In my picture storybooks, I am anticipating the publication of *A Boy like Me.* Suffice to say I am in good hands with the inspired artwork of Bruce Whately and looking forward to the evocative way he will treat this text which is quite a poetic one yet with a simple story about peace. As for my novels, a recent trip to Cambodia—and most especially to Siem Reap, to see the wonder of so many ancient temples there—contributed to the fantasy I have been developing over some years, with its working title of *Shoes.* It is now in the process of editing.

In August September this year I am off to the Somme in France researching part of an as yet untitled novel set during World War I. When my mother was a baby her big brother, then nineteen, went off to Gallipoli. He returned after a battle that ended in defeat, luckily unharmed, only to be sent to France and to the terrible Battle of the Somme, where he was to lose his life in the trenches. This book does not so much tell his story, but a soldier's story—or more to the point, a young man's story.

As mentioned earlier, I am continuing work on my poetry book *Collecting Evidence,* sorting and sampling my recent poetry and poetry from other decades for a collection written for adults.

So as a writer I find there is still much work to be done, and wonderful distractions like grandchildren, and travel in between. And looking back I'm a little intrigued as to why it took me so long to come back to my first love—poetry. But I do feel with this flurry of poetic activity that I have come home.

*   *   *

HEIMBERG, Justin

Personal

Born in MD.

Addresses

Home—Metro Washington, DC. *Agent*—Allan Halderman, United Talent Agency, 44 Montgomery St., San Francisco, CA 94104. *E-mail*—justinheimberg@gmail.com.

Career

Writer, creative director, and improvisational performer. Filmwriter, beginning c. 2001; corporate writer; director of online comedy videos. Seven Footer Entertainment (media company), cofounder and former chief creative officer; Lazoo Worldwide (international transmedia company), cofounder and chief content officer. Inventor of games, including "Would You Rather . . . ?" and "Hollywood Shuffle."

Writings

(With David Gomberg) *Would You Rather . . . ?: Over 200 Absolutely Absurd Dilemmas to Ponder,* Plume (New York, NY), 1997.

(With David Gomberg) *Would You Rather. . .? 2: Electric Boogaloo: Over 300 More Absolutely Absurd Dilemmas to Ponder,* Plume (New York, NY), 1999.

(With David Gomberg) *Do unto Others: 1,000 Hilarious Ways to Screw with People's Heads,* St. Martin's Griffin (New York, NY), 2000.

Shrek (based on the motion picture), Dutton Children's Books (New York, NY), 2001.

The World's Worst . . . Book: 1,000 of the Most Hilarious, Bizarre, and Disgusting Things Never Thought Of, Three Rivers Press (New York, NY), 2002.

(With brother Jason Heimberg) *The Official Movie Plot Generator,* 2003.

The Yo Momma Vocabulary Builder, 2007.

(With David Borgenicht) *The Worst-case Scenario Survival Handbook: Extreme Junior Edition,* illustrated by Chuck Gonzales, Chronicle Books (San Francisco, CA), 2008.

(With David Borgenicht) *The Worst-case Scenario Survival Handbook: Weird Junior Edition,* illustrated by Chuck Gonzales, Chronicle Books (San Francisco, CA), 2010.

Coauthor of screenplays, including to *Ace Ventura: Pet Detective Jr.,* 2009. Writer for *The Cleveland Show* (animated television series), Fox, 2009-10. Contributor to periodicals, including *Details, Esquire, MAD,* and *Men's Journal.*

Biographical and Critical Sources

PERIODICALS

Publishers Weekly, May 29, 2000, review of *Do unto Others: 1,000 Hilarious Ways to Screw with People's Heads,* p. 74.

School Library Journal, November, 2010, Esther Keller, review of *The Worst-Case Scenario Survival Handbook,* p. 136.

ONLINE

Justin Heimberg Home Page, http://www.justinheimberg. com (August 15, 2011).

Writers Store Web site, http://www.writersstore.com/ (August 15, 2011), "The Brothers Heimberg."*

*   *   *

HELLARD, Susan

Personal

Born in England. *Education:* Degree (graphics). *Hobbies and other interests:* Swimming.

Addresses

Home and office—North London, England. *Agent*—Arena Illustration Portfolio, 31 Eleanor Rd., London E15 4AB, England.

Career

Illustrator and designer, beginning 1978.

Writings

SELF-ILLUSTRATED

How to Be Popular with Your Pet, Piccadilly Press (London, England), 1984.

(Adaptor) *Billy Goats Gruff,* Piccadilly Press (London, England) 1986.

(Adaptor) Hans Christian Andersen, *The Ugly Duckling,* Putnam (New York, NY), 1987.

(Adaptor) *Froggie Goes A-Courting,* Putnam (New York, NY), 1988.

(Adaptor) *This Little Piggy,* Putman (New York, NY), 1989.

Time to Get Up, Piccadilly Press (London, England), 1989, Putnam (New York, NY), 1990.

Eleanor and the Babysitter, Little, Brown (Boston, MA), 1991.

Baby Tiger, Piccadilly Press (London, England), 1999.

Baby Panda, Piccadilly Press (London, England), 1999.

Baby Lemur, Holt (New York, NY), 1999.

Baby Elephant, Piccadilly Press (London, England), 2000.

ILLUSTRATOR; FOR CHILDREN

Sam McBratney, *Zesty,* Hamilton (London, England), 1984.

Anita Harper, *It's Not Fair!,* G.P. Putnam's (New York, NY), 1986.

Barbara Iresom, *Fighting in Break, and Other Stories,* Faber & Faber (London, England), 1987.

Sandy Asher, *Where Do You Get Your Ideas?: Helping Young Writers Begin,* Walker (New York, NY), 1987.

Anita Harper, *Just a Minute!,* Putnam (New York, NY), 1987.

Kathy Henderson, *Don't Interrupt!,* Barron's (New York, NY), 1988.

Anita Harper, *What Feels Best?,* Putnam (New York, NY), 1988.

Dick King-Smith, *Friends and Brothers,* Mammoth (London, England), 1989.

Sylvia Woods, *Now Then, Charlie Robinson,* Puffin (London, England), 1989.

Jill Tomlinson, *The Gorilla Who Wanted to Grow Up,* Mammoth (London, England), 1990.

Jill Tomlinson, *The Cat Who Wanted to Go Home,* Mammoth (London, England), 1990.

Terrance Dicks, *Teacher's Pet,* Piccadilly Press (London, England), 1990.

Paul Sidey, *The Dinosaur Diner, and Other Poems,* Piccadilly Press (London, England), 1990.

Jill Tomlinson, *Penguin's Progress,* Mammoth (London, England), 1991.

Jill Tomlinson, *The Hen Who Wouldn't Give Up,* Mammoth (London, England), 1991.

Gwen Grant, *Little Blue Car,* Orchard Books (London, England), 1991.

Jill Tomlinson, *The Aardvark Who Wasn't Sure,* Mammoth (London, England), 1991.

Jill Tomlinson, *The Otter Who Wanted to Know,* Methuen (London, England), 1992.

Jill Tomlinson, *The Owl Who Was Afraid of the Dark,* Methuen (London, England), 1992.

Elizabeth Gouge, *I Saw Three Ships,* Lion (London, England), 1992.

Lucy Coats, *One Hungry Baby: A Bedtime Counting Rhyme,* Orchard Books (London, England), 1992, Crown (New York, NY), 1994.

Mary Hooper, *Spook Spotting,* Walker (London, England), 1993.

Ken Adams, *Samson Superslug,* Lion (London, England), 1993.

Linda Newbery, *The Marmalade Pony,* Hippo (London, England), 1994.

Elizabeth Laird, *Stinker Muggles and the Dazzle Bug,* Collins (London, England), 1995.

Terrance Dicks, *Harvey to the Rescue,* Piccadilly (London, England), 1995.

Phil Roxbee Cox, *Nightmare at Mystery Mansion,* Usborne (London, England), 1995.

W.J. Corbett, *Hamish: Climbing Father's Mountain,* Hodder (London, England), 1995.

Julie Hope and John Hope, *Christmas Carols for Cats,* HarperCollins (New York, NY), 1996.

Terrance Dicks, *Harvey and the Beast of Bodmin,* Piccadilly (London, England), 1996.

Terrance Dicks, *Harvey on Holiday,* Piccadilly (London, England), 1996.

Stan Cullimore, *George's Gang in Trouble,* Piccadilly Press (London, England), 1996.

(With Amanda Hall) Richard Brown and Kate Ruttle, selectors, *A Mosquito in the Cabin* (poems), Cambridge University Press (Cambridge, England), 1996.

Terrance Dicks, *Harvey and the Swindlers,* Piccadilly Press (London, England), 1997.

Terrance Dicks, *Harvey Goes to School,* Piccadilly Press (London, England), 1997.

Bernard Ashley, *Flash,* Orchard (London, England), 1997.

Mary Hooper, *Spooks Ahoy!,* Walker (London, England), 1997.

Julie Hope and John Hope, *Nursery Rhymes for Cats,* Bantam (London, England), 1998.

Mary Hooper, *The Great Twin Trick,* Walker (London, England), 1999.

Julie Hope and John Hope, *Christmas Crackers for Cats,* Bantam (London, England), 2000.

Mary Hooper, *Spook Summer,* Walker (London, England), 2001.

Kate Lum, *Princesses Are Not Quitters!,* Bloomsbury (London, England), 2002, Bloomsbury Children's Books (New York, NY), 2003.

Giles Andreae, *My Grandson Is a Genius!,* Bloomsbury Children's Books (New York, NY), 2003.

Irena Green, *You Can Do It, Stanley,* Corgi Pups (London, England), 2004.

Belinda Hollyer, selector, *She's All That!: Poems about Girls,* Kingfisher (London, England), 2005, Kingfisher (Boston, MA), 2006.

Louise Baum, *The Mouse Who Braved Bedtime,* Bloomsbury Children's Books (New York, NY), 2006.

Angela McAllister, *A Pocketful of Kisses,* Bloomsbury Children's (London, England), 2006, published as *Take a Kiss to School,* Bloomsbury Children's Books (New York, NY), 2006.

Bel Mooney, *Who Loves Mr Tubs?,* Egmont (London, England), 2006.

Louis Baum, *Milo Mouse and the Scary Monster,* Bloomsbury Children's (London, England), 2006.

Morag Cuddleford-Jones, *Mum Stuff: Because Mum Knows Best,* Simon & Schuster (London, England), 2007.

Rupert Kingfisher, *Madame Pamplemousse and Her Incredible Edibles,* Bloomsbury Children's Books (New York, NY), 2008.

James Mayhew, *Where's My Cuddle?,* Bloomsbury (London, England), 2008, published as *Where's My Hug?,* Bloomsbury Children's Books (New York, NY), 2008.

Rupert Kingfisher, *Madame Pamplemousse and the Time-Travelling Café,* Bloomsbury (London, England), 2009.

Kate Lum, *Princesses Are Not Perfect,* Bloomsbury (London, England), 2009, Bloomsbury Children's Books (New York, NY), 2010.

Cora Harrison, *I Was Jane Austen's Best Friend: A Secret Diary,* Delacorte Press (New York, NY), 2010.

ILLUSTRATOR; "T.R. BEAR" SERIES BY TERRANCE DICKS

Enter T.R., Piccadilly (London, England), 1985, Barrons's (New York, NY), 1988.

T.R. Goes to School, Piccadilly (London, England), 1985, Barron's (New York, NY), 1988.

T.R.'s Day Out, Piccadilly (London, England), 1985.

T.R. Afloat, Piccadilly Press (London, England), 1986.

T.R.'s Hallowe'en, Piccadilly Press (London, England), 1986, Barron's (New York, NY), 1988.

T.R.'s Festival, Piccadilly Press (London, England), 1987.

T.R.'s Big Game, Piccadilly Press (London, England), 1987.

T.R. Goes to Hollywood, Piccadilly Press (London, England), 1988.

T.R. Goes Skiing, Piccadilly Press (London, England), 1988.

T.R. Down Under, Piccadilly Press (London, England), 1989.

T.R. in New York, Piccadilly Press (London, England), 1989.

T.R. Bear at the Zoo, Piccadilly Press (London, England), 1990.

ILLUSTRATOR; "RHYMES WITH ME" SERIES BY TONY BRADMAN

Play Time, MacDonald (London, England), 1985.

At the Park, Macdonald (London, England), 1985.

Let's Pretend, Macdonald (London, England), 1985.

Hide and Seek, Macdonald (London, England), 1985.

ILLUSTRATOR; "DILLY THE DINOSAUR" SERIES BY TONY BRADMAN

Dilly the Dinosaur, Piccadilly Press (London, England), 1986, Viking Kestrel (New York, NY), 1987.

Dilly Visits the Dentist, Piccadilly Press (London, England), 1986, published as *Dilly Goes to the Dentist,* Viking Kestrel (New York, NY), 1987.

Dilly's Muddy Day, Mammoth (London, England), 1986, published as *Dilly Gets Muddy!,* 1999.

Dilly and the Horror Film, Piccadilly Press (London, England), 1987, Viking Kestrel (New York, NY), 1989.

Dilly and the Tiger, Piccadilly Press (London, England), 1988.

Dilly: The Worst Day Ever, Piccadilly Press (London, England), 1988.

Dilly Tells the Truth, Viking Kestrel (New York, NY), 1988.

Dilly-Dinosuar, Superstar, Piccadilly Press (London, England), 1989.

Dilly and the Ghost, Piccadilly Press (London, England), 1989.

Dilly Goes on Holiday, Piccadilly Press (London, England), 1990.

Dilly Speaks Up, Piccadilly Press (London, England), 1990, Viking (New York, NY), 1991.

Dilly the Angel, Piccadilly Press (London, England), 1990, published as *Dilly at the Funfair,* Mammoth (London, England), 1999.

Dilly's Birthday Party, Piccadilly Press (London, England), 1991.

Dilly and the Big Kids, Piccadilly Press (London, England), 1991, published as *Dilly to the Rescue,* 1999.

Dilly and His Swamp Lizard, Piccadilly Press (London, England), 1991.

Dilly Goes to School, Mammoth (London, England), 1992.

Dilly and the Pirates, Piccadilly Press (London, England), 1992.

Dilly Goes Swamp Wallowing, Mammoth (London, England), 1993.

Dilly Dinosaur, Detective, Heinemann (London, England), 1994.

Dilly and the Tiger, and Other Stories, Dean (London, England), 1994.

Dilly and the Vampire, Heinemann (London, England), 1995, published as *Dilly Saves the Day,* 1999.

Dilly and the Goody-Goody, Mammoth (London, England), 1996.

Dilly and the Cup Final, Mammoth (London, England), 1997, published as *Dilly and the School Report,* Egmont Children's (London, England), 2001.

Dilly Breaks the Rules, Mammoth (London, England), 1999.

Dilly and the Gold Medal, Mammoth (London, England), 1999.

Dilly and the School Play, Egmont Children's (London, England), 2002.

Dilly's Bumper Book of Stores, Egmont Children's (London, England), 2008.

ILLUSTRATOR; *"WOODSIDE SCHOOL STORIES" SERIES BY JEAN URE*

The Fright, Orchard (London, England), 1988.
Loud Mouth, Orchard (London, England), 1988.
Soppy Birthday, Orchard (London, England), 1988.

ILLUSTRATOR; *"FAMOUS CHILDREN" SERIES*

Ann Rachlin, *Bach,* Barron's (New York, NY), 1992.
Ann Rachlin, *Handel,* Barron's (New York, NY), 1992.
Ann Rachlin, *Haydn,* Barron's (New York, NY), 1992.

Ann Rachlin, *Mozart,* Barron's (New York, NY), 1992.
Ann Rachlin, *Brahms,* Barron's (New York, NY), 1993.
Ann Rachlin, *Chopin,* Barron's (New York, NY), 1993.
Ann Rachlin, *Schumann,* Barron's (New York, NY), 1993.
Ann Rachlin, *Tchaikovsky,* Barron's (New York, NY), 1993.

Ann Rachlin, *Schubert,* Gollancz (London, England), 1993, Barron's (New York, NY), 1994.

Ann Rachlin, *Beethoven,* Gollancz (London, England), 1993, Barron's (New York, NY), 1994.

Tony Hart, *Toulouse-Lautrec,* Gollancz (London, England), 1993, Barron's (New York, NY), 1994.

Tony Hart, *Michelangelo,* Gollancz (London, England), 1993, Barron's (New York, NY), 1994.

Tony Hart, *Leonardo da Vinci,* Barron's (New York, NY), 1994.

Tony Hart, *Picasso,* Barron's (New York, NY), 1994.

ILLUSTRATOR; *"CAMBRIDGE READING" SERIES BY JUNE CREBBIN*

Nibbles, Cambridge University Press (Cambridge, England), 1997.

Apples!, Cambridge University Press (Cambridge, England), 1997.

Wrigglebottom, Cambridge University Press (Cambridge, England), 1997.

The Flying Football, Cambridge University Press (Cambridge, England), 1997.

The Puppy Chase, Cambridge University Press (Cambridge, England), 1997.

Granny's Teeth, Cambridge University Press (Cambridge, England), 1997.

ILLUSTRATOR; *"JENNY DALE'S KITTENS" SERIES BY JENNY DALE*

Star the Snowy Kitten, Macmillan Children's (London, England), 1999, Aladdin (New York, NY), 2001.

Nell the Naughty Kitten, Macmillan Children's (London, England), 1999, Aladdin (New York, NY), 2001.

Bob the Bouncy Kitten, Macmillan Children's (London, England), 1999, Aladdin (New York, NY), 2000.

Patch the Perfect Kitten, Macmillan Children's (London, England), 2000, Aladdin (New York, NY), 2001.

Colin the Clumsy Kitten, Aladdin (New York, NY), 2000.

Felix the Fluffy Kitten, Aladdin (New York, NY), 2000.

Leo the Lucky Kitten, Macmillan Children's (London, England), 2000.

Lucy the Lonely Kitten, Macmillan Children's Books (London, England), 2000.

Snuggles the Sleepy Kitten, Macmillan Children's (London, England), 2001.

Pip the Prize Kitten, Macmillan Children's (London, England), 2001.

Sid the Speedy Kitten, Macmillan Children's (London, England), 2001.

Poppy the Posh Kitten, Macmillan Children's (London, England), 2001.

ILLUSTRATOR; "JENNY DALE'S PUPPIES" SERIES BY JENNY DALE

Spike the Special Puppy, Macmillan Children's (London, England), 2000.
Merlin the Magic Puppy, Macmillan Children's (London, England), 2000.
Snowy the Surprise Puppy, Macmillan Children's (London, England), 2000, Scholastic (New York, NY), 2005.

ILLUSTRATOR; "JENNY DALE'S BEST FRIENDS" SERIES BY JENNY DALE

Bubble and Squeak, Macmillan Children's (London, England), 2001, Scholastic (New York, NY), 2005.
Crumble and Custard, Macmillan Children's (London, England), 2001.
Banger and Mash, Macmillan Children's (London, England), 2001.
Lily at the Beach, Macmillan Children's (London, England), 2001.
Lily Finds a Friend, Macmillan Children's (London, England), 2001.
Amber and Alfie, Macmillan Children's (London, England), 2002.
Snowflake and Sparkle, Macmillan Children's (London, England), 2002.
Bramble and Berry, Macmillan Children's (London, England), 2002.
Skipper and Sky, Macmillan Children's (London, England), 2002.
Pogo and Pip, Macmillan Children's (London, England), 2002.
Carrot and Clover, Macmillan Children's (London, England), 2002.
Blossom and Beany, Macmillan Children's (London, England), 2002, Scholastic (New York, NY), 2004.
Hattie and Henry, Macmillan Children's (London, England), 2003.
Lottie and Ludo, Macmillan Children's (London, England), 2003.

ILLUSTRATOR; "MARVIN REDPOST" SERIES BY LOUIS SACHAR

Marvin Redpost, Class President, new edition, Bloomsbury Children's Books (London, England), 2004.
Is He a Girl?, Bloomsbury Children's Books (London, England), 2004.
Marvin Redpost—Why Pick on Me?, Bloomsbury Children's Books (London, England), 2004.
Marvin Redpost, Kidnapped at Birth, Bloomsbury Children's Books (London, England), 2004.
Super Fast, out of Control!, new edition, Bloomsbury Children's (London, England), 2005.

ILLUSTRATOR; OTHER

Anita Naik, *Single Again: Living Alone and Liking It*, Piccadilly Press (London, England), 1992.

Vida Adamoli, *You and Your Cat: The Ultimate Relationship*, Piccadilly (London, England), 1994.

Biographical and Critical Sources

PERIODICALS

Booklist, October 1, 2010, Francisca Goldsmith, review of *I Was Jane Austen's Best Friend: A Secret Diary*, p. 89.
Children's Bookwatch, December, 2006, reviews of *The Mouse Who Braved Bedtime*.
Horn Book, November, 1995, review of *Chopin*, p. 774; November, 1995, review of *Tchaikovsky*, p. 774.
Kirkus Reviews, September 15, 2006, review of *The Mouse Who Braved Bedtime*, p. 946.
Publishers Weekly, February 9, 1990, review of *Time to Get Up*, p. 58; April 26, 1991, review of *Eleanor and the Babysitter*, p. 59; March 27, 2006, review of *Girl Stuff: A Survival Guide to Growing Up*, p. 81; October 4, 2010, review of *I Was Jane Austen's Best Friend*, p. 48
School Arts, May-June, 2006, Ken Marantz, review of *Leonardo da Vinci*, p. 57.
School Library Journal, August, 1994, review of *Toulouse-Lautrec*, p. 151; August, 1994, Shirley Wilton, review of *Leonardo da Vinci*, p. 151; August, 1994, Shirley Wilton, review of *Michelangelo*, p. 151; August, 1994, Shirley Wilton, review of *Picasso*, p. 151; January, 2000, Michele Snyder, review of *Baby Lemur*, p. 104; November, 2005, Rachael Vilmar, review of *The Little Cupcakes*, p. 96; July, 2006, Jill Heritage, review of *She's All That!: Poems about Girls*, p. 120; October, 2006, Tamara E. Richman, review of *The Mouse Who Braved Bedtime*, p. 102.
Times Educational Supplement, September 25, 1992, Philippa Davidson, review of *Mozart, Bach, Handel,* and *Hayden*, p. 12; July 5, 1996, review of *George's Gang in Trouble*, p. 6; September 20, 1996, review of *Dilly and the Goody-Goody*, p. 16; September 20, 1996, review of *Dilly and the Vampire*, p. 16.

ONLINE

Arena Illustration Web site, http://www.arenaillustration.com/ (August 21, 2011), "Susan Hellard."
Bloomsbury USA Web site, http://www.bloomsburyusa.com/ (August 17, 2006), "Susan Hellard."*

*   *   *

HOWLAND, Naomi

Personal

Born in Englewood, NJ; children: one son, two daughters. *Education:* School of Visual Arts, B.F.A. (photography); attended Art Center College of Design.

Addresses

Home—Claremont, CA. *Agent*—Marietta Zacker, Nancy Gallt Literary Agency, 273 Charlton Ave., South Orange, NJ 07079; mariettanancygallt.com. *E-mail*—naomiphowland@gmail.com.

Career

Author and illustrator. Also worked as a painter and printmaker.

Awards, Honors

Best Children's Books of the Year selection, Bank Street College of Education, 2000, for *Latkes, Latkes, Good to Eat;* Notable Children's Books of Jewish Content selection, Association of Jewish Libraries, 2004, for *The Mystery Bear* by Leone Adelson.

Writings

SELF-ILLUSTRATED

ABCDrive!: A Car Trip Alphabet, Clarion Books (New York, NY), 1994.

Latkes, Latkes, Good to Eat: A Chanukah Story, Clarion Books (New York, NY), 1999.

The Matzah Man: A Passover Story, Clarion Books (New York, NY), 2002.

The Better-than-Best Purim, Marshall Cavendish (New York, NY), 2012.

FOR CHILDREN

Princess Says Goodnight, illustrated by David Small, Harper (New York, NY), 2010.

ILLUSTRATOR

Carin Dewhirst, *Peter and the Wolf,* Friedman/Fairfax Publishers (New York, NY), 1996.

Carin Dewhirst, *The Nutcracker,* Friedman/Fairfax Publishers (New York, NY), 1996.

Leone Adelson, *The Mystery Bear: A Purim Story,* Clarion Books (New York, NY), 2004.

Sidelights

Naomi Howland's books for young readers include *The Matzah Man: A Passover Story* and *Latkes, Latkes, Good to Eat: A Chanukah Story,* both of which feature her original art. Howland has also contributed artwork to stories by others, including *The Mystery Bear: A Purim Story* by Leone Adelson. "With a muted palette and folksy touches, Howland's appealing gouache paintings perfectly capture the flavor of the Jewish festivities," Bina Williams noted in a *School Library Journal* review of Adelson's illustrated tale.

"I love to create picture books," Howland stated on her home page. "A good picture book is the perfect marriage of words and pictures, each dependent on the other yet each interpreting the story in a unique way." Her first published work, *ABCDrive!: A Car Trip Alphabet,* evolved from her coursework at the Art Center

Naomi Howland's story of a feisty young princess is paired with David Small's artwork in the pages of **Princess Says Goodnight.** (Illustration copyright © 2010 by David Small. Reproduced by permission of HarperCollins Children's Books, a division of HarperCollins Publishers.)

College of Design in Pasadena, California. During a ride into the city with his mother, a young boy (modeled after the author's son) witnesses one busy scene after another and focuses his attention on the impressive variety of wheeled vehicles to be seen. Howland's illustrations, inspired by the streetscapes of San Francisco, "show a rich diversity of people, objects, vehicles, and actions that kids can identify," noted *Booklist* critic Hazel Rochman.

In *Latkes, Latkes, Good to Eat* Howland incorporates elements from both folklore and fairytales. Set in a small village, her story focuses on Sadie, a resourceful and kindhearted girl who must care for her four younger brothers while their mother is away. When the boys refuse to gather wood on the chilly first night of Chanukah, Sadie ventures alone into the forest, where she meets a shivering, elderly woman. The girl offers all her firewood to the woman; in exchange, she is given a magical frying pan that will cook as many latkes as the family can eat. When the hungry brothers discover the secret words that activate the pan, humorous chaos ensues. A *Publishers Weekly* critic described *Latkes, Latkes, Good to Eat* as an "agreeable outing" that features "friendly, folk-ish art," and Ilene Cooper noted in *Booklist* that "Howland effectively sets her story in a Russian shtetl, using words, intonation, and especially pictures."

Howland offers her take on a childhood favorite, "The Gingerbread Man," in *The Matzah Man*. As the Jewish holiday approaches, a baker forms a small figure from his last bit of dough, only to watch the creation pop from the heated oven looking for escape. After evading Cousin Tiliie, Auntie Bertha, Grandpapa Solly, and others, the Matzah Man seeks refuge at the home of Mendel Fox, a fluffy-taled fellow who has a few tricks of his own. "The book design has a fresh, springlike feeling," Cooper remarked in *Booklist,* and *School Library Journal* contributor Amy Lilien-Harper wrote that "the gouache, collage, and pencil illustrations" in *The Matzah Man* "are well rendered and amusing." In the words of a *Kirkus Reviews* critic, "Those in search of a light-hearted Passover story will find this enjoyable."

Princess Says Goodnight pairs Howland's story with illustrations by Caldecott Medal winner David Small. As she prepares for bed, a young girl peers into a mirror and imagines herself living in a royal palace, complete with servants that deliver chocolate éclairs to her room and a court jester to amuse her. "Sweet and disarmingly infectious without being cloying, this is a bedtime story full of joy," wrote a contributor in *Publishers Weekly,* and *Booklist* reviewer Diane Foote deemed *Princess Says Goodnight* to be a "fun, sleepy-time read for all little princesses."

"I get my inspiration remembering the stories I loved best as a child," Howland told *SATA*. "My studio is a small sunny room overlooking my garden. It is one of my favorite places to be."

Biographical and Critical Sources

PERIODICALS

Booklist, April 15, 1994, Hazel Rochman, review of *ABCDrive!: A Car Trip Alphabet*, p. 1541; September 1, 1999, Ilene Cooper, review of *Latkes, Latkes, Good to Eat: A Chanukah Story*, p. 149; February 15, 2002, Ilene Cooper, review of *The Matzah Man: A Passover Story*, p. 1020; October 1, 2004, Hazel Rochman, review of *The Mystery Bear: A Purim Story*, p. 346; April 1, 2010, Diane Foote, review of *Princess Says Goodnight*, p. 48.

Kirkus Reviews, February 15, 2002, review of *The Matzah Man*, p. 259; April 15, 2010, review of *Princess Says Goodnight*.

Publishers Weekly, September 27, 1999, review of *Latkes, Latkes Good to Eat*, p. 52; February 18, 2002, review of *The Matzah Man*, p. 65; May 3, 2010, review of *Princess Says Goodnight*, p. 48.

School Library Journal, March, 2002, Amy Lilien-Harper, review of *The Matzah Man*, p. 189; December, 2004, Bina Williams, review of *The Mystery Bear*, p. 96; April, 2010, Marianne Saccardi, review of *Princess Says Goodnight*, p. 128.

ONLINE

Naomi Howland Home Page, http://www.naomihowland.com (July 1, 2011).

*   *   *

HULISKA-BEITH, Laura

Personal

Born in Omaha, NE; married; husband's name Jeff. *Education:* Kansas City Art Institute, degree.

Addresses

Home and office—Kansas City, MO. *Agent*—Mela Bolinao, MB Artists, 775 6th Ave., Ste. No. 6, New York, NY 10001; mela@mbartists.com. *E-mail*—LHBeith@kc.rr.com.

Career

Author and illustrator. Hallmark Cards, Kansas City, MO, former illustrator. *Exhibitions:* Work exhibited in Society of Illustrators Original Art Show, New York, NY, 2000.

Member

Society of Illustrators (New York, NY).

Awards, Honors

Marion Vannet Ridgeway Award, 2000, for *The Book of Bad Ideas;* Oppenheim Toy Portfolio Award, and Bank Street College Best Books citation, both 2002, and numerous child-selected state awards, all for *The Recess Queen* by Alexis O'Neill; Missouri Building Block Award, and Great Lakes Great Books Award, both 2005, both for *Bubble Gum, Bubble Gum* by Lisa Wheeler; Outstanding Alumni Award, Kansas City Art Institute, 2007.

Writings

SELF-ILLUSTRATED

The Book of Bad Ideas, Little, Brown (Boston, MA), 2000.

ILLUSTRATOR

Melanie Gerth, *Ten Little Ladbugs,* Piggy Toes Press (Santa Monica, CA), 2000.

Linda Hayward, *Pepé and Papa,* Golden Books (New York, NY), 2001.

Edward Mendelson, *Edward Lear,* Sterling Publishing (New York, NY), 2001.

Lisa Lebowitz Cader, *When I Wear My Crown,* Chronicle Books (San Francisco, CA), 2002.

Mary Ann Hoberman, *The Looking Book,* Little, Brown (Boston, MA), 2002.

Alexis O'Neill, *The Recess Queen,* Scholastic (New York, NY), 2002.

Kimberly Brubaker Bradley, *Favorite Things,* Dial Books for Young Readers (New York, NY), 2003.

Angela Johnson, *Violet's Music,* Dial Books for Young Readers (New York, NY), 2004.

Alice Low, *Aunt Lucy Went to Buy a Hat,* HarperCollins (New York, NY), 2004.

Lisa Wheeler, *Bubble Gum, Bubble Gum,* Little, Brown (New York, NY), 2004.

Elise Broach, *Hiding Hoover,* Dial Books for Young Readers (New York, NY), 2005.

June Sobel, *The Goodnight Train,* Harcourt (Orlando, FL), 2006.

Mary-Alice Moore, *The Wheels on the School Bus,* HarperCollins (New York, NY), 2006.

Katherine Pebley O'Neal, *The Silly Family,* Zonderkidz (Grand Rapids, MI), 2008.

Katherine Pebley O'Neal, *The Messy Family,* Zonderkidz (Grand Rapids, MI), 2008.

Katherine Pebley O'Neal, *The Loud Family,* Zonderkidz (Grand Rapids, MI), 2008.

Katherine Pebley O'Neal, *Grandpa Grumpy's Family,* Zonderkidz (Grand Rapids, MI), 2008.

Alexis O'Neill, *The Worst Best Friend,* Scholastic Press (New York, NY), 2008.

Kimberly Willis Holt, *The Adventures of Granny Clearwater and Little Critter,* Henry Holt (New York, NY), 2010.

Kate Feiffer, *The Wild Wild Inside: A View from Mommy's Tummy,* Simon & Schuster Books for Young Readers (New York, NY), 2010.

Sara Joseph Hale, *Mary Had a Little Lamb,* Marshall Cavendish (New York, NY), 2011.

Sidelights

Beginning her career creating art for Hallmark Cards, Laura Huliska-Beith has accumulated illustration credits that include more than twenty books for young readers, among them such critically acclaimed tales as *The Goodnight Train* by June Sobel and *The Adventures of Granny Clearwater and Little Critter* by Kimberly Willis Holt. Huliska-Beith also added author to her credits in 2000 with the publication of her self-illustrated debut, *The Book of Bad Ideas,* which was inspired by the antics of her four siblings and follows a variety of harmless acts and their humorous but unintended consequences. According to a *Publishers Weekly* critic, "Huliska-Beith's wry look at such simultaneously embarrassing and hilarious moments will have readers cracking up," while *School Library Journal* reviewer Sheilah Kosco dubbed *The Book of Bad Ideas* "delightfully funny offering."

Alexis O'Neill's *The Recess Queen* features a verse tale that centers on a new student's confrontation with a schoolyard bully. Huliska-Beith's artwork for the story prompted praise from a contributor in *Kirkus Reviews* who stated that her use of "rubbery-limbed figures, rolling perspectives, and neon-bright colors reflect[s] the text's informality." A *Publishers Weekly* critic maintained that the illustrator's use of "humorous details . . . playfully conveys the underlying drama of the situation." *Violet's Music,* a story by Angela Johnson, centers on a youngster's search for others who share her passion for rhythm and melody. Here Huliska-Beith's "lively, undulant multimedia collages" were cited as a highlight of the work by a *Kirkus Reviews* critic.

Laura Huliska-Beith's illustration projects include Aunt Lucy Went to Buy a Hat, *a humorous story by Alice Low.* (Illustration copyright © 2004 by Laura Huliska-Beith. All rights reserved. Reproduced by permission HarperCollins Children's Books, a division of HarperCollins.)

view of *The Goodnight Train* that Huliska-Beith's "acrylic-and-collage artwork curves around the spreads and encourages page turns."

A soon-to-be-born baby girl serves as the narrator of Kate Feiffer's *The Wild Wild Inside: A View from Mommy's Tummy.* Huliska-Beith's acrylic illustrations, with their "sculptural feel and neon colors," effectively match the "exuberance" of Feiffer's tale, remarked a contributor in *Publishers Weekly.* In Holt's tall tale *The Adventures of Granny Clearwater and Little Critter,* a feisty old woman and her grandson survive in the desert after tumbling from a covered wagon, managing to foil a stagecoach robber in the process. In *School Library Journal,* Donna Atmur applauded Huliska-Beith's "colorful collage illustrations" for Holt's story.

Biographical and Critical Sources

PERIODICALS

Booklist, March 1, 2002, Hazel Rochman, review of *The Recess Queen,* p. 1143; July, 2002, Hazel Rochman, review of *The Looking Book: A Hide-and-Seek Counting Story,* p. 1859; March 15, 2004, Gillian Engberg, review of *Violet's Music,* p. 1308; August 1, 2006, Jennifer Mattson, review of *The Wheels on the School Bus,* p. 95; September 1, 2008, Hazel Rochman, review of *The Worst Best Friend,* p. 109; November 1, 2010, Ian Chipman, review of *The Adventures of Granny Clearwater and Little Critter,* p. 72.

Bulletin of the Center for Children's Books, March, 2002, review of *The Recess Queen,* p. 250; March, 2004, Janice Del Negro, review of *Aunt Lucy Went to Buy a Hat,* p. 285; July-August, 2004, Karen Coats, review of *Bubble Gum, Bubble Gum,* p. 489.

Childhood Education, fall, 2002, Jeanie Burnett, review of *The Recess Queen,* p. 52.

Kirkus Reviews, December 15, 2001, review of *The Recess Queen,* p. 1761; March 15, 2002, review of *The Looking Book,* p. 414; June 1, 2003, review of *Favorite Things,* p. 800; December 15, 2003, review of *Violet's Music,* p. 1450; January 1, 2004, review of *Aunt Lucy Went to Buy a Hat,* p. 39; March 1, 2004, review of *Bubble Gum, Bubble Gum,* p. 231; June 15, 2005, review of *Hiding Hoover,* p. 678; June 1, 2006, review of *The Wheels on the School Bus,* p. 577; August 1, 2006, review of *The Goodnight Train,* p. 796; April 15, 2008, review of *The Loud Family;* August 15, 2008, review of *The Worst Best Friend.*

Publishers Weekly, September 11, 2000, review of *The Book of Bad Ideas,* p. 89; January 21, 2002, review of *The Recess Queen* p. 89; April 15, 2002, review of *The Looking Book,* p. 63; October 28, 2002, review of *When I Wear My Crown,* p. 75; May 19, 2003, review of *Favorite Things,* p. 73; January 12, 2004, review of *Violet's Music,* p. 53; February 23, 2004, review of *Aunt Lucy Went to Buy a Hat,* p. 74; February 1, 2010, review of *The Wild, Wide Inside: A View from Mommy's Tummy!,* p. 47.

Kate Feiffer's humorous story in **The Wild, Wild Inside** *gains toddler-friendly humor from Huliska-Beith's accompanying acrylic paintings.*
(Illustration copyright © 2010 by Laura Huliska-Beith. Reproduced by permission of Simon & Schuster for Young Readers, an imprint of Simon & Schuster Publishing Division.)

A youngster's outlandish account of his day is the focus of Kimberly Brubaker Bradley's *Favorite Things.* "Embellished with bits of paper-and-fabric-collage, [Huliska-Beith's] . . . artwork brims with playful curves, cartoonish characters and fanciful touches," reported a *Publishers Weekly* reviewer. In *Aunt Lucy Went to Buy a Hat,* a humorous picture book by Alice Low, an easily distracted woman who thinks she has lost her fancy chapeau makes a series of ill-advised purchases in an attempt to replace it. A critic in *Publishers Weekly* noted that "the stylish swoops of paint and skewed paper collages capture this book's benign carelessness." Focusing on a sticky predicament, Lisa Wheeler's *Bubble Gum, Bubble Gum* also features Huliska-Beith's "vibrant, bouncing illustrations," according to *School Library Journal* critic Andrea Tarr.

In Elise Broach's *Hiding Hoover,* another of Huliska-Beith's illustration projects, two siblings hope to prevent their father from discovering that they now have a pet dragon. *School Library Journal* critic Susan Weitz wrote that "the joyful silliness of each intensely colored and fearlessly cluttered picture drives the story forward." *The Goodnight Train,* a bedtime tale by Sobel, follows a locomotive's rail trip to Dreamland. "There is bountiful fun to be had in the journey's creamy hues," a *Kirkus Reviews* contributor noted of this book, and Amy Lilien-Harper observed in a *School Library Journal* re-

School Library Journal, September, 2000, Sheilah Kosco, review of *The Book of Bad Ideas,* p. 218; March, 2002, Lisa Gangemi Kropp, review of *The Recess Queen,* p. 198; June, 2002, Dona Ratterree, review of *The Looking Book,* p. 97; August, 2003, Marianne Saccardi, review of *Favorite Things,* p. 122; February, 2004, Jane Marino, review of *Violet's Music,* p. 114; March, 2004, Bina Williams, review of *Aunt Lucy Went to Buy a Hat,* p. 176; May, 2004, Andrea Tarr, review of *Bubble Gum, Bubble Gum,* p. 126; May, 2005, Jennifer Ralston, review of *The Recess Queen,* p. 50; August, 2005, Susan Weitz, review of *Hiding Hoover,* p. 86; August, 2006, Suzanne Myers Harold, review of *The Wheels on the School Bus,* p. 107; October, 2006, Amy Lilien-Harper, review of *The Goodnight Train,* p. 128; August, 2008, Amy Lilien-Harper, reviews of *Grandpa Grumpy's Family, The Loud Family, The Messy Family,* and *The Silly Family,* all p. 100; October, 2008, Mary Hazelton, review of *The Worst Best Friend,* p. 117; February, 2010, Amy Lilien-Harper, review of *The Wild, Wild Inside,* p. 82; September, 2010, Donna Atmur, review of *The Adventures of Granny Clearwater and Little Critter,* p. 126.

ONLINE

Laura Huliska-Beith Home Page, http://www.laurahuliska beith.com (July 1, 2011).

MB Artists Web site, http://www.mbartists.com/ (July 1, 2011), "Laura Huliska-Beith."*

                        *   *   *

HYDE, Catherine

Personal

Born in England; married; has children. *Education:* Central St. Martin's College of Art and Design, degree (fine arts painting).

Addresses

Home—Helston, Cornwall, England. *E-mail*—enquiries @catherinehyde.co.uk; chydeart@gmail.com.

Career

Fine-art painter and illustrator. *Exhibitions:* Work exhibited at numerous galleries in England.

Awards, Honors

Aesop Accolade honor, American Folklore Society, 2010, for *Firebird* by Saviour Pirotta.

Illustrator

Carol Ann Duffy, *The Princess's Blankets,* Templar Books (Somerville, MA), 2009.

Saviour Pirotta, *Firebird,* Candlewick Press (Somerville, MA), 2010.

Biographical and Critical Sources

PERIODICALS

Kirkus Reviews, October 15, 2009, review of *The Princess's Blankets.*

Publishers Weekly, November 23, 2009, review of *The Princess's Blankets,* p. 55.

School Librarian, winter, 2010, Diana Barnes, review of *Firebird,* p. 232.

School Library Journal, March, 2010, Miriam Lang Budin, review of *The Princess's Blankets,* p. 117; October, 2010, Margaret Bush, review of *Firebird,* p. 103.

ONLINE

Catherine Hyde Home Page, http://www.catherinehyde. co.uk (July 25, 2011).

Firebird Stories Web site, http://www.firebirdstories.com/ (July 25, 2011), "Catherine Hyde."*

I-K

INNERST, Stacy

Personal
Born in Los Angeles, CA; has children. *Education:* University of New Mexico, B.A., 1980; graduate study at Southern Illinois University.

Addresses
Home—Mt. Lebanon, PA. *Agent*—Susan Cohen, Writers House, 21 W. 26th St., New York, NY 10010; scohen@writershouse.com. *E-mail*—info@stacyinnerst.com.

Career
Illustrator. Freelance illustrator, beginning 1980; *Pittsburgh Post-Gazette,* Pittsburgh, PA, editorial illustrator, beginning 1999.

Member
Society of Children's Book Writers and Illustrators.

Awards, Honors
Editorial work honored by representation in annuals, including *American Illustration, Print,* and *Luerzer's Archive: 200 Best Illustrators Worldwide;* honors from Society of Illustrators, *Communication Arts,* and Corporation for Public Broadcasting; Parents' Choice Gold Medal, and One Hundred Titles for Reading and Sharing selection, New York Public Library, both 2003, both for *M Is for Music* by Kathleen Krull; *Smithsonian* magazine Notable Book for Children selection, 2010, for *Lincoln Tells a Joke* by Krull and Paul Brewer.

Illustrator
Kathleen Krull, *M Is for Music,* Harcourt (Orlando, FL), 2003.

Tony Johnston, *The Worm Family,* Harcourt (Orlando, FL), 2004.

Stacy Innerst (Photograph by Dan DeLong. Reproduced by permission.)

Kathleen Krull and Paul Brewer, *Lincoln Tells a Joke: How Laughter Saved the President (and the Country),* Houghton Mifflin Harcourt (Boston, MA), 2010.

Tony Johnston, *Levi Strauss Gets a Bright Idea: A Fairly Fabricated Story of a Pair of Pants,* Houghton Mifflin Harcourt (Boston, MA), 2011.

Contributor to periodicals, including *Boston Globe, Chicago Tribune, New York Times,* and *Philadelphia Inquirer.*

Sidelights
The artwork of Stacy Innerst, a former editorial illustrator for the *Pittsburgh Post-Gazette,* has graced the pages of such well-received children's books as Kathleen Krull's *M Is for Music* and Tony Johnston's stories in both *The Worm Family* and *Levi Strauss Gets a Bright Idea: A Fairly Fabricated Story of a Pair of Pants.* "It was a bit of a shift to go from editorial newspaper illustration to children's books, but I was eager to try it," Innerst noted in a Harcourt Web site interview. "The subject matter forced me to 'lighten up' and take a breather from the news. It was also fun to create something for an audience that is composed mainly of kids

and their parents—a group for whom I have tremendous respect!" In fact, Innerst's work is noted for its unique approach; for example, in illustrating Johnson's picture-book history about the man who invented blue jeans, he uses denim as the canvas on which he "chronicles the raucous action in acrylic paintings," according to a *Publishers Weekly* critic.

In Krull's offbeat alphabet book *M Is for Music,* the author presents a smorgasbord of musical styles, terms, and names, touching on such diverse individuals as Ludwig von Beethoven and Frank Zappa and such concepts as aria and quadrille. Innerst's "jazzy, oil-and-acrylic collage assemblages include humorous touches to reinforce the concepts," remarked *School Library Journal* critic Jane Marino. A *Publishers Weekly* reviewer similarly noted that the artist's "slyly humorous, slightly abstract oil and acrylic illustrations give the minimal text a sophisticated spin." Writing in the *New York Times Book Review,* Paul O. Zelinsky offered effusive praise for Innerst's "bravura painting" in *M Is for Music.* "A daub of paint here and a smear there, and voilá, a perfect Louis Armstrong in caricature . . . ," wrote Zelinsky. "Graphics as sophisticated as Innerst's often lack what interests children most: well-developed subject matter and a sense of humor. But both are fully in evidence here." Discussing his approach to the work in his Harcourt interview, the artist explained: "I wanted the overall presentation of the book to feel like a musical score, with the kind of scrawled energy that one perceives when looking at a handwritten piece of music."

Johnston's *The Worm Family* offers "a unique take on prejudice," according to *School Library Journal* contributor John Sigwald. Despite their love for one another, the seven skinny, wiggly members of the Worm clan have difficulty establishing permanent roots and face discrimination from a host of creepy-crawly neighbors each time they attempt to settle down. Finally, the worms take a bold stand and assert their rights. Innerst's "antic oil paintings . . . picture the Worms standing tall like fingers or curling in graceful esses," applauded a contributor in reviewing *The Worm Family* for *Publishers Weekly.*

Lincoln Tells a Joke: How Laughter Saved the President (and the Country), a picture-book biography by Krull and her husband, Paul Brewer, affords readers an unique view of Abraham Lincoln by focusing on the way the sixteenth U.S. president used humor to guide him through political and personal crises. "Innerst's colorful and unconventional acrylic illustrations . . . are the perfect complement to both the text and the subject matter," Jody Kopple maintained in her *School Library Journal* review of the book. His "gorgeous, textured paintings, many of them caricatures, are varied and inventive," a critic in *Kirkus Reviews* stated, and a *Publishers Weekly* contributor wrote that the artist's

"stylized acrylics" in *Lincoln Tells a Joke* "underline the image of Lincoln as backwoodsman-turned-politician."

"I was born in Los Angeles, where my father worked for the *LA Times* and taught at UCLA," Innerst told *SATA.* "As a small child I lived in a neighborhood in Santa Monica Canyon that was home to Rod Serling, James Arness, Ray Bradbury, and Noel Neill, the actress who played Lois Lane in the *Superman* TV series. It was no wonder that stories, comics, fantasy, and imagination took root early in my mind. Mr. Serling was in the P.T.A. and yet, there he was on TV, introducing the *Twilight Zone.*

Innerst captures the silliness hidden in Kathleen Krull's informative text in his art for the picture book **M Is for Music.** (Harcourt, 2003. Illustration copyright © 2003 by Stacy Innerst. All rights reserved. Reproduced by permission of Harcourt.)

The personality of a famous U.S. president is reflected in Innerst's illustrations for Kathleen Krull and Paul Brewer's picture book **Lincoln Tells a Joke.** (Harcourt Children's Books, 2010. Illustration copyright © 2010 by Stacy Innerst. Reproduced by permission of Houghton Mifflin Harcourt Publishing Company. All rights reserved.)

"I've nearly always had some sort of drawing or painting implement in my hand and have learned to use those tools judiciously, but there were many defaced walls and books in my parents' home during my childhood. I even left my mark in a copy of *The Wind in the Willows*—apparently I thought picture books were 'interactive' at the time.

"The most gratifying pictures I've made as an adult are those that appear in books that are read by or to children. I now live in Pennsylvania but many of the paintings I've done for books are in the Every Picture Tells a Story gallery in Santa Monica, California. Full circle, I suppose."

Biographical and Critical Sources

PERIODICALS

Booklist, August, 2003, GraceAnne A. DeCandido, review of *M Is for Music,* p. 1985; February 15, 2010, Andrew Medlar, review of *Lincoln Tells a Joke: How Laughter Saved the President (and the Country),* p. 73.

Childhood Education, summer, Maria T. Holder, review of *M Is for Music,* p. 212.
Horn Book, May-June, 2010, Betty Carter, review of *Lincoln Tells a Joke,* p. 109.
Kirkus Reviews, August 1, 2003, review of *M Is for Music,* p. 1019; October 1, 2004, review of *The Worm Family,* p. 963; March 15, 2010, review of *Lincoln Tells a Joke;* July 15, 2011, review of *Levi Strauss Gets a Bright Idea: A Fairly Fabricated Story of a Pair of Pants.*
New York Times Book Review, November 16, 2003, Paul O. Zelinsky, "Letters Entertain You," review of *M Is for Music,* p. 37.
Publishers Weekly, September 8, 2003, review of *M Is for Music,* p. 74; December 6, 2004, review of *The Worm Family,* p. 58; March 22, 2010, review of *Lincoln Tells a Joke,* p. 69; July 18, 2011, review of *Levi Strauss Gets a Bright Idea.*
School Library Journal, September, 2003, Jane Marino, review of *M Is for Music,* p. 200; February, 2005, John Sigwald, review of *The Worm Family,* p. 104; March, 2010, Jody Kopple, review of *Lincoln Tells a Joke,* p. 142.

ONLINE

Harcourt Web site, http://www.harcourtbooks.com/ (July 1, 2011), interview with Innerst.
Society of Children's Book Writers and Illustrators Web site, http://www.scbwi.org/ (July 1, 2011), "Stacy Innerst."
Stacy Innerst Home Page, http://www.stacyinnerst.com (July 1, 2011).

*   *   *

JOHNSON, Christine 1978-

Personal

Born February 2, 1978, in Indianapolis, IN; married; children: two. *Education:* DePaul University, degree. *Hobbies and other interests:* Yoga, cooking.

Addresses

Home—Indianapolis, IN. *Agent*—Caryn Wiseman, Andrea Brown Literary Agency; caryn@andreabrownlit.com.

Career

Writer. Worked variously in human resources and as a library clerk, nanny, yoga instructor, and assistant manager of a tanning salon.

Writings

NOVELS

Claire de Lune, Simon Pulse (New York, NY), 2010.

Nocturne (sequel to *Claire de Lune*), Simon Pulse (New York, NY), 2011.

Sidelights

In her debut novel, *Claire de Lune*, Indiana-based writer Christine Johnson offers an unconventional take on the werewolf literary genre, focusing on a small-town teenager whose world changes dramatically on her sixteenth birthday. Johnson continues her supernatural saga in *Nocturne*.

Described as "a fun and entertaining read" by *School Library Journal* critic Donna Rosenblum, *Claire de Lune* centers on Claire Benoit, a high-school student who discovers a horrific family secret: she is descended from a long line of female werewolves and her transformation from human to wolf is imminent. Claire struggles to keep this knowledge from both best friend Emily and especially from current beau Matthew Engle, whose scientist father is determined to capture and cure werewolves at any cost. "Johnson weaves a page-turning tale of forbidden love, loyalty, friendship, and

Cover of Christine Johnson's young-adult novel **Claire de Lune,** *which features supernatural themes.* (Simon Pulse, 2010. Book cover photographs by Getty Images. Reproduced by permission of Simon & Schuster, Inc.)

deception that will leave readers eager for more," Rosenblum predicted in her review of *Claire de Lune*, and a critic in *Publishers Weekly* remarked that Johnson's novel "glimmers with mystery and a budding romance amid Romeo and Juliet-like complications." "Smooth writing and engaging main characters make for an easy read," Francisca Goldsmith observed in her *Booklist* review and a *Kirkus Reviews* contributor asserted of *Claire de Lune* that Johnson's "unadorned, simple writing style works well."

In *Nocturne* Claire must take drastic action when someone learns of her dual identity. A *Kirkus Reviews* critic noted in a review of this novel that in *Nocturne* Johnson once again treats teen readers to "a solid story with an undeniably likable heroine."

Biographical and Critical Sources

PERIODICALS

Booklist, May 15, 2010, Francisca Goldsmith, review of *Claire de Lune,* p. 46.
Kirkus Reviews, April 15, 2010, review of *Claire de Lune;* July 15, 2011, review of *Nocturne.*
Publishers Weekly, April 26, 2010, review of *Claire de Lune,* p. 111.
School Librarian, winter, 2010, Elizabeth Finlayson, review of *Claire de Lune,* p. 244.
School Library, April, 2010, Donna Rosenblum, review of *Claire de Lune,* p. 160.

ONLINE

Christine Johnson Home Page, http://www.christinejohnsonbooks.com (July 15, 2011).
Simon & Schuster Web site, http://www.simonandschuster.com/ (July 15, 2011), "Christine Johnson."*

*　　*　　*

JOHNSON, Maureen 1973-

Personal

Born February 16, 1973, in Philadelphia, PA. *Education:* University of Delaware, B.A. (writing); Columbia University, M.F.A.

Addresses

Home—New York, NY. *Agent*—Kate Schafer Testerman, kate@ktliterary.com. *E-mail*—maureen@maureenjohnsonbooks.com.

Career

Novelist. Worked variously in a restaurant, as a literary manager, with a stage show in Las Vegas, and as an editor. Presenter at schools.

Awards, Honors

Best Young-Adult Books selection, American Library Association, and Books for the Teen Age selection, New York Public Library, both 2005, both for *The Key to the Golden Firebird; Booksense* selection, 2005, for *Thirteen Little Blue Envelopes.*

Writings

YOUNG-ADULT FICTION

The Bermudez Triangle, Razorbill (New York, NY), 2004.

The Key to the Golden Firebird, HarperCollins (New York, NY), 2004.

Thirteen Little Blue Envelopes, HarperCollins (New York, NY), 2005.

Devilish, Razorbill (New York, NY), 2006.

Girl at Sea, HarperCollins (New York, NY), 2007.

(With John Green and Lauren Myracle) *Let It Snow: Three Holiday Romances,* Speak (New York, NY), 2008.

Suite Scarlett, Point (New York, NY), 2008.

Scarlett Fever, Point (New York, NY), 2010.

The Last Little Blue Envelope, HarperTeen (New York, NY), 2011.

Contributor to anthologies, including *Vacations from Hell,* HarperTeen (New York, NY), 2009, and *Zombies vs. Unicorns,* edited by Holly Black and Justine Larbalestier, Simon & Schuster (New York, NY), 2010.

Author's work has been translated into Catalan, Croatian, Dutch, French, German, Hebrew, Hungarian, Italian, Polish, Romanian, Swedish, and Turkish.

Sidelights

In Maureen Johnson's young-adult novels teenaged girls face unexpected circumstances and transcend them through optimism and love. Her stories, which include *The Key to the Golden Firebird, Thirteen Little Blue Envelopes, Girl at Sea,* and the companion novels *Suite Scarlett* and *Scarlett Fever,* are sometimes realistic and sometimes filled with humor. Critics have consistently praised Johnson's ability to create believable characters with whom teen readers can identify; as Emily Garrett Cassady noted in her *School Library Journal* review of *Suite Scarlett,* the author "blends sibling rivalry and the importance of family, friendship, and romance into a plot that is charming and well delivered."

Born in Philadelphia, Pennsylvania, Johnson knew early on that she wanted to become a writer and she draws on her own growing-up years in several of her books for teens. Her supernatural mystery novel *Devilish,* for instance, was inspired by her experience attending a Roman Catholic high school, an experience that "caused me to develop a lifelong aversion to polyester and knee socks," as Johnson wryly noted on her home page. In

the novel, Jane Jarvis and Allison "Ally" Concord attend St. Teresa's Preparatory School for Girls in Providence, Rhode Island. Ally is a little lost at the school due to her naiveté about social interaction, so Jane looks out for her. When actual demons begin to plague the school, Jane realizes that Ally has also changed somehow. "Well-developed characters are Johnson's forté," Susan Riley noted in a review of *Devilish* for *School Library Journal,* while a *Kirkus Reviews* critic asserted that "Johnson writes with flair, intelligence and humor" and her "well-realized" characters ratchet up the "suspense as deftly as [noted horror novelist] Stephen King."

After graduating from the University of Delaware and Columbia University, Johnson began writing in earnest. In her first novel, *The Bermudez Triangle,* she tells the story of Nina Bermudez's last year in high school. Sent to summer camp prior to her senior year, Nina returns home only to find that her two best friends, Avery and Mel, have begun a homosexual romance. While at camp Nina had started her own relationship with a boy named Steve, whom she still contacts via e-mail and phone. The novel follows Nina and her friends through the

Cover of Maureen Johnson's young-adult novel The Bermudez Triangle, *featuring photography by Dana Edmunds.* (Razorbill, 2007. Reproduced by permission of Razorbill, a division of Penguin Putnam Books for Young Readers.)

school year as they make plans for college and try to deal with the fact that the relationship between Avery and Mel has strained the friendship of all three. Reviewing *The Bermudez Triangle* for the *Bulletin of the Center for Children's Books,* Deborah Stevenson commented that "the omniscient narration slips easily from viewpoint to viewpoint, which helps keep the girls sympathetic through good behavior and bad . . . and makes credible the final restoration and affirmation of friendship." A *Kirkus Reviews* contributor called the book a "warm, humorous, and smoothly readable story" and noted that "the characterizations of love . . . are tender even when painful." Susan Riley, writing in *School Library Journal,* deemed *The Bermudez Triangle* "exceptional" and a novel that "perceptively reflects the real-life ambiguities and shades of gray faced by contemporary adolescents."

The Key to the Golden Firebird finds May's strained family falling apart following the death of her father and her mother's absences due to her need to return to work. Her teenage sisters Brooks and Palmer deal with the family tragedy: Brooks turns to alcohol and hangs out with a bad crowd while Palmer uses television-watching to escape from the fear and anxiety she feels. May deals with the situation better, however, and her longtime friendship with next-door neighbor Peter soon begins to become something more. The sisters' road trip in their father's beloved Pontiac Firebird transforms the way in which each deals with her loss. Miranda Doyle, writing in *School Library Journal,* called *The Key to the Golden Firebird* "poignant and laced with wry humor," adding that Johnson's "wonderfully moving and entertaining novel [is] full of authentic characters and emotions." In a review for *Booklist,* Frances Bradburn deemed the work "a very special, unexpected coming-of-age" tale, while *Bulletin of the Center for Children's Books* contributor Deborah Stevenson called *The Key to the Golden Firebird* "an honest yet highly reassuring account of surviving loss."

The chain of events that play out in both *Thirteen Little Blue Envelopes* and *The Last Little Blue Envelope* begins after eccentric Aunt Peg passes away, leaving seventeen-year-old Ginny with a list of several European destinations to visit, and a stack of sealed, numbered envelopes she must open upon reaching each destination. Along the way, Ginny not only discovers much about her aunt's life that she did not know, but also learns self-reliance. Her adventures in *The Last Little Blue Envelope* conclude during a trip to London and the discovery of Peg's final letter. "As she comes to the last of the letters," wrote Janis Flint-Ferguson in *Kliatt,* "Ginny has grown from the shy teenager she was to one who is more independent, more invested in the life around her." Gillian Engberg maintained in her *Booklist* review of *Thirteen Little Blue Envelopes* that "readers will probably overlook any improbabilities and willingly accompany Ginny through her sensitive, authentically portrayed experiences—uncomfortable, lonely; giddy, and life changing—as she pieces together

Johnson's teen novel Devilish *focuses on a teen whose radical change in luck causes her school friends to worry.* (Photograph of girl © Dimitri Vervits/Getty Images. Photo of cupcake © Royalty-Free/Corbis. Reproduced by permission of Razorbill, a division of Penguin Young Readers Group, a member of Penguin Group (USA) Inc., 345 Hudson St., New York, NY 10014. All rights reserved.)

family mysteries and discovers herself." According to Emily Garrett in *School Library Journal, Thirteen Little Blue Envelopes* "drives home the importance of family, love, and the value of connections that you make with people," while *Voice of Youth Advocates* contributor Liz Sunderman wrote of *The Last Little Blue Envelope* that "this is one of the rare books that will delight both lovers of contemporary adventures and those who prefer realistic romances."

Girl at Sea concerns seventeen-year-old Clio Ford, who is sent to live in Italy with her drifter father while her professor mother is off on a fellowship. Clio and her father created a popular computer game years before, and the family became quite wealthy, but Mr. Ford has since wasted most of that money. Now he hopes to recoup his fortune—and regain the respect of his daughter—by hunting for treasure at the bottom of the Mediterranean Sea. When Claire realizes that the treasure they are searching for is only part of the mystery, she must cope with her father's archeologist girlfriend, decipher clues as to the whereabouts of a shipwreck, and wonder if crewmate Aidan is really romantically interested in her. A critic for *Kirkus Reviews* described *Girl at Sea* as "full of unforgettable moments and much more complicated than readers may grasp as they turn the pages." "There is diving, excitement, adventure, romance—all in a beautiful setting," noted Claire Rosser in her *Kliatt* review of the novel, while Cassady noted in *School Library Journal,* that Johnson "does a great job of peppering enough interesting information and planting enough clues to keep the story moving along." In *Publishers Weekly* a critic concluded of *Girl at Sea* that "spirited Clio is immensely personable and witty," while *Booklist* critic Heather Booth deemed Johnson's novel a "whirlwind of mystery and action, friendship and romance."

Johnson takes readers to her adopted home town of Manhattan in *Suite Scarlett,* and *Scarlett Fever,* both of which focus on the Martins, a resourceful but financially strapped family whose members operate The Hopewell, an ageing residential hotel in the city's Upper East Side. When the Martin children reach age fifteen, they also do their part: each one is assigned to

Cover of Johnson's young-adult novel Scarlett Fever, *a quirky tale about a self-reliant family that operates a run-down hotel in Manhattan.* (Book cover photographs by Image Source Black/Jupiterimages (wallpaper); Image Source/Jupiterimages (key). Reproduced by permission of Scholastic, Inc.)

care for one room in the hotel, along with that room's often-eccentric occupant. Scarlett's fifteenth birthday finds her turning assistant to demanding hotel guest Mrs. Amberson, a wealthy patroness of the city's theatre groups. Mrs. Amberson's support of a fledgling production of Shakespeare's *Hamlet* seems a wise choice, especially since Scarlett's older brother Spencer is involved, but when the woman's interest wanes Scarlett is left to keep the production going. The teen's ability to multi-task allows her to channel some energy into her personal life, namely a budding love affair with one of Spencer's costars.

Mrs. Amberson's dilettantish support of a locally produced television program requires Scarlett's attention in *Scarlett Fever,* and here Spencer is again the beneficiary. While attempting to rein in Mrs. Amberson's efforts to become an actor's agent, the teen also finds herself the primary caregiver to the woman's new dog.

Reviewing *Suite Scarlet,* a *Kirkus Reviews* writer praised "the authentic charm of the characters and the endearing sweetness of their odd familial relationships," and Thom Barthelmess wrote in *Booklist* that Johnson's story serves up an "utterly winning, madcap Manhattan farce, crafted with a winking, urbane narrative and tight, wry dialogue." Although *Scarlett Fever* "may be enjoyed for the light if slightly madcap romance that it is, it is notable for its attention to social class and to the Martins' struggles with money," noted *School Library Journal* contributor Amy S. Pattee of the sequel, and a *Kirkus Reviews* critic dubbed the same novel an "hilarious follow-up" in which "spencer and Mrs. Amberson's antics . . . are uproariously funny."

Biographical and Critical Sources

PERIODICALS

Booklist, September 1, 2004, Frances Bradburn, review of *The Key to the Golden Firebird,* p. 122; November 1, 2004, Frances Bradburn, review of *The Bermudez Triangle,* p. 475; September 15, 2005, Gillian Engberg, review of *Thirteen Little Blue Envelopes,* p. 57; October 15, 2006, Ilene Cooper, review of *Devilish,* p. 40; July 1, 2007, Heather Booth, review of *Girl at Sea,* p. 50; June 1, 2008, Thom Barthelmess, review of *Suite Scarlett,* p. 79; May 1, 2011, Cindy Dobrez, review of *The Last Little Blue Envelope,* p. 116.
Bulletin of the Center for Children's Books, July-August, 2004, Deborah Stevenson, review of *The Key to the Golden Firebird,* p. 471; November, 2004, Deborah Stevenson, review of *The Bermudez Triangle,* p. 128.
Horn Book, July-August, 2008, Claire E. Gross, review of *Suite Scarlett,* p. 450; November-December, 2008, Claire E. Gross, review of *Let It Snow: Three Holiday Romances,* p. 648; March-April, 2010, Claire E. Gross, review of *Scarlett Fever,* p. 60.
Kirkus Reviews, May 1, 2004, review of *The Key to the Golden Firebird,* p. 443; October 1, 2004, review of *The Bermudez Triangle,* p. 962; August 1, 2005, re-

view of *Thirteen Little Blue Envelopes,* p. 851; July 15, 2006, review of *Devilish,* p. 724; May 1, 2007, review of *Girl at Sea;* May 1, 2008, review of *Suite Scarlett;* November 1, 2008, review of *Let It Snow;* February 15, 2010, review of *Scarlett Fever;* March 15, 2011, review of *The Last Little Blue Envelope.*

Kliatt, May, 2004, Claire Rosser, review of *The Key to the Golden Firebird,* p. 10; September, 2004, Janis Flint-Ferguson, review of *The Bermudez Triangle,* p. 12; September, 2005, Janis Flint-Ferguson, review of *Thirteen Little Blue Envelopes,* p. 9; May, 2007, review of *Girl at Sea,* p. 14; July, 2008, Claire Rosser, review of *Suite Scarlett,* p. 16; November, 2008, Sherrie Forgash Ginsberg, review of *Let It Snow,* p. 24.

Publishers Weekly, December 6, 2004, review of *The Bermudez Triangle,* p. 61; September 5, 2005, review of *Thirteen Little Blue Envelopes,* p. 63; June 4, 2007, review of *Girl at Sea,* p. 50; May 12, 2008, review of *Suite Scarlett,* p. 55.

School Library Journal, June, 2004, Miranda Doyle, review of *The Key to the Golden Firebird,* p. 143; November, 2004, Susan Riley, review of *The Bermudez Triangle,* p. 146; October, 2005, Emily Garrett, review of *Thirteen Little Blue Envelopes,* p. 163; October, 2006, Susan Riley, review of *Devilish,* p. 158; June, 2007, Emily Garrett, review of *Girl at Sea,* p. 148; October, 2008, Madeline J. Bryant, review of *Let It Snow,* p. 94, and Emily Garrett Cassady, review of *Suite Scarlett,* p. 150; January, 2010, Amy S. Pattee, review of *Scarlett Fever,* p. 104.

Voice of Youth Advocates, August, 2010, Amy Fiske, review of *Scarlett Fever,* p. 248; April, 2011, Liz Sundermann, review of *The Last Little Blue Envelope,* p. 61.

ONLINE

Maureen Johnson Home Page, http://www.maureen johnsonbooks.com (July 15, 2011).*

*   *   *

KATZ, Karen 1947-

Personal

Born September 16, 1947, in Newark, NJ; daughter of Alex (a furniture manufacturer) and Muriel (a homemaker) Katz; married Gary Richards (a writer), 1999; children: Lena. *Education:* Tyler School of Art, degree, 1969; Yale School of Art and Architecture, M.F.A., 1971.

Addresses

Home—New York, NY. *E-mail*—karen@karenkatz.com.

Career

Author and illustrator of children's books. Has also worked as a costume designer, quilt maker, fabric artist,

Karen Katz (Photo by Gary Richards. Reproduced by permission.)

graphic designer, and toy designer. *Exhibitions:* Work exhibited at Society of Illustrators Picture Book show, 1999, 2002, and Children's Museum of Arts, New York, NY, 1999.

Awards, Honors

Smithsonian, People, and *Parent Guide* magazines Best Books designation, all 1997, all for *Over the Moon;* Bill Martin, Jr., Picture Book Award nomination, Florida Reading Association Award nomination, and *Child* magazine Best Book designation, all 2000, all for *The Colors of Us;* National Parenting Publications Gold Award, and *Child* magazine Best Book designation, both 2001, and Bank Street College School Books Committee Best Book designation, 2002, all for *Counting Kisses;* Oppenheim Toy Portfolio Gold Seal Award, 2002, for both *Counting Kisses* and *Twelve Hats for Lena;* Dollywood Foundation Imagination Library Award, 2004, for *I Can Share!;* National Parenting Publications Award, 2005, for both *Ten Tiny Tickles* and *Daddy Hugs 1 2 3,* and 2006, for *Mommy Hugs;* Children's Choices selection, International Reading Association, 2008, for *Princess Baby;* Oppenheim Toy Portfolio Gold Award, 2009, for *Princess Baby, Night-night.*

Writings

SELF-ILLUSTRATED

Over the Moon: An Adoption Tale, Holt (New York, NY), 1997.
The Colors of Us, Holt (New York, NY), 1999.

Where Is Baby's Belly Button?, Little Simon (New York, NY), 2000.

In Grandmother's Arms, Scholastic (New York, NY), 2001.

Counting Kisses, Margaret K. McElderry Books (New York, NY), 2001.

Where Is Baby's Mommy?, Little Simon (New York, NY), 2001.

Excuse Me!, Grosset & Dunlap (New York, NY), 2002.

Grandma and Me, Little Simon (New York, NY), 2002.

Twelve Hats for Lena: A Book of Months, Margaret K. McElderry Books (New York, NY), 2002.

No Biting!, Grosset & Dunlap (New York, NY), 2002.

My First Kwanzaa, Holt (New York, NY), 2003.

Daddy and Me, Simon & Schuster (New York, NY), 2003.

Counting Christmas, Margaret K. McElderry Books (New York, NY), 2003.

Grandpa and Me, Little Simon (New York, NY), 2004.

What Does Baby Say?, Little Simon (New York, NY), 2004.

My First Chinese New Year, Holt (New York, NY), 2004.

No Hitting!, Grosset & Dunlap (New York, NY), 2004.

I Can Share!, Grosset & Dunlap (New York, NY), 2004.

Ten Tiny Tickles, Margaret K. McElderry Books (New York, NY), 2005.

A Potty for Me!, Little Simon (New York, NY), 2005.

Daddy Hugs 1 2 3, Margaret K. McElderry Books (New York, NY), 2005.

Mommy Hugs, Margaret K. McElderry Books (New York, NY), 2006.

Best-ever Big Brother, Grosset & Dunlap (New York, NY), 2006.

Can You Say Peace?, Holt (New York, NY), 2006.

Where Is Baby's Pumpkin?: A Lift-the-flap Book, Little Simon (New York, NY), 2006.

Best-ever Big Sister, Grosset & Dunlap (New York, NY), 2006.

Wiggle Your Toes, paper engineering by Gene Vosough, Little Simon (New York, NY), 2006.

My First Ramadan, Holt (New York, NY), 2007.

Peek-a-Baby, Little Simon (New York, NY), 2007.

Where Is Baby's Dreidel?: A Lift-the-flap Book, Little Simon (New York, NY), 2007.

Ten Tiny Babies, Margaret K. McElderry Books (New York, NY), 2008.

Princess Baby, Schwartz & Wade (New York, NY), 2008.

Twinkle Toes, Grosset & Dunlap (New York, NY), 2008.

Where Are Baby's Easter Eggs?: A Lift-the-flap Book, Little Simon (New York, NY), 2008.

Where Is Baby's Birthday Cake?: A Lift-the-flap Book, Little Simon (New York, NY), 2008.

Beddy-bye, Baby: A Touch-and-feel Book, Little Simon (New York, NY), 2009.

Shake It Up, Baby!, Little Simon (New York, NY), 2009.

Superhero Me!, Grosset & Dunlap (New York, NY), 2009.

Where Is Baby's Beach Ball?: A Lift-the-flap Book, Little Simon (New York, NY), 2009.

Where Is Baby's Christmas Present?: A Lift-the-flap Book, Little Simon (New York, NY), 2009.

Princess Baby, Night-night, Schwartz & Wade (New York, NY), 2009.

Baby's Colors, Little Simon (New York, NY), 2010.

Baby's Shapes, Little Simon (New York, NY), 2010.

Princess Baby on the Go, Schwartz & Wade (New York, NY), 2010.

Babies on the Bus, Henry Holt (New York, NY), 2011.

Author's books have been published in Spanish.

ILLUSTRATOR

Marion Dane Bauer, *Toes, Ears, and Nose!*, Little Simon (New York, NY), 2003.

Anastasia Suen, *Subway*, Viking (New York, NY), 2004.

Jayne C. Shelton, *In Grandma's Arms*, Scholastic (New York, NY), 2007.

Margaret Wise Brown, *A Child's Good Morning Book*, HarperCollins (New York, NY), 2009.

Margaret Wise Brown, *Sleepy ABC*, Harper (New York, NY), 2010.

Sidelights

A former costume designer and quilter, Karen Katz now writes and illustrates picture books and lift-the-flap books for young readers. Katz, a graduate of the Yale School of Art and Architecture, is the creator of such critically acclaimed works as *Over the Moon: An Adoption Tale*, *Mommy Hugs*, and *Babies on the Bus*. For her efforts, she has earned a number of National Parenting Publications awards as well as several other honors. "I am living my dream," Katz remarked in an interview on the Random House Web site. "I couldn't think of anything I'd rather do than children's books."

Published in 1997, Katz's debut picture book *Over the Moon* was inspired by events from her own life. As she stated in her Random House interview, "After my husband and I adopted our daughter from Guatemala, I de-

Katz's rambunctious young characters star in picture books such as **Twelve Hats for Lena,** *which features her original collage art.* (Copyright © 2002 by Karen Katz. Reprinted by permission of Margaret K. McElderry Books, an imprint of Simon & Schuster Children's Publishing Division.)

cided I wanted to illustrate children's books. I had been a graphic designer for many years. For nine months, I painted pictures of kids and anything that looked like it could be in a children's book. Then I put together a portfolio to show." A senior editor at a New York City publishing house eventually encouraged Katz to write a book about adoption. "That was the beginning of my career," the author/illustrator noted. "I was very lucky to meet someone who had great vision and was willing to trust in my potential."

Marked by elements of fantasy, *Over the Moon* follows a couple's journey to a distant land to adopt the tiny baby they both had seen in their dreams. "Bold colors and lively patterns swirl across the pages of *Over the Moon*," noted *Booklist* critic Stephanie Zvirin, and a *Publishers Weekly* reviewer praised the "contagious exuberance" of Katz's "playfully stylized collage, gouache and colored pencil illustrations, which display a vibrant palette and all the energy of a flamenco dance."

The Colors of Us is another picture-book tribute to Katz's daughter. In this picture work, a young girl wants to use brown paint for her self-portrait. The girl's mother, an artist, takes her daughter for a walk through their neighborhood, pointing out the many different shades of brown skin on the people they meet. In the words of *Booklist* contributor Hazel Rochman, Katz's illustrations "celebrate the delicious colors of the individual people, all brown, and each one different."

A fussy baby is the star of *Counting Kisses,* a "delightfully simple, interactive story," according to *Childhood Education* reviewer Susan A. Miller. In this book the titular infant is coaxed to sleep by a series of kisses from her mother and father, her grandmother, her older sister, and even the family pets. "With buoyant cartoons rendered in a bouquet of vibrant pastel tones, Katz creates a book as irresistible as a baby's smile," observed a contributor in reviewing *Counting Kisses* for *Publishers Weekly*. In another family-centered work, *Counting Christmas*, a family prepares lights, presents, and cookies for their holiday celebration. "The collage, gouache, and colored-pencil illustrations are cheery and have a nice textural feel," wrote Linda Israelson in her *School Library Journal* review of this work.

A young girl creates a different style of headgear for each month of the year in *Twelve Hats for Lena: A Book of Months.* January's stocking cap is adorned with pictures of snowmen and sleds; March's hat is decorated with shamrocks. When December arrives, Lena cannot decide which end-of-the-calendar holiday to emphasize, so she designs an oversized headpiece that includes symbols from Hanukkah, Kwanzaa, and Christmas. "Katz's mixed-media artwork, primarily a combination of gouache and collage, has a kicky brightness that refreshes such traditional subjects as valentines, a spring flower garden, [and] American flags," remarked a contributor in *Publishers Weekly*.

Katz captures the affection between a mother and child in the art for her illustrated picture-book story Counting Kisses. (Illustration copyright © 2001 by Karen Katz. Reprinted by permission of Margaret K. McElderry Books, an imprint of Simon & Schuster Children's Publishing Division.)

Katz looks at holiday celebrations in *My First Kwanzaa* and *My First Chinese New Year*. In the former, a preschooler discusses the seven underlying principles of Kwanzaa, and her text and illustrations "combine to convey the wider sense of community that is the essence of the holiday," according to Rochman. In the latter, a young girl makes an altar to honor her ancestors, enjoys a meal with her relatives, and attends a parade through Chinatown. Katz "introduces readers to the traditions and importance of this holiday," noted a reviewer in *Publishers Weekly*. A number of critics offered praise for Katz's collage and mixed-media illustrations for *My First Chinese New Year*; for example, a contributor in *Kirkus Reviews* remarked that these pictures "capture the excitement that surrounds the celebration." In a more-recent work, *My First Ramadan*, Katz looks at the traditional holiday through the eyes of a young Muslim boy. "Children will appreciate the warm, personal narrative," Rochman observed.

To celebrate the United Nations International Day of Peace, Katz offered the self-illustrated *Can You Say Peace?*, "a simple, buoyantly illustrated look at the wonderful variety of lifestyles across the globe and the similarities of children everywhere," remarked Shelley B. Sutherland in *School Library Journal*. The work depicts children from a host of nations, including India, France, and Mexico, all who teach readers how to say "peace" in their native languages. While complimenting the "vibrantly colored patterns" and "soothing rhythmic lines" in Katz's illustrations, a *Kirkus Reviews* contributor stated that this "primer on nonviolence works in its simplicity." As Katz once remarked to *SATA*, "I am . . . fascinated by people from all over the world—what they look like, how they live, and the differences that make us all unique."

Katz once told *SATA*: "I am fascinated by babies and little kids. The simplest words and gestures can make them laugh. Sometimes while I'm standing in line at the supermarket and watching kids sitting in grocery carts, my best ideas are born." *Daddy Hugs 1 2 3* focuses on the warm relationship between a father and his infant. Describing the collage, gouache, and colored-pencil illustrations, *School Library Journal* reviewer Rachael Vilmar noted that the pictures "are made up of Katz's signature patterned objects and cutesy round-headed figures." In a companion volume, *Mommy Hugs*, Katz follows a baby and her mother through a busy day. "The sunny pictures capture familiar activities," remarked Linda Ludke in her reviw of this book for *School Library Journal.*

In the counting book *Ten Tiny Tickles* a baby's caregivers, including her parents, siblings, and grandparents, gently touch and tickle the infant as they bathe, diaper, and dress her. Katz's "illustrations depict loving family members with round faces, happy smiles, and rosy cheeks," as Maryann H. Owen stated in her *School Library Journal* review. A set of playful babies wriggles their toes, splashes in the tub, and cuddles before bedtime in *Ten Tiny Babies,* a companion counting book that employs rhyming couplets to describe infants' boundless energy. Writing in *Booklist,* Rochman noted that Katz's "folk art collages, very colorful," would en-

courage repeated readings of the title. In the words of a *Publishers Weekly* contributor, the work "is a solid addition to Katz's extensive oeuvre of adorableness."

In *Princess Baby* a toddler who has grown tired of such nicknames as "Cupcake" and "Giggly Goose" dons a shiny crown and fabulous jewels to firmly establish her "big girl" identity. Here Katz's artwork "supports the book's messages about children's rich fantasy life and their desire to assert themselves," commented Abby Nolan in *Booklist,* while Blair Christolon, writing in *School Library Journal,* applauded Katz's "cheerful view of a youngster's world." In a follow-up, *Princess Baby Night-Night,* the energetic protagonist cleverly resists her parents' efforts to get her into bed. "The simple, dialogue-based text is accessible and humorous," Shelle Rosenfeld noted in her *Booklist* review.

Shake It Up, Baby!, a self-illustrated title that comes complete with a small, plastic rattle embedded in its spine, encourages youngsters to bounce and wiggle along with the rhyming text. A critic in *Kirkus Reviews* complimented Katz's artwork here, citing her use of "varicolored backgrounds against which the babies romp." In *The Babies on the Bus,* the author/illustrator offers her take on the classic childhood song, "The Wheels on the Bus." According to Carolyn Janssen in *Booklist,* "Katz's familiar round-faced youngsters of different ethnicities will delight readers," and a *Kirkus Reviews* contributor commended the "endearing energy" of the bus-riding toddlers, describing the cast of characters in *The Babies on the Bus* as "lovingly unpretentious in their soft, enthusiastic movements."

In addition to her self-illustrated titles, Katz has provided artwork for books by other authors, among them *Subway* by Anastasia Suen. A work told in verse, *Subway* depicts a young girl's trip uptown with her mother. "Katz creates a merry metropolis that is both multicolored and multicultural," remarked a critic in *Publishers Weekly,* and *Booklist* contributor Gillian Engberg noted that the "jelly-bean colors in the artwork extend the sense of sunny excitement" in *Subway.*

Originally published in 1952, Margaret Wise Brown's *A Child's Good Morning Book* gets a fresh reinterpretation thanks to Katz's "profusion of bold colors, shapes, and patterns," as Carolyn Phelan stated in *Booklist.* "Katz's legions of fans will certainly rejoice to see her signature kewpie doll-like characters," a *Publishers Weekly* critic remarked. Katz also provided new illustrations for *Sleepy ABC,* a work by Brown that was first released in 1953. Katz's "cheerful, cuddly illustrations" for *Sleepy ABC* drew praise from a *Kirkus Reviews* contributor, and Amy Lilien-Harper predicted in *School Library Journal* that the "brightly colored mixed-media illustrations are likely to appeal to young children."

Katz's illustration projects include an updated edition of Margaret Wise Brown's **Sleep ABC.** (Illustration copyright © 2010 by Karen Katz. Reproduced by permission of HarperCollins Children's Books, a division of HarperCollins Publishers.)

"I have always loved to paint and experiment with pattern, texture, collage, and color," Katz once told *SATA*. "I have always been interested in folk art from around the world, Indian miniatures, Mexican ceramics, fabrics, Marc Chagall, Henri Matisse, children's art, and primitive painting. My careers have included costume design, quilt making, fabric artistry, and graphic design. Looking back, I can see that all of these passions and career choices have had a part in influencing me to become a children's book author and illustrator.

"When an idea for a story pops into my head, I ask these questions: Will a child want to read this book? Will parents want to read this book with their children? Will this book make a child laugh? Will this book make a parent and child feel something? Is there something visual here that will hold a child's interest? Will a child see something in a different way after reading this book? If the answer to most of those questions is 'yes,' then I know I'm on the right track.

"I am very lucky to get to do what I do. Everyday I go into my studio and have fun. Don't get me wrong: some days are very frustrating. Sometimes the colors are all wrong and the words don't sound right, but after I work at it for a while . . . and try to do it a different way . . . and think . . . and change the words or colors . . . and try some more . . . suddenly, there it is: a great page of writing or a great illustration. And nothing is more satisfying than that."

Biographical and Critical Sources

PERIODICALS

Booklist, September 1, 1997, Stephanie Zvirin, review of *Over the Moon: An Adoption Tale,* p. 133; September 15, 1999, Hazel Rochman, review of *The Colors of Us,* p. 268; February 1, 2001, Lauren Peterson, review of *Counting Kisses,* p. 1056; September 1, 2003, Hazel Rochman, review of *My First Kwanzaa,* p. 134; November 1, 2003, Hazel Rochman, review of *Counting Christmas,* p. 501; February 1, 2004, Gillian Engberg, review of *Subway,* p. 982; February 1, 2005, Linda Perkins, review of *My First Chinese New Year,* p. 965; July, 2005, Ilene Cooper, review of *Ten Tiny Tickles,* p. 1929; February 15, 2006, Ilene Cooper, review of *Mommy Hugs,* p. 102; May 15, 2006, Hazel Rochman, review of *Can You Say Peace?,* p. 50; June 1, 2007, Hazel Rochman, review of *My First Ramadan,* p. 83; January 1, 2008, Abby Nolan, review of *Princess Baby,* p. 95; July 1, 2008, Hazel Rochman, review of *Ten Tiny Babies,* p. 74; November 15, 2006, Carolyn Phelan, review of *A Child's Good Morning Book,* p. 51; December 1, 2008, Shelle Rosenfeld, review of *Princess Baby, Night-Night,* p. 58.

Childhood Education, spring, 2002, review of *Counting Kisses,* p. 173.

Kirkus Reviews, August 1, 2002, review of *Twelve Hats for Lena: A Book of Months,* p. 1134; November 1, 2003, review of *My First Kwanzaa,* p. 1317; November 15, 2004, review of *My First Chinese New Year,* p. 1090; June 1, 2006, review of *Can You Say Peace?,* p. 575; November 15, 2008, review of *A Child's Good Morning Book;* December 15, 2008, review of *Shake It Up, Baby!;* November 15, 2009, review of *Sleepy ABC;* June 1, 2011, review of *The Babies on the Bus.*

Publishers Weekly, August 4, 1997, review of *Over the Moon,* p. 73; June 5, 2000, review of *Where Is Baby's Belly Button?,* p. 96; November 27, 2000, review of *Counting Kisses,* p. 75; April 29, 2002, review of *Grandma and Me,* p. 73; July 15, 2002, review of *Twelve Hats for Lena,* p. 72; September 22, 2003, review of *Counting Christmas,* p. 69; February 2, 2004, review of *Subway,* p. 75; December 20, 2004, review of *My First Chinese New Year,* p. 61; June 25, 2007, review of *My First Ramadan,* p. 63; December 17, 2007, review of *Princess Baby,* p. 50; June 23, 2008, review of *Ten Tiny Babies,* p. 53; December 8, 2008, review of *A Child's Good Morning Book,* p. 57.

School Library Journal, February, 2001, Kathleen Kelly MacMillan, review of *Counting Kisses,* p. 102; October, 2002, Joy Fleishhacker, review of *Twelve Hats for Lena,* p. 114; October, 2003, Linda Israelson, review of *Counting Christmas,* and Virginia Walter, review of *My First Kwanzaa,* both p. 64; December, 2004, Rachel G. Payne, review of *My First Chinese New Year,* p. 112; February, 2004, Margaret R. Tassia, review of *Subway,* p. 124; June, 2005, Rachael Vilmar, review of *Daddy Hugs 1 2 3,* p. 118; July, 2005, Maryann H. Owen, review of *Ten Tiny Tickles,* p. 75; April, 2006, Linda Ludke, review of *Mommy Hugs,* p. 110; September, 2006, Shelley B. Sutherland, review of *Can You Say Peace?,* p. 174; August, 2007, Kristin Anderson, review of *My First Ramadan,* p. 82; March, 2008, Blair Christolon, review of *Princess Baby,* p. 168; September, 2008, Linda Ludke, review of *Ten Tiny Babies,* p. 151; January, 2009, Blair Christolon, reviews of *A Child's Good Morning Book,* p. 72, and *Princess Baby, Night-Night,* p. 78; January, 2010, Amy Lilien-Harper, review of *Sleepy ABC,* p. 69; June, 2011, Carolyn Janssen, review of *The Babies on the Bus,* p. 88.

ONLINE

Karen Katz Home Page, http://www.karenkatz.com (July 1, 2011).

Random House Web site, http://www.randomhouse.com/ (December 1, 2008), "Author Spotlight: Karen Katz."

Simon & Schuster Web site, http://www.simonandschuster.com/ (July 1, 2011), "Karen Katz Revealed."*

*   *   *

KIM, Susan 1958-

Personal

Born 1958; partner of Laurence Klavan (a writer). *Education:* Wesleyan University, B.A. (English and theatre).

Addresses

Home—New York, NY. *E-mail*—Susankim212@gmail.com.

Career

Writer and educator. Scriptwriter for animation studios, including Jumbo Pictures, 1994-96, Disney Channel, 2000-06, Vodka Capital, 2009-10, Anker Productions, 2010, and Little Airplane Productions. Producer and director of short films; former story editor. Goddard College, Plainfield, VT, teacher of writing in low-residency M.F.A. program, beginning 2006. Member, Ensemble Studio Theatre, beginning 1990.

Awards, Honors

Five Emmy award nominations; four Writers Guild award nominations; Writers Guild Award for Best Documentary, 1996; (with Laurence Klavan) American Library Association Quick Picks for Young Adults selection, and YALSA Great Graphic Novel for Teens selection, both 2010, both for *Brain Camp.*

Writings

FOR YOUNG ADULTS

(With Elissa Stein) *Flow: The Cultural Story of Menstruation,* St. Martin's Griffin (New York, NY), 2009.
(With partner, Laurence Klavan) *City of Spies,* illustrated by Pascal Dizinf, Roaring Book Press (New York, NY), 2010.
(With Laurence Klavan) *Brain Camp,* illustrated by Faith Erin Hicks, Roaring Book Press (New York, NY), 2010.

OTHER

(Adaptor) *The Joy Luck Club* (play; based on the novel by Amy Tan; produced in New York, NY), Dramatists Play Service (New York, NY), 1999.
Four from E.S.T. Marathon, '99 (collected one-act play), Dramatists Play Service (New York, NY), 2000.

Author of one-act plays *Death and the Maiden, Rapid Eye Movement, Dreamtime for Alice,* and *Memento Mori.* Author of film documentaries, including *Imaginary Witness: Hollywood and the Holocaust, Paving the Way,* and *Icebound,* and of scripts for television series, including *Square One TV,* 1987, *Mathnet,* 1991, *Happily Ever After,* 1997, *The Mystery Files of Shelby Woo,* 1997-98, *Fix and Foxi,* 2002, *Dragon Tales,* 2001-02, *Stanley,* 2002-03, *Third and Bird,* 2008, *Mama Mirabelle's Home Movies,* 2007-08, *Ni Hao, Kai-Lan,* 2008, *Martha Speaks,* 2008, *Speed Racer: The Next Generation,* 2008-09, *Arthur,* 2008-10, *Reading Rainbow,* and *Are You Afraid of the Dark?* Adapter of animated films into picture-book texts, including *Baby Beaver Rescue,* Simon & Schuster. Contributor to Web sites, including *Huffington Post* and *New Yorker* Online.

Adaptations

Several of Kim's teleplays have been adapted into book form, among them: *Hide and Seek,* adapted by Laura F. Marsh, National Geographic (Washington, DC), 2009; *Big Enough,* adapted by Marsh, National Geographic, 2009; *Play Ball!,* adapted by Marcy Goldberg Sacks, Houghton Mifflin Harcourt (Boston, MA), 2009; *What's in a Tail?,* adapted by Marsh, National Geographic, 2009; and *Kai-lan's Beach Day,* adapted by Maggie Testa, illustrated by Dave Walston, Simon Spotlight/Nickelodeon (New York, NY), 2010.

Sidelights

An award-winning playwright, television scriptwriter, blotter, and the author of several film documentaries, Susan Kim has also teamed up with her partner, award-winning mystery writer and playwright Laurence Klavan, to create the graphic novels *City of Spies* and *Brain Camp,* the latter featuring cartoon art by Faith Erin Hicks. Turning to nonfiction, Kim has also coauthored the thought-provoking *Flow: The Cultural Story of Menstruation,* joining fellow playwright Elissa Stein to chronicle the history of menses throughout history with a sometimes irreverent eye toward how it has shaped the role of women in various cultures. "There is probably no better book for moms who want their daughters to respect themselves in every aspect," concluded Donna Chavez in her laudatory review of *Flow* for *Booklist.* Based in New York City, Kim divides her time between writing, blogging, and teaching dramatic writing at Goddard Collage, where she instructs students in the school's low-residency M.F.A. writing program.

Featuring artwork by Pascal Dizin, *City of Spies* mixes history and intrigue into a story that draws readers into the life of two preteens who are caught up in America's spy hysteria during World War II. Kim was inspired to begin the story for the graphic novel after speaking with an elderly friend "who grew up in a wealthy but dysfunctional household, much like Evelyn in our book," as the coauthor later explained to *Comic Book Reporter Online* contributor Alex Dueben. "She said that when she was a kid, she used to hunt for Nazi spies on the upper east side of Manhattan during the early 1940s. I casually told [fellow writer] Laurence this over dinner one night, and he immediately said, 'That would make a great movie.' We stayed late at the restaurant, sketching out the rough story on the tablecloth, then spent the next year writing it."

City of Spies serves up a mix of what a *Publishers Weekly* reviewer characterized as "a good old-fashioned adventure story and rip-roaring fun." Living in relative isolation in a wealthy section of New York City, ten-year-old Evelyn spends a lot of time creating comics drawings featuring cartoon superhero Zirconium Man in order to bring excitement to her life. When she is sent to stay with an aunt living in the city's German neighborhood, the girl makes friends with the son of a resident of Aunt Lia's building. The friends' imaginative natures allow them to imagine that German spies are living all around them, and they decide to help their country by becoming spy hunters. In typical "the boy who cried wolf" fashion, Evelyn and Tony eventually stumble on a real ring of actual Nazi spies, but no adult will believe them.

Praising Dizin's "expressive" retro-styled *ligne claire* illustrations for *City of Spies,* Jesse Karp added that "Kim and Klavan put a sophisticated spin on classic boys' adventure story elements and handle issues of friendship, economic class, and abandonment." In *Kirkus Reviews* a critic characterized the graphic novel as "well-paced" and "well-drawn," predicting that Kim and Klavan's story "will surely appeal to thoughtful young readers." For Douglas P. Davey, writing in *School Library Journal, City of Spies* stands as a "complex, well-executed work [that] combines a modern, emotional narrative with a European comic style." Davey went on to laud Dizin's decision to vary his illustration style, moving from the two-dimensional, Hergé-inspired drawing to a "more traditional American style" when depicting Evelyn's own Zirconium Man comics.

Another collaboration between Kim and Klavan, the graphic novel *Brain Camp,* introduces fourteen-year-olds Jenna and Lucas, whose misfit status makes each of them ineligible even for admission to their local summer camp. When the teens are among a larger group of underachievers accepted into a high-profile S.A.T. preparatory camp, their parents are surprised but relieved. Unfortunately, Camp Fielding has a hidden agenda: to transform slackers into brilliant zombies, and Jenna and Lucas must now team up to battle the powers of evil for the right to goof off. A "fun" read for mature younger teens, according to Davey in *School Library Journal, Brain Camp* boasts a plot that "moves well and is illustrated with excellent full-color artwork." In *Publishers Weekly* a reviewer also praised the "bright and expressive drawing" Hicks contributes to *Brain Camp,* while Karp concluded in *Booklist* that the coauthors' "far-out . . . climax mixes with genuine insight into . . . handling the pressures of [school] performance."

Biographical and Critical Sources

PERIODICALS

Booklist, November 15, 2009, Donna Chavez, review of *Flow: The Cultural Story of Menstruation,* p. 6; March 15, 2010, Jesse Karp, review of *City of Spies,* p. 60; May 15, 2010, Jesse Karp, review of *Brain Camp,* p. 33.
Bulletin of the Center for Children's Books, October, 2010, April Spisak, review of *Brain Camp,* p. 79.
Kirkus Reviews, April 15, 2010, review of *City of Spies.*
Marie Claire, December, 2009, Lauren Iannotti, interview with Kim and Elissa Stein, p. 86.
Publishers Weekly, April 5, 2010, review of *City of Spies,* p. 64; June 14, 2010, review of *Brain Camp,* p. 55.
School Library Journal, May, 2010, Douglas P. Davey, review of *City of Spies,* p. 141; July, 2010, Douglas P. Davey, review of *Brain Camp,* p. 106.

ONLINE

Comic Book Resources Web site, http://www.comicbook resources.com/ (April 29, 2010), Alex Dueben, interview with Kim and Laurence Klavan.
Ensemble Studio Theatre Web site, http://ensemblestudio theatre.org/ (August 15, 2011), "Susan Kim."*

L

LAGOS, Alexander

Personal

Born in NJ; married; has children.

Addresses

Home—Brooklyn, NY. *Agent*—Jill Grinberg, Anderson Grinberg Literary Management, 244 5th Ave., 11th FL, New York, NY 10001; jill@grinbergliterary.com. *E-mail*—info@thesonsoflibertybook.com.

Career

Musician and writer. Toured with rock band FEEL; Barnes & Noble, Brooklyn, NY, former manager.

Writings

"SONS OF LIBERTY" GRAPHIC-NOVEL SERIES

(With brother Joseph Lagos) *The Sons of Liberty,* illustrated by Steve Walker and Oren Kramek, Random House Children's Books (New York, NY), 2010.
(With Joseph Lagos) *Death and Taxes,* illustrated by Steve Walker and Oren Kramek, Random House Children's Books (New York, NY), 2011.

Sidelights

Alexander Lagos teamed up with his older brother, Joseph Lagos, to create and write the "Sons of Liberty" graphic-novel series, which weaves together superhero elements of classic adventure comics with actual events and people from U.S. history. Brought to life through dramatic sequential artwork by Steve Walker and Oren Kramek, the "Sons of Liberty" books were designed by the Lagos brothers as a way to attract the interest of comic-book fans, history buffs, and even reluctant readers. In addition to conveying Joseph Lagos's fasci-

nation with colonial-era history, the stories also prompt readers to ponder the actions and choices that determined the course of the nation's founding. In a review of the first installment in the Lagos brothers' graphic-novel series, a *Kirkus Reviews* writer cited the "Sons of Liberty" books for their "distinctly different take on the American Revolution."

Born in Elizabeth, New Jersey, as the son of Uruguayan immigrants, Lagos moved with his family to Texas as a young child. His passion was music while growing up, and he performed with the alternative rock band FEEL for several years before settling down in Brooklyn, New York, finding a job, and beginning his family. When Joseph began working on his idea for a history novel that would feature superhero elements, he enlisted his creative younger brother to help with the brainstorming, plotting, and writing. Because Alexander had left the Lone Star State and now lived in Brooklyn, the two brothers often relied on communication technology to engage in their literary endeavor.

The Sons of Liberty is set in the tobacco-growing region of rural Pennsylvania, outside the city of Philadelphia. Brothers Graham and Brody are slaves brought from Africa, and they decide to escape from their work in the tobacco fields after their master behaves particularly cruelly. Advised to search for a man named Benjamin, they first locate and are befriended by inventor and statesman Benjamin Franklin. Franklin has a son, William, who shares his father's inventive genius, but he employs it to destructive ends. After he uses Graham and Brody in an experiment, the brothers are left with unusual powers that they must now learn to harness. Still in hiding, they continue their search for the proper Benjamin and find him in the person of Quaker abolitionist Benjamin Lay. Lay channels the brothers' new abilities by instructing them in the African fighting technique called Dambe. Now able to defend themselves, Graham and Brody decide to do battle against roaming slave hunters. When tragedy strikes, they must also avenge the death of Lay, their friend and mentor. The brothers' adventures continue in *Death and Taxes,* as tensions over British policies within the North American colonies begin to flare into violence.

Predicting that the colorful digitized artwork in *The Sons of Liberty* will attract younger readers, Jesse Karp added in his *Booklist* review of the first volume in the Lagos brothers' series that the incorporation of "well-researched (but embellished) history" with well-realized characters and a cliffhanger ending "makes for an uncommonly complex, literate, and satisfying adventure." Reviewing the same installment in *Voice of Youth Advocates,* Kat Kan suggested that the brothers' decision to mix "historical fiction with super hero elements . . . could attract reluctant readers," and a *Publishers Weekly* critic predicted that anyone other than a stickler for historical veracity "should appreciate the fast pace and creativity" on exhibit in the pages of the illustrated saga. "Not a source of accurate history," the *Kirkus Reviews* contributor admitted, *The Sons of Liberty* is nonetheless "hard to put down."

Biographical and Critical Sources

PERIODICALS

Booklist, June 1, 2010, Jesse Karp, review of *The Sons of Liberty* p. 70.
Kirkus Reviews, April 15, 2010, review of *The Sons of Liberty.*
Library Journal, March 15, 2011, Martha Cornog, review of *Death and Taxes,* p. 104.
Publishers Weekly, May 3, 2010, review of *The Sons of Liberty,* p. 55.
School Library Journal, July, 2010, Douglas P. Davey, review of *The Sons of Liberty,* p. 106.
Voice of Youth Advocates, August, 2010, Kat Kan, review of *The Sons of Liberty,* p. 238.

ONLINE

Andrew and Joseph Lagos Home Page, http://thesonsof libertybook.com (July 15, 2011).
Melissa Buron Web log, http://melissaburon.livejournal. com/ (March 20, 2010), Melissa Buron, interview with Joseph Lagos.*

*   *   *

LEE, Y.S. 1974-
(Ying S. Yee)

Personal

Born 1974, in Singapore; immigrated to Canada; married; has children. *Education:* B.A.; M.A.; Ph.D. (Victorian literature and culture), 2004. *Hobbies and other interests:* Yoga.

Addresses

Home—Kingston, Ontario, Canada. *Agent*—Rowan Lawton, Peters, Fraser & Dunlop, 34-43 Russell St., London WC2B 5HA, England; rlawton@pdf.co.uk. *E-mail*—ying@yslee.com.

Career

Writer.

Awards, Honors

John Spray Mystery Award nomination, Canadian Children's Book Centre, 2011, for *A Spy in the House.*

Writings

(As Ying S. Lee) *Masculinity and the English Working Class: Studies in Victorian Autobiography and Fiction,* Routledge (New York, NY), 2007.

"THE AGENCY" NOVEL SERIES

A Spy in the House, Candlewick Press (Somerville, MA), 2010.
The Body at the Tower, Candlewick Press (Somerville, MA), 2010.
The Traitor and the Tunnel, Walker Books (London, England), 2011, Candlewick Press (Somerville, MA), 2012.

Author's work has been translated into several languages, including French, German, Italian, and Spanish.

Sidelights

Readers are drawn back to the streets of Victorian London in Canadian writer Y.S. Lee's four-part "The Agency" novel series, which includes *A Spy in the House, The Body at the Tower,* and *The Traitor and the Tunnel.* Born in Singapore, Yee was raised in Ontario with a fascination for nineteenth-century British society and history. While earning her Ph.D. in Victorian literature and culture, she produced a thesis that she eventually published as *Masculinity and the English Working Class: Studies in Victorian Autobiography and Fiction.* She was also inspired by her research into the subject to develop the idea for a story featuring a detective agency operating during the late 1800s, an agency run solely by women. This idea, combined with Lee's own experiences living and studying in London, became her "The Agency" novels, featuring talented detective Mary Quinn.

Cover of Y.S. Lee's historical mystery **A Spy in the House,** *part of her "Agency" series.* (Candlewick Press, 2010. Book jacket photograph copyright © 2010 by Scott Nobles. Reproduced by permission of Candlewick Press, Somerville, MA.)

When readers meet her in *A Spy in the House,* seventeen-year-old Quinn is a street-smart orphan and convicted thief who is alive only because she was rescued from the hangman's noose by a female prison warden who took pity on her. For the last five years, she has lived at Miss Scrimshaw's Academy for Girls, getting an education in knowledge and manners. Quinn now learns that this education has been to prepare her to work as an undercover investigator and Quinn's first Agency assignment is to infiltrate the household of a wealthy London merchant. Disguised as a hired companion for the merchant's spoiled daughter, she quickly learns the lay of the land in the Thorold home, but her assignment to bring to light information regarding Mr. Thorold's lost cargo ships is soon put on the back burner when murder is done and Quinn's heart is captured by handsome fellow sleuth James Easton. Drawing readers into what a *Publishers Weekly* critic described as "the richly described underbelly of Victorian London," *A Spy in the House* features a plot with a "feminist tenor." Quinn story is studded with "classic elements of Victorian mystery and melodrama," added *School Library Journal* contributor Cheri Dobbs, and "historical details

are woven seamlessly into the plot." Comparing Lee's characters to those in the Regency novels of Jane Austen, Ilene Cooper added in *Booklist* that the story's "mystery is solid" and "the secret of Mary's parentage" serves as "an interesting string to run through succeeding books" in the "Agency" series.

The Body at the Tower finds Quinn working undercover as a boy apprentice builder, where she hopes to unmask a murderer at a construction site located near London's Houses of Parliament. Now she must draw on her knowledge of the rough ways of street life as she bunks in low-rent lodgings and brawls with the rest of the crew. In *The Traitor and the Tower* a petty thief infiltrates Buckingham Palace and Queen Victoria hires the Agency to ferret him or her out. Quinn now plays the part of palace domestic, but her search for the thief is sidelined when a murder involving a friend of the Prince of Wales exposes a connection between the murderer and Quinn's own father. As she watches the Royal Family manipulate the facts to protect its interest, Mary also draws on her friendship with Easton as she searches for answers of her own, particularly to the source of a secret tunnel underneath Buckingham Palace. "Lee does a wonderful job . . . taking the reader deep into another time and place," asserted Lona Trulove in her *Voice of Youth Advocates* review of *The Body at the Tower,* and *School Library Journal* critic Necia Blundy noted the "fiery relationship" between Quinn and Easton that also adds romantic tension to Yee's story. "Smart and suspenseful," according to *Booklist* critic Cooper, *The Body at the Tower* casts a "solid heroine" in a story that effectively evokes "life in Victorian England."

Biographical and Critical Sources

PERIODICALS

Booklist, January 1, 2010, Ilene Cooper, review of *A Spy in the House,* p. 70; December 15, 2010, Ilene Cooper, review of *The Body at the Tower,* p. 54.
Bulletin of the Center for Children's Books, April, 2010, Elizabeth Bush, review of *A Spy in the House,* p. 344.
Kirkus Reviews, February 15, 2010, review of *A Spy in the House.*
Publishers Weekly, February 1, 2010, review of *A Spy in the House,* p. 51.
School Librarian, winter, 2010, D. Telford, review of *The Body at the Tower,* p. 244.
School Library Journal, April, 2010, Cheri Dobbs, review of *A Spy in the House,* p. 162; September, 2010, Necia Blundy, review of *The Body at the Tower,* p. 157.
Voice of Youth Advocates, June, 2010, Lona Trulove, review of *A Spy in the House,* p. 156; October, 2010, Lona Trulove, review of *The Body at the Tower,* p. 352.

ONLINE

Y.S. Lee Home Page, http://yslee.com (August 11, 2011).

LEVY, Debbie 1957-
(Deborah Marian Levy)

Personal

Born 1957, in Silver Spring, MD; daughter of Harold and Jutta Levy; married Richard S. Hoffman; children: Alex Hoffman, Ben Hoffman. *Education:* University of Virginia, B.A. (government and foreign affairs); University of Michigan, J.D./M.A. (law and world politics). *Religion:* Jewish. *Hobbies and other interests:* Kayaking, swimming, fishing, walking in the woods, reading, gardening, bowling.

Addresses

Home—MD. *E-mail*—debbi@debbielevybooks.com.

Career

Author, journalist, and attorney. Wilmer, Cutler & Pickering, Washington, DC, attorney for six years, specializing in international trade and immigration law; American Lawyer Media/Legal Times, editor and vice president for six years.

Member

Society of Children's Book Writers and Illustrators, Authors Guild, Children's Book Guild of Washington, DC.

Awards, Honors

Parents' Choice Award, 2010, Sydney Taylor Award Notable Book for Older Readers selection, Association of Jewish Libraries, and Cooperative Children's Book Center Choices listee, both 2011, and Charlotte Award nomination, State of New York, 2012, all for *The Year of Goodbyes.*

Writings

Underwater, Darby Creek Publishing (Plain City, OH), 2007.
Maybe I'll Sleep in the Bathtub Tonight, and Other Funny Bedtime Poems, illustrated by Stephanie Buscema, Sterling Publishing (New York, NY), 2010.
The Year of Goodbyes: A True Story of Friendship, Family, and Farewells, Disney-Hyperion Books (New York, NY), 2010.

Contributor of stories to periodicals, including *Highlights for Children.*

NONFICTION

Kidding around Washington, D.C.: A Fun-filled, Fact-packed Travel and Activity Book, John Muir Publications (Santa Fe, NM), 1997, second edition, 2000.

Civil Liberties, Lucent Books (San Diego, CA), 2000.
Medical Ethics, Lucent Books (San Diego, CA), 2001.
Bigotry, Lucent Books (San Diego, CA), 2002.
Lyndon B. Johnson, Lerner Publications (Minneapolis, MN), 2003.
Maryland, Kidhaven Press (San Diego, CA), 2004.
Slaves on a Southern Plantation, Kidhaven Press (San Diego, CA), 2004.
The Berlin Wall, Blackbirch Press (Farmington Hills, MI), 2004.
The Vietnam War, Lerner Publications (Minneapolis, MN), 2004.
James Monroe, Lerner Publications (Minneapolis, MN), 2005.
John Quincy Adams, Lerner Publications (Minneapolis, MN), 2005.
Sunken Treasure, KidHaven Press (Farmington Hills, MI), 2005.
The World Trade Center, KidHaven Press (Farmington Hills, MI), 2005.
Rutherford B. Hayes, Lerner Publications (Minneapolis, MN), 2007.
Richard Wright: A Biography, Twenty-first Century Books (Minneapolis, MN), 2008.
The Signing of the Magna Carta, Twenty-first Century Books (Minneapolis, MN), 2008.

Sidelights

A former newspaper editor and attorney, Debbie Levy has established a third career as the author of nonfiction books that include *Richard Wright: A Biography, The Berlin Wall,* and *Bigotry,* as well as of the verse work *The Year of Goodbyes: A True Story of Friendship, Family, and Farewells,* a Sydney Taylor Award Notable Book. "I think in some ways fiction is most challenging," Levy remarked in a *Teacher Librarian* interview with Julie Prince, discussing her ability to transition between several genres. Although her law training taught her to enjoy research and scouting for sources that are solid and varied, Levy also indulges her whimsical side in *Maybe I'll Sleep in the Bathtub Tonight, and Other Funny Bedtime Poems,* in which she teams up with artist Stephanie Buscema to create "a fun, hip take on traditional bedtime books," according to a *Publishers Weekly* reviewer.

Levy's debut title, *Kidding around Washington, D.C.: A Fun-filled, Fact-packed Travel and Activity Book,* was followed by *Civil Liberties,* which examines the right to privacy, book banning, religious freedoms, and other issues. According to *Booklist* critic Shelle Rosenfeld, the author's "well-chosen examples of events and court cases effectively illustrate terms and concepts." In *Medical Ethics* Levy explores the controversies surrounding genetic engineering and assisted suicide, among other topics, while in *Bigotry* she focuses her study on racism, anti-Semitism, and homophobia. "The text is clear and accessible," Mary R. Hofmann commented in her *School Library Journal* review of *Medical Ethics,* while *Booklist* reviewer Roger Leslie deemed *Bigotry* an "informative, forthright overview" of a perennial social ill.

Cover of Debbie Levy's The Year of Goodbyes: A True Story of Friendship, Family, and Farewells. *(Disney-Hyperion Books, 2010. Reproduced by permission of Disney-Hyperion, an imprint of Disney Book Group LLC. All rights reserved.)*

Levy's biographical works includes *Lyndon B. Johnson,* a balanced portrait of the thirty-sixth president of the United States that discusses his successes in the legislative arena as well as his struggles to find a peaceful resolution in Vietnam. "Levy affirms LBJ's legacy as the strongest civil-rights advocate who ever occupied the White House," remarked William McLoughlin in a *School Library Journal* appraisal. In *Richard Wright* the author chronicles the life of the celebrated African-American writer who remains best known for his searing novel *Native Son* and his autobiography *Black Boy.* Levy "does a fine job of placing Wright's personal life in the context of black history," Hazel Rochman stated in her *Booklist* review of Levy's profile.

Underwater, Levy's first work of fiction, centers on Gabe Livingston, a lonely, temperamental youth who escapes from life's problems by caring for his pet fish and playing his favorite computer game. Writing in *School Library Journal,* Laura Lutz noted that the complex work "deserves an audience and should find one with male readers."

The Year of Goodbyes combines excerpts from Levy's German-born mother's childhood *poesiealbum* (poetry album) as well as an original free verse to create "a poignant portrait of . . . life in 1938 Nazi Germany that crackles with adolescent vitality," in the words of a *Publishers Weekly* critic. The work depicts the growing specter of anti-Semitism under German chancellor Adolf Hitler as seen through the eyes of twelve-year-old Hamburg resident Jutta Salzburg (Levy's mother), whose family desperately seeks refuge in the United States. *The Year of Goodbyes* presents "not only the history of that era but also a universal experience that readers young and old would find compelling," Levy explained to Prince: "living as a member of a scorned group, clinging to normalcy in the face of a crazy world, wanting desperately both to flee and to stay in the place that is your home but also your oppressor." Jennifer Schultz, writing in *School Library Journal,* described the work as "a verse novel slim in length but long on beauty, power, and anguish."

"Since I write in a variety of genres (nonfiction, fiction, and poetry) and for a variety of ages (from young children to young adults) I often am asked which type of writing I enjoy the most," Levy commented to *SATA.* "I can't answer that question because I love them all! But I can answer a related question, which is what I hope my writing does, at least in some small way, for readers of different ages. Let's take the question one group at a time: Small, Medium, and Large.

"Small: For the youngest children, I hope to excite them about words, language, stories, and reading.

"Medium: For the middle group, I hope to do what I try to do for the 'Small' group, plus give them reasons to engage in the important practice of immersion in books. Why? Because reading books involves sustained periods of thought and interpretation of another person's point of view, and these are very good and important abilities.

"Large: For the young adults, I hope to take them outside of themselves, an exercise that can also lead them back to themselves, with new perspective. I want to be honest about the world without being oppressive. And—I still hope to excite them about words, language, stories, and reading."

Biographical and Critical Sources

PERIODICALS

Booklist, February 1, 2000, Shelle Rosenfeld, review of *Civil Liberties,* p. 1013; February 1, 2002, Roger Leslie, review of *Bigotry,* p. 933; December 1, 2005, Hazel Rochman, review of *The World Trade Center,* p. 59; December 1, 2007, Hazel Rochman, review of *Richard Wright: A Biography,* p. 33; February 15,

2010, Kay Weisman, review of *The Year of Goodbyes: A True Story of Friendship, Family, and Farewells,* p. 75; March 1, 2010, Hazel Rochman, review of *Maybe I'll Sleep in the Bathtub Tonight and Other Funny Bedtime Poems,* p. 75.

Kirkus Reviews, February 15, 2010, review of *The Year of Goodbyes.*

Publishers Weekly, January 25, 2010, review of *The Year of Goodbyes,* p. 119; February 8, 2010, review of *Maybe I'll Sleep in the Bathtub Tonight and Other Funny Bedtime Poems,* p. 48.

School Library Journal, April, 2001, Mary R. Hofmann, review of *Medical Ethics,* p. 163; February, 2003, William McLoughlin, review of *Lyndon B. Johnson,* p. 162; April, 2005, Anne Chapman Callaghan, review of *The Berlin Wall,* p. 155; December, 2007, Carol Jones Collins, review of *Richard Wright,* p. 154; January, 2008, Karen Scott, review of *The Signing of the Magna Carta,* p. 140; April, 2008, Laura Lutz, review of *Underwater,* p. 144; April, 2010, Julie Roach, review of *Maybe I'll Sleep in the Bathtub Tonight and Other Funny Bedtime Poems,* p. 147; May, 2010, Jennifer Schultz, review of *The Year of Goodbyes,* p. 118.

Teacher Librarian, June, 2010, Julie Prince, "Lawyer, Journalist, Spinmeister? An Interview with Debbie Levy," p. 68.

Washington Post, November 8, 1998, Debbie Levy, "Last Train Out: A 60-year-old Diary Says Nothing of the Terror, but Its Message Is Crystal Clear."

Washington Post Magazine, January 16, 2011, Kris Coronado, "Whatever Happened to . . . the Woman Who Kept a Diary in Nazi Germany?"

ONLINE

Debbie Levy Home Page, http://www.debbielevybooks. com (July 1, 2011).

Debbie Levy Web log, http://www.debbielevy.blogspot. com/ (July 1, 2011).

Year of Goodbyes Web log, http://theyearofgoodbyes. blogspot.com/ (July 1, 2011).

*   *   *

LEVY, Deborah Marian
See LEVY, Debbie

M

MAGUIRE, Eden

Personal

Born in England; children: two daughters. *Education:* Birmingham University, Ph.D. (English literature). *Hobbies and other interests:* Horseback riding, travel, cinema, theatre, art history, painting.

Addresses

Home—CO; Yorkshire, England.

Career

Novelist.

Writings

"BEAUTIFUL DEAD" YOUNG-ADULT NOVEL SERIES

Jonas, Sourcebooks Fire (Naperville, IL), 2009.
Arizona, Hodder Children's (London, England), 2009, Sourcebooks Fire (Naperville, IL), 2010.
Summer, Hodder Children's (London, England), 2009, Sourcebooks Fire (Naperville, IL), 2011.
Phoenix, Hodder Children's (London, England), 2009, Sourcebooks Fire (Naperville, IL), 2011.

"DARK ANGEL" YOUNG-ADULT NOVEL SERIES

Dark Angel, Hachette (New York, NY), 2011.
Twisted Heart, Hachette (New York, NY), 2011.

Also author of screenplay adaptation of *Jonas.*

Sidelights

British writer Eden Maguire taps the paranormal romance tradition established in Emily Brontë's classic *Wuthering Heights* in her "Beautiful Dead" novel series, which includes *Jonas, Arizona, Summer,* and *Phoenix.* A second series of paranormal romances, which begins with the novels *Dark Angel* and *Twisted Heart,* focuses on the passion shared by Tania and Orlando and the efforts of reclusive rock legend Zoran to use his power as a Dark Angel to lure Tania away to the dark side.

Readers are transported to Ellerton High in *Jonas,* as Phoenix becomes the fourth student to meet a tragic and unusual death. Jonas was the first, dying in a motorcycle accident less than a year before. Then came the deaths of Summer and Arizona. While family and friends mourn the young man's death in a knife fight, his girlfriend Darina begins to have visions of the dead teens. Soon Phoenix appears to her, transformed into a zombie, and explains that the four have been welcomed into the Beautiful Dead: a group of young people unjustly killed who are allowed ten days to return to earth and seek justice before moving on to their spiritual resting place. Darina is given permission to visit Phoenix while his soul is in this limbo: in exchange, she promises to help each of the four Beautiful Dead to resolve things left undone at their deaths. Jonas returns first, followed by Arizona (a tragic drowning), Summer (a random shooting), and Phoenix. Each appears in human form but is recognizable to Darina due to their tattoo of angel wings.

Several readers noted the influences of Stephenie Meyer's "Twilight" books on Maguire's "Beautiful Dead" novels. A *Publishers Weekly* critic wrote in a review of *Jonas* that the author's saga plays out in "a series of emotional confrontations, sweet interludes between the lovers, and adrenaline-urging moments of physical threat." "A fun read that blends elements of several genres," according to *School Library Journal* critic Kathleen E. Graver, the first "Beautiful Dead" novel will attract teenage romance fans who "will empathize with Darina and her love and grief for Phoenix."

The first installment in Eden Maguire's "Beautiful Dead" series, **Jonas** *features cover art by Julia Starr.* (Sourcebooks Fire, 2010. Book cover design by Julia Starr. Reproduced by permission of Sourcebooks, Inc.)

Biographical and Critical Sources

PERIODICALS

Booklist, October 1, 2010, Cindy Welch, review of *Arizona,* p. 83.
Kirkus Reviews, March 1, 2010, review of *Jonas.*
Publishers Weekly, February 8, 2010, review of *Jonas,* p. 52.
School Librarian, spring, 2010, Sandra Bennett, review of *Arizona,* p. 51.
School Library Journal, March, 2010, Kathleen E. Graver, review of *Jonas,* p. 162; December, 2010, Chris Shoemaker, review of *Arizona,* p. 120.

ONLINE

Cynsations Web log, http://cynthialeitichsmith.blogspot.com/ (September 17, 2010), Cynthia Leitich Smith, interview with Maguire.
Eden Maguire Home Page, http://www.beautifuldead.com. (August 15, 2011).*

MARTÍNEZ, Rueben 1940-

Personal

Born 1940, in Miami, AZ; son of copper miners; children: three. *Education:* Attended barber school.

Addresses

Office—Librería Martinez Book & Art Galleries, 216 N. Broadway, Santa Ana, CA 92701.

Career

Bookstore owner, literacy advocate, barber, and writer. Worked variously as a grocery clerk and crane operator in Los Angeles, CA; barber and hair stylist in Los Angeles and Santa Ana, CA; Librería Martínez Book & Art Galleries, Santa Ana, owner and founder, 1993—; Libros para Niños (children's bookstore), Santa Ana, owner and founder, 2000. Cofounder of Latino Book & Family Festival. Member of board of directors, *Críticas* magazine and Families in School; member of advisory board, L.A. Best; founding member, Santa Ana's Reading City committee. Chapman University, presidential fellow, 2008—. Regular contributor to television shows on Univision, Telemundo, and PBS; weekly guest reader for *El Club de Libritos,* Univision.

Awards, Honors

Named Spanish Language Community Advocate of the Year, *Críticas,* 2002; MacArthur fellowship, John D. and Catherine T. MacArthur Foundation, 2004; named among 100 People Who Shaped Orange County, *Orange County Register,* 2005; honorary L.H.D., Whittier College, 2005; Authors Guild Award for Distinguished Service to the Literary Community, 2006; Local Heroes Award, Union Bank/KCET, 2009; Latino Spirit Award, California Latino Legislative Caucus; Small Business of the Year award, Hispanic Chamber of Commerce; HEEF Golden Apple Award; commendations from United Way, State of California, City of Los Angeles, U.S. Congress, California Teachers Association, California Library Association, Orange County Human Relations Commission, City of Santa Ana, Santa Ana Unified School District, Rancho Santiago Community College District, Chapman University, California State University at Fullerton, and University of California at Irvine.

Writings

Once upon a Time: Traditional Latin American Tales/ Había una vez: Cuentos tradicionales latinoamericanos, illustrated by Raúl Colón, translated by David Unger, Rayo (New York, NY), 2010.

Sidelights

Barber-turned-bookseller Rueben Martínez is the founder and owner of Santa Ana, California-based Librería Martínez Book & Art Galleries, one of the most

Rueben Martínez's bilingual story collection Once upong a Time: Traditional Latin-American Tales *features artwork by Raúl Colón.* (Rayo, 2010. Illustration copyright © 2010 by Raúl Colón. Reproduced by permission of Rayo, an imprint of HarperCollins Publishers.)

successful retailers of Spanish-language publications in the United States. A tireless advocate for literacy within the North-American Hispanic community, Martínez received a MacArthur fellowship—known as a "genius grant"—in 2004 for his efforts, becoming the first bookseller to be so honored. "I tell students to read one story a day," he remarked to *Publishers Weekly* interviewer Bridget Kinsella. "If you read 20 minutes every day, then you will read a million words in a year. We try to make reading contagious, like a bad cold."

Born in 1940 in the small mining town of Miami, Arizona, Martínez became an avid reader at a young age, rising early each day to pore over his neighbor's newspaper before they awoke. At age eighteen he ventured to Los Angeles, California, working as a crane operator and a grocery-store clerk and then attending barber school. Recalling the lackluster selection of reading materials that were available at the barbershop he frequented while growing up, Martínez vowed to do better for his own customers, and when he opened his salon in Santa Ana, he started bringing copies of his favorite books into the store, a collection that eventually grew to 200 titles.

Soon, Martínez was lending both English-and Spanish-language books to his patrons, and in 1993 he opened a small bookstore inside the barbershop. The venture proved tremendously successful, and he moved to larger quarters in 1999; he has more recently opened a second store in nearby Linwood. Martínez also owns Libros para Niños in Santa Ana, where he specializes in children's books. Each of his stores comes equipped with its own barber chair. "It's a symbol for our people, especially kids, that you can do anything you desire," he told *USA Today* contributor Marco R. della Cava.

As Martínez's reputation has soared, he has become a much-sought-after speaker, appearing at schools and bookstores across the nation, as well as at England's Oxford University and the Sorbonne in Paris, France. He also joined with actor Edward James Olmos to establish the Latino Book & Family Festival, which recognizes the work of Chicano and Latino authors. Despite his increasing fame, Martínez remains humble about his mission, promoting a love of books. "We are a community-based business," he stated to *Reading Today* contributor John Micklos, Jr. "We are the mountain that goes to Muhammad with good literature. Those pages, they talk. We want to give people the opportunity to continue having those pages talk to them. Education is freedom."

In 2010 Martínez joined the ranks of published authors with the release of *Once upon a Time: Traditional Latin American Tales/Había una vez: Cuentos tradicionales latinoamericanos*. A collection of seven classic folktales told in both English and Spanish, this book includes "The Wedding Rooster," a cumulative tale, and "The Tlacuache and the Coyote," a trickster story. Narda McCarthy, writing in *School Library Journal*, applauded

Martínez's "pleasant, uncomplicated prose," and *Booklist* critic Andrew Medlar observed that the stories in *Once upon a Time* "make a strong contribution to a still relatively empty canon of bilingual, Latin American folktale offerings."

Biographical and Critical Sources

PERIODICALS

Booklist, February 15, 2010, Andrew Medlar, review of *Once upon a Time: Traditional Latin American Tales/ Había una vez: Cuentos tradicionales latinoamericanos*, p. 73.

Entrepreneur, April, 2005, April Y. Pennington, "Well-read: From Cutting Hair to Inspiring Hispanic Readership, Rueben Martínez's Novel Idea Is a Story for All Ages," p. 172.

Kirkus Reviews, March 1, 2010, review of *Once upon a Time*.

Los Angeles Times, April 28, 1996, Dennis McLellan and Alex Garcia, "'The Best in Books and Hair': Rueben Martínez Is a Barber and a Bookseller, but His Real Job Is Keeping Kids in School," p. E1; October 20, 2002, Jennifer Mena, "Passion That Speaks Volumes"; September 28, 2004, James Ricci, "Sowing Literacy Brings Windfall," p. 1.

New American, March 21, 2005, Warren Mass, "Grooming Minds," p. 32.

Orange County Register, August 11, 2006, Justino Aguila, "His Next Chapter."

People, November 8, 2004, "¡Viven los libros! Rueben Martínez Turns a Bookstore That Began in His Barbershop into a Crusade to Give Hispanics More to Read," p. 132.

Reading Today, February-March, 2006, John Micklos, Jr., "The Barber Who Loved Books," p. 11.

Publishers Weekly, November 29, 2004, Bridget Kinsella, "Rueben's Reading Revolution: Aiming to Spread Latino Culture, Genius Bookseller Plans to Open 25 More Bookstores," p. 15.

School Library Journal, December, 2009, Narda McCarthy, review of *Once upon a Time*, p. 103.

USA Today, October 11, 2004, Marco R. della Cava, "Barber Grooms Love of Books," p. 1D.

ONLINE

Families in Schools Web site, http://www.familiesinschools. org/ (July 15, 2011), "Rueben Martínez."

Librería Martínez Book & Art Galleries Web site, http://libreriamartinez.net/ (July 15, 2011).*

*   *   *

MILLER, Debbie S. 1951-

Personal

Born August 14, 1951, in San Francisco, CA; daughter of Frederic E. and Jacqueline Supple; married Dennis

Debbie S. Miller (Photograph by Dennis C. Miller. Reproduced by permission.)

C. Miller (a wildlife survey pilot), September 8, 1973; children: Robin, Casey. *Education:* University of Denver, B.A., 1973; attended University of Alaska. *Hobbies and other interests:* Hiking, camping, cross-country skiing.

Addresses

Home—Fairbanks, AK. *E-mail*—debbiesmiller@hotmail.com.

Career

Author, journalist, educator, and conservationist. Elementary schoolteacher in Alaska and California, 1973-79; State of Alaska Legislative Branch, Fairbanks, investigator and writer, 1982-86; Caribou Enterprises, Fairbanks, photojournalist 1986—; freelance writer, beginning 1986. Artist-in-residence at Gates of the Arctic National Park and Preserve. Presenter at schools; volunteer in conservation community.

Member

Alaska Wilderness League (founding board member).

Awards, Honors

Outstanding Science Trade Book for Children selection, National Science Teacher's Association/Children's Book Council (NSTA/CBC), and Notable Book designation, International Society of School Librarians, both 1995, both for *A Caribou Journey;* NSTA/CBC Outstanding Science Trade Book for Children selection, and Outstanding Book from a Learning Perspective listee, Parents Council, both 1997, both for *Flight of the Golden Plover;* Children's Literature Choice listee, and Notable Book nomination, American Library Association, both 1998, both for *Disappearing Lake;* National Press Award nomination in environmental reporting, 2001, for "Ground Zero"; Charlotte Award nomination, 2002, and CBC Outstanding Trade Book in the Field of Social Studies selection, and Recommended Title selection, National Council of Teachers of English, both 2003, all for *The Great Serum Race;* Teacher's Choice Award, International Reading Association, 2003, for *Are Trees Alive?;* Pacific Northwest Booksellers Book Award nomination, Society of School Librarians International Book Award Honor Book selection, and John Burroughs Nature Book for Young Readers selection, all 2003, and NSTA/CBC Outstanding Science Trade Book for Students selection, 2004, all for *Arctic Lights, Arctic Nights;* NSTA/CBC Outstanding Science Trade Book for Students selection, 2007, and Forget-Me-Not Book Award, Alaska State Literacy Association, 2009, both for *Big Alaska;* Refuge Hero Award, U.S. Fish & Wildlife Service, for nature writing and education and conservation efforts; several Notable Book and Children's Choice listee.

Writings

FOR CHILDREN

A Caribou Journey, illustrated by Jon Van Zyle, Little, Brown (Boston, MA), 1994, new edition, University of Alaska Press (Fairbanks, AK), 2010.

Flight of the Golden Plover: The Amazing Migration between Hawai'i and Alaska, illustrated by Daniel Van Zyle, Alaska Northwest (Anchorage, AK), 1996.

Disappearing Lake: Nature's Magic in Denali National Park, illustrated by Jon Van Zyle, Walker (New York, NY), 1997.

A Polar Bear Journey, illustrated by Jon Van Zyle, Little, Brown (Boston, MA), 1997.

River of Life, illustrated by Jon Van Zyle, Clarion (New York, NY), 2000.

A Woolly Mammoth Journey, illustrated by Jon Van Zyle, Little, Brown (Boston, MA), 2001, new edition, University of Alaska Press (Fairbanks, AK), 2010.

Are Trees Alive?, illustrated by Stacey Schuett, Walker (New York, NY), 2002.

The Great Serum Race: Blazing the Iditarod Trail, illustrated by Jon Van Zyle, Walker (New York, NY), 2002.

Arctic Lights, Arctic Nights, illustrated by Jon Van Zyle, Walker (New York, NY) 2003.

Big Alaska: Journey across America's Most Amazing State, illustrated by Jon Van Zyle, Walker & Company (New York, NY), 2006.

Survival at Forty Below, illustrated by Jon Van Zyle, Walker & Company (New York, NY), 2010.

OTHER

Midnight Wilderness: Journeys in the Arctic National Wild-life Refuge, Sierra Club Books (San Francisco, CA), 1990, tenth anniversary edition, foreword by Margaret E. Murie, Alaska Northwest (Portland, OR), 2000.

(With Loren MacArthur) *Audubon Guide to the National Wildlife Refuges, Alaska and the Northwest: Alaska, Oregon, Washington,* foreword by Theodore E. Roosevelt IV, St. Martin's Press (New York, NY), 2000.

Contributor to books, including *Seasons of Life and Land: Arctic National Wildlife Refuge,* Mountaineers Books, 2003; *Arctic Wings: Birds of the Arctic National Wildlife Refuge,* edited by Stephen Brown, Mountaineers Books, 2006; and *Wild Moments: Adventures with Animals of the North,* edited by Michael Engelhard, University of Alaska Press. Contributor to magazines and newspapers, including *Wilderness, Amicus Journal, Alaska Geographic,* and *Alaska.*

Sidelights

A respected writer, educator, and conservationist, Debbie S. Miller has garnered critical acclaim for her non-fiction picture books, many of which focus on the state of Alaska. Miller, who has testified before the U.S. Congress about the importance of the Arctic National Wildlife Refuge, is the recipient of the Refuge Hero Award from the U.S. Fish & Wildlife Service for her conservation efforts. She has also received a host of honors for her children's books, among them *A Caribou Journey, Arctic Lights, Arctic Nights,* and *Big Alaska: Journey across America's Most Amazing State.*

Miller once explained to *SATA* how she began her writing career: "After spending thirteen years exploring the Arctic National Wildlife Refuge, I was motivated to write a book about the region, based on our extraordinary wilderness adventures and the fact that the area is threatened with proposed oil development. The Arctic Refuge is the largest and most isolated protected block of wilderness remaining in North America." In *Mid-*

In A Polar Bear Journey Miller joins artist Jon Van Zyle in introducing children to the Arctic-dwelling creatures in the story of a mother bear and her two growing cubs traveling in search of food. (Illustration copyright © 1997 by Jon Van Zyle. Reproduced by permission of Little, Brown & Company.)

night Wilderness, a book written for adults, she "describes vividly the wonders of this magnificent nineteen million-acre preserve in Alaska's northeastern corner, from its coastal plain to its mountains, glaciers and rivers," noted a reviewer for *Publishers Weekly.*

Miller's experience, knowledge, and respect for Alaska's wilderness and wildlife are also reflected in her books for children. *A Caribou Journey* takes the reader traveling with a herd of caribou through Northern Alaska. The land as well as the life and habits of this migratory animal are revealed as readers follow the caribou along the trails. Set against a beautiful landscape, the wild creatures traverse a hostile environment, search for food under the snow, and flee from their enemies. *Appraisal* reviewer Elizabeth Irish called *A Caribou Journey* delightful and "full of accurate, fascinating, and unusual information." While the "story is simply told," claimed *School Librarian* critic Sybil Hannavy, "it contains a lot of information." Other commentators noted that *A Caribou Journey* serves as an effective vehicle for Miller's extensive knowledge of caribou and habitat. "She knows the terrain and the animals first hand," concluded a reviewer for *Junior Bookshelf,* and "feels deeply about her subject."

In *Flight of the Golden Plover* Miller takes readers on another extraordinary migration as she describes the dramatic journey of the Pacific golden plover, a shorebird that flies across the Pacific Ocean between Alaska and Hawaii. *Flight of the Golden Plover* and *A Caribou Journey* were both recognized as Outstanding Science Trade Books for Children by the National Science Teachers Association and the Children's Book Council.

Published in 1997, *A Polar Bear Journey* is an "engrossing" presentation of the life cycle of polar bears, according to *Booklist* reviewer Ilene Cooper. Here Miller's narrative begins in November with a mother bear seeking a cozy den in order to give birth to two young bears during January. The bear's journey continues as the mother and her two offspring leave the den in March to forage for food. Miller brings the reader into the bears' world of survival as they travel over a sea of ice. Ellen M. Riordan, writing in *School Library Journal,* praised the book for its "informative and lyrical text," noting that facts about the polar bears are "smoothly integrated into the satisfying narrative."

In *Disappearing Lake* Miller once again renders the cycle of life, this time in Alaska's Denali National Park. As spring melts the winter snow, the water coming down from the mountains forms a lake which sustains a variety of animals and birds. Summer eventually dries up these waters, transforming the area into a meadow where new plant and animal life thrives, until, once again, winter covers the region with snow. "Miller describes [the wildlife residents'] comings and goings and the lake's metamorphosis in smooth, often poetic prose," Elizabeth Bush asserted in her review of *Disappearing Lake* for *Bulletin of the Center for Children's Books.* Also praising the book, *School Library Journal* critic Roz Goodman applauded the author's use of "simple, yet descriptive, action-packed words" to reveal the ever-changing life of the ephemeral lake.

River of Life follows the life of a river through the seasons in an Alaskan year, beginning and ending in winter. Illustrated by Jon Van Zyle, the book features the lives of both animals and humans that live near the river, including a young boy who watches the animals and builds snowmen on the river's banks. "This book reveals the vibrancy of the natural world," proclaimed Shelley Townsend-Hudson in her review for *Booklist.* Arwen Marshall pointed out in her *School Library Journal* article that in *River of Life* readers will notice "the author and illustrator's obvious affection for and excitement about their subject."

Miller takes readers back in time in *A Woolly Mammoth Journey.* She explained how she got the idea on her home page: "One day a friend handed me a mammoth tooth that he discovered while gold mining in a nearby river. The molar was the size of a brick and weighed about four pounds. This sparked my imagination. How could I hold this giant tooth and not further research these shaggy creatures that lived near my home as 'recently' as 10,000 to 12,000 years ago?" The mammoths in her story deal with multiple threats, from Ice Age hunters (both human and animal) to rough terrain. Margaret Bush, writing in *School Library Journal,* noted that *A Woolly Mammoth Journey* is designed to "convey the impressive bodies and probable social behavior of these early cousins of the elephant."

Miller's daughter prompted her next book, *Are Trees Alive?,* which features not only Alaskan trees, but trees from other parts of the world. "One day I hiked near a forest with my four-year-old daughter, Casey. She looked up at a tall tree and asked, 'Are trees alive?' I answered yes, and explained that trees were living things. She responded, 'But how do they breathe? They don't have noses.'" In order to answer these questions and others in a way that young readers can understand, Miller compares trees to the human body. While questioning some aspects of this metaphor, a *Kirkus Reviews* critic wrote that Miller "succeeds in conveying a warm feeling for trees and the environment" in her "feel-good story." Lucinda Snyder Whitehurst, in her *School Library Journal* review of *Are Trees Alive?,* called Miller's language "simple but poetic."

Returning to Alaska and another collaboration with Van Zyle, Miller's *The Great Serum Race: Blazing the Iditarod Trail* focuses on the original event that the 1,000-mile sled-dog race commemorates. In 1925, sled-dog teams and their owners made the long trek from Anchorage to Nome, Alaska, in order to deliver an antitoxin serum to fight a deadly outbreak of diphtheria. Miller spends some time on the most well-known of the heroic dogs, such as Balto, but also focuses on the larger history of the monumental sporting event. A critic for

Kirkus Reviews commented that *The Great Serum Race* "offers a more complete history of the serum race and all the heroic players within a more general context" than other books about the subject. Susan Oliver, writing in *School Library Journal,* deemed *The Great Serum Race* "an excellent account told with lots of detail and drama," while *Booklist* reviewer Todd Morning asserted that "Miller's telling is exciting, and her details are compelling."

Arctic Lights, Arctic Nights focuses on the natural cycle of light in the Alaskan year, giving readers an idea, month by month, of what amount and duration of daylight can be expected, as well as what temperatures are normal during any given season. A *Kirkus Reviews* contributor called the book "a lovely treatment of a difficult concept and of a very special place," and Patricia Manning wrote in *School Library Journal* that Miller includes "lyrical messages about light and its partner, darkness," while describing how wildlife deals with these changes in temperature and light. Carolyn Phelan, writing in *Booklist,* pointed out the "unusually good glossary" contained at the end of the book. Discussing what prompted her to write *Arctic Lights, Arctic Nights,* Miller commented on her home page: "One of the reasons why I love living in Alaska is the light, through all of our seasons."

Big Alaska, which was selected as an Outstanding Science Trade Book for Students, offers a tour of the "Last Frontier" through the eyes of a majestic bald eagle. Here Miller introduces readers to such scenic wonders as the Arctic National Wildlife Refuge, Tongass National Forest, Glacier Bay, Denali National Park, and the Iditarod Trail while also supplying facts about the state's climate, symbols, population, and economy. Writing in *School Library Journal,* Amelia Jenkins called *Big Alaska* "a special treasure both for readers already interested in the subject and newcomers," and a contributor in *Kirkus Reviews* predicted that the work "may spur the curiosity of armchair adventurers and naturalists."

Set in Alaska's Gates of the Arctic National Park and Preserve, *Survival at Forty Below* examines the ways in which a variety of animals adapt to the brutal winters above the Arctic Circle, winters that can last from October to May. While serving as the park's artist-in-residence, Miller hiked seventy-five miles through the wilderness. As she stated on her home page, "Through my research and interviews with scientists I learned that animals of the Arctic have unusual and unique ways of combating and escaping the cold." In her book she discusses animals both large and small, including the wood frog, which lies frozen most of the year beneath the snow; the Arctic ground squirrel; and the willow ptarmigan, as well as musk oxen and caribou. "The text moves smoothly and quickly, offering interesting glimpses of varied hibernation patterns and the physical characteristics" of each animal, Margaret Bush reported in *School Library Journal.* A *Kirkus Reviews* critic described *Survival at Forty Below* as a "fascinating look at the great diversity of animal adaptations, as well as an introduction to some lesser-known species."

When not researching or writing, Miller enjoys visiting elementary schools in different regions of the United States as a guest author. She shares the beauty of Alaska and her life as a nature writer through slides and hands-on materials. "As a former teacher, I love sharing Alaska's natural world with my own children and with students in schools around the country. . .," she explained on her home page. "It's my hope that readers will truly experience the environment of Alaska and the lives of animals when reading my books."

Biographical and Critical Sources

PERIODICALS

Appraisal, winter, 1995, Elizabeth Irish, review of *A Caribou Journey,* pp. 47-48.
Booklist, December 15, 1997, Ilene Cooper, review of *A Polar Bear Journey,* p. 701; December 1, 1998, Sally Estes and Carolyn Phelan, review of *A Polar Bear Journey,* p. 676; March 15, 2000, Shelley Townsend-Hudson, review of *River of Life,* p. 1384; May 1, 2001, Carolyn Phelan, review of *A Woolly Mammoth Journey,* p. 1686; June 1, 2002, Todd Morning, review of *Are Trees Alive?,* p. 1727; January 1, 2003, Todd Morning, review of *The Great Serum Race: Blazing the Iditarod Trail,* p. 884; October 1, 2003, Carolyn Phelan, review of *Arctic Lights, Arctic Nights,* p. 314; March 1, 2006, Carolyn Phelan, review of *Big Alaska: Journey across America's Most Amazing State,* p. 96; December 1, 2009, Carolyn Phelan, review of *Survival at Forty Below,* p. 57.
Bulletin of the Center for Children's Books, February, 1997, Elizabeth Bush, review of *Disappearing Lake: Nature's Magic in Denali National Park,* p. 215.
Childhood Education, spring, 2003, review of *The Great Serum Race,* p. 177; summer, 2004, Gina Hoagland, review of *Arctic Lights, Arctic Nights,* p. 212.
Junior Bookshelf, February, 1995, review of *A Caribou Journey,* p. 11.
Kirkus Reviews, March 15, 2002, review of *Are Trees Alive?,* p. 419; October 1, 2002, review of *The Great Serum Race,* p. 1476; June 1, 2003, review of *Arctic Lights, Arctic Nights,* p. 808; February 15, 2006, review of *Big Alaska,* p. 188; January 15, 2010, review of *Survival at Forty Below.*
Publishers Weekly, February 9, 1990, review of *Midnight Wilderness: Journeys in the Arctic National Wildlife Refuge,* p. 52.
School Librarian, May, 1995, Sybil Hannavy, review of *A Caribou Journey,* p. 65.
School Library Journal, April, 1997, Roz Goodman, review of *Disappearing Lake,* p. 129; October, 1997, Ellen M. Riordan, review of *A Polar Bear Journey,* pp. 120-121; July, 2000, Arwen Marshall, review of

River of Life, p. 96; June, 2001, Margaret Bush, review of *A Woolly Mammoth Journey,* p. 140; May, 2002, Lucinda Snyder Whitehurst, review of *Are Trees Alive?,* p. 141; November, 2002, Susan Oliver, review of *The Great Serum Race,* p. 130; August, 2003, Patricia Manning, review of *Arctic Lights, Arctic Nights,* p. 183; May, 2006, Amelia Jenkins, review of *Big Alaska,* p. 115; January, 2010, Margaret Bush, review of *Survival at Forty Below,* p. 88.

ONLINE

Debbie S. Miller Home Page, http://www.debbiemiller alaska.com (July 1, 2011).
EcoSpeakers.com, http://www.ecospeakers.com/ (July 1, 2011), "Debbie S. Miller."*

* * *

MORA, Pat 1942-

Personal

Born January 19, 1942, in El Paso, TX; daughter of Raul Antonio (an optician and business owner) and Estela (a homemaker) Mora; married William H. Burnside, Jr., July 27, 1963 (divorced 1981); married Vernon Lee Scarborough (an archaeologist and professor), May 25, 1984; children: (first marriage) William Roy, Elizabeth Anne, Cecilia Anne. *Education:* Texas Western College (now University of Texas—El Paso), B.A., 1963; University of Texas—El Paso, M.A., 1967. *Politics:* Democrat. *Religion:* "Ecumenical." *Hobbies and other interests:* Reading, walking, cooking, gardening, museums, traveling, visiting with family and friends.

Addresses

Home—Santa Fe, NM. *Agent*—Elizabeth Harding, Curtis Brown Ltd., Ten Astor Pl., New York, NY 10003.

Career

Writer, educator, administrator, lecturer, and activist. El Paso Independent School District, El Paso, TX, teacher, 1963-66; El Paso Community College, part-time instructor in English and communications, 1971-78; University of Texas—El Paso, part-time lecturer in English, 1979-81, assistant to vice president of academic affairs, 1981-88, director of university museum and assistant to president, 1988-89; full-time writer, 1989—. Distinguished Visiting Professor, Garrey Carruthers chair in honors, University of New Mexico, 1999; Civitella Ranieri fellow to Umbria, Italy, 2003. Member of Ohio Arts Council panel, 1990. W.K. Kellogg Foundation, consultant, 1990-91, and member of advisory committee for Kellogg National Fellowship Program, 1991-94. Assisted in promotion of National Poetry Month, beginning 1997; cofounder of Estela and Raúl Mora Award, National Association to Promote Library Service to the

Pat Mora (Photograph by Cynthia Farah-Haines. Reproduced by permission.)

Spanish-speaking and Latinos, 2000; judge of poetry fellowship for National Endowment for the Arts. Host of radio program *Voices: The Mexican-American in Perspective,* KTEP, 1983-84; gives poetry readings and presentations throughout the world.

Member

Academy of American Poets, International Reading Association, National Association of Bilingual Educators, Society of Children's Book Writers and Illustrators, Texas Institute of Letters, Friends of the Santa Fe Library, Museum of New Mexico Foundation, Spanish Colonial Arts Society, National Council of La Raza.

Awards, Honors

Award for Creative Writing, National Association for Chicano Studies, 1983; Poetry Award, *New America,* 1984; Harvey L. Johnson Book Award, Southwest Council of Latin American Studies, 1984; Southwest Book Award, Border Regional Library, 1985, for *Chants,* 1987, for *Borders,* 1994, for *A Birthday Basket for Tía;* W.K. Kellogg National Leadership fellowship, 1986-89; Leader in Education Award, El Paso Women's Employment and Education, 1987; Chicano/Hispanic Faculty and Professional Staff Association Award, University of Texas—El Paso, 1987; named to Writers Hall of Fame,

El Paso Herald-Post, 1988; Poetry Award, Conference of Cincinnati Women, 1990; National Endowment for the Arts fellowship in creative writing, 1994; Américas Award commendation, Consortium of Latin Americas Studies Program, Choice designation, Cooperative Children's Book Center (CCBC), Children's Books Mean Business listee, Children's Book Council, and Notable Books for a Global Society designation, International Reading Association, all 1996, all for *Confetti;* Premio Aztlan Literature Award, and Women of Southwest Book Award, both 1997, both for *House of Houses;* Washington Children's Choice Picture Book Award nomination, 1997, for *Pablo's Tree* illustrated by Cecily Lang; Tomás Rivera Mexican-American Children's Book Award, Southwest Texas State University, 1997, *Skipping Stones* Book Award, 1998, and Apollo Children's Book Award nomination, Apollo Reading Center (FL), 2002, all for *Tomás and the Library Lady;* Book Publishers of Texas Award, Texas Institute of Letters, 1998, and PEN Center USA West Literary Award finalist, 1999, both for *The Big Sky;* Pellicer-Frost Binational Poetry Award, 1999, for collection of odes; Alice Louis Wood Memorial Ohioana Award for Children's Literature, 2001; Teddy Award, Writers' League of Texas, and Books for the Teen Age selection, New York Public Library, both 2001, both for *My Own True Name;* named Literary Light for Children, Associates of the Boston Library, 2002; named Distinguished Alumna, 2004, University of Texas—El Paso; Golden Kite Award, Society of Children's Book Writers and Illustrators, 2005, and Pura Belpré Honor Book selection, American Library Association (ALA), and ALA Notable Book designation, 2006, both for *Doña Flor;* National Hispanic Cultural Center Literary Award, 2006; honorary D.L., State University of New York, Buffalo, 2006; Roberta Long Medal for Distinguished Contributions to Celebrating the Cultural Diversity of Children, University of Alabama at Birmingham, 2007; International Latino Book Award for Best Poetry in English, Spur Poetry Award finalist, Western Writers of America, and Bronze Medal in Poetry, Independent Publisher Book Awards, all 2007, all for *Adobe Odes;* Best of the Best selection, Chicago Public Library, 2008, for both *Sweet Dreams/Dulces sueños* and *¡Let's Eat!/¡A comer!;* named honorary member, American Library Association, 2008; Américas Book Award, ALA Notable Book designation, Best of the Best selection, Chicago Public Library, and Best Children's Books of the Year selection, Bank Street College of Education, all 2008, all for *¡Yum!¡Mmmm! ¡Qué Rico!;* Best Children's Picture Book—English, International Latino Book Awards, 2009, for *Abuelos;* Notable Book designation, ALA, Best Children's Books of the Year selection, Bank Street College of Education, and Choice designation, CCBC, all 2010, all for *Gracias/Thanks;* ALA Notable Book designation, CCBC Choice designation, Américas Commended selection, and Notable Children's Books in the Language Arts selection, Children's Literature Assembly, all 2010, all for *Book Fiesta!,* Américas Commended selection, 2010, for *A Piñata in a Pine Tree;* ALA Quick Picks for Reluctant Young-Adult Readers

selection, and Américas Commended listee, both 2011, both for *Dizzy in Your Eyes;* awards from numerous state reading associations.

Writings

PICTURE BOOKS; FOR CHILDREN

A Birthday Basket for Tía, illustrated by Cecily Lang, Macmillan (New York, NY), 1992.

Listen to the Desert/Oye al desierto, illustrated by Francesco X. Mora, Clarion Books (New York, NY), 1994.

Agua, Agua, Agua (concept book), illustrated by José Ortega, GoodYear Books (Reading, MA), 1994.

Pablo's Tree, illustrated by Cecily Lang, Macmillan (New York, NY), 1994.

(With Charles Ramirez Berg) *The Gift of the Poinsettia,* Piñata Books (Houston, TX), 1995, adapted as the play *Los posadas and the Poinsettia.*

(Reteller) *The Race of Toad and Deer,* illustrated by Maya Itzna Brooks, Orchard Books (New York, NY), 1995, revised edition, illustrated by Domi, Groundwood/Douglas & McIntyre (Toronto, Ontario, Canada), 2001.

Tomás and the Library Lady (biography), illustrated by Raúl Colón, Knopf (New York, NY), 1997, published as *Thomas and the Library Lady,* Dragonfly Books (New York, NY), 1997.

Delicious Hullabaloo/Pachanga deliciosa, illustrated by Francesco X. Mora, Piñata Books (Houston, TX), 1998.

The Rainbow Tulip, illustrated by Elizabeth Sayles, Viking (New York, NY), 1999.

(Reteller) *The Night the Moon Fell,* illustrated by Domi, Groundwood/Douglas & McIntyre (Toronto, Ontario, Canada), 2000.

The Bakery Lady/La señora de la panadería, illustrated by Pablo Torrecilla, Piñata Books (Houston, TX), 2001.

A Library for Juana: The World of Sor Juana Inés (biography), illustrated by Beatriz Vidal, Knopf (New York, NY), 2002.

Maria Paints the Hills, illustrated by Maria Hesch, Museum of New Mexico Press (Santa Fe, NM), 2002.

Doña Flor: A Tall Tale about a Giant Woman with a Great Big Heart, illustrated by Raúl Colón, Knopf (New York, NY), 2005.

The Song of Francis and the Animals, illustrated by David Frampton, Eerdmans (Grand Rapids, MI), 2005.

Let's Eat!/¡A comer!, illustrated by Maribel Suárez, Rayo (New York, NY), 2008.

Here, Kitty, Kitty!/¡Ven, gatita, ven!, illustrated by Maribel Suárez, Rayo (New York, NY), 2008.

Sweet Dreams/Dulces sueños, illustrated by Maribel Suárez, Rayo (New York, NY), 2008.

Abuelos, illustrated by Amelia Lau Carling, Groundwood Books (Toronto, Ontario, Canada), 2008.

Book Fiesta!: Celebrate Children's Day/Book Day/Celebremos el día de los niños/el día de los libros, illustrated by Rafael López, Rayo (New York, NY), 2009.

Gracias/Thanks, illustrated by John Parra, Lee & Low (New York, NY), 2009.

A Piñata in a Pine Tree: A Latino Twelve Days of Christmas, illustrated by Magaly Morales, Clarion Books (Boston, MA), 2009.

Wiggling Pockets/Los bolsillos saltarines, illustrated by Maribel Suárez, Rayo (New York, NY), 2009.

POETRY; FOR CHILDREN

The Desert Is My Mother/El desierto es mi madre, art by Daniel Lechon, Piñata Books (Houston, TX), 1994.

Confetti: Poems for Children, illustrated by Enrique O. Sanchez, Lee & Low Books (New York, NY), 1995.

Uno, dos, tres/One, Two, Three, illustrated by Barbara Lavallee, Clarion (New York, NY), 1996.

The Big Sky, illustrated by Steve Jenkins, Scholastic (New York, NY), 1998.

My Own True Name: New and Selected Poems for Young Adults, 1984-1999, illustrated by Anthony Accardo, Piñata Books (Houston, TX), 2001.

Love to Mama: A Tribute to Mothers (anthology), illustrated by Paula S. Barragán, Lee & Low (New York, NY), 2001.

Marimba!: Animales from A to Z, illustrated by Doug Cushman, Clarion (New York, NY), 2006.

¡Yum! ¡Mmmm! ¡Qué Rico!: Americas' Sproutings (haiku), illustrated by Rafael López, Lee & Low (New York, NY), 2007.

Join Hands!: The Ways We Celebrate Life, illustrated by George Ancona, Charlesbridge (Watertown, MA), 2008.

Dizzy in Your Eyes: Poems about Love, Knopf (New York, NY), 2010.

POETRY; FOR ADULTS

Chants, Arte Público Press (Houston, TX), 1984.

Borders, Arte Público Press (Houston, TX), 1986.

Communion, Arte Público Press (Houston, TX), 1991.

Agua Santa/Holy Water, Beacon Press (Boston, MA), 1995.

Aunt Carmen's Book of Practical Saints, Beacon Press (Boston, MA), 1997.

Adobe Odes, University of Arizona Press (Tucson, AZ), 2006.

FOR ADULTS

Nepantla: Essays from the Land in the Middle, University of New Mexico Press (Albuquerque, NM), 1993.

House of Houses (memoir), Beacon Press (Boston, MA), 1997.

Zing!: Seven Creativity Practices for Educators and Students, Corwin Press (Thousand Oaks, CA), 2010.

Work represented in anthologies, including *New Worlds of Literature,* Norton (New York, NY); *Revista Chicano-Ripueña: Kikirikí/Children's Literature Anthology,* Arte Público (Houston, TX), 1981; *Tun-Ta-Ca-Tún,* Arte Público, 1986; *The Desert Is No Lady: Southwestern*

Landscapes in Women's Writing and Art (also see below), edited by Vera Norwood and Janice Monk, University of Arizona Press (Tucson, AZ), 1997; *Many Voices: A Multicultural Reader,* edited by Linda Watkins-Goffman and others, Prentice-Hall (Englewood Cliffs, NJ), 2001; and *¡Wachale! Poetry and Prose about Growing up Latino in America,* edited by Ilan Stevens, Cricket Books, 2001. Contributor of poetry and essays to periodicals, including *Best American Poetry 1996, Calyx, Daughters of the Fifth Sun, Horn Book, Kalliope, Latina, Ms., New Advocate,* and *Prairie Schooner.*

Mora's books have been translated into several languages, including Bengali and Italian.

Sidelights

One of the most distinguished Hispanic writers working in the United States, Pat Mora also endeavors to promote cultural appreciation and literacy as well as conservation. Described by Jeanette Larson in *Booklist* as "a champion of bilingual literacy," Mora dedicates her writing to advance the recognition and preservation of Mexican-American culture. In books such as *Pablo's Tree, Adobe Odes, Book Fiesta!: Celebrate Children's Day/Book Day/Celebremos el día de los niños/el día de los libros,* and *Join Hands!: The Ways We Celebrate Life,* Mora works to instill in young Latinos pride in their heritage. "Seamlessly incorporating Spanish words into text that is mostly in English," Larson stated, "Mora's writing often mirrors the natural code-switching speech patterns of children who grow up in bilingual communities."

Characteristically, Mora's books are set in the southwestern United States, often in her birthplace of El Paso, Texas, and the surrounding desert. Celebrating the Mexican-American experience while also encouraging unity among all cultures, her written work for children includes picture books, biographies, concept books, and retellings of Mayan folktales. In titles such as *The Gift of the Poinsettia, Let's Eat!/¡A comer!,* and *Abuelos,* she shares Hispanic history, customs, and traditions with children of all cultures. "Like any writer," she related to Larson, "I consciously and unconsciously choose topics, stories, and ideas that are influenced by who I am, where and how I was raised, where I've traveled, what I've experienced. Ideally, we bring ourselves to the page." As a poet, Mora has also compiled verse anthologies for both children and young adults and has edited or contributed to poetry collections for more general readers.

In her children's books, Mora addresses several of the subjects and themes that constitute her books for adults, such as Mexican-American culture, nature (especially the desert), and the importance of family. Her spare but evocative prose is filled with descriptions and imagery; she also includes basic Spanish phrases in her works, most of which are published in both English and

Spanish. A *Dictionary of Hispanic Biography* essayist noted that "Mora has been essential to the movement to understand and uphold Mexican-American culture. . . . She provides an excellent model for young Hispanics who are just beginning to understand the past and are about to experience promising futures. . . . As a successful Hispanic writer, and a writer who writes about and for Hispanics, Mora is an exemplary role model for the young people of an increasingly multicultural America."

Born in El Paso to parents of Mexican descent, Mora and her siblings were taught both English and Spanish while growing up, and she frequently acknowledges the influence of her maternal grandmother and aunt, both who resided with the family. She attended a Roman Catholic grade school and devoured, equally, comic books, novels, and biographies of famous Americans such as Clara Barton, Davy Crockett, Amelia Earhart, Betsy Ross, William Penn, Dolly Madison, and Jim Bowie. In high school Mora began writing poetry, mostly religious in focus. As she later related in a *Scholastic* interview, "I always liked reading, and I always liked writing, but I don't think I thought of being a writer."

Although she enjoyed her family's Mexican traditions, Mora downplayed her ethnicity at school and did not reveal to her friends that she was bilingual. "There were times when I wished that my Mexican heritage were a part of my school day," she recalled in her *Scholastic* interview. "I wished that we had had books that had Spanish in them. And I wished that I had seen things about Mexican culture on the bulletin boards and in the library. One of the reasons that I write children's books is because I want Mexican culture and Mexican-American culture to be a part of our schools and libraries."

After graduating from high school, Mora thought about becoming a doctor, then decided to be a teacher. She attended Texas Western College (now the University of Texas—El Paso) and received her bachelor's degree in 1963. Shortly after graduation, she married William H. Burnside, Jr., with whom she would have three children: William, Elizabeth, and Cecilia. Mora began to teach English and Spanish at grade and high schools in El Paso. She earned her master's degree in 1967, and then became a part-time instructor in English and communications at El Paso Community College. In 1981, she moved into administration. Several years later, after going through a divorce, she turned to her past: in addition to writing, she also began to educate herself about her heritage. Awarded for her early efforts, she published her first adult poetry collection, *Chants,* in 1984, the same year she married Vernon Lee Scarborough, an archeologist and professor whom she had met at college. Five years later she left her administrative job to become a full-time writer and speaker.

In 1992, Mora produced her first book for children, *A Birthday Basket for Tía.* A picture book inspired by an incident involving her aunt, the story describes how

Barbara Lavallee's colorful artwork brings to life Mora's Mexican-inspired bilingual concept book Uno, Dos Tres: One, Two, Three.

young narrator Cecilia finds the perfect present for her ninety-year-old great-aunt, Tía, by collecting objects that recall the many happy times they have shared. Featuring a repetitive text, *A Birthday Basket for Tía* is both a story and a concept book that helps readers count from one to ninety. A *Publishers Weekly* reviewer described the work as "poignant" and added that Mora's text "flows smoothly from one event to the next, and clearly presents the careful planning behind Cecilia's gift-gathering mission." Writing in *School Library Journal,* Julie Corsaro deemed *A Birthday Basket for Tía* a "warm and joyful story," while *Horn Book* critic Maeve Visser Knoth called Cecilia "an irrepressible child."

Featuring a multigenerational focus, *Pablo's Tree* takes place during the fifth birthday of its protagonist, a boy who has been adopted and now lives with his single mother. Pablo is excited because he is going to be with his abuelito, or grandfather, for whom he is named. Lito has established a tradition for his grandson: every year, he decorates a special tree in the boy's honor, leaving the decorations as a surprise. In past years, the tree has been festooned with balloons, colored streamers, paper lanterns, and even bird cages; this year, Lito has chosen bells and wind chimes as his theme. Pablo and Lito celebrate the day by eating apples and listening to the music coming from the tree; Lito also tells Pablo the story of the tree, which was planted when Pablo's mother adopted him. Writing in the *Bulletin of the Center for Children's Books,* Deborah Stevenson commented that *Pablo's Tree* "has a celebratory aspect that makes it appealing not just to adoptees but to kids generally.'" In *Booklist,* Annie Ayres called the picture book "lovely and resonant," with a story that "rings with happiness and family love."

Based on a family story from Mora's mother, *The Rainbow Tulip* is set in El Paso during the 1920s and features Estelita, a first grader caught between two cultures. Estelita realizes that her heritage sets her apart: she sees her mother, who speaks no English and dresses in dark clothes, as old-fashioned. The girls in Estelita's class are dressing as tulips for the upcoming May Day parade, and she wants her costume to be different from the others. When the big day arrives, she comes dressed in all the colors of the rainbow, then successfully executes a maypole dance and wins her teacher's approval. The girl's mother then explains that being different can be both sweet and sour, much like the lime sherbet that is their favorite dessert, and Estelita recognizes her mother's quiet love for her. According to *Library Journal* critic Ann Welton, in *The Rainbow Tulip* "Mora succeeds in creating a quiet story to which children will respond. . . . This tale of family love and support crosses cultural boundaries and may remind youngsters of times when their families made all the difference."

Another picture book, *Tomás and the Library Lady*, combines two of Mora's characteristic themes: the joy of reading and the special quality of intergenerational relationships. Based on an incident in the life of Hispanic author and educator Tomás Rivera, Mora's fictionalized biography describes how young Tomás, the son of migrant workers, is introduced to the world of books by a sympathetic librarian. Tomás's grandfather has told him wonderful stories, but has run out of them; he tells Tomás to go to the library for more. At the library, Tomás meets a kindly librarian who gives him books in English—signed out on her own card. In return, Tomás teaches Spanish to the librarian. In *Publishers Weekly* a critic predicted that "young readers and future librarians will find this an inspiring tale." Interestingly, *Tomás and the Library Lady* was the first of Mora's stories to be accepted for publication; due to the difficulty in finding an appropriate illustrator, it was delayed for almost a decade before it was published, together with Raul Colón's evocative art.

Mora transports readers back to seventeenth-century Mexico in *A Library for Juana: The World of Sor Juana Inés*. The story focuses on the childhood of Sor Juana Inéz de la Cruz, a nun and noted intellectual who became known for her poetry, songs, and stories and who is acknowledged as one of Mexico's most noted women writers. Reviewing *A Library for Juana* in *Kirkus Reviews,* a critic praised the book as a "magnificent offering" that is enhanced by "exquisite gouache-and-watercolor" paintings that are "filled with authentic details" by illustrator Beatriz Vidal. "Mora laces her narrative with lively anecdotes," noted a *Publishers Weekly* writer, and in *Booklist* Gillian Engberg praised the author's "inspiring . . . account of a Latin American woman who loved learning during a time when few women were educated." "Mora's beautifully crafted text does credit to its subject," concluded Ann Welton in *School Library Journal,* calling *A Library for Juana* "an exceptional introduction to an exceptional woman."

As a girl, Sor Juana loved to read, and in *Doña Flor: A Tall Tale about a Giant Woman with a Great Big Heart* Mora introduces another enthusiastic reader. Set in the American Southwest, *Doña Flor* focuses on a giantess who is beloved by the normal-sized children living nearby. When a loud, mysterious sound is heard, terrifying the locals, the giant woman tracks down what proves to be its very surprising source. Mora graces her "economical, poetic text with vivid, fanciful touches," in the opinion of Engberg, and Colón's "signature" art injects "texture and movement," according to *School Library Journal* contributor Linda M. Kenton.

Folk tales and other traditional stories take center stage in books such as *The Gift of the Poinsettia* and *The Song of Francis and the Animals*. Praised by a *Publishers Weekly* contributor as a "celebratory" work, *The Song of Francis and the Animals* introduces readers to the Catholic saint who was able to communicate with animals, while *The Gift of the Poinsettia* tells the story of the young Mexican girl whose search for a gift for the baby Jesus is transformed into the brilliant red plant that comes into bloom during the Christmas season. In *School Library Journal,* Jane Barrer described Mora's text for *The Song of Francis and the Animals* as "more poetry than story," and Engberg concluded that Mora's

In Marimba! *Doug Cushman's high-energy animal characters keep pace with Mora's rhythmic storyline as they dance through the alphabet.* (Illustration © 2006 by Doug Cushman. Reproduced by permission of Houghton Mifflin Company. All rights reserved.)

text "brings close the spiritual connection between Francis and the animals." As Barrer added, David Frampton's woodcut illustrations accentuate this focus, depicting the saint's faith in the gentleness of all creatures.

Mora's first verse collection for young readers, *Confetti: Poems for Children,* features free-verse narrative poems that describe the American Southwest as seen through the eyes of a young Mexican-American girl. The child, who lives in the desert, describes the region and its inhabitants throughout the space of a day, from early morning to nightfall. The sun, clouds, leaves, and wind are the focus of some poems, while others feature a wood sculptor, a grandmother, and a baker. In *Kirkus Reviews* a critic noted that the "best of these poems that mix English and Spanish . . . warmly evokes familiar touchstones of Mexican-American life." Writing in *School Library Journal,* Sally R. Dow called *Confetti* a "welcome addition" and stated that the poems "capture the rhythms and uniqueness of the Southwest and its culture."

Marimba!: Animales from A to Z follows an after-hours party at a city zoo in Mora's rhyming bilingual text, as animals of all sorts turn to song while the zookeepers take a nap. In *¡Yum! ¡Mmmm! ¡Qué Rico!: Americas' Sproutings* she includes a baker's dozen of haiku introducing thirteen foods unique to the Americas. In *Kirkus Reviews,* a critic dubbed *Marimba!* as "an inviting introduction to both Spanish and the animal kingdom," and also praised the energetic, high-contrast cartoon art by Doug Cushman. Described by *Booklist* contributor Julie Cummins as an "inventive stew," *¡Yum! ¡Mmmm! ¡Qué Rico!* features "stylized Mexican" art by Rafael Lopez. Working on *¡Yum! ¡Mmmm! ¡Qué Rico!* was a labor of love for its author. "For many years I have been interested in indigenous languages, cultures, and foods," Mora told a *Lee & Low Books* interviewer. "I had never tried haiku before, but I purchased a beautiful book of haiku, and the . . . interests came together."

Another verse collection, *The Big Sky,* celebrates the land, people, and creatures of the Southwest in fourteen poems, and also includes poems set in Mora's then home state of Ohio. Subjects include the sky, a grandmother, a huge mountain, an old snake, a horned lizard, and coyotes. A *Publishers Weekly* reviewer predicted that the poems in *The Big Sky* "will delight readers of all ages with their playfully evocative imagery," and in *School Library Journal* Lisa Falk dubbed it a "gem [that] is both a lovely poetry book and an evocative look at a magical place." Calling Mora's words "wonderful," Marilyn Courtot commented in *Children's Literature* that the collection's "spare and dramatic poems transport readers to the American Southwest." In *Join Hands!* Mora introduces readers to the pantoum, a Malayasian poetic form that emphasizes rhyme and repetition. Illustrated with photographs by George Ancona, the work trumpets the joys of creative play, depicting children marching in a parade and participating

One of the most important of family relationships is Mora's focus in Love to Mama: A Tribute to Mothers, *featuring ethnic-inspired paintings by Paula S. Barragán.* (Illustration © 2001 by Paula S. Barragán. Reproduced by permission of Lee & Low Books, Inc.)

in a masquerade. Susan Lissim, writing in *School Library Journal,* offered praise for the "lively and beautiful book."

My Own True Name: New and Selected Poems for Young Adults, 1984-1999 contains sixty poems primarily selected by Mora from among those published in her adult books. The metaphor of a cactus, which represents human existence, joins the poems thematically: blooms represent love and joy, thorns represent sorrow and hardship, and roots represent family, home, strength, and wisdom. Autobiographical, the poems address Mora's life as a Latina in the Southwest, her search for identity, and her experience as a mother. She also weaves Mexican phrases, historical figures, and cultural symbols into her poems. Calling the poems "powerful," Gillian Engberg noted in *Booklist* that "the rich, symbolic imagery, raw emotion, and honesty will appeal to mature teens." Another work aimed at a young-adult audience, *Dizzy in Your Eyes: Poems about Love* contains fifty poems focusing on the most universal of emotions. Mora's verses explore not only romantic but also platonic, filial, and fraternal love, "picturing each variation as a strong force that strikes, blesses, empowers and beautifies" a teenager's life, observed a critic in *Kirkus Reviews.* "The quiet lyricism of some lines will prompt many readers to roll them over and over on their tongues," Jill Heritage Maza commented in *School Library Journal.*

Mora and illustrator Maribel Suárez collaborated on a series of easy-to-read bilingual works centering on the activities of the Rosa family, which includes three siblings Isabel, Tina, and Danny. In *Let's Eat!/¡A comer!* the family and their lively pup gather for a simple dinner of tortillas, beans, cheese, and chile. According to a *Kirkus Reviews* contributor, readers who are familiar with either English or Spanish can be "encouraged to try to learn some words or sentences in the unfamiliar language." *Sweet Dreams/Dulces sueños* focuses on Abuelita's efforts to lull her grandchildren to sleep, and in *Here, Kitty, Kitty!/¡Ven, gatita, ven!* the Rosa children have fun with a new pet. A critic in *Kirkus Reviews* noted that *Sweet Dreams/Dulces sueños* "brings a soothing tone to a nightly ritual universal in any language or culture," and Hazel Rochman maintained in *Booklist* that *Here, Kitty, Kitty!/¡Ven, gatita, ven!* would be [f]un for preschoolers speaking and learning both languages."

A traditional New Mexican festival is the subject of *Abuelos,* an award-winning picture book by Mora. Amelia warily prepares for her first midwinter fiesta, a Halloween-like celebration in which villagers masquerading as scary old men descend from the mountains and chase youngsters around huge bonfires. During the festivities, Amelia's older brother is grabbed by one of the costumed performers, and she comes to his rescue by grabbing the mask of the abuelos, revealing his true—and none-too-frightening—identity. A contributor in *Kirkus Reviews* applauded the "gently scary story embedded in a fascinating and little-known 'bogeyman' tradition," and a *Publishers Weekly* critic described *Abuelos* as a "playful tale." Referencing a better-known

holiday, Mora presents a "zippy spin" on a familiar holiday song, as *Horn Book* reviewer Chelsey Philpot put it, in *A Piñata in a Pine Tree: A Latino Twelve Days of Christmas.* A *Kirkus Reviews* critic deemed this work "absolutely entertaining."

In *Gracias/Thanks,* a bilingual tale illustrated by John Parra, a young boy joyfully recounts the people and things for which he is most grateful, including his soft pajamas, his uncle's guitar playing, and ladybugs. *Booklist* contributor Linda Perkins complimented the "originality and liveliness of language and art" found in Mora's work, and Shannon Dye Gemberling maintained in *School Library Journal* that the narrative "carries a sense of happiness brought by the simple things in life." According to *Horn Book* reviewer Jennifer M. Brabander, "Mora's text is presented in Spanish first, then English, a respectful nod to Spanish-speaking readers."

In 1997, Mora lobbied successfully to establish a national day to celebrate childhood and bilingual literacy. Called El día de los niños/El día de los libros, the day is part of National Poetry Month. In 2000, Mora and her siblings established the Estela and Raúl Mora Award, a prize named in honor of their parents and coordinated by the National Association to Promote Library Service to Latinos (REFORMA) to promote El día de los niños/El día de los libros. In *Book Fiesta!* Mora showcases the joys of reading, depicting children enjoying their books while riding aboard a train, flying in an airplane, and even sitting atop an elephant. "The cheery and effortless dual English/Spanish text instills a festival atmosphere," a critic noted in a review of the work for *Kirkus Reviews.*

John Parra takes on illustrator duties in Mora's imaginative bilingual picture book Gracias/Thanks! (Illustration copyright © 2009 by John Parra. Reproduced by permission of Lee & Low Books, Inc.)

In an essay in *Horn Book,* Mora explained what has motivated her to write: "I write because I am a reader. I want to give to others what writers have given me, a chance to hear the voices of people I will never meet . . . I enjoy the privateness of writing and reading. I write because I am curious. I am curious about me. Writing is a way of finding out how I feel about anything and everything. . . . Writing is my way of saving my feelings. . . . I write because I believe that Hispanics need to take their rightful place in American literature. I will continue to write and to struggle to say what no other writer can say in quite the same way."

Biographical and Critical Sources

BOOKS

Children's Literature Review, Volume 58, Gale (Detroit, MI), 2000.

Dictionary of Hispanic Biography, Gale (Detroit, MI), 1996.

Dictionary of Literary Biography, Volume 209: *Chicano Writers,* 3rd series, Gale (Detroit, MI), 1996.

Ikas, Karen Rosa, *Chicana Ways: Conversations with Ten Chicana Writers,* University of Nevada Press (Reno, NV), 2001.

Mora, Pat, *House of Houses,* Beacon Press (Boston, MA), 1997.

Mora, Pat, *Nepantla: Essays from the Land in the Middle,* University of New Mexico Press (Albuquerque, NM), 1993.

This Is about Vision: Interviews with Southwestern Writers, edited by William Balassi and others, University of New Mexico Press (Albuquerque, NM), 1990.

PERIODICALS

Book Links, January 1, 2011, Jeanette Larson, interview with Mora, p. S23.

Booklist, November 1, 1994, Annie Ayres, review of *Pablo's Tree,* p. 507; November 15, 1998, Isabel Schon, review of *Tomás and the Library Lady,* p. 599; March 15, 2000, Gillian Engberg, review of *My Own True Name: New and Selected Poems for Young Adults, 1984-1999,* p. 1377; November 15, 2002, Gillian Engberg, review of *A Library for Juana: The World of Sor Juana Inéz,* p. 605; December 15, 2002, Hazel Rochman, review of *Maria Paints the Hills,* p. 760; October 15, 2005, Gillian Engberg, review of *The Song of Francis and the Animals,* p. 58; December 1, 2005, Gillian Engberg, review of *Doña Flor: A Tall Tale about a Giant Woman with a Great Big Heart,* p. 55; December 1, 2007, Julie Cummins, review of *¡Yum! ¡Mmmm! ¡Qué Rico!: Americas' Sproutings,* p. 45; October 15, 2008, Hazel Rochman, review of *Here, Kitty, Kitty! ¡Ven, gatita, ven!,* p. 46; January 1, 2009, Andrew Medlar, review of *Book Fiesta!: Celebrate Children's Day/Book Day/Celebremos el día de los niños/el día de los libros,* p. 90; November 1, 2009, Linda Perkins, review of *Gracias/Thanks,* p. 35; November 1, 2009, Andrew Medlar, review of *A Piñata in a Pine Tree: A Latino Twelve Days of Christmas,* p. 51.

Bulletin of the Center for Children's Books, September, 1994, Deborah Stevenson, review of *Pablo's Tree,* p. 20; February, 2006, Hope Morrison, review of *Doña Flor,* p. 276.

Horn Book, July-August, 1990, Pat Mora, "Why I Am a Writer," pp. 436-437; January-February, 1993, Maeve Visser Knoth, review of *A Birthday Basket for Tía,* pp. 76-77; November-December, 1994, Maeve Visser Knoth, review of *Pablo's Tree,* pp. 723-724; July, 2001, Nell D. Beram, review of *Love to Mama: A Tribute to Mothers,* p. 468; September-October, 2005, Deirdre F. Baker, review of *The Song of Francis and the Animals,* p. 565; November-December, 2009, Chelsey Philpot, review of *A Piñata in a Pine Tree,* p. 646; January-February, 2010, review of *Gracias/Thanks,* p. 77.

Kirkus Reviews, October 1, 1996, review of *Confetti: Poems for Children,* p. 1476; November 15, 2002, review of *A Library for Juana,* p. 1699; August 1, 2005, review of *The Song of Francis and the Animals,* p. 854; September 15, 2005, review of *Doña Flor,* p. 1031; October 15, 2006, review of *Marimba!: Animales from A to Z,* p. 1075; September 15, 2007, review of *¡Yum! ¡Mmmm! ¡Qué Rico!;* February 15, 2008, review of *Let's Eat!;* May 1, 2008, review of *Sweet Dreams;* June 15, 2008, review of *Join Hands!: The Ways We Celebrate Life;* August 1, 2008, review of *Here, Kitty, Kitty!;* September 15, 2008, review of *Abuelos;* February 1, 2009, review of *Book Fiesta!;* September 15, 2009, review of *A Piñata in a Pine Tree;* December 15, 2009, review of *Dizzy in Your Eyes: Poems about Love.*

New Advocate, fall, 1998, Pat Mora, "Confessions of a Latina Author," pp. 279-289.

Publishers Weekly, August 31, 1992, review of *A Birthday Basket for Tía,* p. 77; July 21, 1997, review of *Tomás and the Library Lady,* p. 201; March 23, 1998, review of *The Big Sky,* p. 99; October 28, 2002, review of *A Library for Juana,* p. 71; June 27, 2005, review of *The Song of Francis and the Animals,* p. 67; October 27, 2008, review of *Abuelos,* p. 53.

School Library Journal, September 15, 1992, Julie Corsaro, review of *A Birthday Basket for Tía,* p. 156; November, 1996, Sally R. Dow, review of *Confetti,* p. 100; July, 1998, Lisa Falk, review of *The Big Sky,* p. 90; November, 1999, Ann Welton, review of *The Rainbow Tulip,* p. 126; July, 2000, Nina Lindsay, review of *My Own True Name,* p. 119; April, 2001, Ann Welton, review of *Love to Mama,* p. 165; November, 2002, Ann Welton, review of *A Library for Juana,* p. 146; October, 2005, Linda M. Kenton, review of *Doña Flor,* p. 122, and Jane Barrer, review of *The Song of Francis and the Animals,* p. 123; September, 2007, Marilyn Taniguchi, review of *¡Yum! ¡Mmmm! ¡Qué Rico!;* p. 185; April, 2008, Donna Atmur, review of *Let's Eat!,* p. 117; July, 2008, Madeline Walton-Hadlock, review of *Sweet Dreams/Dulces sueños,* p.

78; November, 2008, Susan Lissim, review of *Join Hands!*, p. 111; October, 2009, Diane Olivo-Posner, review of *A Piñata in a Pine Tree*, p. 82; December, 2009, Shannon Dye Gemberling, review of *Gracias/ Thanks*, p. 103; January, 2010, Jill Heritage Maza, review of *Dizzy in Your Eyes*, p. 124.

Voice of Youth Advocates, April, 2001, Delia Culberson, review of *My Own True Name*, p. 20.

ONLINE

Children's Literature Web site, http://www.childrenslit. com/ (January 9, 2008), Marilyn Courtot, "Pat Mora."

Lee & Low Books Web site, http://www.leeandlow.com/ (July 15, 2011), "BookTalk with Pat Mora."

Pat Mora Home Page, http://www.patmora.com (July 15, 2011).

National Book Festival Web site, http://www.loc.gov:8081/ bookfest/kids-teachers/authors/ (July 15, 2011), interview with Mora.

Scholastic Web site, http://www2.scholastic.com/ (May 19, 2002), interview with Mora.

Voices from the Gaps: Women Writers of Color Web site, http://voices.cla.umn.edu/ (May 19, 2002), Delia Abreu and others, "Pat Mora."

OTHER

The Desert Is No Lady (film), Women Who Make Movies, 1995.*

* * *

MORSTAD, Julie

Personal

Born in Canada.

Addresses

Home—Vancouver, British Columbia, Canada.

Career

Author/illustrator, designer, and animator. *Exhibitions:* Work exhibited at Atelier Gallery.

Awards, Honors

Amelia Frances Howard-Gibbon Illustrator's Award shortlist, and Marilyn Baillie Picture Book Award, Canadian Children's Book Centre, both 2007, both for *When You Were Small* by Sara O'Leary; Alcuin Society Award, and *ForeWord* magazine Book of the Year Award finalist, both 2008, both for *Where You Came From* by O'Leary; Marilyn Baille Award finalist, Amelia Frances Howard-Gibbon Illustrator's Award shortlist, Ruth and Sylvia Schwartz Children's Book Award finalist, and Chocolate Lily Award shortlist, all 2011, all for *Singing away the Dark* by Caroline Woodward.

Writings

SELF-ILLUSTRATED

Milk Teeth and Others, Drawn & Quarterly/Petits livres (Montréal, Québec, Canada), 2007.

Also illustrator of *ABC* flashcard set.

ILLUSTRATOR

Sara O'Leary, *When You Were Small*, Simply Read Books (Vancouver, British Columbia, Canada), 2006.

Sara O'Leary, *Where You Came From*, Simply Read Books (Vancouver, British Columbia, Canada), 2008.

Mélikah Abdelmoumen, *Premières amours: des histoires de filles*, La Courte échelle (Montréal, Québec, Canada), 2008.

Jon Arno Lawson, *Think Again*, KCP Poetry (Toronto, Ontario, Canada), 2010.

Caroline Woodward, *Singing away the Dark*, Simply Read Books (Vancouver, British Columbia, Canada), 2010.

Sara O'Leary, *When You Were Small Too*, Simply Read Books (Vancouver, British Columbia, Canada), 2011.

Sidelights

Evoking the same muse as twentieth-century illustrator Edward Gorey, award-winning Canadian artist Julie Morstad weaves a subtle surrealism into her detailed pen-and-tint renderings. Paired with texts by writers that include Sara O'Leary, Jon Arno Lawson, and Caroline Woodward, Morstad's listless, dreamlike human characters encourage close examination and often appear to morph into birds, animals, and trees in the pages of her picture books. In addition to her work for other writers, Morstad has collected her drawings of slightly off-kilter children, flowers and trees, animals, and other objects in the art book *Milk Teeth and Others*. Praising Morstad's illustrations for Lawson's poetry collection *Think Again*, a *Kirkus Reviews* writer noted that her "spare grayscale drawings curiously stitch . . . a narrative thread through the volume," and *Booklist* contributor Daniel Kraus concluded that the artist's "wistful line art" helps make *Think Again* "an ideal book for wandering, wondering romantics."

O'Leary's quirky story for *When You Were Small* finds a little boy named Henry sitting with his father in the livingroom and asking for stories about "when I was small." The question inspires his dad to begin a nonsensical journey into a magical past wherein Henry was small enough to live in his father's slipper, ride on the back of the family cat, and be carried about in his father's shirt pocket. The author/artist collaboration continues in *Where You Came From*, as Henry's curiosity prompts questions about where he came from. To avoid a serious discussion of the birds and bees, his parents answer with a range of whimsical possibilities: Henry may have been delivered in the mail, discovered in the window of a local pet shop, left by aliens, delivered by the fairies, or purchased on sale at a nearby department store.

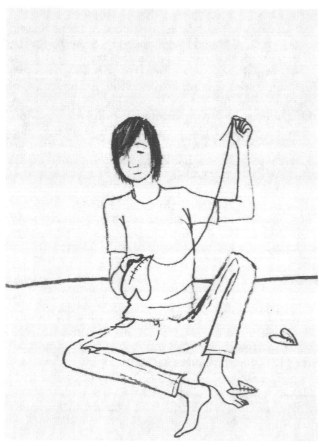

Julie Morstad's artwork appears in books such as JonArno Lawson's **Think Again.** (KCP Poetry, 2010. Illustration copyright © 2010 by Julie Morstad. Reproduced by permission of Kids Can Press Ltd., Toronto.)

Expanding on O'Leary's text, Morstad's "whimsical, crosshatched line illustrations, washed with gently shadowed colors, appear to float on white pages," noted *Booklist* reviewer GraceAnne A. DeCandido in appraising *When You Were Small,* while a *Publishers Weekly* critic noted the "midcentury" effect achieved by the artist's contribution of "homespun sketches" interspersed with larger pen-and-ink drawings with "drop caps, delicately tinted . . . and airy with negative space." Appraising *Where You Came From,* Madeline Walton-Hadlock wrote in *School Library Journal* that the book's "whimsical pen-and-ink drawings with watercolor accents and a lovely minimalist design complement [O'Leary's] simple, poetic text."

Biographical and Critical Sources

PERIODICALS

Booklist, May 1, 2006, GraceAnne A. DeCandido, review of *When You Were Small,* p. 93; March 15, 2010, Daniel Kraus, review of *Think Again,* p. 40.

Kirkus Reviews, March 1, 2010, review of *Think Again.*

Publishers Weekly, May 22, 2006, review of *When You Were Small,* p. 50.

Resource Links, April, 2006, Lori Lavallee, review of *When You Were Small,* p. 8.

School Library Journal, October, 2006, Wendy Woodfill, review of *When You Were Small,* p. 120; October, 2008, Madeline Walton-Hadlock, review of *Where You Came From,* p. 117.

ONLINE

Julie Morstad Home Page, http://www.juliemorstad.com (May 11, 2011).*

*   *   *

MYERS, Laurie

Personal

Born October 29, in Anderson, SC; daughter of Betsy Byars (an author); married, 1974; children: three. *Education:* Clemson University, degree.

Addresses

Home—Los Angeles, CA.

Career

Writer, beginning 1990. Presenter at schools.

Awards, Honors

International Reading Association (IRA) Children's Choice selection, 1994, for *Earthquake in the Third Grade;* American Library Association Notable Book designation, 2002, for *Surviving Brick Johnson;* Mountain and Plains Booksellers Association Book Award nomination, 2002, IRA Teachers Choice and Parent's Choice selections, both 2003, and Texas Christian Schools Association/Children's Crown Award nomination, 2005, all for *Lewis and Clark and Me;* South Carolina Children's Book Award, 2004, for *My Dog, My Hero;* (with Betsy Duffey and Betsy Byars) Best Book selection, Bank Street College of Education, 2008, for *Dog Diaries;* nominated for several state-sponsored children's choice awards.

Writings

Earthquake in the Third Grade, illustrated by Karen Ritz, Clarion Books (New York, NY), 1993.

Garage Sale Fever, illustrated by Kathleen Collins Howell, HarperCollins (New York, NY), 1993.

Guinea Pigs Don't Talk, illustrated by Cheryl Taylor, Clarion Books (New York, NY), 1994.

(With mother Betsy Byars and sister Betsy Duffey) *My Dog, My Hero,* illustrated by Loren Long, Holt (New York, NY), 2000.

Surviving Brick Johnson, illustrated by Dan Yaccarino, Clarion Books (New York, NY), 2000.

Lewis and Clark and Me: A Dog's Tale, illustrated by Michael Dooling, Henry Holt (New York, NY), 2002.

(With Betsy Byars and Betsy Duffey) *The SOS File,* illustrated by Arthur Howard, Henry Holt (New York, NY), 2004.

(With Betsy Byars and Betsy Duffey) *Dog Diaries: Secret Writings of the WOOF Society,* illustrated by Erik Brooks, Henry Holt (New York, NY), 2007.

(With Betsy Byars and Betsy Duffey) *Cat Diaries: Secret Writings of the MEOW Society,* illustrated by Erik Brooks, Henry Holt (New York, NY), 2010.

Escape by Night: A Civil War Adventure, illustrated by Amy June Bates, Henry Holt (New York, NY), 2011.

Adaptations

Surviving Brick Johnson was adapted for audiobook read by Joel Leffert, Recorded Books, 2004.

Sidelights

The daughter of noted children's author Betsy Byars and the sister of fellow author Betsy Duffey, Laurie Myers has continued in the family tradition, beginning her career writing for children in 1990. In addition to creating a number of original stories that range in focus, from the historical themed *Lewis and Clark and Me: A Dog's Tale* and *Escape by Night: A Civil War Adventure* to contemporary stories such as *Earthquake in the Third Grade, Guinea Pigs Don't Talk,* and *Surviving Brick Johnson,* Myers has teamed up with her mother and sister to produce several entertaining picture-book collaborations.

One of Myers' earliest published stories, the chapter book *Guinea Pigs Don't Talk,* finds Lisa hoping to make new friends as the new student in Mrs. Flower's third-grade class. Although two classmates attempt to make Lisa the subject of their jokes, Traci comes to the new girl's aid and by the end of the day the four children are on their way to becoming friends. Another spate of bullying takes place in *Surviving Brick Johnson,* as Alex becomes convinced that the school bully has him in his crosshairs. Fortunately, the smaller fifth grader finds a useful remedy in karate, which ultimately forges an unexpected friendship. *Guinea Pigs Don't Talk* was praised by *Booklist* contributor Kay Weisman, who noted that "Myers handles typical childhood issues with a humorous touch." *Surviving Brick Johnson* is enlivened by "frequently witty dialogue and snappy one-liners," according to Todd Morning, another *Booklist* contributor, while in *School Library Journal* Elaine E. Knight predicted that "readers . . . attracted by the short length and humor" of Myers' chapter book "will receive an important and painless message about the nature of respect and friendship."

Several of Myers' stories focus on dogs, and she introduces a famous canine from history in *Lewis and Clark and Me.* Meriwether Lewis accompanied William Clark on the famous three-year trek from Missouri to the Pacific Ocean during the first decade of the nineteenth century, and he brought along his dog Seaman. Basing her account of this journey on research into Lewis and Clark's actual journals and letters, as well as her own trips along the explorers' trail through Montana and across the Pacific Northwest, Myers gives her story added interest by having Seaman provide the narration. In addition to helping with hunting and tracking, Lewis's dog "served as . . . guard dog as well as a peacemaker with the Indians," according to *Booklist* critic Karen Hutt, "and his story offers an interesting perspective on a familiar piece of U.S. history." Brought to life in oil paintings by Michael Dooling, *Lewis and Clark and Me* brings a doggy realism to the journey. "It really does feel as if a dog is relating the tale," asserted a *Kirkus Reviews* writer, who added that the author's "dog's eye view [of history] is well done and refreshing."

Myers again turns to history in *Escape by Night,* which is based on a story taken from the childhood of former U.S. president Woodrow Wilson. Set in Augusta, Georgia, in the fall of 1863, Myers' story focuses on nine-year-old Tommy, a pastor's son, as he befriends a wounded soldier named Red while helping out at a Confederate Army hospital set up in his father's church. As he gets to know Red, he discovers that the man actually hails from Ohio. Through their talks, the boy learns about the Yankee's perspective on the war and slavery, and when the man asks for help in escaping before he is revealed as a Union soldier and transferred to a brutal prison camp, Tommy has a difficult decision to make. "Realistic pencil sketches" by Amy June Bates "highlight pivotal scenes," noted a *Kirkus Reviews* writer, the critic predicting that readers will share Tommy's moral dilemma in Myers' "suspenseful Civil War vignette." A *Publishers Weekly* critic recommended *Escape by Night* as "sharp historical fiction, adeptly streamlined for reluctant readers," while *Booklist* critic Ian Chipman noted the author's "light touch" in presenting the moral message in her "quick and exciting chapter book."

Joining Byars and Duffey, Myers is also the coauthor of *The SOS File,* a humorous chapter book that allows readers to sit in on Mr. Magro's class as twelve students read extra-credit essays in which they recount a time when they had to ask for help from others. One of the essays has not earned the hoped-for extra grade points, and readers can help decide which one it is. The stories range from the adventurous—coming face to face with a bear, or seeing sharks swimming nearby—to the mundane—misplacing a favorite hat—to the fanciful—being discovered in a dumpster and going on a search for one's birth parents—and are brought to life in what a *Kirkus Reviews* critic described as "spot-on funny and frightening" art by Arthur Howard. In *School Library Journal,* Maria B. Salvadore praised *The SOS File* as an "engaging, plausible, and highly readable collection of anecdotes," and a *Publishers Weekly* critic suggested that the book "may well boost the confidence of reluctant readers."

Laurie Myers collaborates with mother Betsy Byars and sister Betsy Duffey on the entertaining Cat Diaries, *a story featuring artwork by Erik Brooks.*
(Illustration copyright © 2010 by Erik Brooks. Reproduced by permission of Henry Holt & Company, LLC.)

Other collaborations by the mother-daughters trio include *My Dog, My Hero, Dog Diaries: Secret Writings of the WOOF Society,* and *Cat Diaries: Secret Writings of the MEOW Society. My Dog, My Hero* contains eight tales that are purported entries for the My Hero award. The courageous canines competing for this title range from a pup that rescues a young child and a dog who makes a lonely person's life more joyful to a brave canine that locates several people lost during a tornado. In addition to capturing a diverse selection of voices in their essays for *My Dog, My Hero,* the coauthors "highlight . . . the common themes of gratitude, admiration, and love," according to *School Library Journal* contributor Pat Leach.

Illustrated by Erik Brooks, *Dog Diaries* and *Cat Diaries* also feature a collection of animal-centered stories, but here the authors take a whimsical approach by including tales told by the animals themselves. The WOOF Society (WOOF stands form Words of Our Friends) assembles to share stories told by dogs from all over the world, and the eleven tales included in *Dog Diaries* "cover many aspects of the animals' lives and are by turns touching, funny, and sad," according to *School Library Journal* contributor Terrie Dorio. Cats' perspectives on life are given equal time in *Cat Diaries,* which includes stories related during a meeting of the Memories Expressed in Our Writing (or MEOW) Society. The international convocation includes Chico, the smallest cat in the world, who requires a translator to share his crimestopping tale, and Miu, a cat worshiped in ancient Egypt. "Sure to please cats and the people who love them," according to a *Kirkus Reviews* writer, *Cat Diaries* was also recommended by the critic as "a great choice for newly independent readers."

"When I grew up I wanted to be a detective, not an author," Myers admitted on her home page. "Although an author could be creative, I didn't think an author's life would be very exciting. I was wrong. Now, I'm Seaman fighting off bears in the western wilderness. I'm Alex frantically trying to escape from Brick Johnson. I'm Buster racing across the yard to save that baby. I am all of those characters and more, without ever leaving my house. All I have to do is start writing."

Biographical and Critical Sources

PERIODICALS

Booklist, October 15, 1994, Kay Weisman, review of *Guinea Pigs Don't Talk,* p. 427; September 15, 2000, Todd Morning, review of *Surviving Brick Johnson,* p. 242; September 1, 2002, Karen Hutt, review of *Lewis and Clark and Me: A Dog's Tale,* p. 125; April 15, 2011, Ian Chipman, review of *Escape by Night: A Civil War Adventure,* p. 64.

Horn Book, September-October, 2002, Betty Carter, review of *Lewis and Clark and Me,* p. 577.

Kirkus Reviews, June 15, 2002, review of *Lewis and Clark and Me,* p. 886; May 1, 2004, review of *The SOS File,* p. 439; April 1, 2010, review of *Cat Diaries: Secret Writings of the MEOW Society;* May 15, 2011, review of *Escape by Night.*

Publishers Weekly, July 29, 2002, review of *A Leader of the Pack,* p. 74; May 17, 2004, review of *The SOS File,* p. 50; April 25, 2011, review of *Escape by Night,* p. 137.

School Library Journal, October, 2000, Elaine E. Knight, review of *Surviving Brick Johnson,* p. 131; January, 2001, Pat Leach, review of *My Dog, My Hero,* p. 92; September, 2002, Nancy Collins-Warner, review of *Lewis and Clark and Me,* p. 230; June, 2004,B. Allison Gray, review of *Surviving Brick Johnson,* p. 74; Maria B. Salvadore, review of *The SOS File,* p. 103; June, 2007, Terrie Dorio, review of *Dog Diaries: Secret Writings of the WOOF Society,* p. 92.

ONLINE

Laurie Myers Home Page, http://www.lauriemyers.com (August 1, 2011).

N-O

NAYERI, Daniel

Personal
Born in Iran; immigrated to United States. *Education:* New York University, degree.

Addresses
Home—New York, NY. *Agent*—Anderson Literary Management, 12 W. 19th St., 2nd Fl., New York, NY 10011. *E-mail*—daniel.nayeri@gmail.com.

Career
Writer and editor. Worked variously as a used bookstore clerk, children's librarian, storyteller, carpenter, and pastry chef. Former literary agent in New York, NY; HarperCollins Publisher, New York, NY, associate editor, 2004-05; Houghton Mifflin Harcourt, New York, NY, editor, beginning 2009.

Writings
Straw House, Wood House, Brick House, Blow (short fiction), illustrated by Regina Roff, Candlewick Press (New York, NY), 2011.

Author of film *The Cult of Sincerity.*

"ANOTHER" YOUNG-ADULT NOVEL SERIES; WITH SISTER DINA NAYERI

Another Faust, Candlewick Press (Somerville, MA), 2009.
Another Pan, Candlewick Press (Somerville, MA), 2010.
Another Jeykll, Candlewick Press (Somerville, MA), 2010.

Adaptations
Another Faust and *Another Pan* were adapted for audiobook, read by Katherine Kellgren, Brilliance Audio, 2009.

Sidelights
Writer, editor, and filmmaker Daniel Nayeri collaborates with his sister, Dina Nayeri, on the novels *Another Faust, Another Pan,* and *Another Jeykll.* Geared for teen readers, these books are part of the Nayeris' "Another" series, in which elements from literary classics are woven into stories featuring a group of students attending an elite New York City prep school. Nayeri's solo work, the short-story collection *Straw House, Wood House, Brick House, Blow,* treats readers to examples of stories in four classic literary genres: Westerns, science fiction, detective stories, and lighthearted romance. Interestingly, Nayeri managed to compose *Straw House, Wood House, Brick House, Blow* primarily on the keypad of his iPhone, setting perhaps a new "first" in Y.A. literature.

Nayeri was born in Iran but left as a young child when his family fled that country for religious reasons. After a period in which the Nayeris lived as refugees, he and his family immigrated to the United States, and he has continued to make his home here. After completing his degree at New York University, Nayeri worked for a literary agent and eventually found a job as an assistant editor with a major New York City publisher. He also worked on several creative endeavors, one of which was writing and producing *The Cult of Sincerity,* a feature film that was the first of its kind to have its world premier on YouTube. He was working as an associate editor when he got a phone call from Dina explaining that it was time she pursue her lifelong dream of writing a novel and would Daniel help. Over two weeks the siblings expanded Dina's idea into an outline; the manuscript of their first novel took them another twelve months and was eventually released as *Another Faust.*

Another Faust, like the other books in the "Almost" series, is liberally salted with world history as well as literary references to writers ranging from James Barrie, Johann Wolfgang von Goethe, and Lord Byron to

Cover of Daniel and Dina Nayeri's prep-school thriller Another Faust, *a story with literary origins that features artwork by Scott Nobles.* (Jacket photograph copyright © 2010 by Scott Nobles. Reproduced by permission of Candlewick Press, Somerville, MA.)

Nathaniel Hawthorne, Robert Louis Stevenson, and Laura Ingalls Wilder. *Another Faust* follows the story of five kidnaped ten year olds who have been selected for their special talents, then kidnaped and groomed in avarice and ambition by the mysterious Madame Nicola Vileroy. Now age fifteen, they emerge from seclusion and arrive at Manhattan's exclusive Marlowe School, where Madame has enrolled them. Trained to cheat, lie, and steal without any moral quibbles, the five soulless Fausts—Valentin, Victoria, Christian, and twins Bella and Bice—quickly take control and begin to pursue their endless ambitions, until secrets are revealed that cause them to see the true consequences of acquiescing to their driven natures. "Telling the story from alternate viewpoints keeps the action moving," noted *Booklist* contributor Shauna Yusko, and a *Publishers Weekly* critic dubbed the Nayeris' prose "clever and stylish." Noting the references to Goethe's *Faust* that appear throughout the novel, Hayden Bass asserted in *School Library Journal* that the story's "well-timed twists" will attract "fans of dark contemporary fantasy." "By switching character viewpoints often," wrote a *Kirkus Reviews* writer, the Nayeris "keep the pace [of their debut novel] moving to an ending full of action, revelation and horror."

A perennial favorite by English writer J.M. Barrie, *Peter Pan,* is the Nayeris' jumping-off point in *Another Pan.* This time the Marlowe School counts Wendy and John Darling among its students. The siblings know that their admission is a result of their Egyptologist father's place on the school's faculty; most of the other students are wealthy and look down on the poorer Darlings, even though Wendy is dating the popular Connor Wirth. Then a new student, Peter, arrives, aided by the sinister Madame Vileroy and bringing with him the mysterious *Book of Gates.* Wendy and John are seduced by Peter's stories of magic, only to find themselves trapped in an underworld containing an ancient mystery. Captain Hook, the Lost Boys, and teenage romance mix with Egyptian myths, mystical pyramids, and the lure of eternal youth in the Nayeris' intriguing story. Readers will enjoy "Wendy's emergence as a compelling heroine seeking her own identity," according to Judith A. Hayn in *Voice of Youth Advocates,* and a *Kirkus Reviews* writer commented that the story's "adventure and Egypt-as-life parallels keep the pages turning." In *Booklist* Shauna Yusko predicted of *Another Pan* that "this unique twist on a classic story should find even wider appreciation" than the siblings' debut, and Sue Giffard asserted in her *School Library Journal* review that "the authors succeed in creating a sense of danger that builds to a suspenseful climax."

Discussing their collaborative writing career Dina Nayeri explained the siblings' working relationship. "Writing with two people is actually a lot harder than writing alone," she noted, especially because she spends most of the year living outside the United States. Weeks are spent in the planning stages, establishing narrative voice and the story's tone, "so that when we begin writing, we can both be shooting for the same mark. Then we divide up the chapters and write a draft, and each person gets to thoroughly edit the other person's chapter. We do that a couple more times until the voice is smooth. I can't imagine being able to pull it off with a non-family member."

Biographical and Critical Sources

PERIODICALS

Booklist, September 15, 2009, Shauna Yusko, review of *Another Faust,* p. 49; November 15, 2010, Shauna Yusko, review of *Another Pan,* p. 47.

Bulletin of the Center for Children's Books, October, 2009, Karen Coats, review of *Another Faust,* p. 76.

Kirkus Reviews, review of *Another Faust;* September 15, 2010, review of *Another Pan.*

Publishers Weekly, August 3, 2009, review of *Another Faust,* p. 46.

School Library Journal, September, 2009, Hayden Bass, review of *Another Faust,* p. 168; December, 2010, Sue Giffard, review of *Another Pan,* p. 122.

Voice of Youth Advocates, August, 2009, Jennifer Miskec, review of *Another Faust,* p. 241; December, 2010, Judith A. Hayn, review of *Another Pan,* p. 474.

ONLINE

Anderson Literary Management Web site, http://www.ander sonliterary.com/ (February 15, 2011).
Candlewick Press Web site, http://www.candlewick.com/ (February 15, 2011), interview with Daniel and Dina Nayeri.
Daniel Nayeri Home Page, http://danielnayeri.com (August 15, 2011).*

*   *   *

NEWHOUSE, Maxwell 1947-

Personal

Born August 1, 1947, in Campbell River, British Columbia, Canada; married; wife's name Lillian; children: two sons, one daughter. *Education:* Attended Vancouver School of Art. *Hobbies and other interests:* Building furniture out of driftwood.

Addresses

Home—Cultus Lake, Brtish Columbia, Canada. *E-mail*—max.newhouse@telus.net.

Career

Author and illustrator. Formerly worked in construction. Presenter at schools and libraries. *Exhibitions:* Work exhibited throughout Canada, beginning 1971, including at Vancouver Art Gallery, Vancouver, British Columbia; Equinox Gallery, Vancouver; Victoria Art Gallery, Victoria, British Columbia; Doheny Gallery, Vancouver, Woltjen Gallery, Edmonton, Alberta; Petley Jones Gallery, Vancouver; Gallery of Canadian Folk Art, Calgary, Alberta; and North Vancouver Community Art Gallery. Mural installation at Manning Provincial Park, British Columbia, Canada. Work included in permanent collection, Canada House Gallery, Banff, Alberta.

Awards, Honors

Information Book Award Honour Book selection, Children's Literature Roundtables of Canada, 2004, for *Emily Carr: At the Edge of the World* by Jo Ellen Bogart; Governor General's Award for Children's Illustration nomination, 2006, for *Let's Go for a Ride.*

Writings

SELF-ILLUSTRATED

The RCMP Musical Ride, Tundra Books (Plattsburgh, NY), 2004.

Let's Go for a Ride, Tundra Books (Toronto, Ontario, Canada), 2006.
The House That Max Built, Tundra Books (Plattsburgh, NY), 2008.
Counting on Snow, Tundra Books (Plattsburgh, NY), 2010.
The Weber Street Wonder Work Crew, Tundra Books (Plattsburgh, NY), 2010.

ILLUSTRATOR

Janet Lunn, *Laura Secord: A Story of Courage,* Tundra Books (Plattsburgh, NY), 2001.
Jo Ellen Bogart, *Emily Carr: At the Edge of the World,* Tundra Books (Plattsburgh, NY), 2003.

Sidelights

Based in British Columbia, Canada, painter Maxwell Newhouse has paired his folk-style artwork with original texts in his illustrated books *The RCMP Musical Ride, Let's Go for a Ride, The House That Max Built, Counting on Snow,* and *The Weber Street Wonder Work Crew.* In addition to his original, self-illustrated books, Newhouse has also illustrated several biographies of famous Canadian women. Reviewing his work for *Emily Carr: At the Edge of the World* by Jo Ellen Bogart, *Booklist* critic Gillian Engberg praised "Newhouse's small, appealing ink drawings" that capture scenes from the life of the noted Canadian artist. *Laura Secord: A Story of Courage,* Janet Lunn's biography of a nineteenth-century Canadian patriot, features folk-art-style oil paintings that *School Library Journal* contributor Linda Ludke recommended as "a perfect match for this tale of an ordinary woman in extraordinary circumstances."

Born in British Columbia in the late 1940s, Newhouse exhibited an early talent for art, and he began to take this talent seriously in his late teens. As a young man he designed his own course of art study, experimenting with sketching and drawing, designing poster art, and embarking on a variety of traditional craft projects. When he decided to formalize his education, Newhouse was able to bypass two years of college and start his education at the Vancouver School of Art as a junior.

After working as a fine-art painter for over a decade, Newhouse began to search for new creative avenues in the late 1970s, and he found one in folk art, where he was able to capture elements of everyday life with a combination of whimsy and nostalgia. A group of oil paintings he originally exhibited in 2001 that commemorates a musical touring performance of the Royal Canadian Mounted Police eventually became his first book, *The RCMP Musical Ride.* In *School Library Journal* Corrina Austin praised Newhouse's picture-book debut as a "beautifully illustrated" profile of the popular equestrian exhibition, which was first performed in 1887 and features mounties astride rare all-black horses. "Horse lovers and fans of the Musical Ride will enjoy this information picture book, as will those interested in

Maxwell Newhouse combines a toddler-friendly story with his detailed illustrations in his nature-themed picture book Counting on Snow. (Illustration copyright © 2010 by Maxwell Newhouse. Reproduced by permission of Tundra Books.)

various aspects of Canada's history," predicted Victoria Pennell in her review of *The RCMP Musical Ride* for *Resource Links.*

Newhouse moves from horses to automobiles in *Let's Go for a Ride,* an illustrated history of the modern age of motorized road travel. Along with the twenty oil paintings featured in the book, he creates what *School Library Journal* contributor Wendy Lukehart described as "a conversational, first-person" narrative that "conveys the challenges of the early driving days," when Model T's shared the road with horse-drawn buggies and also draws readers forward in time to the mid-twentieth century. Progress of a different sort is the focus of *The House That Max Built,* as a man's dream of owning a home near a lake is brought to fruition as an army of specialists—from architects to framers, electricians, plumbers, roofers, finish carpenters, and landscapers—all take their turn in the process, helped by Max's curious dog. In *School Library Journal* Steven Engelfield recommended *The House That Max Built* for

its combination of "strong visual appeal and just enough detail," and Carolyn Phelan remarked in *Booklist* that the author/illustrator's own knowledge of construction "pays off for young readers" in a book that is both "fresh and informative."

The combination of detailed folk-style paintings and Newhouse's child-centered text has also resulted in *The Weber Street Wonder Work Crew* and *Counting on Snow,* the latter which uses Canadiana to introduce young children to the numbers one through ten. The artist casts what *School Library Journal* critic Heidi Estrin characterized as "a multicultural group of intensely helpful children" in his story about neighborliness and volunteerism in *The Weber Street Wonder Work Crew.* If everyone pitches in and helps out, everyone is better off, readers find, and children can help by weeding gardens, walking dogs, babysitting, and helping with cleaning, cooking, and manning the neighborhood garage sale. By following the efforts of the eleven young people in his story, Newhouse "sends an encouraging and positive message to children about the volume of working together," asserted *Resource Links* contributor Tanya Boudreau.

Biographical and Critical Sources

PERIODICALS

Booklist, November 1, 2003, Gillian Engberg, review of *Emily Carr: At the Edge of the World,* p. 510; April 15, 2008, Carolyn Phelan, review of *The House That Max Built,* p. 48.

Horn Book, March-April, 2002, Mary M. Burns, review of *Laura Secord: A Story of Courage,* p. 214.

Kirkus Reviews, April 15, 2010, review of *The Weber Street Wonder Work Crew.*

Resource Links, December, 2003, Victoria Pennell, review of *Emily Carr,* p. 24; April, 2004, Victoria Pennell, review of *The RCMP Musical Ride,* p. 34; April, 2008, Isobel Lang, review of *The House That Max Built,* p. 5; February, 2010, Tanya Boudreau, review of *The Weber Street Wonder Work Crew,* p. 4.

School Library Journal, April, 2002, Linda Ludke, review of *Laura Secord,* p. 152; December, 2003, Cris Riedel, review of *Emily Carr,* p. 164; September, 2004, Corrina Austin, review of *The RCMP Music Ride,* p. 230; April, 2006, Wendy Lukehart, review of *Let's Go for a Ride,* p. 130; May, 2008, Steven Engelfield, review of *The House That Max Built,* p. 116; June, 2010, Heidi Estrin, review of *The Weber Street Wonder Work Crew,* p. 81; December, 2010, Grace Oliff, review of *Counting on Snow,* p. 96.

ONLINE

Maxwell Newhouse Home Page, http://www.maxwellnew house.com (July 12, 2011).

*   *   *

O'BRIEN, Caragh M.

Personal

Born in St. Paul, MN; married; children: two sons, one daughter. *Education:* Williams College, B.A.; Johns Hopkins University, M.A. (writing).

Addresses

Home—Storrs, CT. *Agent*—Kirby Kim, William Morris Endeavor, 152 W. 57th St., 25th Fl., New York, NY 10022. *E-mail*—cob@caraghobrien.com.

Career

Educator and writer. Teacher of high school in Tolland, CT, until 2011.

Awards, Honors

CYBILS Young-Adult Fantasy/Science Fiction Award nomination, 2010, and Best Fiction for Young Adults selection, YALSA/American Library Association, and Amelia Bloomer List selection, both 2011, all for *Birthmarked.*

Writings

YOUNG-ADULT NOVELS

Birthmarked, Roaring Brook Press (New York, NY), 2010.
Prized (sequel to *Birthmarked*), Roaring Brook Press (New York, NY), 2011.

Author's books have been translated into French and German.

OTHER

Master Touch (adult novel), Bantam Books (New York, NY), 1998.
North Star Rising (adult novel), Bantam Books (New York, NY), 1998.
Kissing Lessons (adult novel), Kensington Pub. (New York, NY), 2000.

Sidelights

After earning her M.A. in writing from Johns Hopkins University, Caragh M. O'Brien authored several adult romances while continuing her career as a high-school teacher. Things changed after O'Brien switched genres and began to focus on young-adult fiction. With the critical success of her science-fiction-themed *Birthmarked,* O'Brien was able to leave teaching and devote her full time to her writing.

O'Brien grew up in Minnesota, but moved to New England when she began her undergraduate education at Massachusetts's Williams College. She came up with the idea for her first novel while on a road trip south with her husband and children. "There was a severe drought," O'Brien recalled on her home page, "and the lakes were so low the landscape seemed like a wasteland. That started me imagining what political and social things might happen after climate change, and the first ideas for Gaia's story began there. I wrote the first chapter as a sort of experiment, and quickly realized I needed to write more to see what happened."

In *Birthmarked* O'Brien takes readers to a near-future Earth in which the problems of climate change have become pronounced over the past three centuries. Sixteen-year-old Gaia Stone lives in Wharfton, a village on the north shore of Unlake Superior that is outside the Enclave, a city walled in to provide relative safety and stability to its inhabitants. As a midwife working alongside her mother, Gaia is obligated to select three healthy newborns for transportation into the Enclave each month. After one mother refuses to relinquish her infant, Gaia's mother is arrested in retaliation. Finding her way behind the wall, Gaia endeavors to locate her mother, but what she finds within the Enclave signals a society that is lulled into submission by a controlling and corrupt government. "Genetics and medical knowledge play a large role," noted a *Kirkus Reviews* writer, explaining that a secret code used to rank infants of genetic merit also figures in O'Brien's plot. Gaia's story continues in *Prized* as the teenaged midwife and her infant sister ultimately find themselves living, under coercion, in a matriarchal society called Sylum where another oppressive government uses environmental threats to subdue its people.

Although Daniel Kraus noted in *Booklist* that O'Brien's dystopian novels incorporate many elements of science fiction, the author's "concerns are corporeal; her impulsive and spirited heroine . . . is the kind readers adore." Reviewing *Birthmarked*, a *Publishers Weekly* critic noted that the author's future world allows her to "explore complex issues of morality and survival" in a story that treats readers to "a brisk and sometimes provocative read." "Readers who enjoy adventures with a strong heroine standing up to authority against fire odds will enjoy this compelling tale," predicted *School Library Journal* contributor Sue Giffard in her review of O'Brien's Y.A. debut.

Biographical and Critical Sources

PERIODICALS

Booklist, February 15, 2010, Daniel Kraus, review of *Birthmarked,* p. 47.
Bulletin of the Center for Children's Books, September, 2010, April Spisak, review of *Birthmarked,* p. 36.
Kirkus Reviews, March 15, 2010, review of *Birthmarked.*
Publishers Weekly, February 15, 2010, review of *Birthmarked,* p. 132.
School Library Journal, May, 2010, Sue Giffard, review of *Birthmarked,* p. 120.
Voice of Youth Advocates, April, 2010, Etienne Vallee, review of *Birthmarked,* p. 74.

ONLINE

Caragh O'Brien Home Page, http://www.caraghobrien.com (August 11, 2011).*

P

PALMER, Robin 1969-

Personal

Born 1969. *Education:* Boston University, degree.

Addresses

Home—New York, NY. *Agent*—Kate Lee, ICM, 825 8th Ave., New York, NY 10019. *E-mail*—robin@robinpalmeronline.com.

Career

Television producer and author. William Morris Agency, Los Angeles, CA, assistant in television literary department, then literary agent; Lifetime Television, producer and developer; freelance writer, beginning 2001.

Writings

YOUNG-ADULT NOVELS

Cindy Ella, Speak (New York, NY), 2008.
Geek Charming, Speak (New York, NY), 2009.
Little Miss Red, Speak (New York, NY), 2009.

"YOURS TRULY, LUCY B. PARKER" MIDDLE-GRADE NOVEL SERIES

Girl vs. Superstar, G.P. Putnam's Sons (New York, NY), 2010.
Sealed with a Kiss, G.P. Putnam's Sons (New York, NY), 2010.

Adaptations

Geek Charming was adapted as a television film produced for the Disney Channel.

Sidelights

Robin Palmer lived in California and worked as a producer and developer for television until rekindling her interest in fiction writing. Now based in New York City, Palmer entertains middle-grade and older teens with novels that include *Cindy Ella, Geek Charming,* and *Little Miss Red* as well as sharing the chronicles of an adventurous sixth grader in her "Yours Truly, Lucy B. Parker" series.

Palmer was raised in the northeastern United States and earned her college degree at Boston University. A jump to the West Coast led to a job at the William Morris Agency, and from there she moved to an executive position at Lifetime Television, where she helped develop and produce the original films airing on that network. In 2001 she decided to make her break from the fast-paced, highly competitive Hollywood culture by leveraging her writing talent. Palmer's first novel, *Cindy Ella,* was published seven years later.

Set in Los Angeles, *Cindy Ella* finds high-school sophomore Cindy less than enthusiastic about the upcoming school prom. Her twin stepsisters are in hyperdrive in their preparations for the special day, however, and Cindy's stepmother encourages their drama. When Cindy writes a letter to the school newspaper in which she notes the relative insignificance of the prom in relation to the Earth's environmental woes, she becomes an outcast among most of her peers . . . with the exception of her two best friends and her online pal "BklynBoy." Although *Cindy Ella* was judged to be a somewhat "formulaic, fairy-tale-based romance" by *School Library Journal* critic Susan Riley, Palmer's heroine is "a wonderful character—thoughtful, intelligent, pretty, and kind."

Palmer returns readers to Los Angeles in *Geek Charming,* as Castle Heights High School diva Dylan Schoenfield seems to have the best of everything: the best boyfriend, the best girlfriends, and the most coveted handbag in school to boot. When her prized handbag is accidentally tossed into a fountain during a trip to the shopping mall, Dylan finds herself in debut to its rescuer, nerdish classmate Josh Rosen. In return, she agrees to appear in Josh's current film about teen popularity, a film he hopes will be his ticket to a film-school

A preteen East Coast transplant gives her impressions of the California lifestyle in Girl vs. Superstar, *a novel by Robin Palmer that features artwork by Anne Cresci.* (Cover art copyright © 2010 by Anne Cresci. Reproduced by permission of G.P. Putnam's Sons, a division of Penguin Young Readers Group, a member of Penguin Group (USA) Inc., 345 Hudson St., New York, NY 10014. All rights reserved.)

scholarship. As Josh trails the beautiful and popular young woman through the social milieu of the popular cliques, each gains a new perspective as their flaws, vulnerabilities, and strengths come to the fore, especially after Dylan is dumped by her current beau. Reviewing *Geek Charming* in *Publishers Weekly,* a critic noted that Palmer's "lighthearted" second novel is "filled with snappy dialogue" and the alternating narratives of Dylan and Josh wind to a "more original and plausible" ending than the standard teen romance. In *School Library Journal* Brandy Danner noted that, while the novel's "plot is predictable," Palmer's "writing is sharp" and her humorous touch will add to "teens' enjoyment of this riches-to-rags title."

Dubbed by *Booklist* critic Debbie Carton a "frothy addition to the modern fairy-tale genre," Palmer's *Little Miss Red* introduces Sophie Greene, a seventeen-year-old high schooler whose history of good grades and loyalty to a humdrum but likeable boyfriend do not

seem to be leading her to a life that compares with those of Devon Devoreaux, the heroine of her favorite romance novels. Everything changes when Sophie is forced out of her comfort zone while on a trip east to visit her grandmother. On the plane to Florida she finds herself seated next to Jack, a handsome and suave nineteen year old who seems to be worthy of Devon herself. As she gains the confidence to step out of her comfort zone, Sophie also learns to deal with real life rather than fantasy.

Geared for slightly younger readers, Palmer's "Yours Truly, Lucy B. Parker" novels focus on a twelve year old who is trying to find her own place in a family under the celebrity spotlight. Lucy just wants life to be normal, but that is not likely to happen now that her mom is marrying the father of preteen television actress and singing sensation Laurel Moses. In *Girl vs. Superstar* Lucy has been dropped by her best friends, and she feels even worse when photographed by the paparazzi standing next to her glam soon-to-be stepsister. Desperate e-mails to Dr. Maude, the star of a television advice show, help the preteen articulate her troubles while life with Laurel slowly reveals some surprises that make *Girl vs. Superstar* both "funny" and "fast-paced," according to *Booklist* critic Kara Dean. "Palmer does a great job of showing the glitter of stardom as well as the downsides of fame," noted Wendy E. Dunn in her *School Library Journal* review of the same novel, while Dean predicted of the sequel, *Sealed with a Kiss,* that "fans will look forward to future installments" of Lucy's Hollywood adventures.

Biographical and Critical Sources

PERIODICALS

Booklist, February 1, 2010, Debbie Carton, review of *Little Miss Red,* p. 38; June 1, 2010, Kara Dean, review of *Girl vs. Superstar,* p. 83; December 15, 2010, Kara Dean, review of *Sealed with a Kiss,* p. 54.

Bulletin of the Center for Children's Books, June, 2009, Karen Coats, review of *Geek Charming,* p. 413.

Publishers Weekly, January 26, 2009, review of *Geek Charming,* p. 121; January 11, 2010, review of *Little Miss Red,* p. 49.

School Library Journal, February, 2008, Susan Riley, review of *Cindy Ella,* p. 124; September, 2009, Brandy Danner, review of *Geek Charming,* p. 170; February, 2010, Tina Zubak, review of *Little Miss Red,* p. 121; April, 2010, Wendy E. Dunn, review of *Girl vs. Superstar,* p. 165.

Voice of Youth Advocates, April, 2009, Debbie Clifford, review of *Geek Charming,* p. 56; April, 2010, Mary Ann Darby, review of *Little Miss Red,* p. 61.

ONLINE

Robin Palmer Home Page, http://www.robinpalmeronline.com (June 12, 2011).

Robin Palmer Web log, http://robinpalmer.blogspot.com (June 12, 2011).*

*   *   *

PEIRCE, Lincoln

Personal

Born in Ames, IA; father a college professor; married; children: two. *Education:* Attended Skowhegan School of Painting and Sculpture; Colby College, B.A. (art); Brooklyn College, M.F.A.

Addresses

Home—Portland, ME. *E-mail*—bignate@harpercollins. com.

Career

Cartoonist, author, and illustrator. Creator of "Big Nate" comic strip through United Features Syndicate, beginning 1991; teacher of art in New York City high schools; animator of short cartoon films.

Writings

"BIG NATE" SERIES; SELF-ILLUSTRATED

Big Nate Strikes Again, Harper (New York, NY), 2010.
Big Nate: In a Class by Himself, Harper (New York, NY), 2010.
Big Nate Out Loud (originally published in syndication, 2007), Andrews McMeel (Kansas City, MO), 2011.
Big Nate from the Top (originally published in syndication, 2006-07), Andrews McMeel (Kansas City, MO), 2011.
Big Nate: A Cartoon Collection, Andrews McMee (Kansas City, MO), 2011.
Big Nate Boredom Buster: Super Scribbles, Cool Comix, and Lots of Laughs, Harper (New York, NY), 2011.
Big Nate: On a Roll, Harper (New York, NY), 2011.

Comics also collected as *I Smell a Pop Quiz: A Big Nate Book* and *Add More Babes!*

Author's work has been published in Chinese, Czech, Dutch, French, Germany, Hebrew, Indonesian, Italian, Japanese, Portuguese, Spanish, and Turkish.

Sidelights

Cartoonist Lincoln Peirce wields the pen behind the "Big Nate" comic strip, which can be found in more than 250 U.S. newspapers, posted on *Comics.com,* and collected in *Big Nate from the Top* and *Big Nate Out Loud.* The eleven-year-old brainiac who stars in Peirce's popular strip has also made appearances in several well-illustrated chapter books, among them *Big Nate: In a*

Class by Himself, Big Nate Strikes Again, and *Big Nate: On a Roll.* In chronicling the preteen's comic exploits, Peirce draws on memories of his own childhood and his experience as a high-school art teacher. Reviewing *Big Nate Strikes Again* in *Booklist,* Ian Chipman dubbed the book "fun for boys," noting that the author/illustrator's addition of "cartoon tidbits make the pages fly past with punch lines galore."

Peirce was born in Iowa but spent his formative years in northern New England, where he developed a talent for cartooning. After earning an art degree at Colby College, Peirce taught high school in New York City and also earned an M.F.A. at Brooklyn College. His first "Big Nate" comic strip appeared in 1991 and ran for over two decades before attracting the interest of major book publishers. After the comic was posted on the popular *Poptropica* Web site in February of 2009, however, requests to view the online comic crashed the site. News of "Big Nate"'s popularity made it to editors at HarperCollins and resulted in Peirce's first book contract. "One of my goals was to write a book that I would have loved to read when I was a kid," Peirce told Maine-based *Portland Press Herald* contributor Tom Atwell in describing Big Nate's move to chapter books. "Kids are so visual. That is how I looked at books as a kid when I went to the library. I'd flip through the book to check out the pictures. This is a book for kids who like comics and who like a good story."

Nate Wright, the outgoing preteen star of the comic that bears his name, has too much going to be tied down by school schedules. For him, middle-school life seems to alternate between the desperately tedious and the horribly challenging, with teachers thrown into the mix to add to the frustration. In his first graphic-novel outing, *Big Nate: In a Class by Himself,* Nate's belief that he is exceptional is reinforced by a fortune cookie, and although he spends his school hours hoping to discover his special talent, his only measurable success is in accumulating detentions. *Big Nate Strikes Again* finds Nate teamed up with insufferable straight-A student Gina Hemphill-Toms to prepare a presentation on Ben Franklin for Mrs. Godfrey's class. The chance to help his fleeceball team win an upcoming tournament buoy's Nate's spirits . . . until he realizes that Gina is also on his team and has named it the Kuddle Kittens.

Reviewing Peirce's first chapter book, a *Publishers Weekly* critic praised Nate as a "sharp-witted and unflappable protagonist" that will find fans among Peirce's target audience of eight-to-twelve-year-olds, and *School Library Journal* reviewer Lora Van Marel predicted the popularity of the "laugh-out-loud" story among reluctant readers. "Peirce gets all the details of a sixth-grade boy just right," wrote Robin L. Smith in her *Horn Book* review of *Big Nate Strikes Again,* the critic predicting that "even the most jaded middle-schooler will find much to laugh about" in Nate's second book-length outing. Calling the same book "clever and funny,"

Lincoln Peirce's cartoon character "Big Nate" has found his way into several entertaining stories, among them **Big Nate: In a Class by Himself.** (Illustration copyright © 2010 Lincoln Peirce. Reproduced by permission of HarperCollins Children's Books, a division of HarperCollins Publishers, Ltd.)

School Library Journal critic Patty Saidenberg added that Peirce's loosely drawn comics and well-paced text combine to "give the story a fun and carefree rhythm."

Biographical and Critical Sources

PERIODICALS

Booklist, March 1, 2010, Ian Chipman, review of *Big Nate: In a Class by Himself,* p. 70; February 1, 2011, Ian Chipman, review of *Big Nate Strikes Again,* p. 78.

Bulletin of the Center for Children's Books, May, 2010, Karen Coats, review of *Big Nate: In a Class by Himself,* p. 393.

Horn Book, November-December, 2010, Robin L. Smith, review of *Big Nate Strikes Again,* p. 101; July-August, 2010, Robin L. Smith, review of *Big Nate: In a Class by Himself,* p. 118.

Kirkus Reviews, March 1, 2010, review of *Big Nate: In a Class by Himself.*

Portland Press Herald (Portland, ME), May 30, 2010, Tom Atwell, interview with Peirce.

Publishers Weekly, April 12, 2010, review of *Big Nate: In a Class by Himself,* p. 49.

School Library Journal, April, 2010, Lora van Marel, review of *Big Nate: In a Class by Himself,* p. 166; December, 2010, Patty Saidenberg, review of *Big Nate Strikes Again,* p. 122.

Washington Post, June 27, 2010, Michael Cavna, interview with Peirce.

ONLINE

Lincoln Peirce Home Page, http://www.bignatebooks.com (June 12, 2011).

United Features Syndicate Web site, http://unitedfeatures.com/ (August 3, 2011), "Lincoln Peirce."

*   *   *

PERRY, M. LaVora

Personal

Born in Cleveland, OH; married Cedric Richardson; children: three. *Education:* Attended Ithaca College and City College of New York; Cleveland State University, B.S. (elementary education; cum laude), 1995. *Religion:* Buddhist. *Hobbies and other interests:* Nature walks, bicycling, ice skating and rollerskating, reading, dancing, watching movies, spending time with family.

Addresses

Home—East Cleveland, OH. *Office*—Forest Hill Publishing, 13200 Forest Hill Ave., East Cleveland, OH 44112. *E-mail*—mlavoraperry@mlavoraperry.com.

Career

Writer, publisher, and journalist. Former actor; neighborhood activist; American Greetings, staff writer, beginning 1995; Forest Hill Publishing, founder, 2004. Presenter at schools and workshop.

Member

Society of Children's Book Writers and Illustrators (marketing coordinator of Northern Ohio chapter), Soka Gakkai International.

Awards, Honors

Creative Excellence Award, American Greetings, 1999, 2000.

Writings

Successful Self-publishing: From Children's Author to Independent Publisher, a Guide for Writers, Forest Hill Pub. (East Cleveland, OH), 2005.
Taneesha Never Disparaging, Wisdom Publications (Boston, MA), 2008.
Peacebuilders, Forest Hil Pub. (East Cleveland, OH), 2011.

Contributor to books, including *Illuminations: Expressions of the Personal Spiritual Experience,* Celestial Arts, 2006, and *Bumbo for the Soul: The Recipe for Literacy in the African-American Community,* 2007. Columnist and contributor to *Greater University Circle Neighborhood Voice* (Cleveland, OH); contributor to periodicals, including *Catalyst—Ohio* and *Living Buddism.*

Biographical and Critical Sources

PERIODICALS

Kirkus Reviews, March 1, 2010, review of *Peacebuilders.*

ONLINE

M. LaVora Perry Home Page, http://www.mlavoraperry.com (May 11, 2011).
Brown Bookshelf Web site, http://thebrownbookshelf.com (February 18, 2010), interview with Perry.

*   *   *

PETERS, Lisa Westberg 1951-

Personal

Born October 19, 1951, in Minneapolis, MN; daughter of Walter M. (an inventor) and Naomi (a nurse) Westberg; married David G. Peters (a journalist), August 16, 1975; children: Emily, Anna. *Education:* University of Minnesota, B.A., 1974. *Hobbies and other interests:* Hiking, canoeing, swimming, reading, gardening, travel.

Addresses

Home—Minneapolis, MN. *E-mail*—lwpeters@comcast.net.

Career

Writer. The Loft, instructor in children's-book writing; speaker at schools and conferences.

Member

Children's Literature Network, Geological Society of Minnesota, Loft Literary Center, Minneapolis Institute of Arts, International Sand Collectors Society.

Awards, Honors

Outstanding Science Trade Book designation, National Science Teachers Association, and Minnesota Book Award nomination, both 1988, both for *The Sun, the Wind, and the Rain*; Notable Children's Trade Book in Social Studies selection, Children's Book Council (CBC), 1990, for *Good Morning, River!*; CBC Children's Choice selection, and Children's Book of the Year designation, Child Study Children's Book Committee, both 1992, both for *Water's Way;* International Reading Association (IRA) Children's Choice selection, 1995, for *Meg and Dad Discover Treasure in the Air;* Outstanding Science Trade Book for Children selection, 1995, for *When the Fly . . . ;* American Library Association Notable Book designation, and IRA Children's Choice selection, both 2001, both for *Cold Little Duck, Duck, Duck*; Minnesota Book Award, 2003, and *Riverbank Review* book of distinction honor, 2004, both for *Our Family Tree;* Minnesota Book Award nomination, *Riverbank Review* Book of Distinction honor, and *School Library Journal* Best Book designation, all 2004, all for *Earthshake.*

Writings

The Sun, the Wind, and the Rain, illustrated by Ted Rand, Holt (New York, NY), 1988.
Serengeti, Macmillan (New York, NY), 1989.
Tania's Trolls, illustrated by Sharon Wooding, Arcade (New York, NY), 1989.
The Condor, Macmillan (New York, NY), 1990.
Good Morning, River!, illustrated by Deborah Kogan Ray, Arcade (New York, NY), 1990.
Water's Way, illustrated by Ted Rand, Arcade (New York, NY), 1991.
Purple Delicious Blackberry Jam, illustrated by Barbara McGregor, Arcade (New York, NY), 1992.
This Way Home, illustrated by Normand Chartier, Holt (New York, NY), 1993.

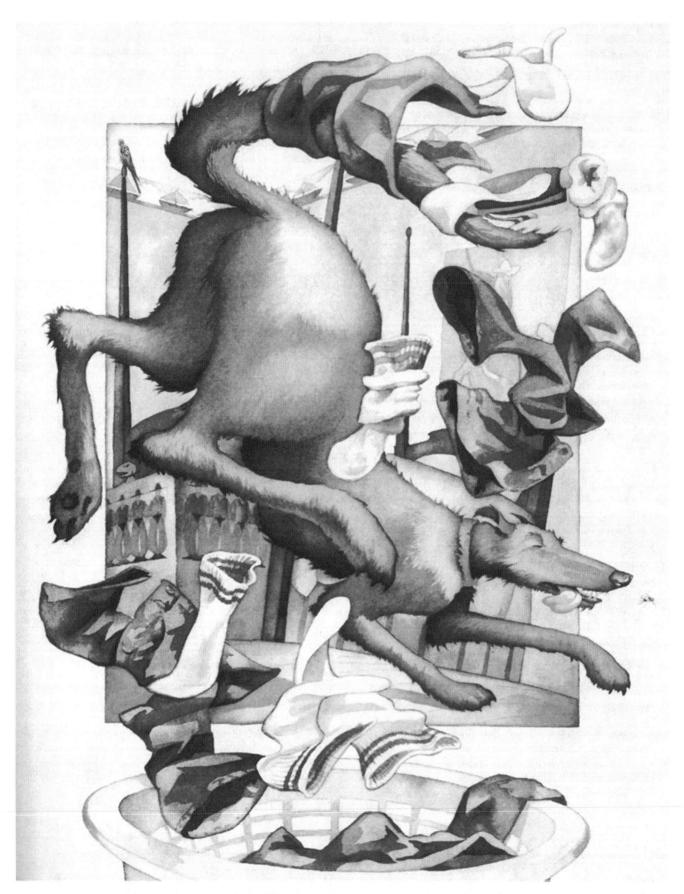

***Lisa Westberg Peters teams up with artist Brad Sneed to tell an imaginative story in* When the Fly Flew In.** (Illustration copyright © 1994 by Brad Sneed. Reproduced by permission of Dial Books for Young Readers, a division of Penguin Young Readers Group, a member of Penguin Group (USA) Inc., 345 Hudson St., New York, NY 10014. All rights reserved.)

When the Fly Flew in . . ., illustrated by Brad Sneed, Dial Books for Young Readers (New York, NY), 1994.

The Hayloft, illustrated by K.D. Plum, Dial Books for Young Readers (New York, NY), 1995.

Meg and Dad Discover Treasure in the Air, illustrated by Deborah Durland DeSaix, Holt (New York, NY), 1995.

October Smiled Back, illustrated by Ed Young, Holt (New York, NY), 1996.

Cold Little Duck, Duck, Duck, illustrated by Sam Williams, Greenwillow Books (New York, NY), 2000.

Our Family Tree: An Evolution Story, illustrated by Lauren Stringer, Harcourt (San Diego, CA), 2003.

Earthshake: Poems from the Ground Up, illustrated by Cathie Felstead, Greenwillow Books (New York, NY), 2003.

We're Rabbits!, illustrated by Jeff Mack, Harcourt (Orlando, FL), 2004.

Sleepyhead Bear, illustrated by Ian Schoenherr, Greenwillow Books (New York, NY), 2006.

Frankie Works the Night Shift, illustrated by Jennifer Taylor, Greenwillow Books (New York, NY), 2010.

Volcano Wakes Up!, illustrated by Steve Jenkins, Henry Holt (New York, NY), 2010.

Sidelights

Lisa Westberg Peters writes stories, poems, and novels aimed at a young audience. Paired with well-known illustrators such as Ed Young, Ted Rand, Deborah Kogan Ray, Jeff Mack, Lauren Stringer, and Steve Jenkins, her picture-book stories include *Earthshake: Poems from the Ground Up, We're Rabbits!, Sleepyhead Bear,* and *Frankie Works the Night Shift.* Stories for older readers include *The Condor* and *Serengeti.*

Peters was born and raised in Minnesota, where she often spent the summers in a cabin on the banks of the St. Croix River. Her father was an engineer with the 3-M Company, and he successfully inspired his daughter with an interest in science at an early age. Peters attended the University of Minnesota, where she met her husband, David Peters, while the two of them were working on the staff of the school newspaper. Although she had been writing for years, she began writing for children because, as she explained in an interview posted at her home page, "I like to tell them about the things I've discovered about the world. I also like to make them smile." Peters credits her two daughters, Emily and Anna, with giving her ideas for stories when the girls were young. The Peters sisters became a deep well of both character and story ideas for their writer mother, and they told Peters when a story she was writing was moving too slowly or was too scary.

In *Our Family Tree: An Evolution Story* Peters presents, in picture-book format, a family album of Man's ancient ancestors. Beginning by describing the early, single-cell creatures that first lived in the sea, Peters traces the journey of life on Earth from these simple beginnings to the human beings of the modern day.

Along the way, she takes what a critic for *Publishers Weekly* called an "outside/inside approach," describing the outward appearance and then the genetic foundations of each creature in the evolutionary story.

As Peters explained in an article for *Riverbank Review,* it took her "about thirteen years" to develop the idea and text for *Our Family Tree.* The idea for the book had been waiting in the back of her mind since she and her husband went on a camping trip in the mountains near Seattle. Out in the natural world, Peters began to wonder about the idea of evolution and "what it means to be human." Actually writing about the topic took years of research and reading, as Peters learned all she could about evolution, geology, and fossils. Finally, when it was time to write the story, "I sat on my back porch surrounded by a struggling Minnesota spring. . . . It took less than an hour to write the manuscript that was to become *Our Family Tree.* I knew it was the story I wanted to tell." Praising Peters' effort, a critic for *Kirkus Reviews* called the book "a lyrical, carefully researched look into our deep past," and a *St. Paul Pioneer Press* contributor asserted that *Our Family Tree* "provides the perfect way to introduce a complex scientific concept to young children."

Peters' lifelong interest in geology led her to write *Earthshake!: Poems from the Ground Up.* The twenty-

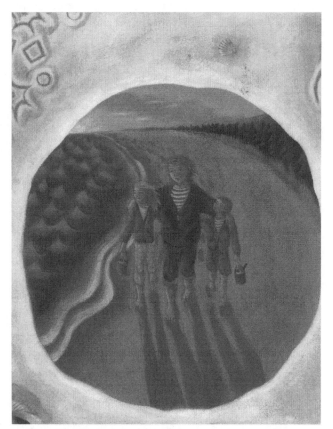

Peters presents the theory of evolution to young readers by describing the interrelationship of all human life on Earth in **Our Family Tree,** *illustrated by Lauren Stringer.* (Illustration copyright © 2003 by Lauren Stringer. Reproduced by permission of Harcourt, Inc.)

two poems in the collection cover everything from the movement of tectonic plates and the creation of fossils to such humble subjects as simple rocks and the course of a mountain stream. Cris Riedel, writing in *School Library Journal,* called the poems in the book "exuberant, silly, and serious by turns," while *Booklist* critic Carolyn Phelan recommended *Earthshake!* as "a creative addition to earth science units." A critic for *Kirkus Reviews* was particularly forward-looking in the book's usefulness, observing that Peters' book "could be used in the classroom for the next 10,000 years."

Earth science also inspired Peters' text for *Volcano Wakes Up!,* a collaboration with noted cut-paper-collage artist Jenkins that focuses on one of the most visually dramatic geological manifestations. In lighthearted rhyme, the book's sixteen poems take a "day-in-the-life" approach to a growing volcano, showing the environment that exists near a slowly erupting volcano. "From clever acrostics to bantering text messages, Peters playfully mixes poetry forms," wrote a *Kirkus Reviews* writer in discussing the volume, and Phelan noted that Jenkins' "dramatic compositions" featuring "varied hues and textures create visual interest even in scenes with no living characters." Noting Peters' inclusion of a fact-filled afterword, *School Library Journal* contributor Patricia Manning recommended *Volcano Wakes Up!* as "a way to connect geology and poetry in an interdisciplinary curriculum."

Animals figure in several of Peters' stories for young children. In *We're Rabbits!* a trio of garden-munching bunnies stays one hop ahead of a hard-working gardener, while *Sleepyhead Bear* pairs illustrations by Ian Schoenherr with a story about a drowsy bear cub that hopes to take an afternoon nap but is kept awake by the relentless buzzing of woodland insects. The counting book *Frankie Works the Night Shift* is illustrated with Jennifer Taylor's digital art and follows an orange cat on its nightly rounds keeping the mice at bay in a family's hardware story. Reviewing *We're Rabbits!* in *Kirkus Reviews,* a critic dubbed the picture book "a new-or pre-reader's delight," while *Booklist* critic Terry Glover wrote that Peters' "lilting, rhyming text" teams with Jeff Mack's colorful to "perfectly capture the story's rough-and-tumble action." A "warm bedtime rhyme," in the words of *Booklist* critic Hazel Rochman, *Sleepyhead Bear* "will have toddlers . . . snuggling down, soft and warm," and *Frankie Works the Night Shift* was characterized by a *Kirkus Reviews* writer as an "enormously entertaining" work that "is given a huge boost of silliness and adrenalin by . . . Taylor's photo-based digital collages."

"Perhaps because I spent childhood summers on a river, I especially like to write picture books involving nature or the natural sciences," Peters once commented. "The woods and rivers of Minnesota and Wisconsin left a strong impression on me as a child, and my writing career started with poetry on the beach on lazy summer afternoons. Eventually I chose the more practical field of journalism, but after my children were born, I wandered away from newspapering in order to linger over the sounds, patterns, and rhythms found in children's books.

"Because I'm not a scientist, I recognize the need to make scientific subjects appealing and understandable. For the sake of young minds, I blend the facts of science with the pull of story. I also try to use simple and expressive language. My ideas come from my own experiences as a mountain climber, a bird watcher, a fossil finder, and from what I hope is a lifelong curiosity about the earth and its creatures. I'm simply trying to gather kids around and help them discover what I am discovering for myself.

"Besides picture-book science, I also write children's fiction. My ideas for those stories come from my childhood, my children, my travels, and from a place in my mind where ideas simmer until they're ready. My inspiration to write often comes from a different source—reading great books or listening to great music."

Jennifer Taylor creates the detailed illustrations for Peters' **Frankie Works the Night Shift,** *which finds a retired kitty pulling its weight as a factory guard cat.* (Illustration copyright © 2010 by Jennifer Taylor. Reproduced by HarperCollins Children's Books, a division of HarperCollins Publishers.)

Biographical and Critical Sources

PERIODICALS

Booklist, March 15, 2003, Hazel Rochman, review of *Our Family Tree: An Evolution Story,* p. 1326; November 15, 2003, Carolyn Phelan, review of *Earthshake: Poems from the Ground Up,* p. 596; March 15, 2004,

Sam Williams takes up illustration duties in Peters' engaging picture book Cold Little Duck, Duck, Duck. (Greenwillow Books, an imprint of HarperCollins Publishers, 2000. Illustration copyright © 2003 by Sam Williams. Reproduced by permission of HarperCollins Children's Books, a division of HarperCollins Publishers.)

Terry Glover, review of *We're Rabbits!*, p. 1310; March 1, 2010, Carolyn Phelan, review of *Volcano Wakes Up!*, p. 69; April 15, 2010, Ilene Cooper, review of *Frankie Works the Night Shift*, p. 51.

Kirkus Reviews, April 1, 2003, review of *Our Family Tree*, p. 538; July 15, 2003, review of *Earthshake*, p. 967; January 1, 2004, review of *We're Rabbits!*, p. 40; February 15, 2010, review of *Volcano Wakes Up!*

Publishers Weekly, February 17, 2003, review of *Our Family Tree*, p. 73.

Riverbank Review, spring, 2003, Lisa Westberg Peters, "The Evolution of *Our Family Tree*."

Ruminator Review, fall, 2003, Lisa Bullard, review of *Our Family Tree.*

St. Paul Pioneer Press, April 29, 2003, review of *Our Family Tree.*

School Library Journal, May, 2003, Patricia Manning, review of *Our Family Tree*, p. 140; September, 2003, Cris Riedel, review of *Earthshake*, p. 204; February, 2010, Mary Jean Smith, review of *Frankie Works the Night Shift*, p. 92.

ONLINE

Children's Literature Network Online, http://www.childrens literaturnetwork.org/ (July 15, 2011), "Lisa Westberg Peters."

Lisa Westberg Peters Home Page, http://www.lisawestberg peters.com (July 15, 2011).*

*   *   *

PURVIS, Leland

Personal

Married; wife's name Elizabeth. *Education:* Portland State University, B.A. (history), 1991.

Addresses

Home—Brooklyn, NY. *E-mail*—leland.purvis@gmail. com.

Career

Illustrator and sequential artist.

Awards, Honors

Xeric Foundation grant, 2000, for *Vóx: Collected Works*; Ignatz Award nomination for Promising New Talent, 2004, for *Suspended in Language.*

Writings

SELF-ILLUSTRATED

Pubo (originally published in comic-book format), Dark Horse Comics (Milwaukie, OR), 2003.

Vóx: Collected Works, 1999-2003 (originally published in comic-book format), Absence of Ink Comics, 2004.

ILLUSTRATOR

Jim Ottaviani, *Suspended in Language: Niels Bohr's Life, Discoveries, and the Century He Shaped,* GT Labs (Ann Arbor, MI), 2004.

Marshall Poe, *Sons of Liberty* ("Turning Points" graphic-novel series), Aladdin Paperbacks (New York, NY), 2008.

Marshall Poe, *A House Divided* ("Turning Points" graphic-novel series), Aladdin Paperbacks (New York, NY), 2008.

Douglas Rushkoff, *Program or Be Programmed: Ten Commands for a Digital Age,* OR Books (New York, NY), 2010.

Illustrator of "Vulcan and Vishnu" (online comic). Contributor to anthologies, including *The Monon Street Power Collective 1,* Welsh El Dorado Press, 2004; *24seven,* Image Comics, 2006; and *Smut Peddler,* volume three, Saucy Goose Press, 2006.

ILLUSTRATOR; "RESISTANCE" GRAPHIC-NOVEL SERIES BY CARLA JABLONSKI

Resistance, First Second (New York, NY), 2010.

Defiance, First Second (New York, NY), 2011.

Victory, First Second (New York, NY), 2011.

Sidelights

A self-taught artist with a degree in history, award-winning comics creator Leland Purvis is best known as the talent behind the "Vóx" and "Pubo" comics series, both of which feature his detailed black-and-white sequential line art. Purvis's illustrations also appear along-

Leland Purvis has created the art for **Resistance,** *the first installment in Carla Jablonsi's three-part graphic-novel World-War-II history.* (First Second Books, 2010. Illustration copyright © 2010 by Leland Purvis. Reproduced by permission of Henry Holt & Company, LLC.)

side texts by other writers, among them *Suspended in Language: Niels Bohr's Life, Discoveries, and the Century He Shaped,* Jim Ottaviani's graphic biography of the noted atomic physicist, and several volumes in historian Marshall Poe's "Turning Points" middle-grade graphic-novel series about young boys who experience dramatic epochs in U.S. history. "The personal nature" of Poe's history-based adventure along with Purvis's "loose, sketchy art will invite young readers into this fascinating time and place," concluded Douglas P. Davey in his review of "Turning Points" installment *Sons of Liberty* for *School Library Journal.* For Steve Raiteri, reviewing Ottaviani's biography in *Library Journal,* "Purvis capably illustrates the main story" by choreographing the author's shifts between the real world and the fantastical in a work that the critic judged "inventive, sophisticated, and sometimes subtle."

One of Purvis's major illustrated works has been the graphic-novel trilogy comprised of *Resistance, Defiance,* and *Victory* and featuring a text by Carla Jablonski. Set during World War II, the "Resistance" books focus on Paul Tessier, a young teen whose father is taken prisoner by the German forces invading his native France. In addition to trying to hold his family together in the face of tragedy and fear, Paul also joins his sister Marie and their Jewish friend Henri Levy as perhaps the youngest members of the valiant French resistance. In his art for the "Resistance" books, Purvis mixes sepia-toned drawings that represent Paul's own sketches within the full-color images that comprise the story's narrative, creating "a visual thread that readers can follow to see the action through his [Paul's] eyes," according to *School Library Journal* contributor Andrea Lipinski. In *Kirkus Reviews* a critic commented of the first novel in the series that "Purvis's knack for facial expressions conveys a depth . . . missing" in Jablonski's text, while a *Publishers Weekly* critic remarked that his "rough, expressive line . . . works nicely for his frequent close-ups on characters' faces." Praising *Resistance* as a "stirring graphic novel," *Booklist* contributor Hazel Rochman added that "readers will be held by the realistic characterizations and grim events, all fleshed out in Purvis's quavery artwork."

Biographical and Critical Sources

PERIODICALS

Booklist, August, 2004, Ray Olson, review of *Suspended in Language: Niels Bohr's Life, Discoveries, and the Century He Shaped,* p. 1916; March 15, 2010, Hazel Rochman, review of *Resistance,* p. 57.

Kirkus Reviews, April 15, 2010, review of *Resistance.*

Library Journal, November 1, 2004, Steve Raiteri, review of *Suspended in Language,* p. 66.

Publishers Weekly, March 1, 2010, review of *Resistance,* p. 55.

School Library Journal, July, 2008, Douglas P. Davey, review of *Sons of Liberty,* p. 121; March, 2009, Lisa Goldstein, review of *A House Divided,* p. 174; May, 2010, Andrea Lipinski, review of *Resistance,* p. 140.

ONLINE

Leland Purvis Home Page, http://www.lelandpurvis.com (July 20, 2011).

Leland Purvis Web log, http://lelandpurvis.blogspot.com (July 20, 2011).

R

RITTER, Lukas
See SAMPSON, Jeff

* * *

ROBERTS, Laura Peyton

Personal
Born in Newport Beach, CA; married. *Education:* San Diego University, B.S. (geological science), M.A. (English).

Addresses
Home—San Diego, CA. *E-mail*—laura@laurapeyton roberts.com.

Career
Geologist and author.

Writings

YOUNG-ADULT NOVELS

Ghost of a Chance, Delacorte Press (New York, NY), 1997.
The Queen of Second Place, Delacorte Press (New York, NY), 2005.
Queen B (companion to *The Queen of Second Place*), Delacorte Press (New York, NY), 2006.
Green, Delacorte Press (New York, NY), 2010.

"CLEARWATER CROSSING" YOUNG-ADULT NOVEL SERIES

Get a Life, Bantam Books (New York, NY), 1998.
Reality Check, Bantam Books (New York, NY), 1998.
Heart & Soul, Bantam Books (New York, NY), 1998.
Promises, Promises, Bantam Books (New York, NY), 1998.
Just Friends, Bantam Books (New York, NY), 1998.
Keep the Faith, Bantam Books (New York, NY), 1998.
New Beginnings, Bantam Books (New York, NY), 1999.
One Real Thing, Bantam Books (New York, NY), 1999.
Skin Deep, Bantam Books (New York, NY), 1999.
No Doubt, Bantam Books (New York, NY), 1999.
More than This, Bantam Books (New York, NY), 1999.
Hope Happens, Bantam Books (New York, NY), 2000.
Dream On, Bantam Books (New York, NY), 2000.
Love Hurts, Bantam Books (New York, NY), 2000.
What Goes Around, Bantam Books (New York, NY), 2000.
Tried & True, Bantam Books (New York, NY), 2000.
Special Edition: The Diaries, Bantam Books (New York, NY), 2000.
Just Say Yes, Bantam Books (New York, NY), 2001.
Prime Time, Bantam Books (New York, NY), 2001.
Now & Always, Bantam Books (New York, NY), 2001.
Don't Look Back, Bantam Books (New York, NY), 2001.

Sidelights
Laura Peyton Roberts was born and raised in southern California, where she pursued a career as a geologist before becoming an author. Roberts uses her native California as the setting for several of her young-adult novels, which have been praised for their focus on upbeat characters, strong friendships, and a touch of whimsy. Among Roberts' books are standalone novels such as *Ghost of a Chance, Queen B,* and *Green* as well as the twenty-one books in her "Clearwater Crossing" series, which focuses on eight high schoolers whose strong faith and compassion prove transformational to both themselves and others. "I was always a huge reader, and I always loved writing short things, but I didn't believe I'd ever be able to write a novel," Roberts noted on her home page in discussing her unusual career path. "In my job as a geologist . . . I wrote hundreds of reports, some of them quite long. When I went back to college to get an English degree, I had to

write a lengthy master's thesis. With so many nonfiction pages behind me, writing a novel seemed more possible and I decided to give it a try."

Roberts' first novel, *Ghost of a Chance,* was published in 1997; it would be followed by four years' work on her "Clearwater Crossing" books. Although the novel's heroine, Chloe, is wealthy, beautiful, and self-assured, she is also best friends with Melissa, and that friendship is a boon when Melissa's parents decide to divorce and throw her family into a tailspin. Another distraction comes in the form of James, a handsome ghost who haunts the halls of Chloe's manorial home. The fact that he is handsome, aloof, and unavailable makes James instantly appealing to both young women, but with the help of some flesh-and-blood boyfriend alternatives Melissa and Chloe realize that their friendship is more important. Reviewing *Ghost of a Chance,* a *Publishers Weekly* critic dubbed it a "sweet, low-key ghost story" enlivened by "girl talk" and "adolescent wit."

Red haired Cassie Howard, the main character in *The Queen of Second Place,* is fifteen years old and determined to make the grade with the elite clique at Hilltop High School. When the handsome Kevin transfers into her sophomore class, his instant popularity makes him a potential boyfriend target. Unfortunately, this romantic interest puts Cassie in the cross-hairs of the beautiful but jealous Sterling Carter, who effectively controls who is in and who is out. Cassie returns in *Queen B,* as her runner-up status for Snow Queen improves her social standing. Although her relationship with Kevin is going well, new girl Tiffany seems to be positioning herself as a romantic rival. Meanwhile, the continued rebuffs by Sterling and her minions present Cassie with serious challenges. When the chance comes to take charge of an upcoming school talent show, the sophomore begins to realize that there are other ways to build a base of strong friends, and she explores these in a first-person narration that captures the ups and downs of high-school life.

While Cassie has to change her priorities before she will appeal to Roberts' readers, her "bumpy ride into Kevin's heart" is mapped out in *The Queen of Second Place* "with a tone [that] is light and funny," according to Cindy Welch in *Booklist.* The story's "unexpected twists and turns . . . will keep readers turning pages," predicted *School Library Journal* critic Catherine Ensley, the reviewer adding of *The Queen of Second Place* that "Roberts clearly takes the crown for this witty and inventive offering." Citing *Queen B* as a "frothy" preteen novel, Debbie Carton added in *Booklist* that "short chapters with cute titles help move the book along." In *Kliatt,* Myrna Marler recommended the same book as "a fun read that should appeal to teens" dealing with "the first joys and trials of young love."

Roberts turns to middle-grade readers in *Green,* which opens on the day Lilybet Green turns thirteen years old. When a special present dramatically explodes and leaves her disoriented and holding a gold-and-emerald key, Lily also receives her inheritance: the knowledge that she is a "lepling"—a human with leprechaun ancestry—whose destiny is to follow her late grandmother as caretaker of a clan of wealthy leprechauns. Of course, the job of guarding the clan's pot of gold can only be won if the girl passes three tests. As Lily sets out to do so it becomes clear that someone does not wish her good luck in a novel that *Booklist* critic Welch described as "a fun, fresh take on leprechaun lore" that "young readers will enjoy following." Reviewing *Green,* a *Kirkus Reviews* writer praised Roberts' heroine as "likable and well-drawn," and through her experience she "challenges herself, gains confidence, and learns the true meaning of friendship," according to *School Library Journal* contributor Cheryl Ashton.

Biographical and Critical Sources

PERIODICALS

Booklist, June 1, 2005, Cindy Welch, review of *The Queen of Second Place,* p. 1788; June 1, 2006, Debbie Carton, review of *Queen B,* p. 64; December 1, 2009, Cindy Welch, review of *Green,* p. 44.
Kirkus Reviews, July 15, 2005, review of *The Queen of Second Place,* p. 795; December 15, 2009, review of *Green.*
Kliatt, July, 2005, Myrna Marler, review of *The Queen of Second Place,* p. 15; July, 2006, Myrna Marler, review of *Queen B,* p. 13.
Publishers Weekly, August 25, 1997, review of *Ghost of a Chance,* p. 73; October 10, 2005, review of *The Queen of Second Place,* p. 62; January 4, 2010, review of *Green,* p. 47.
School Library Journal, September, 2005, Catherine Ensley, review of *The Queen of Second Place,* p. 212; November, 2006, Linda L. Plevak, review of *Queen B,* p. 148; February, 2010, Cheryl Ashton, review of *Green,* p. 123.

ONLINE

Laura Peyton Roberts Home Page, http://www.laurapeyton roberts.com (June 12, 2011).

*　　*　　*

ROOT, Barry

Personal

Married Kimberly Bulcken (an illustrator); children: three.

Addresses

Home and office—Quarryville, PA.

Career

Illustrator. *Exhibitions:* Solo exhibits include at Demuth Museum, Lancaster, PA, 2011.

Awards, Honors

Best Illustrated Children's Book selection, *New York Times,* for *Someplace Else* by Carol P. Saul; Carolyn W. Field Award Notable Book designation, 2001, for *Brave Potatoes* by Toby Speed; Oppenheim Toy Portfolio Gold Award, 2004, for *By My Brother's Side* by Tiki and Ronde Barber; Best Books of the Year selection, Bank Street College of Education, Children's Choice selection, International Reading Association/Children's Book Council, and Christopher Award, all 2006, all for *Game Day* by Tiki and Ronde Barber.

Writings

SELF-ILLUSTRATED

Gumbrella, Putnam (New York, NY), 2002.

ILLUSTRATOR

Sam Swope, *The Araboolies of Liberty Street,* Potter (New York, NY), 1989.

Roberto Piumini, *The Saint and the Circus* (translation of *Grazie di san Tonio* by Olivia Holmes), Tambourine (New York, NY), 1991.

JoAnne Stewart Wetzel, *The Christmas Box,* Knopf (New York, NY), 1992.

Marti Stone, *The Singing Fir Tree: A Swiss Folktale,* Putnam (New York, NY), 1992.

Mary Lyn Ray, *Pumpkins: A Story for a Field,* Harcourt (San Diego, CA), 1992.

Michael O. Tunnell, *Chinook!,* Tambourine (New York, NY), 1993.

Bill Martin, Jr., *Old Devil Wind,* Harcourt (San Diego, CA), 1993.

Mary Lyn Ray, *Alvah and Arvilla,* Harcourt (San Diego, CA), 1994.

Lee Bennett Hopkins, editor, *April, Bubbles, Chocolate: An ABC of Poetry,* Simon & Schuster (New York, NY), 1994.

M.L. Miller, *Those Bottles!,* Putnam (New York, NY), 1994.

Jennifer Armstrong, *Wan Hu Is in the Stars,* Tambourine (New York, NY), 1995.

Toby Speed, *Two Cool Cows,* Putnam (New York, NY), 1995.

Carol P. Saul, *Someplace Else,* Simon & Schuster (New York, NY), 1995.

Timothy R. Gaffney, *Grandpa Takes Me to the Moon,* Tambourine (New York, NY), 1996.

Tony Johnston, *Fishing Sunday,* Tambourine (New York, NY), 1996.

Toby Speed, *Whoosh! Went the Wish,* Putnam (New York, NY), 1997.

Jan Peck, *The Giant Carrot,* Dial (New York, NY), 1998.

Charlotte Towner Graeber, *Nobody's Dog,* Hyperion (New York, NY), 1998.

Kathi Appelt, *Cowboy Dreams,* HarperCollins (New York, NY), 1999.

Lee Wardlaw, *Saturday Night Jamboree,* Dial (New York, NY), 2000.

Toby Speed, *Brave Potatoes,* Putnam (New York, NY), 2000.

Robert Burleigh, *Messenger, Messenger,* Atheneum (New York, NY), 2000.

Susan Hill, *Backyard Bedtime,* HarperFestival (New York, NY), 2001.

Laura Godwin, *Central Park Serenade,* HarperCollins (New York, NY), 2002.

Terry Farish, *The Cat Who Liked Potato Soup,* Candlewick (Cambridge, MA), 2003.

Tiki and Ronde Barber, with Robert Burleigh, *By My Brother's Side,* Simon & Schuster (New York, NY), 2004.

Elizabeth Loredo, *Giant Steps,* Putnam (New York, NY), 2004.

Tiki and Ronde Barber, with Robert Burleigh, *Game Day,* Simon & Schuster (New York, NY), 2005.

Tiki and Ronde Barber, with Robert Burleigh, *Teammates,* Simon & Schuster (New York, NY), 2006.

Sarah Martin Busse and Jacqueline Briggs Martin, *Banjo Granny,* Houghton Mifflin (Boston, MA), 2006.

Mary Lyn Ray, *Christmas Farm,* Harcourt (Orlando, FL), 2008.

Paul Fleischman, *The Birthday Tree,* Candlewick Press (Cambridge, MA), 2008.

Ted Kooser, *Bag in the Wind,* Candlewick Press (Somerville, MA), 2010.

Sarah Sullivan, *Passing the Music Down,* Candlewick Press (Somerville, MA), 2010.

(With Kimberly Bulcken Root) Verla Kay, *Whatever Happened to the Pony Express?,* G.P. Putnam's Sons (New York, NY), 2010.

Jan Peck, *Giant Peach Yodel!,* Pelican Publishing (Gretna, LA), 2011.

Contributor to periodicals, including *New York Times Magazine, Forbes,* and *Sports Illustrated.*

Sidelights

Award-winning illustrator Barry Root has provided the artwork for numerous picture books for young readers, and he served as both illustrator and writer for his original picture-book story in *Gumbrella.* Root has worked with a number of well-known authors, such as Paul Fleischman, Lee Bennett Hopkins, and Verla Kay, and he has also illustrated picture books by famous football-star siblings Tiki and Ronde Barber. From fables to tall tales to historical works, Root's illustration projects range widely in subject, earning him praise from both critics and readers alike.

Gumbrella is the story of an elephant that creates a hospital for smaller animals that are injured. Gumbrella enjoys the company of his charges so much that he will not let patients return home once they have recovered. "Root cleverly depicts Gumbrella's single-minded altruism with visual winks . . . coupled with a sly voice," wrote a *Publishers Weekly* contributor. "The tone is light, the pictures are bright," noted a critic for *Kirkus Reviews*, while Anita L. Burkam maintained in *Horn Book* that "Root fully exploits the humor inherent in an elephant with a Florence Nightingale complex." Jody McCoy, reviewing *Gumbrella* for *School Library Journal*, predicted that "children will enjoy Root's first endeavor as both illustrator and author," and in *Booklist* Ilene Cooper recommended the same book as "a story hour choice that might spark discussion among little ones."

Root's "zany depictions of the portly circus star and his startled menagerie are executed with a panache befitting the big top," wrote a *Publishers Weekly* critic in appraising the artist's contributions to Roberto Piumini's *The Saint and the Circus*, while his art for Michael O. Tunnel's *Chinook!* prompted *Horn Book* critic Nancy Vasilakis to predict that "children will relish the illustrations." Of Jennifer Armstrong's picture book *Wan Hu Is in the Stars*, a *Publishers Weekly* critic wrote that Root's "full-bleed gouaches perfectly complements the gentle buoyancy of the narrative," and Jan Peck's retelling of a Russian folk tale in *The Giant Carrot* benefits from the illustrator's "depiction of the family's dirt farm and ramshackle log cabin [as] . . . full of sunshine and energy," according to a *Publishers Weekly* contributor. Writing of Elizabeth Laredo's picture book *Giant Steps*, *Booklist* critic Jennifer Mattson wrote that "the real stars" of the picture book "are Root's goofy, snaggletooth giants."

Beyond tall tales and fairy stories, Root has illustrated collections of poetry as well as contemporary tales. In *April, Bubbles, Chocolate: An ABC of Poetry*, editor Lee Bennett Hopkins's "random mix of moods and styles . . . is expressed in Root's bright, clear watercolor paintings," according to Hazel Rochman in *Booklist*. Reviewing the illustrator's work for *Central Park Serenade*, Laura Godwin's celebration of New York City, *Horn Book* contributor Roger Sutton noted that "Root's bird's-eye vision of Central Park" serves as an invitation "into a beautiful part of the world." A *Publishers Weekly* critic also complimented the artist's "vibrantly hued, intentionally hazy paintings" for Godwin's story, while *School Library Journal* contributor Susan Marie Pitard concluded of the book that "verbal

Barry Root's illustration projects include Jan Peck's folk-style story in **The Giant Carrot.** (Illustration copyright © 1998 by Barry Root. Used by permission of Dial Books for Young Readers, a division of Penguin Young Readers Group, a member of Penguin Group (USA) Inc., 345 Hudson St., New York, NY, 10014. All rights reserved.)

images and illustrations . . . work together seamlessly to present a joyful, busy portrait." Karla Kushkin, also reviewing *Central Park Serenade,* wrote in *Horn Book* that "Root paints . . . with a skilled hand, using a palette so lush you can smell the warmth of summer in it."

Banjo Granny, a contemporary tall tale by Jacqueline Briggs Martin and daughter Sarah Martin Busse, concerns a sprightly grandmother who embarks on a long journey to visit a bluegrass-loving toddler. "Root's fluid artwork brings warmth, movement, and color to the rhythmic text," Tamara E. Richman commented in her *School Library Journal* review of the picture book, and a *Publishers Weekly* critic applauded Root's depiction of the "gold-flecked, majestic landscapes" that Granny encounters during her voyage. Root teamed with Mary Lyn Ray to create *Christmas Farm,* the story of a New England farmer who, with assistance from her young neighbor, spends five years nurturing hundreds of balsam seedlings until they are ready to sell as full-sized Christmas trees. "Root's appealing watercolor-and-gouache illustrations invite inspection," Abby Nolan commented in *Booklist,* while *Horn Book* critic Kitty Flynn maintained that the paintings "honor the characters' warm intergenerational friendship." In *Kirkus Reviews* a critic praised the winter landscapes in *Christmas Farm,* writing that they feature "deep blue skies with speckles of falling snow, deep green trees and glowing lights from distant farmhouses."

Paul Fleischman's *The Birthday Tree,* a book first published in 1979, was reissued nearly thirty years later with new artwork by Root. After three of their sons die at sea, a sailor and his wife move inland and plant a tree to commemorate the birth of their fourth child. The boy and the tree appear linked in an odd manner, however: as the boy grows, so does the tree, its health mirroring the well-being of the child who, despite his parents' concerns, chooses a seafaring life. Writing in *Booklist,* Carolyn Phelan remarked that the "timeless quality" of *The Birthday Tree* "is echoed in the expressive watercolor artwork," and a *Kirkus Reviews* contributor observed that Root's "muted colors add lyrical touches, and . . . evoke the couple's lonely isolation." A *Publishers Weekly* critic also applauded Root's rustic landscapes, stating that the illustrator "evokes soft hills and wide skies with calm authenticity."

Bag in the Wind, a picture book by former U.S. poet laureate Ted Kooser, offers a gentle environmental message in its tale of a plastic grocery bag that escapes from a landfill and drifts through the countryside, where it is alternately used and discarded by a host of individuals. "The muted, dappled colors of Root's gouache and watercolor illustrations are a perfect complement" to Kooser's thoughtful narrative, Kristen McKulski reported in *Booklist,* and Bob Minzesheimer noted in *USA Today* that *Bag in the Wind* "is beautifully illustrated by . . . Root's gentle watercolors."

In his artistic contribution to the football-related tales by the brothers Barber, "Root's sunny watercolors, often accented with lush, green trees, capture action on

Root teams up with popular athletes Tiki and Ronde Barber to create a series of inspiring picture books that include **Teammates.** (Illustration copyright © 2006 by Barry Root. Reprinted by permission of Simon & Schuster Books for Young Readers, an imprint of Simon & Schuster Publishing Division.)

and off the field," according to a *Publishers Weekly* critic, referencing *By My Brother's Side.* In *Game Day,* another of the Barbers' sports-themed stories, the illustrator's "earth-toned watercolors capture the speed, action and colors" of the book's autumn setting, according to a *Publishers Weekly* writer. Carolyn Phelan, in her *Booklist* review of *Teammates,* maintained that "Root's vibrant watercolor-and-gouache paintings kick the story over the goalposts."

Root's collaboration with his artist wife Kimberly Bulcken Root has produced the illustrations for Verla Kay's *Whatever Happened to the Pony Express?,* a story set in the nineteenth century. Kay uses a series of letters exchanged by siblings who live in different regions of the United States to explore the evolution of transportation and delivery methods during the period, focusing on the legendary mail service that relied on swift horses and fearless riders. The Roots' illustrations, "rendered in pencil, ink, gouache, and watercolor, are crucial in developing the personal drama of the siblings and their families," commented Lucinda Whitehurst Snyder in her *School Library Journal* review of the book. The pictures "burst with vigor, especially those of a Pony Express rider jetting across the page," a critic maintained in reviewing *Whatever Happened to the Pony Express?* for *Publishers Weekly.*

Bag in the Wind, *a story by former U.S. poet laureate Ted Kooser, is brought to life in Root's evocative art.* (Illustration copyright © 2010 by Barry Root. Reproduced by permission of Candlewick Press, Somerville, MA.)

Biographical and Critical Sources

PERIODICALS

Booklist, August, 1992, Hazel Rochman, review of *The Christmas Box,* p. 2020; October 15, 1992, Ellen Mandel, review of *Pumpkins: A Story for a Field,* p. 441; December 15, 1992, Janice Del Negro, review of *The Singing Fir Tree: A Swiss Folktale,* p. 742; April 15, 1993, Deborah Abbott, review of *Chinook!,* p. 1524; October 1, 1993, Carolyn Phelan, review of *Old Devil Wind,* p. 353; February 1, 1994, Ilene Cooper, review of *Those Bottles!,* p. 1010; May 1, 1994, Hazel Rochman, review of *April, Bubbles, Chocolate: An ABC of Poems,* p. 1603; June 1, 1995, Ilene Cooper, review of *Two Cool Cows,* p. 1789; June, 1995, Lauren Peterson, review of *Wan Hu Is in the Stars,* p. 1781; November 15, 1995, Lauren Peterson, review of *Someplace Else,* p. 565; May 15, 1996, Kay Weisman, review of *Fishing Sunday,* p. 1592; June 1, 1997, review of *The Araboolies of Liberty Street,* p. 1675; March 15, 1998, Hazel Rochman, review of *The Giant Carrot,* p. 1246; August, 1998, Ellen Mandel, review of *Nobody's Dog,* p. 2004; January 1, 1999, Il-

ene Cooper, review of *Cowboy Dreams,* p. 885; September 15, 2000, Shelle Rosenfeld, review of *Brave Potatoes,* p. 250; December 15, 2000, Amy Brandt, review of *Saturday Night Jamboree,* p. 829; February 15, 2001, Hazel Rochman, review of *Messenger, Messenger,* p. 1152; June 1, 2002, Lauren Peterson, review of *Central Park Serenade,* p. 1737; November 15, 2002, Ilene Cooper, review of *Gumbrella,* p. 612; April 15, 2003, Carolyn Phelan, review of *The Cat Who Liked Potato Soup,* p. 1477; February 1, 2004, Jennifer Mattson, review of *Giant Steps,* p. 981; September 1, 2004, Todd Morning, review of *By My Brother's Side,* p. 114; September 1, 2005, Ilene Cooper, review of *Game Day,* p. 119; September 1, 2006, Carolyn Phelan, review of *Teammates,* p. 116; November 1, 2006, Hazel Rochman, review of *Banjo Granny,* p. 58; January 1, 2008, Carolyn Phelan, review of *The Birthday Tree,* p. 90; September 15, 2008, Abby Nolan, review of *Christmas Farm,* p. 56; January 1, 2010, Kristen McKulski, review of *Bag in the Wind,* p. 90; May 1, 2010, John Peters, review of *Whatever Happened to the Pony Express?,* p. 87.

Bulletin of the Center for Children's Books, July, 1994, review of *April, Bubbles, Chocolate,* p. 360; July, 1995, review of *Wan Hu Is in the Stars,* p. 376; October,

1995, review of *Someplace Else,* p. 68; October, 1996, review of *Grandpa Takes Me to the Moon,* p. 58; September, 1997, review of *Whoosh! Went the Wish,* p. 27; March, 1998, review of *The Giant Carrot,* p. 255; September, 1998, review of *Nobody's Dog,* p. 14; June, 2000, review of *Brave Potatoes,* p. 374; November, 2000, review of *Messenger, Messenger,* p. 98, review of *Saturday Night Jamboree,* p. 125; December, 2002, review of *Gumbrella,* p. 171; June, 2003, review of *The Cat Who Liked Potato Soup,* p. 387; February, 2004, Janice Del Negro, review of *Giant Steps,* p. 239; January, 2006, Elizabeth Bush, review of *Game Day,* p. 218; January, 2007, Deborah Stevenson, review of *Banjo Granny,* p. 205.

Horn Book, January-February, 1992, Nancy Vasilakis, review of *The Saint and the Circus,* p. 61; November-December, 1992, Nancy Vasilakis, review of *The Christmas Box,* p. 714, Ellen Fader, review of *Pumpkins,* p. 719; July-August, 1993, Nancy Vasilakis, review of *Chinook!,* p. 451; January-February, 1994, Mary M. Burns, review of *Old Devil Wind,* p. 65; July-August, 1994, Nancy Vasilakis, review of *April, Bubbles, Chocolate,* p. 467; November-December, 1994, Ellen Fader, review of *Alvah and Arvilla,* p. 725; November-December, 1995, Nancy Vasilakis, review of *Someplace Else,* p. 737; May, 2000, review of *Brave Potatoes,* p. 300; September-October, 2002, Roger Sutton, "Not Just a Walk in the Park," p. 499, Karla Kuskin, review of *Central Park Serenade,* p. 552, and Anita L. Burkham, review of *Gumbrella,* p. 559; March-April, 2008, Joanna Rudge Long, review of *The Birthday Tree,* p. 201; November-December, 2008, Kitty Flynn, review of *Christmas Farm,* p. 652.

Kirkus Reviews, March 15, 2002, review of *Central Park Serenade,* p. 411; September 15, 2002, review of *Central Park Serenade,* p. 1399; May 1, 2003, review of *The Cat Who Liked Potato Soup,* p. 676; January 1, 2004, review of *Giant Steps,* p. 38; September 15, 2004, review of *By My Brother's Side,* p. 909; September 15, 2005, review of *Game Day,* p. 1020; September 15, 2006, review of *Teammates,* p. 946; November 1, 2006, review of *Banjo Granny,* p. 1121; January 1, 2008, review of *The Birthday Tree;* November 1, 2008, review of *Christmas Farm;* February 15, 2010, review of *Bag in the Wind.*

New York Times Book Review, November 12, 1989, Carol Muske, review of *The Araboolies of Liberty Street,* p. 38; October 25, 1992, review of *Pumpkins,* p. 28; May 22, 1994, Julie Zuckerman, review of *Those Bottles!,* p. 29; May 14, 2000, review of *Messenger, Messenger,* p. 26; September 21, 2003, review of *The Cat Who Liked Potato Soup,* p. 26.

Publishers Weekly, August 11, 1989, review of *The Araboolies of Liberty Street,* p. 457; November 1, 1991, review of *The Saint and the Circus,* p. 80; September 7, 1992, review of *The Christmas Box,* p. 66, review of *Pumpkins,* p. 92; October 12, 1992, review of *The Singing Fir Tree,* p. 78; March 15, 1993, review of *Chinook!,* p. 87; September 20, 1993, review of *Old Devil Wind,* p. 29; March 7, 1994, review of *Those Bottles!,* p. 69; September 5, 1994, review of *Alvah and Arvilla,* p. 109; May 8, 1995, review of *Two Cool Cows,* p. 294, and *Wan Hu Is in the Stars,* p. 295; Au-gust 14, 1995, reviews of *Someplace Else,* p. 82; April 21, 1997, review of *Whoosh! Went the Wish,* p. 71; July 22, 1996, review of *Grandpa Takes Me to the Moon,* p. 241; December 8, 1997, review of *Two Cool Cows,* p. 74; December 22, 1997, review of *Someplace Else,* p. 61; February 16, 1998, review of *The Giant Carrot,* p. 210; June 15, 1998, review of *Nobody's Dog,* p. 59; January 18, 1999, review of *Cowboy Dreams,* p. 338; May 22, 2000, review of *Brave Potatoes,* p. 92; June 19, 2000, review of *Messenger, Messenger,* p. 79; April 30, 2001, review of *The Araboolies of Liberty Street,* p. 80; February 25, 2002, review of *Central Park Serenade,* p. 64; September 9, 2002, review of *Gumbrella,* p. 67; May 5, 2003, review of *The Cat Who Liked Potato Soup,* p. 221; February 23, 2004, review of *Giant Steps,* p. 76; August 30, 2004, review of *By My Brother's Side,* p. 55; October 3, 2005, review of *Game Day,* p. 70; October 30, 2006, review of *Banjo Granny,* p. 60; February 4, 2008, review of *The Birthday Tree,* p. 55; January 4, 2010, review of *Bag in the Wind,* p. 45; May 10, 2010, review of *Whatever Happened to the Pony Express?,* p. 44.

Quill & Quire, December, 1994, review of *Alvah and Arvilla,* p. 35.

School Library Journal, December, 1989, Shirley Wilton, review of *The Araboolies of Liberty Street,* p. 90; November, 1991, Karen James, review of *The Saint and the Circus,* p. 106; October, 1992, review of *The Christmas Box,* p. 45; February, 1993, Cyrisse Jaffee, review of *The Singing Fir Tree,* p. 91; March, 1993, Susan Scheps, review of *Pumpkins,* p. 184; June, 1993, Lisa Dennis, review of *Chinook!,* p. 91; November, 1993, Joy Fleishhacker, review of *Old Devil Wind,* p. 86; April, 1994, Susan Scheps, review of *Those Bottles!,* p. 110; September, 1994, Sally R. Dow, review of *April, Bubbles, Chocolate,* p. 208; January, 1995, Martha Rosen, review of *Alvah and Arvilla,* p. 92; June, 1995, Kathy Piehl, review of *Two Cool Cows,* p. 95; July, 1995, Margaret A. Chang, review of *Wan Hu Is in the Stars,* p. 54; January, 1996, Betty Teague, review of *Someplace Else,* p. 95; April, 1996, review of *April, Bubbles, Chocolate,* p. 39; June, 1996, Virginia Golodetz, review of *Fishing Sunday,* p. 102; September, 1996, Kathy East, review of *Grandpa Takes Me to the Moon,* p. 178; September, 1997, Judith Constantinides, review of *Whoosh! Went the Wish,* p. 195; February, 1998, Beth Tegart, review of *The Giant Carrot,* p. 103; June, 1998, Lisa Dennis, review of *Nobody's Dog,* p. 106; February, 1999, Steven Engelfried, review of *Cowboy Dreams,* p. 77; June, 2000, Nina Lindsay, review of *Messenger, Messenger,* p. 102; July, 2000, Ruth Semrau, review of *Brave Potatoes,* p. 88; September, 2000, Jody McCoy, review of *Saturday Night Jamboree,* p. 211; May, 2002, Susan Marie Pitard, review of *Central Park Serenade,* p. 114; November, 2002, Jody McCoy, review of *Gumbrella,* p. 134; July, 2003, Steven Engelfried, review of *The Cat Who Liked Potato Soup,* p. 95; March, 2004, Eve Ortega, review of *Giant Steps,* p. 176; November, 2004, Ann M. Holcomb, review of *By My Brother's Side,* p. 122; January, 2006, Mary Hazelton, review of *Game Day,* p. 116; November, 2006, Rachel

G. Payne, review of *Teammates,* p. 117; December, 2006, Tamara E. Richman, review of *Banjo Granny,* p. 95; February, 2008, Marianne Saccardi, review of *The Birthday Tree,* p. 88; October, 2008, Mara Alpert, review of *Christmas Farm,* p. 97; January, 2010, Marianne Saccardi, review of *Bag in the Wind,* p. 105; June, 2010, Lucinda Snyder Whitehurst, review of *Whatever Happened to the Pony Express?,* p. 76.

Science Books & Films, August, 1997, review of *Grandpa Takes Me to the Moon,* p. 163.

Smithsonian, November, 1992, review of *Pumpkins,* p. 201.

Tribune Books (Chicago, IL), June 23, 2002, review of *Central Park Serenade,* p. 5; May 18, 2003, review of *The Cat Who Liked Potato Soup,* p. 5.

USA Today, April 8, 2010, Bob Minzesheimer, review of *Bag in the Wind,* p. 4D.

Wilson Library Bulletin, April, 1992, Donnarae MacCann and Olga Richard, review of *The Saint and the Circus,* p. 94; December, 1993, Donnarae MacCann and Olga Richard, review of *Old Devil Wind,* p. 112.

ONLINE

Simon & Schuster Web site, http://www.simonandschuster.com/ (July 15, 2011), "Barry Root."*

*   *   *

RUTLAND, J.
(Jarrett Rutland)

Personal

Born in AL. *Education:* Maryland Institute College of Art, B.F.A.

Addresses

Home—Asheville, NC. *Agent*—Prospect Agency, 511 Valley Rd., Upper Montclair, NJ 07043. *E-mail*—jarrettrutland@gmail.com.

Career

Illustrator. A.L.I.V.E. Art Program, Asheville, NC, founder, 2009.

Member

Society of Children's Book Writers and Illustrators.

Illustrator

Nancy Jewell, *Alligator Wedding,* Henry Holt (New York, NY), 2010.

Illustrator of "Spatz" reader series, written by Sherry Fair.

Biographical and Critical Sources

PERIODICALS

Kirkus Reviews, April 15, 2010, review of *Alligator Wedding.*

School Library Journal, March, 2010, Barbara Elleman, review of *Alligator Wedding,* p. 120.

ONLINE

J. Rutland Web Log, http://www.rutlandart.blogspot.com (June 12, 2011).*

*   *   *

RUTLAND, Jarrett
See RUTLAND, J.

S

SAMPSON, Jeff 1982-
(Lukas Ritter)

Personal
Born July 15, 1982, in Nuremberg, Germany; U.S. citizen. *Hobbies and other interests:* Movies, video games, pop culture.

Addresses
Home—Seattle, WA. *Agent*—Michael Stearns, Upstart Crow Literary, P.O. Box 25404, Brooklyn, NY 11202. *E-mail*—jeff@jeffsampsonbooks.com.

Career
Novelist, beginning 2000.

Writings

"DRAGONLANCE: THE NEW ADVENTURES" MIDDLE-GRADE FANTASY NOVEL SERIES

Dragon Spell, illustrated by Vinod Rams, Mirrorstone (Renton, WA), 2005.
The Wayward Wizard ("Suncatcher Trilogy"), illustrated by Vinod Rams, Mirrorstone (Renton, WA), 2006.
Wizard's Betrayal ("Trinistyr Trilogy"), Mirrorstone (Renton, WA), 2006.
The Ebony Eye ("Suncatcher Trilogy"), illustrated by Vinod Rams, Mirrorstone (Renton, WA), 2007.
The Stolen Sun ("Suncatcher Trilogy"), illustrated by Vinod Rams, Wizards of the Coast (Renton, WA), 2007.
(Under name Lukas Ritter) *Monster Slayers,* Mirrorstone (Renton, WA), 2010.
(Under name Lukas Ritter) *Monster Slayers: Unleashed,* Mirrorstone (Renton, WA), 2011.

"DEVIANTS" YOUNG-ADULT NOVEL SERIES

Vesper, Balzer & Bray (New York, NY), 2011.
Havoc, Balzer & Bray (New York, NY), 2012.

Author's work has been translated into German.

Biographical and Critical Sources

PERIODICALS

Booklist, January 1, 2011, Francisca Goldsmith, review of *Vesper,* p. 100.
Publishers Weekly, January 3, 2011, review of *Vesper,* p. 52.

ONLINE

Jeff Sampson Home Page, http://jeffsampsonbooks.com (June 12, 2011).

* * *

SCHLITZ, Laura Amy

Personal
Female. *Education:* Goucher College, B.A. (aesthetics), 1977. *Hobbies and other interests:* Theatre, reading, baking, quilting, playing folk harp, making marionettes and origami.

Addresses
Home—Baltimore, MD. *E-mail*—lschlitz@parkschool. net.

Career
Librarian, storyteller, and author. Enoch Pratt Free Library, Baltimore, MD, children's librarian, until mid-1980s; Children's Theatre Association (theatre company), Baltimore, playwright for two years; Park School, Baltimore, MD, lower school librarian, beginning 1991; professional storyteller.

Awards, Honors
Great Lakes Good Books Award for Nonfiction, c. 2006, for *The Hero Schliemann;* Judy Lopez Honor Book designation, 2006, and CYBILS Award for Children's Lit-

erature in Middle-School Fiction Category, 2007, both for *A Drowned Maiden's Hair;* CYBILS Award for Poetry nomination, *School Library Journal* Best Books designation, and *Booklist* Editor's Choice designation, all 2007, and Newbery Medal, 2008, all for *Good Masters! Sweet Ladies!*

Writings

A Drowned Maiden's Hair: A Melodrama, Candlewick Press (Cambridge, MA), 2006.

The Hero Schleimann: The Dreamer Who Dug for Troy, illustrated by Robert Byrd, Candlewick Press (Cambridge, MA), 2006.

Good Masters! Sweet Ladies! Voices from a Medieval Village (monologues), illustrated by Robert Byrd, Candlewick Press (Cambridge, MA), 2007.

(Adaptor) *The Bearskinner: A Tale of the Brothers Grimm* (based on "Der Bärenhäuter"), illustrated by Max Grafe, Candlewick Press (Cambridge, MA), 2007.

The Night Fairy, illustrated by Angela Barrett, Candlewick Press (Cambridge, MA), 2010.

Also author of short plays for children that have been produced throughout the United States.

Sidelights

Laura Amy Schlitz made a name for herself in 2006, when her first two books were published to widespread critical acclaim. A librarian at privately run Park School in Baltimore, Maryland, Schlitz had been writing for many years when Candlewick Press decided to release her novel *A Drowned Maiden's Hair: A Melodrama* as well as her nonfiction title *The Hero Schleimann: The Dreamer Who Dug for Troy.* Two years later, she made the news again, this time when her play anthology *Good Masters! Sweet Ladies! Voices from a Medieval Village* was honored with the prestigious Newbery Award.

Schlitz grew up in Baltimore and gained a love of theatre after she was cast in her first play at age eight. She continued to be involved in the stage during high school and college, where she earned a degree from Goucher College. Her first job, as a librarian at Baltimore's Enoch Pratt Free Library, came about after she applied for the government-funded position of storyteller but did not meet the requirements. Schlitz left her job as a librarian for a few years during the mid-1980s to work as a playwright for the city's Children's Theatre Association, but returned to the job in 1991, when she joined the staff of Park School.

The Newbery Award-winning *Good Masters! Sweet Ladies!* had its original incarnation as a performance project for a group of fifth graders who were studying the Middle Ages. "I wanted them to have something to perform, but no one wanted a small part," Schlitz commented in a profile of her work on the Park Street

School Web site. "I decided to write monologues instead of one long play, so that for three minutes at least, every child could be a star." By adopting the persona of the leading role in short vignettes such as "Jack, the Half-wit," "Mariot and Maud, the Glassblower's Daughters," and "Hugo, the Lord's Nephew," a performer can gain an intimate understanding of what life was like on an English manorial estate during the thirteenth century. Writing that Schlitz's book "gives teachers a refreshing option for enhancing the study of the European Middle Ages," Deirdre F. Baker added in *Horn Book* that *Good Masters! Sweet Ladies!* also features "pristine, elegant" watercolor art by Robert Byrd. "Bolstered by lively asides and unobtrusive [author's] notes," Schlitz's twenty-two monologues successfully "bring to life a prototypical English village in 1255," concluded a *Publishers Weekly* reviewer.

Although *Good Masters! Sweet Ladies!* may be Schlitz's best-known work, she has also created widely acclaimed novels and picture-book texts. Described by *Horn Book* contributor Kathleen Isaacs as an "irreverent" look at one of the major advances in modern archaeology, *The Hero Schleimann* follows the life of the

Cover of Laura Amy Schlitz's highly praised novel **A Drowned Maiden's Hair,** *featuring artwork by Tim O'Brien.* (Jacket illustration copyright © 2006 by Tim Lott. Reproduced by permission of Candlewick Press, Somerville, MA.)

German who, in 1870, rediscovered the ancient city of Troy by following the directions as set forth in Homer's epic Iliad. Schlitz's book "attempts to disentangle" the legends from the facts surrounding Heinrich Schleimann's colorful life, Isaacs added, writing that the cartoon illustrations provided by Byrd "add to the appeal of the gently humorous text." Noting Schlitz's inclusion of information regarding archeological techniques of a past era, Gillian Engberg predicted that *The Hero Schleimann* will likely "spark interesting class discussions about how history is made and slanted over time."

As its subtitle unabashedly pronounces, *A Drowned Maiden's Hair* is an old-fashioned melodrama in which an unsuspecting heroine finds herself in the clutches of ne'er-do-wells until, despite all odds, she ultimately escapes. In Schlitz's story, which is set in 1909, the heroine is an eleven-year-old orphan named Maud Flynn. Headstrong Maud is considered troublesome by the staff at the Barbary Asylum for Orphans and no one is more surprised than she when she is selected to be adopted by three unmarried sisters of obvious financial means. Moving to the Hawthorne sisters' large home, Maud is given pretty dresses and good food. Oddly, though, she must remain hidden from the many people who come to visit. Soon Maud realizes why: the sisters make their living as fake spiritualists, performing mechanically orchestrated séances in order to tap into the bank accounts of the sad, lonely, and grief stricken. Because of her resemblance to the recently deceased daughter of a wealthy widow, Maud is expected to join in their plan to con this woman of her substantial fortune. Although gratitude for her material comforts and a need for affection motivate Maud to willingly join in the sisters' scheme, as events progress she begins to have second thoughts. Ultimately, a taste of freedom and her growing friendship with the sisters' deaf housemaid, Muffet, inspires Maud to take her life into her own hands.

"Schlitz's well-written narrative . . . captures melodrama at its best," concluded a *Kirkus Reviews* writer in a review of *A Drowned Maiden's Hair,* the critic commenting in particular on the author's detailed account of how the fake spiritualists created optical illusions during their pretend séances. Calling Maud a "charismatic, three-dimensional character" whose moral battle is believable, Melissa Moore added in her *School Library Journal* review that the novel "will find an audience with fans of gothic tales," and *Horn Book* reviewer Anita L. Burkham maintained that "Schlitz realizes both characters and setting . . . with unerring facility." "People throw the word 'classic' about rather a lot, but *A Drowned Maiden's Hair* genuinely deserves to become one," concluded Meghan Cox Gurdon in her review for the *Wall Street Journal,* and Elizabeth Spires wrote in the *New York Times Book Review* that Schlitz's "delightful" debut novel "provides a satisfying, if slightly creepy, look behind the scenes at how spiritual-

Enhanced with artwork by Robert Byrd, Schlitz's intriguing historical plays in **Good Masters! Sweet Ladies!** *won her a prestigious Newbery medal.* (Illustration copyright © 2007 by Robert Byrd. Reproduced by permission of Candlewick Press, Somerville, MA.)

ists accomplished some of their haunting effects. But it is also about love in all of its guises, deceptions and disappointments."

Schlitz turns to younger readers in her books *The Bearskinner: A Tale of the Brothers Grimm* and *The Night Fairy,* the latter illustrated by Angela Barrett. Featuring what *School Library Journal* critic Kirsten Cutler praised as "atmospheric" artwork by Max Grafe in which "murky brown tones showcase the interplay of light and shadow," *The Bearskinner* focuses on a fairy-tale staple: a pact between a man and the devil. In Schlitz's retelling, a war-weary soldier with no hope for the future is promised riches if he will wear a filthy and shaggy bearskin both day and night for seven years, neither taking it off to bathe nor cutting his hair all that time. Quickly cast out from society, the Bearskinner rescues another man and finds his bargain hard to keep when he is rewarded for his good deed with the love of the rescued man's daughter. Also praising Grafe's "textured, atmospheric illustrations," Gillian Engberg noted in *Booklist* that "Schlitz's skillful words present a tale that is rarely retold for youth."

An original story rather than a retelling, *The Night Fairy* finds Schlitz's imagination once again soaring. In the tale, a thimble-high young fairy named Flory is learning to fly when a collision with a bat knocks her to earth in a strange, walled garden. Although Flory has always been nocturnal, she now learns to make her way in the daylight, and she gradually builds a rapport with the squirrels, birds, and other creatures that share the cherry tree in which she makes her garden home. In *Booklist* Carolyn Phelan found much to admire in the author's "finely crafted and unusually dynamic fairy story," noting that "Schlitz writes with strength of vision and delicate precision of word choice." A *Publishers Weekly* critic dubbed *The Night Fairy* "a whimsical and cozy tale" that demonstrates to children that "handicaps can be overcome through quick thinking and determination," and *Horn Book* contributor Robin L. Smith predicted that young storytime audiences "will enjoy Flora's wit and derring do."

Discussing her work as a writer during an online interview for the *CYBILS Award Web site*, Schlitz noted of the vivid characters she creates: "I'm not sure why, but I almost never write about people I know. On those rare occasions that I use real people as models, they're people that I don't understand. I think in order to write about something, you have to find it mysterious. Too much knowledge leaves the writer at a disadvantage."

Biographical and Critical Sources

PERIODICALS

Booklist, June 1, 2006, Gillian Engberg, review of *The Hero Schleimann: The Dreamer Who Dug for Troy,* p. 100; December 15, 2006, Hazel Rochman, review of *A Drowned Maiden's Hair: A Melodrama,* p. 43; November 15, 2007, Gillian Engberg, review of *The Bearskinner: A Tale of the Brothers Grimm,* p. 40; January 1, 2010, Carolyn Phelan, review of *The Night Fairy,* p. 81.
Bulletin of the Center for Children's Books, October, 2006, Elizabeth Bush, review of *The Hero Schleimann,* p. 93; November, 2006, Elizabeth Bush, review of *A Drowned Maiden's Hair,* p. 144; September, 2007, review of *Good Masters! Sweet Ladies! Voices from a Medieval Village,* p. 51.
Christian Science Monitor, March 14, 2008, Elaine F. Weiss, "Shy School Librarian Finds Success as Author," p. 20.
Horn Book, July-August, 2006, Kathleen Isaacs, review of *The Hero Schleimann,* p. 469; November-December, 2006, Anita L. Burkam, review of *A Drowned Maiden's Hair,* p. 725; November-December, 2007, Deirdre F. Baker, review of *Good Masters! Sweet Ladies!,* p. 699; March-April, 2010, Robin L. Smith, review of *The Night Fairy,* p. 72.
Kirkus Reviews, July 15, 2006, review of *The Hero Schleimann,* p. 730; October 15, 2006, review of *A Drowned Maiden's Hair,* p. 1079; July 15, 2007, review of *Good Masters! Sweet Ladies!*; January 15, 2010, review of *The Night Fairy.*
Magpies, March, 2007, Rayma Turton, review of *A Drowned Maiden's Hair,* p. 40.
New York Times Book Review, December 3, 2005, Elizabeth Spires, review of *A Drowned Maiden's Hair,* p. 66.
Publishers Weekly, August 27, 2007, review of *Good Masters! Sweet Ladies!,* p. 90; January 4, 2010, review of *The Night Fairy,* p. 47.
School Library Journal, September, 2006, Rita Soltan, review of *The Hero Schleimann,* p. 236; October, 2006 Melissa Moore, review of *A Drowned Maiden's Hair,* p. 170; August, 2007, Alana Abbott, review of *Good Masters! Sweet Ladies!,* p. 138; December, 2007, Kirsten Cutler, review of *The Bearskinner,* p. 157; April, 2008, Mary Grace Gallagher, "A Tall Tale," p. 34; April, 2010, Sarah Polace, review of *The Night Fairy,* p. 139.
Wall Street Journal, November 11, 2006, Meghan Cox Gurdon, review of *A Drowned Maiden's Hair.*

ONLINE

CYBILS Award Web site, http://dadtalk.typepad.com/cybils/2007/ (March 12, 2007), interview with Schlitz.
Park School Web site, http://www.parkschool.net/ (September 22, 2008), "Laura Amy Schlitz Wins Newbery Medal for Children's Literature."
School Library Journal Online, http://www.schoollibraryjournal.com/ (November 5, 2007), Elizabeth Bird, interview with Schlitz.

*   *   *

SCHORIES, Pat 1952-

Personal

Born July 30, 1952, in Batavia, NY; daughter of Alfred (a mechanical engineer) and Beatrice (a nurse) Schories; married Harry Bolick (a photographer and musician), July 11, 1998; children: Elizabeth (stepdaughter). *Education:* Kent State University, B.F.A., 1974. *Politics:* Democrat.

Addresses

Home—Hopewell Junction, NY. *E-mail*—pat@patschories.com.

Career

Children's book author and illustrator. Has also worked as a freelance graphic designer and botanical illustrator, 1976—.

Member

Society of Children's Book Writers and Illustrators, Authors Guild, Authors League, Guild of Natural Science Illustrators.

Pat Schories (Photograph by Harry Bolick. Reproduced by permission.)

Awards, Honors

Parents magazine Best Children's Book of the Year designation, and New York Public Library Title for Reading and Sharing selection, both 1991, both for *Mouse Around;* Outstanding Science Trade Book for Children designation, Children's Book Council/National Science Teachers Association, 1997, for *Over under in the Garden;* Garden State Children's Book Award, 2001, for *Bathtime for Biscuit;* Cooperative Children's Book Center Choice selection, 2007, for *Jack and the Night Visitors;* Best Children's Book selection, Bank Street College of Education, 2007, for *Jack and the Night Visitors,* 2008, for *Jack Wants a Snack.*

Writings

SELF-ILLUSTRATED

Mouse Around, Farrar, Straus (New York, NY), 1991.
He's Your Dog!, Farrar, Straus (New York, NY), 1993.
Over under in the Garden: A Botanical Alphabet Book, Farrar, Straus (New York, NY), 1996.
Breakfast for Jack, Front Street (Asheville, NC), 2004.
Jack and the Missing Piece, Front Street (Asheville, NC), 2004.
Jack and the Night Visitors, Front Street (Asheville, NC), 2006.
Jack Wants a Snack, Front Street (Asheville, NC), 2008.
When Jack Goes Out, Boyds Mills Press (Honesdale, PA), 2010.

ILLUSTRATOR

Louis Ross, *Puddle Duck,* Dutton (New York, NY), 1979.
Kit Schorsch, reteller, *The Town Mouse and the Country Mouse,* Checkerboard Press, 1989.
Kit Schorsch, reteller, *Stone Soup,* Checkerboard Press, 1989.

Linda Leuck, *Teeny, Tiny Mouse,* Bridgewater Books (Mahwah, NJ), 1998.

ILLUSTRATOR; "BISCUIT THE PUPPY" SERIES BY ALYSSA SATIN CAPUCILLI

Biscuit (also see below), HarperCollins (New York, NY), 1996, reprinted, 2007.
Biscuit Finds a Friend, HarperCollins (New York, NY), 1997.
Bathtime for Biscuit, HarperCollins (New York, NY), 1998.
Biscuit's Picnic (also see below), HarperCollins (New York, NY), 1999.
Hello, Biscuit, HarperCollins (New York, NY), 1999.
Happy Birthday, Biscuit! (also see below), HarperCollins (New York, NY), 1999.
Happy Halloween, Biscuit! (also see below), Harper-Festival (New York, NY), 1999.
Happy Thanksgiving, Biscuit! (also see below), Harper-Festival (New York, NY), 1999.
Biscuit's New Trick (also see below), HarperCollins (New York, NY), 2000.
Biscuit's Christmas: A Scratch-and-Sniff Book, Harper-Festival (New York, NY), 2000.
Happy Easter, Biscuit! HarperFestival (New York, NY), 2000.
Time to Paint, Biscuit! (also see below), HarperCollins (New York, NY), 2001.
Merry Christmas, from Biscuit, HarperFestival (New York, NY), 2001.
Biscuit's Valentine's Day, HarperFestival (New York, NY), 2001.
Biscuit's Day at the Beach (also see below), HarperCollins (New York, NY), 2001.
Biscuit Wants to Play, HarperCollins (New York, NY), 2001.
Biscuit Visits the Farm, HarperFestival (New York, NY), 2002.
Biscuit Meets the Neighbors (also see below), Harper-Collins (New York, NY), 2002.
Biscuit Loves You, HarperCollins (New York, NY), 2002.
Biscuit Goes to the Park (also see below), HarperCollins (New York, NY), 2002.
Biscuit Goes to School, HarperCollins (New York, NY), 2002.
Biscuit and the Bunny (also see below), HarperCollins (New York, NY), 2002.
Happy Hanukkah, Biscuit!, HarperCollins (New York, NY), 2002.
What Is Love, Biscuit?, HarperCollins (New York, NY), 2003.
Biscuit Loves School, HarperFestival (New York, NY), 2003.
Biscuit's Big Friend, HarperCollins (New York, NY), 2003.
Biscuit Is Thankful, HarperCollins (New York, NY), 2003.
Biscuit Wins a Prize (also see below), HarperCollins (New York, NY), 2004.
Biscuit Gives a Gift (also see below), HarperFestival (New York, NY), 2004.
Biscuit Visits the Pumpkin Patch, HarperFestival (New York, NY), 2004.

Biscuit Loves Father's Day, HarperFestival (New York, NY), 2004.

Biscuit Loves Mother's Day, HarperFestival (New York, NY), 2004.

Meet Biscuit, HarperCollins (New York, NY), 2005.

Biscuit's Graduation Day, HarperCollins (New York, NY), 2005.

Biscuit's Fourth of July, HarperCollins (New York, NY), 2005.

Biscuit and the Baby, HarperCollins (New York, NY), 2005.

Biscuit's Snowy Day, HarperCollins (New York, NY), 2005.

Biscuit: Storybook Collection (includes *Biscuit, Biscuit Wins a Prize, Biscuit's New Trick, Biscuit's Picnic, Time to Paint, Biscuit!, Biscuit Goes to the Park, Happy Birthday, Biscuit!, Biscuit's Day at the Beach, Biscuit Meets the Neighbors,* and *Biscuit and the Bunny*), HarperFestival (New York, NY), 2005.

Biscuit's Hanukkah, HarperCollins (New York, NY), 2005.

Biscuit Visits the Big City, HarperCollins (New York, NY), 2006.

Biscuit's Day at the Farm, HarperCollins Children's Books (New York, NY), 2007.

Biscuit's Fun with Friends, HarperFestival 2007.

Biscuit and the Little Pup, HarperCollins Children's Books (New York, NY), 2008.

Biscuit Takes a Walk, HarperCollins Children's Books (New York, NY), 2009.

Biscuit Meets the Class Pet, HarperCollins Children's Books (New York, NY), 2010.

Biscuit and the Lost Teddy Bear, HarperCollins Children's Books (New York, NY), 2011.

Sidelights

Trained as a graphic artist, Pat Schories has become best known for her work within the field of children's books, particularly her illustrations for Alyssa Satin Capucilli's "Biscuit the Puppy" series. The frisky yellow puppy in this long-running series is based on one of Schories' own dogs, and another family pet provides the inspiration for her original picture-book series about a lovable terrier pup named Jack. Other original self-illustrated stories by Schories include *Mouse Around, He's Your Dog!,* and *Over under in the Garden: A Botanical Alphabet Book.*

Born in 1952, Schories started her love affair with books and bookbinding while growing up in Ohio. As she once admitted to *SATA,* "I started writing and illustrating my own books early on [and] still have one from second grade, complete with cloth binding and endpapers." At Kent State University she majored in graphic design and illustration, then moved to New York City with the intent to "live in a loft, create books, [and] live a bohemian lifestyle." However, her dreams quickly confronted reality: "I had no idea lofts were expensive or hard to come by and ended up in a shoe-box apartment, far from midtown." Undaunted by such less-than-ideal surroundings, Schories began freelancing for a small book-design studio while scouting for illustration assignments from book publishers. Her efforts were rewarded with her first job: Louis Ross's *Puddle Duck,* a baby's cloth book that was published in 1979. "Not the highbrow children's literature I had planned for myself, but a step in the door," Schories later recalled, "and I was thrilled with the opportunity to illustrate anything!"

In 1989 Schories was given the go ahead for her first major illustration assignment, the wordless picture book *Mouse Around.* "I was overjoyed!" she recalled. Published in 1991, *Mouse Around* depicts a young mouse and his foray into the world outside his quiet mouse hole in the basement. Calling Schories' effort "an engaging, wordless" story, a *Publishers Weekly* reviewer also described *Mouse Around* as a story told "effectively and with great charm, . . . offering [readers] the fun and challenge of hunting for the mouse on each page."

The spunky yellow puppy that stars in Alyssa Satin Capucilli's popular picture-book series is brought to life in Schories' colorful art for Biscuit.
(HarperTrophy 1996. Illustration copyright © 1996 by Pat Schories. Reproduced by permission of HarperCollins Children's Books, a division of HarperCollins Publishers.)

Schories followed *Mouse Around* with two other original picture-book assignments until, "finally I was able to quit my day job and work on my own books full

Schories modeled the lovable animal characters in **Bathtime for Biscuit** *and others in Capucilli's series on her own pets.* (HarperTrophy, 1998. Illustration copyright © 1998 by Pat Schories. Reproduced by permission of Harper-Collins Children's Books, a division of HarperCollins Publishers.)

time. Glorious!" In *Over under in the Garden: An Alphabet Book* she draws on her expertise as a botanical illustrator and crafts a text consisting of the names of twenty-six different plants and animals, each one beginning with a different letter of the alphabet. *Over under in the Garden* also serves as an introduction to nature for young children. Praising the detail used by Schories in her drawings, *Horn Book* reviewer Elizabeth Watson noted that through the "carefully drawn and faithfully colored" pictures" in the book "youngsters will "have their first encounter with kohlrabi and mandrake . . . [and] will be able to recognize both if they ever meet them again." *School Library Journal* contributor Carolyn Noah praised Schories' "striking artwork" for *Over under in the Garden* as well as citing the book's "handsome design."

Since Capucilli's first "Biscuit the Puppy" book appeared in 1996, Schories' image of a golden puppy has become an icon for beginning readers. Biscuit has appeared as a stuffed toy, and has made character appearances at story hours. The "Biscuit the Puppy" series has also won praise from critics: *Booklist* contributor Ilene Cooper considered Schories' illustrations "appealing" in *Biscuit's Valentine's Day,* while Wendy S. Carroll noted in her *School Library Journal* review of *Biscuit Wants*

to Play that the book's "soft watercolor illustrations . . . convey the action of the text." In a review of the same book, *Booklist* contributor Hazel Rochman noted that "the pictures extend the words." *Biscuit Goes to School* is characterized by "a warmly and invitingly drawn school environment" according to a critic for *Kirkus Reviews,* while Cooper commented in *Booklist* that Schories' "friendly watercolor" illustrations bring out the story's action. The "Biscuit the Puppy" books have appeared as easy-readers, beginning-readers, and lift-the-flap books. To satisfy serious fans, ten of the "Biscuit the Puppy" stories have also been collected as *Biscuit: Storybook Collection.*

With the success of the "Biscuit the Puppy" books, Schories has gone on to craft her own series of picture books about a raffish brown-and-white puppy named Jack. "Jack is an appealing character with perky ears and a variety of beguiling expressions," a *Kirkus Reviews* contributor explained in describing the star of *Breakfast for Jack, Jack and the Missing Piece, Jack Wants a Snack, Jack and the Night Visitor,* and *When Jack Goes Out,* among others. These wordless books follow the adventures of the titular puppy and his human family. In *Breakfast for Jack,* for example, Jack's family is busy rushing around, trying to get ready for school and work, and they seem to have forgotten to give *him* breakfast! Food also plays a role in *Jack Wants a Snack,* as the pup becomes intrigued by the pretend

Schories' work for Capucilli's long-running "Biscuit" series includes **Biscuit Wants to Play.** *(Illustration copyright © 2001 by Pat Schories. Reproduced by permission of HarperCollins Children's Books, a division of HarperCollins Publishers.)*

tea party one of his young family members is hosting in the back yard. In *Jack and the Missing Piece* Jack's boy and his friend are playing with blocks when a piece goes missing and the pup finds himself a suspect, while the puppy and his young owner make friends of a group of friendly robot alien visitors in both *Jack and the Night Visitors* and *When Jack Goes Out.*

"The suspenseful action—and the pacing of it—is just right," praised Jennifer M. Brabander in her review of *Breakfast for Jack* and *Jack and the Missing Piece* for *Horn Book.* A *Publishers Weekly* reviewer also praised the pacing in the first two "Jack" stories, citing the artist's "skillful combination of spot drawings and full page renderings." "Schories does a masterful job of creating a clear plot that children will be able to follow" in *Jack Wants a Snack,* asserted *School Library Journal* contributor Susan E. Murray, while Stacy Dillon noted in the same periodical that the colorful pastel illustrations in *When Jack Goes Out* "are full of whimsy" and give the book "a timeless quality." Reviewing *Jack and the Night Visitors,* Sally R. Dow noted in *School Library Journal* that Schories' book would be useful in "helping [children] . . . to develop pre-reading skills such as sequencing and employing descriptive language," while Phelan cited the author's "strong visual storytelling skills" and "accessible artwork." For Brabander, "the humorous details in the art" for *Jack and the Night Visitors* team with "the story's brief suspense, and the book's small trim size [to] make this exactly right for pre-readers to 'read' to an adult or enjoy on their own." Gay Lynn Van Vleck predicted in her *School Library Journal* review that the "Jack" books will "appeal to young listeners" and might even "prove useful to teachers practicing story writing" in their classrooms.

Married to photographer and old-time fiddler Harry Bolick, Schories is a wife and a stepmother in addition to pursuing her career as author and illustrator. "I make time to cook dinner, garden, exercise, play a little music," she remarked. "But books continue to occupy the largest space in my life, and I imagine they always will. I keep a notebook with ideas, and have a lifetime of picture book making ahead of me!"

Biographical and Critical Sources

PERIODICALS

Booklist, February 15, 2001, Ilene Cooper, review of *Biscuit's Valentine's Day,* p. 1139; November 1, 2001, Hazel Rochman, review of *Biscuit Wants to Play,* pp. 485-486; August, 2002, Ilene Cooper, review of *Biscuit Goes to School,* p. 1969; July, 2003, Stephanie Zvirin, review of *Biscuit's Big Friend,* p. 1899; April 15, 2006, Carolyn Phelan, review of *Jack and the Night Visitors,* p. 55; February 15, 2010, Carolyn Phelan, review of *When Jacks Goes Out,* p. 81.

Horn Book, July-August, 1996, Elizabeth Watson, review of *Over under in the Garden: A Botanical Alphabet Book,* pp. 455-456; January-February, 2005, Jennifer

Schories shares her original, self-illustrated dog story in her "Jack" books, one of which is **Jack Wants a Snack.** (Illustration copyright © 2008 by Pat Schories. Reproduced by permission of Boyds Mills Press.)

M. Brabander, reviews of *Breakfast for Jack* and *Jack and the Missing Piece,* both p. 86; July-August, 2006, Jennifer M. Brabander, review of *Jack and the Night Visitors,* p. 430; September-October, 2008, Jennifer M. Brabander, review of *Jack Wants a Snack,* p. 572; May-June, 2010, Jennifer M. Brabander, review of *When Jack Goes Out,* p. 71.

Kirkus Reviews, June 15, 2002, review of *Biscuit Goes to School,* p. 877; November 1, 2002, review of *Happy Hanukkah, Biscuit!,* p. 1515; October 1, 2004, review of *Breakfast for Jack,* p. 968; April 1, 2006, review of *Jack and the Night Visitors,* p. 357; January 15, 2010, review of *When Jack Goes Out.*

Publishers Weekly, May 24, 1991, review of *Mouse Around,* p. 56; December 20, 2004, reviews of *Breakfast for Jack* and *Jack and the Missing Piece,* both p. 57.

School Library Journal, June, 1996, Carolyn Noah, review of *Over under in the Garden,* p. 118; December, 1999, Laura Santoro, review of *Happy Thanksgiving, Biscuit,* p. 88; June, 2000, Janie Schomberg, review of *Biscuit's New Trick,* p. 102; April, 2001, Wendy S. Carroll, review of *Biscuit Wants to Play,* p. 105; October, 2002, Ilene Abramson, review of *Happy Hanukkah, Biscuit!* p. 58; November, 2004, Gay Lynn Van Vleck, review of *Breakfast for Jack,* pp. 117-118; June, 2006, Sally R. Dow, review of *Jack and the Night Visitors,* p. 126; September, 2008, Susan E. Murray, review of *Jack Wants a Snack,* p. 159; February, 2010, Stacy Dillon, review of *When Jack Goes Out,* p. 94.

ONLINE

Pat Schories Home Page, http://www.patschories.com
    (July 20, 2011).*

* * *

SCHUBERT, Leda 1945-
(Leda Deirdre Schubert)

Personal

Born 1945, in Washington, DC; father an academic, mother a business owner; married Bob Rosenfeld. *Education:* Brandeis, B.A.; Harvard University, M.A.T. (English); Vermont College, M.F.A. (writing for children and young adults), 2004. *Hobbies and other interests:* Reading, playing traditional music, gardening, discussing politics, spending time with her dogs and her friends.

Addresses

Home—Plainfield, VT. *Agent*—Steven Chudney, Chudney Agency, 72 N. State Rd., Ste. 501, Briarcliff Manor, NY 10510. *E-mail*—leda@ledaschubert.com.

Career

Author and educator. Cabot School, Cabot, VT, librarian, beginning 1980; also librarian at Kellogg-Hubbard Library, Montpelier, VT; formerly worked as a teacher, librarian, and preschool director. Vermont Department of Education, school library consultant, 1986-2003. Vermont College of Fine Arts, member of core M.F.A. faculty in writing for children and young adults program. Former member of award committees for Caldecott, Arbuthnot, *Boston Globe/Horn Book,* and Vermont State book awards.

Member

Society of Children's Book Writers and Illustrators, Authors Guild, American Library Association, Association of Library Services for Children.

Awards, Honors

Book Sense Winter Pick, 2005, for *Here Comes Darrell;* New York Public Library 100 Titles for Reading and Sharing designation, and *New York Times* Editors' Choice title, both 2006, both for *Ballet of the Elephants.*

Writings

FOR CHILDREN

Winnie All Day Long, illustrated by William Benedict, Candlewick Press (Cambridge, MA), 2000.

Winnie Plays Ball, illustrated by William Benedict, Candlewick Press (Cambridge, MA), 2000.
Here Comes Darrell, illustrated by Mary Azarian, Houghton Mifflin (Boston, MA), 2005.
Ballet of the Elephants, illustrated by Robert Andrew Parker, Roaring Brook Press (New Milford, CT), 2006.
Feeding the Sheep, illustrated by Andrea U'Ren, Farrar, Straus & Giroux (New York, NY), 2008.
Reading to Peanut, illustrated by Amanda Haley, Holiday House (New York, NY), 2011.
The Princess of Borscht, illustrated by Bonnie Christensen, Roaring Brook Press (New York, NY), 2011.
Monsieur Marceau, illustrated by Gerard DuBois, Roaring Brook Press (New York, NY), 2012.

Also author of six-part serialized novel *Nathan's Song* published in *Boston Globe Online* as part of spring, 2007, Newspapers in Education project. Contributor to periodicals, including *Horn Book* and *School Library Journal.*

Sidelights

Children's book author Leda Schubert lives in Vermont, and her stories for young children are inspired by her personal curiosity as well as by her colorful New England surroundings. Although she has enjoyed writing since childhood, Schubert viewed it as a hobby for many years while working as a teacher, librarian, and library consultant. Working as a librarian allowed her to learn what kinds of books her young patrons liked, and her subsequent job as a library consultant for the Vermont Department of Education gave her a familiarity with almost every book published for children. Benefiting from this experience, Schubert's picture books, which include *Here Comes Darrell, Ballet of the Elephants, Feeding the Sheep,* and the beginning readers *Winnie All Day Long* and *Winnie Plays Ball,* have received critical accolades as well as awards.

"I was lucky that all of my jobs involved reading to children," Schubert explained of her background to *Seven Days Vermont* interviewer Margot Harrison. "I started writing a little bit, but I had no idea what I was doing. I never gave up this dream." Her "Winnie" books, which were written while Schubert worked as a library consultant, were designed to fill what she saw as a specific need: "more trade books for kids that they could buy at the bookstore that would encourage reading, but that were funny and not didactic." Based on the antics of Schubert's own dog, *Winnie All Day Long* introduces a large, rambunctious pup named Winnie and her human playmate Annie and follows the interaction between the two as Winnie's high spirits, napping, mealtimes, and desire for attention affect Annie and her family throughout the day. The oversized pooch celebrates a birthday in *Winnie Plays Ball,* and the toy balls she receives generate several games with Annie. After her "Winnie" stories were accepted for publication by Candlewick Press as part of the publisher's "Brand New

Readers" series, Schubert "got more and more convinced that [writing for children] . . . was what I had to do." She left her job in education and turned to writing.

Schubert's collaboration with Caldecott Medal-winning illustrator Mary Azarian on *Here Comes Darrell* is also based on the author's life: in this case a generous neighbor who plowed driveways in her town so that local working folk could be at their jobs on time during snowstorms. Set amid the northern New England seasons that both author and illustrator know so well, the story focuses on a man who takes time out from his own chores to help out neighbors with backhoe work and snowplowing and also shares his supply of wood. When a severe storm hits the area and destroys the roof of Darrell's barn, his kindness is returned, "celebrat-[ing] . . . a way of life in a rural community where neighbors help each other through the year," according to a *Publishers Weekly* contributor. Calling the collaboration between author and illustrator "delightful," *School Library Journal* contributor Teresa Pfeifer cited Azarian's "distinguished, detailed woodcuts and concluded that *Here Comes Darrell* "will be a pleasure to pair with many other books on the seasons, neighbors, and communities" during story hours.

Ballet of the Elephants was inspired by a television special about the life of renowned twentieth-century ballet choreographer George Balanchine and was written fol-

lowing Schubert's completion of Vermont College's M.F.A. degree in writing for children and young adults. The book follows the efforts of Balanchine and circus promoter John Ringling North to stage North's dream of a "Circus Polka," a dance involving fifty elephants and fifty ballerinas. Set to music by Russian composer Igor Stravinsky, the mammoth undertaking premiered in 1942 as part of the famous Ringling Brothers and Barnum & Bailey Circus. It starred the famous elephant Modoc and prima ballerina Vera Zorina. In her fact-filled text, Schubert brings to life the international proportions of the undertaking, as well as the daunting task of costuming fifty rotund pachyderms in fluffy pink tutus and glittering tiaras.

In *Booklist,* Hazel Rochman praised Schubert's "simple and lyrical" text for *Ballet of the Elephants* as well as her inclusion of an afterword that answers the questions of curious readers. Robert Andrew Parker's ink-and-water color images "capture the movement and vitality of this creative undertaking," added Carol Schene in her *School Library Journal* review of the same book, the critic concluding that Schubert's "clearly written" story "provides a unique introduction to . . . a curious moment in musical history." "Schubert's deft, incisive way of telling the incredible story will set young minds spinning," announced Jed Perl, hailing *Ballet of the Elephants* in the *New York Times Book Review.* "Woven through this casually opulent volume is an inspiriting idea," Perl added: "that boys and girls will be tantalized by the works . . . of geniuses like Balanchine and Stravinsky, men whose achievements our dumb-it-down era sometimes regards as too demanding even for adults."

Brought to life in ink-and-color artwork by Andrea U'Ren, *Feeding the Sheep* shows the path from sheep to sweater as a child watches her mother care for and shear the family sheep, then clean, card, and spin the wool in preparation for dyeing and knitting the resulting yarn into a warm sweater. With its question-and-answer text, the book will inspire young readers through its depiction of "the cozy family bond between parent and child, working together and caring for their free-range animals," noted Rochman. In *School Library Journal* Susan Weitz wrote that "Schubert's text has a predictable, soothing structure" that pairs well with U'Ren's detail-filled illustrations. The book's mix of story and art "is seamless and . . . completely accessible and understandable to young readers," asserted a *Kirkus Reviews* critic, the reviewer going on to dub *Feeding the Sheep* "lovely."

For Lucy, the young star of *Reading to Peanut,* the skill of reading is also the result of a long process. In this case, the process includes sticky notes and pencils, imagination and curiosity, and a parent's patient humor. Together with her helpful dog Peanut, the enthusiastic Lucy draws and labels everything of importance in her kid-sized world, adding the appropriate spellings with her parents' help. Another determined young girl is in-

Leda Schubert joins with illustrator and fellow Vermonter Mary Azarian to create the picture book **Here Comes Darrell.** (Illustration © 2005 by Mary Azarian. All rights reserved. Reproduced by permission of Houghton Mifflin Company. All rights reserved.)

Andrea U'Ren's striking artwork brings to life Schubert's homespun story in **Feeding the Sheep.** (Illustration copyright © 2010 by Andrea U'Ren. Reproduced by permission of Farrar, Straus & Giroux, LLC.)

troduced in *The Princess of Borscht,* a story by Schubert that finds little Ruthie aided by neighbors in her attempt to cook up a mug of hot borscht for her Russian-born grandmother. Illustrated by Amanda Haley, *Reading to Peanut* treats young audiences to an "appealing" heroine in a "warm family story" that gains added interest from its "mild suspense."

Biographical and Critical Sources

PERIODICALS

Booklist, October 1, 2005, Ilene Cooper, review of *Here Comes Darrell,* p. 66; April 1, 2006, Hazel Rochman, review of *Ballet of the Elephants,* p. 46; March 15, 2010, Hazel Rochman, review of *Feeding the Sheep,* p. 47.

Bulletin of the Center for Children's Books, November, 2005, Elizabeth Bush, review of *Here Comes Darrell,* p. 155; May, 2006, Deborah Stevenson, review of *Ballet of the Elephants,* p. 421.

Horn Book, July-August, 2006, Betty Carter, review of *Ballet of the Elephants,* p. 469.

Kirkus Reviews, October 15, 2005, review of *Here Comes Darrell,* p. 1146; March 15, 2006, review of *Ballet of the Elephants,* p. 299; January 15, 2010, review of *Feeding the Sheep;* July 15, 2011, review of *Reading to Peanut.*

New York Times Book Review, May 14, 2006, Jed Perl, "The Big Dance," p. 20.

Publishers Weekly, October 31, 2005, review of *Here Comes Darrell,* p. 55; April 10, 2006, review of *Ballet of the Elephants,* p. 70.

School Library Journal, November, 2005, Teresa Pfeifer, review of *Here Comes Darrell,* p. 107; April, 2006, Carol Schene, review of *Ballet of the Elephants,* p. 132; March, 2010, Susan Weitz, review of *Feeding the Sheep,* p. 132.

ONLINE

Cynsations Web Log, http://cynthialeitichsmith.blogspot. com/ (February 22, 2006), Cynthia Leitich-Smith, interview with Schubert.

Leda Schubert Home Page, http://www.ledaschubert.com (July 15, 2011).

Seven Days Vermont Online, http://www.sevendaysvt.com/ (September 13, 2006), Margot Harrison, interview with Schubert.

*   *   *

SCHUBERT, Leda Deirdre
See SCHUBERT, Leda

*   *   *

SCHWARTZ, John 1957-

Personal

Born 1957, in Galveston, TX; married Jean Mixon; children: three. *Education:* University of Texas at Austin, bachelor's degree, J.D.

Addresses

Home—NJ.

Career

Journalist and author. *Newsweek,* New York, NY, journalist, then senior writer, 1985-2003; journalist for *Washington Post; New York Times,* New York, NY, science journalist, national legal correspondent, beginning 2009. Called to the bar of the State of Texas.

Writings

(With others) *College Financial Aid,* College Research Group of Concord, Massachusetts/Prentice Hall (New York, NY), 1991.

College Scholarships and Financial Aid, Wintergreen/ Orchard House/Macmillan USA (New York, NY), 1995.

(Editor) *College Scholarships and Financial Aid,* Wintergreen/Orchid House/Macmillan USA (New York, NY), 1997.

(With Michael T. Osterholm) *Living Terrors: What America Needs to Know to Survive the Coming Bio-Terrorist Catastrophe,* Delacorte Press (New York, NY), 2000.

Short: Walking Tall When You're Not Tall at All, Rb Flash Point (New York, NY), 2010.

Sidelights

As a journalist, John Schwartz has worked for *Newsweek* and the *Washington Post,* and he now serves as national legal correspondent for the *New York Times,* where he is able to draw on the knowledge he gained during law school. Schwartz has pursued several subjects in more detail, joining Michael Osterholm in investigating biological terrorism in *Living Terrors: What America Needs to Know to Survive the Coming Bio-Terrorist Catastrophe.* In *Short: Walking Tall When You're Not Tall at All,* he writes from a personal perspective: Schwartz has been considered short all his life and as an adult stands five feet three inches tall, seven inches shorter than the average U.S. man.

In *Short* Schwartz challenges the cultural assumption that shorter adults are viewed as less happy, less successful in their careers, and less wealthy than taller individuals, particularly as far as men are concerned. Marshaling the same statistics used to prompt parents to consider human growth hormone treatments for their shorter children, he "breaks down related studies and explains the real statistics behind the headlines and hype," according to *School Library Journal* contributor Jody Kopple. In addition to including inspiring biographies of successful short individuals, other topics addressed by Schwartz in *Short* include how genetics determines height and the psychological issues that may develop, particularly as a result of grade-school bullying.

The inclusion of interviews and anecdotes from the author's own experiences help make *Short* "part memoir, part self-help book, and part treatise" on the representation of short people in the media. The author's "investigation of the relationship between height, wealth, and happiness" is "rich with examples of his own life," asserted a *Publishers Weekly* contributor, the critc deeming *Short* a "down-to-earth and hopeful account." "Short kids will want every word," predicted *Booklist* critic Hazel Rochman, "whether it is about tall guys with problems or about Schwartz's own dating failures and successes."

Biographical and Critical Sources

PERIODICALS

Booklist, February 15, 2010, Hazel Rochman, review of *Short: Walking Tall When You're Not Tall at All,* p. 75.
Publishers Weekly, March 29, 2010, review of *Short,* p. 61.
School Library Journal, March, 2010, Jody Kopple, review of *Short,* p. 180.

Tablet, August 16, 2010, Anat Even-Or, review of *Short.*

ONLINE

New York Times Web site, http://www.nytimes.com/ (August 15, 2011), "John Schwartz."

*   *   *

SEFTON, Catherine
See WADDELL, Martin

*   *   *

SIDDALS, Mary McKenna

Personal

Born in Canada; married; has children. *Education:* Attended college. *Hobbies and other interests:* Nature, spending time with family.

Addresses

Home—Prince George, British Columbia, Canada. *Agent*—Karen Grencik, Karen Grencik, Red Fox Literary, 129 Morro Ave., Shell Beach, CA 93449.

Career

Educator and author. Formerly worked as a teacher.

Awards, Honors

Our Choice selection, Canadian Children's Book Centre, and Best of the Best selection, Chicago Public Library, both 1998, both for *Millions of Snowflakes.*

Writings

Tell Me a Season, illustrated by Petra Mathers, Clarion Books (New York, NY), 1997.
Millions of Snowflakes, illustrated by Elizabeth Sayles, Clarion Books (New York, NY), 1998.
I'll Play with You, illustrated by David Wisniewski, Clarion Books (New York, NY), 2000.
Morning Song, illustrated by Elizabeth Sayles, Henry Holt (New York, NY), 2001.
Compost Stew: An A to Z Recipe for the Earth, illustrated by Ashley Wolff, Tricycle Press (Berkeley, CA), 2010.

Contributor of poems, stories, and articles to periodicals. Former author of "Puzzles 'n' Fun" column for *Owl* magazine.

Sidelights

Based in British Columbia, Canada, Mary McKenna Siddals is a former teacher who has also written picture books such as *Tell Me a Season, Millions of Snow-*

flakes, I'll Play with You, Morning Song, and *Compost Stew: An A to Z Recipe for the Earth.* Crafted carefully with an eye toward rhythm and story-hour readability, Siddals' books showcase artwork by illustrators such as Petra Mathers, Elizabeth Sayles, Ashley Wolff, and David Wisniewski. Reviewing *I'll Play with You* in *Booklist,* Gillian Engberg wrote that Siddals' "words are poetic, mixing humor and glee into the reverence for nature," while a *Publishers Weekly* critic observed that the author's depiction of children enjoying nature reflects "a comforting solitude that suggests a fresh connection with the world." *Tell Me a Season,* Siddals' first picture book, features a rhyming text about the an-

nual cycle of nature that Susan Dove Lempke hailed in her *Booklist* review as "cheerful yet elegant, spare yet satisfying, compact yet enveloping."

Siddals makes a seasonal shift to winter in *Millions of Snowflakes,* a picture book featuring artwork by Elizabeth Sayles. Described by Kathy Broderick in *Booklist* as a "playful poem about the natural world," *Millions of Snowflakes* finds a child imagining all the wonderful fun that can be had outside on a snowy day, from making snow angels to catching snowflakes on one's nose. Coming alive in Sayles pastel-toned paintings, *Millions of Snowflakes* "will get an enthusiastic reaction from active young children," predicted Kathy Broderick in

Cover of Mary McKenna Siddals' winter-themed picture book **Millions of Snowflakes,** *featuring artwork by Elizabeth Sayles.* (Illustration copyright © 1998 by Elizabeth Sayles. Reproduced by permission of Clarion Books, an imprint of Houghton Mifflin Publishing Company. All rights reserved.)

her *Booklist* review. Siddals' text also features a counting element, and her use of "rhyme is not obvious and therefore more effective," according to *Resource Links* critic Lynda Curnoe. Author and illustrator also collaborate on *Morning Song,* which captures first light during a warmer season and pairs Siddals' engaging rhyme with what *School Library Journal* contributor Sally R. Dow described as Sayles' "luminous illustrations." In *Publishers Weekly* a critic praised *Morning Song* as "a winning evocation of a boy's awakening."

A gardener, Siddals learned to compost as a young woman, encouraged by her mother, and she shares what she has learned about this all-natural mode of recycling in *Compost Stew.* Employing what Engberg described as her characteristic "bouncing, rhyming lines" along with a sing-song refrain, the author lists the many things that can be tossed atop a backyard compost pile, from apple cores to Zinnia blossoms. Ashley Wolff accompanies the text with colorful collage art that includes both found objects and compostable materials—from flower petals and leaves to seeds, eggshells, and worms—and also features children of many cultures. *Compost Stew* "provides a lighthearted introduction to an earth-and kid-friendly activity," according to Engberg, and a *Kirkus Reviews* writer dubbed the book "a rollicking, rhyming alphabetical recipe for making successful compost" that will be enjoyed by "budding environmentalists."

Biographical and Critical Sources

PERIODICALS

Booklist, April 1, 1997, Susan Dove Lempke, review of *Tell Me a Season,* p. 1339; November 1, 1998, Kathy Broderick, review of *Millions of Snowflakes,* p. 505 October 1, 2000, Gillian Engberg, review of *I'll Play with You,* p. 350; February 15, 2010, Gillian Engberg, review of *Compost Stew: An A to Z Recipe for the Earth,* p. 88.

Kirkus Reviews, March 1, 2010, review of *Compost Stew.*

Publishers Weekly, January 6, 1997, review of *Tell Me a Season,* p. 72; July 31, 2000, review of *I'll Play with You,* p. 93; December 3, 2001, review of *Morning Song,* p. 58.

Resource Links, April, 1999, review of *Millions of Snowflakes,* p. 6.

School Library Journal, November, 2000, Melinda Schroeter, review of *I'll Play with You,* p. 134; December, 2001, Sally R. Dow, review of *Morning Song,* p. 111; April, 2010, Mary Hazelton, review of *Compost Stew,* p. 149.

ONLINE

Mary McKenna Siddals Home Page, http://www.siddals.com (May 11, 2011).*

STEAD, Erin E. 1982-

Personal

Born December 27, 1982, in Farmington Hills, MI; married Philip C. Stead (a writer), September, 2005. *Education:* Attended art school.

Addresses

Home—Ann Arbor, MI.

Career

Illustrator. Books of Wonder, New York, NY, member of staff; HarperCollins Children's Books, New York, NY, former assistant to the creative director; freelance illustrator and author of children's books.

Awards, Honors

Caldecott Medal, Chicago Public Library Best of the Best designation, New York Public Library Book for Reading and Sharing selection, and Best Illustrated Books selection, *New York Times,* all 2010, all for *A Sick Day for Amos McGee* by Philip C. Stead.

Illustrator

Philip C. Stead, *A Sick Day for Amos McGee,* Roaring Brook (New York, NY), 2010.

Julie Fogliano, *And Then It's Spring,* Roaring Brook Press (New York, NY), 2012.

Sidelights

When Erin E. Stead met her future husband in the art room at her Michigan high school, she had no idea that their meeting would put her on the path to winning the prestigious Caldecot Medal for picture-book illustration. Philip C. Stead has since become an illustrator in his own right in addition to writing stories for children, but when he wrote the manuscript for *A Sick Day for Amos McGee* he knew that the story required his wife's lighter creative touch. Described by *School Library Journal* contributor Mary Jean Smith as a "quiet tale of good deeds rewarded," *A Sick Day for Amos McGee* provided Erin Stead the encouragement she needed to start her own career in picture books.

Stead grew up Farmington Hills, a suburb of Detroit, Michigan, and she met Philip when she was a sophomore and both attended Divine Child High School in nearby Dearborn.They separated during college, Philip attending a Michigan university while Erin moved to the east coast to attend art school. The couple lived in New York City for several years, and there Erin followed her interest in children's books through jobs at a city book store and as an assistant to the creative director at HarperCollins Children's Books. After they returned to Michigan to establish their home, Philip presented Erin with the manuscript for *A Sick Day for Amos McGee.* The couple now lives and works in a renovated, century-old barn in downtown Ann Arbor, where they share studio space and frequently help each other on their respective projects. "There are actually moments when you can see us copying each other, sometimes on paper, sometimes not," Stead explained to *Publishers Weekly* online interviewer Rachel Steinberg.

Brought to life by Erin Stead in softly toned woodblock prints overdrawn with detailed penciled images, *A Sick Day for Amos McGee* focuses on a zookeeper who treats each of his exotic charges like friends, enjoying a game with Elephant, chatting with Penguin, reading soothing bedtime stories to Owl, and boosting Tortoise's self-confidence by challenging it to a race and letting Tortoise win. When Amos comes down with a cold that prevents him from coming to work, the animals decide to visit him at home and care for him as he has cared for them. Philip Stead's gentle story, with its fresh take on "the familiar pet-bonding theme will have great appeal," predicted Hazel Rochman in her *Booklist* review of *A Sick Day for Amos McGee,* and a *Publishers Weekly* cited Erin's illustrations as "breathtaking in their delicacy" and resonating a "quiet affection." In *Horn Book* Kitty Flynn asserted that "Erin Stead's "attentively detailed . . . illustrations reveal character and enhance the cozy mood of Philip Stead's gentle text."

Biographical and Critical Sources

PERIODICALS

Booklist, May 1, 2010, Hazel Rochman, review of *A Sick Day for Amos McGee,* p. 92.

Horn Book, May-June, 2010, Kitty Flynn, review of *A Sick Day for Amos McGee,* p. 72.

Kirkus Reviews, April 15, 2010, review of *A Sick Day for Amos McGee.*

New York Times Book Review, November 7, 2010, Lisa Von Drasek, review of *A Sick Day for Amos McGhee,* p. 34.

Erin E. Stead teamed up with her writer husband, Philip C. Stead, to create the award-winning picture book **A Sick Day for Amos McGee.** (Neal Porter Book, 2010. Illustration copyright © 2010 by Erin E. Stead. Reproduced by permission of Henry Holt & Company, LLC.)

Publishers Weekly, May 10, 2010, review of *A Sick Day for Amos McGee,* p. 41.

School Library Journal, May, 2010, Mary Jean Smith, review of *A Sick Day for Amos McGee,* p. 92.

Todedo Blade, January 23, 2011, Gary T. Pakulski, "Artist Overcomes Doubts to Capture Prestigious Caldecott Medal."

ONLINE

Erin Stead Web log, http://blog.erinstead.com (August 15, 2011).

Publishers Weekly Online, http://www.publishersweekly. com/ (June 28, 2010), Rachel Steinberg, "Erin Stead."*

V-Y

VANDERPOOL, Clare 1964-

Personal

Born 1964, in Wichita, KS; married; husband's name Mark (an engineer); children: four. *Education:* Newman University, B.S. (elementary education), B.A. (English).

Addresses

Home—Wichita, KS. *Agent*—Andrea Cascardi, Transatlantic Literary Agency, P.O. Box 349, Rockville Center, NY 11571-0349; andrea@tla1.com. *E-mail*—clare@ clarevanderpool.com.

Career

Writer. Wichita Catholic Diocese, Wichita, KS, director of youth ministries.

Member

Scoiety of Children's Book Writers and Illustrators.

Awards, Honors

John Newbery Medal, American Library Association, 2011, for *Moon over Manifest.*

Writings

Moon over Manifest (novel), Delacorte Press (New York, NY), 2010.

Sidelights

Clare Vanderpool received the prestigious Newbery Medal for children's literature for her debut novel, *Moon over Manifest,* which was described as a "memorable coming-of-age story" by a *Publishers Weekly* critic. Vanderpool's surprising victory was the culmination of almost ten years of effort on the work for the Kansas-based author, who credits her mother and father with modeling both diligence and optimism. "My parents are both Depression-era children, one born on a farm and one raised in a little house next to the railroad tracks," Vanderpool remarked on the *School Library Journal* Web site. "They raised my siblings and me with a can-do attitude. 'You'll figure it out. You can make it work. Keep at it. Anything is possible.' And I believed them."

Vanderpool was born in Wichita, Kansas, in 1964; she still lives in the College Hill neighborhood where she grew up and her four children attend the same schools she did. "If you ask anyone who knows me," the author remarked on her home page, "they will tell you that I have a very strong connection to place." An avid reader from a very young age, Vanderpool recalls taking her books with her into the most unlikely of places, including department-store dressing rooms and church confessionals. After graduating from Wichita Collegiate School, she attended Newman University, earning degrees in English and elementary education. Vanderpool spent a number of years as the director of youth ministries for the Wichita Catholic Diocese and began writing seriously after the birth of her first child.

Moon over Manifest was inspired by a line from Herman Melville's *Moby Dick:* "It is not down in any map; true places never are," as Vanderpool noted, and the concept of a "true place conjured up ideas of home." "But I wondered, what would a 'true place' be for someone who has never lived anywhere for more than a few weeks or months at a time?" Interestingly, the fictional town of Manifest is based on a real place: the southeastern Kansas town of Frontenac, which was home to both of Vanderpool's maternal grandmothers. During the writing of the novel, the author traveled to Frontenac, scouring through old newspapers and yearbooks and visiting graveyards. "As I started doing research, that's when the story started to take off," she told *New York Times* contributor Julie Bosman. "It really is the story of a young girl looking for clues of her father, wondering if he's coming back to get her and trying to figure out for herself what home means to her."

Set in 1936, *Moon over Manifest* centers on Abilene Tucker, a twelve year old who who has spent most of her life riding the rails. She is sent to live with relatives in her father's hometown of Manifest, Kansas, after he takes a railroad job in Iowa. Once there, the girl blossoms under the care of Shady Howard, an old family friend. When she discovers a box of keepsakes dating to 1917, Abilene stumbles on a mystery from the mining town's past involving bootleggers, the Ku Klux Klan, and a mysterious individual known as the "Rattler." With the help of new friends Lettie and Ruthanne, as well as Miss Sadie, a Hungarian fortune-teller, Abilene begins to piece together the truth about her father's upbringing. "Ingeniously plotted and gracefully told," as Elizabeth Bush commented in the *Bulletin of the Center for Children's Books*, *Moon over Manifest* "will resonate with any reader who's ever wondered whether those old family stories really tell the whole truth." Writing in *Booklist*, Kathleen Isaacs deemed the work a "rich and rewarding first novel," while *School Library Journal* contributor Renee Steinberg stated that Vanderpool's "thoroughly enjoyable, unique page-turner is a definite winner."

Biographical and Critical Sources

PERIODICALS

Booklist, October 15, 2010, Kathleen Isaacs, review of *Moon over Manifest*, p. 63.
Bulletin of the Center for Children's Books, November, 2010, Elizabeth Bush, review of *Moon over Manifest*, p. 152.
Dodge Globe (Dodge, KS), March 7, 2011, Suzanne Perez Tobias, "Wichita's Clare Vanderpool wins the John Newbery Medal."
New York Times, January 11, 2011, Julie Bosman, "Newbery Awarded to Debut Author," p. C1.
Publishers Weekly, September 27, 2010, review of *Moon over Manifest*, p. 60.
School Library Journal, November, 2010, Renee Steinberg, review of *Moon over Manifest*, p. 131.
Washington Post, February 8, 2011, interview with Vanderpool.
Wichita Eagle, January 10, 2011, Erin Brown, "Wichita Author Clare Vanderpool Calls Newbery Medal "Great Honor.'"

ONLINE

BookPage.com, http://www.bookpage.com (January, 2011), Eliza Bourné, interview with Vanderpool.
Clare Vanderpool Home Page, http://www.clarevanderpool.com (July 1, 2011).
Society of Children's Book Writer and Illustrators Web site, http://www.scbwi.org/ (July 1, 2011), "Clare Vanderpool."

School Library Journal Web site, http://www.schoollibrary journal.com/ (June 27, 2011), "ALA Annual 2011: Stead, Vanderpool at Newbery, Caldecott Dinner."*

*   *   *

van EEKHOUT, Greg

Personal
Born in Los Angeles, CA. *Education:* College degree.

Addresses
Home—San Diego, CA. *Agent*—Caitlin Blasdell, Liza Dawson Associates, 350 7th Ave., Ste. 2003, New York, NY 10001. *E-mail*—gregvan@gmail.com.

Career
Author. Worked variously as an ice-cream scooper, telemarketer, bookstore clerk and assistant manager; teacher of college-level English and multimedia development. Presenter at schools and conferences.

Writings

Norse Code, Ballantine Books (New York, NY), 2009.
Kid vs. Squid, Bloomsbury (New York, NY), 2010.
The Boy at the End of the World, Bloomsbury Children's Books (New York, NY), 2011.

Contributor of short fiction to periodicals, including *Amazing Stories, Asimov's Science Fiction, Exquisite Corpse, Flytrap, Magazine of Fantasy & Science Fiction, New Skies, Polyphony, Realms of Fantasy, Scholastic Scope*, and *Strange Horizons*. Work included in anthologies *New Skies: An Anthology of Today's Science Fiction*, edited by Patrick Nielsen Hayden, Tor (New York, NY), 2003; *Year's Best Fantasy 7*, edited by David G. Hartwell and Kathryn Cramer, Tachyon, 2007; *Paper Cities: An Anthology of Urban Fantasy*, edited by Ekaterina Sedia, Senses Five, 2008; and *Other Words*, DAW Books, 2009.

Sidelights
Inspired by his love of comic books, Saturday-morning cartoons, and science-fiction stories by classic writers such as Ray Bradbury, Greg van Eekhout has crafted his own career as a writer. The California native first became known for his short fiction, which has been anthologized and included in several magazines. Van Eekhout's first novel, *Norse Code*, spins a futuristic fantasy that merges Norse myths with the adventures of a rogue warrior and her efforts to stop the destruction of mankind, while his middle-grader novels *Kid vs. Squid* and *The Boy at the End of the World* treat readers to fast-moving, humorous stories that are designed to at-

tract even reluctant readers. Reviewing *Norse Code,* a *Publishers Weekly* critic noted that the book's "compelling prose and epic blend of mythological and modern elements make . . . van Eekhout . . . an author to watch."

Van Eekhout grew up with the urge to tell stories, but he did not immediately gravitate to novel-writing. "I really wanted to be some kind of cartoonist or comic book artist," he noted on his home page, "but I kind of got to a point where I could draw a very few things well and most things not well at all. If I'd worked harder at it, I might have gotten better, and maybe even good enough to do it professionally. That's the approach I took with writing: I started out not being able to write well and kept at it until I got good enough that people were willing to pay for my stories." "I think most kids start out as fantasy fans," he noted in discussing his chosen genre with online interviewer Cynthia Leitich Smith. "Even if the fantasy they're into isn't necessarily Tolkien-style with swords and wizards and eating stew with elves. Dr. Seuss is fantasy. *Toy Story* is fantasy. Spider-Man is fantasy. Most entertainment for kids features an elevated reality in which people have abilities that we don't have in real life or the laws of physics don't resemble what goes on in the real world or animals talk. . . . A walking, talking sea sponge? Total fantasy. So basically, I've been a fantasy fan all my life."

Van Eekhout shares his love of the fantasy genre with upper-elementary-grade readers in *Kid vs. Squid,* a "humorous fantasy that will rush over [readers] . . . like a tidal wave," according to *School Library Journal* critic Walter Minkel. In the story, Thatcher Hill is spending the summer helping out at Uncle Griswald's Museum of Curiosities, which caters to the tourist trade in their coastal California town. The teen's worries that the summer will be long and uneventful end after a pretty young woman breaks into the museum and steals a shrunken witch's head. Tracking her down, Thatcher winds up in a strange undersea world full of monsters and epic quests. Soon he has joined the young woman—actually an Atlantean princess named Shoal—in her effort to rescue her people from a diabolical curse that forces them to spend each summer working at the midway games and food concessions. "The internal logic of [van Eekhout's] . . . story is joyfully convoluted and not even close to airtight," quipped *Booklist* critic Ian Chipman, the critic going on to praise the fanciful humor in *Kid vs. Squid.*

In *The Boy at the End of the World* Fischer awakens from a sleep in an underground pod and reaches Earth's surface only to discover that he is the only human remaining on the planet. With the help of Click, a robot, and a shaggy young mammoth, the boy learns to survive the planet's harsh, jungle-like environment. In his search for others of his kind, he wanders throughout what was once North American. In addition to locating other arks, Fischer discovers that the seeds of destruc-

tion that mankind once sewed have now reseeded, prompting what *Booklist* critic John Peters described as a "quirky, high-stakes adventure hung about with oddball ideas and life-threatening hazards." Describing *The Boy at the End of the World* as a mix between speculative science fiction and a wilderness adventure, a *Kirkus Reviews* writer added that van Eekhout's "diverting tale" benefits from "a brisk pace and clever and snappy dialogue."

Biographical and Critical Sources

PERIODICALS

Booklist, May 15, 2010, Ian Chipman, review of *Kid vs. Squid,* p. 53; May 15, 2011, John Peters, review of *The Boy at the End of the World,* p. 56.
Kirkus Reviews, May 15, 2011, review of *The Boy at the End of the World.*
Publishers Weekly, April 20, 2009, review of *Norse Code,* p. 38.
School Library Journal, July, 2010, Walter Minkel, review of *Kid vs. Squid,* p. 98.

ONLINE

Cynsations Web log, http://cynthialeitichsmith.blogspot. com/ (December 30, 2010), Cynthia Leitich Smith, interview with van Eekhout.
Greg van Eekhout Home Page, http://writingandsnacks. com (June 12, 2011).*

*   *   *

WADDELL, Martin 1941-
(Catherine Sefton)

Personal

Born April 10, 1941, in Belfast, Northern Ireland; son of Mayne (a linen manufacturer) and Alice (a homemaker) Waddell; married Rosaleen Carragher (a teacher), December 27, 1969; children: Thomas Mayne, David Martin, Peter Matthew. *Religion:* "Troubled agnostic." *Hobbies and other interests:* Chess.

Addresses

Home—Newcastle, County Down, Northern Ireland. *Agent*—Gina Pollinger, 222 Old Brompton Rd., London SW5 OB2, England.

Career

Writer, beginning 1966. Worked variously at other occupations, including book-selling and junk-stalling.

Member

Society of Authors, Children's Literature Association of Ireland, Irish Writers Union.

Martin Waddell (Reproduced by permission.)

Awards, Honors

Federation of Children's Book Club Award runner-up, 1982, for *The Ghost and Bertie Boggin;* Carnegie Medal nomination, 1984, for *Island of the Strangers; Guardian* Award runner-up, 1984, and Other Award, 1986, both for *Starry Night;* Nestlée Smarties Grand Prize, 1988, and prix des Critiques de Livres pour Enfants (Belgium), 1989, both for *Can't You Sleep, Little Bear?;* Kurt Maschler/Emil Award, 1989, for *The Park in the Dark;* Best Book for Babies Award, 1990, for *Rosie's Babies;* Smarties Prize, 1991, and shortlist, 1992; Hans Christian Andersen Award, International Board on Books for Young People, 2004.

Writings

Ernie's Chemistry Set, illustrated by Ronnie Baird, Blackstaff (Belfast, Northern Ireland), 1978.

Ernie's Flying Trousers, illustrated by Ronnie Baird, Blackstaff (Belfast, Northern Ireland), 1978.

The Great Green Mouse Disaster, illustrated by Philippe Dupasquier, Andersen (London, England), 1981.

The House under the Stairs, Methuen (London, England), 1983.

(Editor) *A Tale to Tell,* Northern Ireland Arts Council, 1983.

Going West, illustrated by Philippe Dupasquier, Andersen (London, England), 1983, Harper (New York, NY), 1984.

Big Bad Bertie, illustrated by Glynis Ambrus, Methuen (London, England), 1984.

The Budgie Said GRRRR, illustrated by Glynis Ambrus, Methuen (London, England), 1985.

The School Reporter's Notebook, Beaver, 1985.

The Day It Rained Elephants, illustrated by Glynis Ambrus, Methuen (London, England), 1986.

Our Wild Weekend, Methuen (London, England), 1986.

Owl and Billy, Methuen (London, England), 1986.

The Tough Princess, illustrated by Patrick Benson, Walker Books (London, England), 1986, Putnam (New York, NY), 1987.

The Tall Story of Wilbur Small, Blackie & Son (London, England), 1987.

Alice the Artist, illustrated by Jonathan Langley, Dutton (New York, NY), 1988.

Can't You Sleep, Little Bear?, illustrated by Barbara Firth, Walker Books (London, England), 1988, Candlewick Press (Cambridge, MA), 1992, reprinted, Walker Books, 2004.

Class Three and the Beanstalk, illustrated by Toni Goffe, Blackie & Son (London, England), 1988.

Great Gran Gorilla and the Robbers, illustrated by Dom Mansell, Walker Books (London, England), 1988.

Great Gran Gorilla to the Rescue, illustrated by Dom Mansell, Walker Books (London, England), 1988.

Our Sleepysaurus, Walker Books (London, England), 1988.

Owl and Billy and the Space Days, Methuen (London, England), 1988.

Tales from the Shop That Never Shuts, illustrated by Maureen Bradley, Viking Kestrel (London, England), 1988.

Fred the Angel, Walker Books (London, England), 1989.

Judy the Bad Fairy, Walker Books (London, England), 1989.

Once There Were Giants, illustrated by Penny Dale, Delacorte (New York, NY), 1989.

The Park in the Dark, illustrated by Barbara Firth, edited by D. Briley, Lothrop (New York, NY), 1989.

Amy Said, illustrated by Charlotte Voake, Little Brown (Boston, MA), 1990.

Daisy's Christmas, illustrated by Jonathan Langley, Ideals, 1990.

The Ghost Family Robinson, illustrated by Jacqui Thomas, Viking Kestrel (London, England), 1990.

The Hidden House, illustrated by Angela Barrett, Putnam (New York, NY), 1990.

My Great Grandpa, illustrated by Dom Mansell, Putnam (New York, NY), 1990.

Rosie's Babies, illustrated by Penny Dale, Walker Books (London, England), 1990, Candlewick Press (Cambridge, MA), 1999.

We Love Them, illustrated by Barbara Firth, Lothrop (New York, NY), 1990.

Grandma's Bill, illustrated by Jane Johnson, Simon & Schuster, 1990, Orchard Books (New York, NY), 1991.

Coming Home, illustrated by Neil Reed, Simon & Schuster (New York, NY), 1991.

Farmer Duck, illustrated by Helen Oxenbury, Walker Books (London, England), 1991, Candlewick Press (Cambridge, MA), 1992, reprinted, Walker Books, 2006.

The Happy Hedgehog Band, illustrated by Jill Barton, Walker Books (London, England), 1991, Candlewick Press (Cambridge, MA), 1992.

Herbie Whistle, illustrated by Anthony Ian Lewis, Viking Kestrel (London, England), 1991.

Let's Go Home, Little Bear, Candlewick Press (Cambridge, MA), 1991.

Little Obie and the Kidnap, illustrated by Elsie Lennox, Walker Books (London, England), 1991, Candlewick Press (Cambridge, MA), 1994.

Man Mountain, illustrated by Claudio Muñoz, Viking Kestrel (London, England), 1991, illustrated by Jane Massey, Ladybird (London, England), 2001.

Squeak-a-Lot, illustrated by Virginia Miller, Greenwillow (New York, NY), 1991.

The Ghost Family Robinson at the Seaside, illustrated by Jacqui Thomas, Viking Kestrel (London, England), 1992.

Little Obie and the Flood, illustrated by Elsi Lennox, Candlewick Press (Cambridge, MA), 1992.

Owl Babies, illustrated by Patrick Benson, Candlewick Press (Cambridge, MA), 1992, published with audio CD, Walker (London, England), 2006.

The Pig in the Pond, illustrated by Jill Barton, Candlewick Press (Cambridge, MA), 1992.

Sailor Bear, illustrated by Virginia Miller, Candlewick Press (Cambridge, MA), 1992.

Sam Vole and His Brothers, illustrated by Barbara Firth, Candlewick Press (Cambridge, MA), 1992.

The Toymaker: A Story in Two Parts, illustrated by Terry Milne, Candlewick Press (Cambridge, MA), 1992.

Baby's Hammer, illustrated by John Watson, Walker Books (London, England), 1993.

The Big Bad Mole's Coming!, illustrated by John Bendall-Brunello, Walker Books (London, England), 1993.

The Fishface Feud, illustrated by Arthur Robins, Walker Books (London, England), 1993.

Little Mo, illustrated by Jill Barton, Candlewick Press (Cambridge, MA), 1993.

The Lucky Duck Song, illustrated by Judy Brown, Puffin (London, England), 1993.

Rubberneck's Revenge, illustrated by Arthur Robins, O'Brien Press (Dublin, Ireland), 1993.

The School That Went to Sea, illustrated by Leo Hartas, O'Brien Press (Dublin, Ireland), 1993.

Stories from the Bible: Old Testament Stories, illustrated by Geoffrey Patterson, Ticknor & Fields (New York, NY), 1993.

Shipwreck at Old Jelly's Farm, Ginn (Aylesbury, England), 1994.

Upside Down Harry Brown, Ginn (Aylesbury, England), 1994.

The Big, Big Sea, illustrated by Jennifer Eachas, Candlewick Press (Cambridge, MA), 1994.

The Kidnapping of Suzie Q, Hamish Hamilton (London, England), 1994, Candlewick Press (Cambridge, MA), 1996.

When the Teddy Bears Came, illustrated by Penny Dale, Candlewick Press (Cambridge, MA), 1995.

John Joe and the Big Hen, illustrated by Paul Howard, Candlewick Press (Cambridge, MA), 1995.

Tango's Baby, Candlewick Press (Cambridge, MA), 1995.

Mimi and the Dream House, Candlewick Press (Cambridge, MA), 1995.

Mimi and the Picnic, Candlewick Press (Cambridge, MA), 1996.

Cup Final Kid, illustrated by Jeff Cummins, Walker (London, England), 1996.

Bears Everywhere, Candlewick Press (Cambridge, MA), 1996.

You and Me, Little Bear, illustrated by Barbara Firth, Candlewick Press (Cambridge, MA), 1996.

What Use Is a Moose?, illustrated by Arthur Robins, Candlewick Press (Cambridge, MA), 1996.

Small Bear Lost, illustrated by Virginia Austin, Candlewick Press (Cambridge, MA), 1996.

Mimi's Christmas, Candlewick Press (Cambridge, MA), 1997.

Little Frog and the Dog, illustrated by Trevor Dunton, Sundance (Littleton, MA), 1997.

Little Frog and the Frog Olympics, illustrated by Trevor Dunton, Sundance (Littleton, MA), 1997.

Little Frog and the Tadpoles, illustrated by Trevor Dunton, Sundance (Littleton, MA), 1997.

Little Frog in the Throat, illustrated by Trevor Dunton, Sundance (Littleton, MA), 1997.

The Adventures of Pete and Mary Kate, illustrated by Terry Milne, Walker (London, England), 1997.

We Love Them, illustrated by Barbara Firth, Candlewick Press (Cambridge, MA), 1997.

The Life and Loves of Zoe T. Curley, Walker (London, England), 1997.

Yum, Yum, Yummy, illustrated by John Bendall-Brunello, Candlewick Press (Cambridge, MA), 1998.

Who Do You Love?, illustrated by Camilla Ashforth, Candlewick Press (Cambridge, MA), 1999.

Good Job, Little Bear!, illustrated by Barbara Firth, Candlewick Press (Cambridge, MA), 1999.

The Hollyhock Wall, illustrated by Salley Mavor, Candlewick Press (Cambridge, MA), 1999.

A Kitten Called Moonlight, illustrated by Christian Birmingham, Walker Books (London, England), 2000, Candlewick Press (Cambridge, MA), 2001.

Night, Night Cuddly Bear, illustrated by Penny Dale, Candlewick Press (Cambridge, MA), 2000.

Webster J. Duck, illustrated by David Parkins, Candlewick Press (Cambridge, MA), 2001.

Tom Rabbit, illustrated by Barbara Firth, Candlewick Press (Cambridge, MA), 2001.

Milly Bean, Jungle Queen, illustrated by Ana Martin Larrañaga, Walker Books (London, England), 2001.

Mimi and the Blackberry Pies, illustrated by Leo Hartas, Walker Books (London, England), 2001.

The Little Bear Stories, illustrated by Barbara Firth, Walker Books (London, England), 2001.

Mimi and the Picnic, illustrated by Leo Hartas, Walker Books (London, England), 2001.

Give It to Joe!, illustrated by Katherine McEwen, Walker Books (London, England), 2001.

(Reteller) *Two Folk Tales: The Apple Tree Man, The Bogie,* illustrated by Jenny Press, Pearson Education (Harlow, England), 2001.

Herbie Monkey, illustrated by Russell Ayto, Walker Books (London, England), 2001.

Hi, Harry!, illustrated by Barbara Firth, Candlewick Press (Cambridge, MA), 2002.

Snow Bears, illustrated by Sarah Fox-Davies, Candlewick Press (Cambridge, MA), 2002.

Farmer Skiboo Stories, Oxford University Press (Oxford, England), 2002.

Ernie and the Fishface Gang, Walker (London, England), 2002.

(Reteller) *The Adventures of Odysseus: From the Odyssey to Homer,* illustrated by Stuart Harrison, Pearson Education (Harlow, England), 2002.

The Tough Princess, illustrated by Patrick Benson, Oxford University Press (Oxford, England), 2002.

Two Brown Bears, illustrated by Steve Lavis, Oxford University Press (Oxford, England), 2002.

Ronald the Tough Sheep, illustrated by Chris Mould, Oxford University Press (Oxford, England), 2002, published as *Tough Ronald,* Picture Window Books (Minneapolis, MN), 2007.

Hi, Harry!, illustrated by Barbara Firth, Walker Books (London, England), 2003.

Going Up!, illustrated by Russell Ayto, Walker Books (London, England), 2003.

Star Striker Titch, illustrated by Russell Ayto, Walker Books (London, England), 2003.

Cup Run, illustrated by Russell Ayto, Walker Books (London, England), 2003.

Tiny's Big Adventure, illustrated by John Lawrence, Candlewick Press (Cambridge, MA), 2004.

Room for a Little One: A Christmas Tale, illustrated by Jason Cockcroft, Orchard (London, England), 2004, Margaret K. McElderry Books (New York, NY), 2006.

Shooting Star, Walker Books (London, England), 2004.

It's Quacking Time, illustrated by Jill Barton, Candlewick Press (Cambridge, MA), 2005.

Something so Big, illustrated by Charlotte Canty, Oxford University Press (Oxford, England), 2005.

Soft Butter's Ghost and Himself, illustrated by James Mayhew, Orchard (London, England), 2005.

Gallows Hill; and, The Ghostly Penny, illustrated by James Mayhew, Orchard (London, England), 2005.

Sleep Tight, Little Bear!, illustrated by Barbara Firth, Candlewick Press (Cambridge, MA), 2005.

The Ghost Ship, illustrated by Scoular Anderson, Oxford University Press (Oxford, England), 2006.

The Big Little Dinosaur, illustrated by Tim Archbold, Oxford University Press (Oxford, England), 2006.

The Orchard Book of Goblins, Ghouls, and Ghosts, and Other Magical Stories, illustrated by Tony Ross, Orchard (London, England), 2006.

(With Deborah Chancellor) *Dinosaurs,* Cambridge University Press (Cambridge, England), 2007.

Bee Frog, illustrated by Barbara Firth, Candlewick Press (Cambridge, MA), 2007.

Charlie's Tasks, illustrated by Daniel Postgate, Picture Window Books (Minneapolis, MN), 2007.

The Dirty Great Dinosaur, illustrated by Leonie Lord, Orchard (London, England), 2009, published as *The Super Hungry Dinosaur,* Dial Books for Young Readers (New York, NY), 2009.

Captain Small Pig, illustrated by Susan Varley, Andersen (London, England), 2009, Peachtree Publishers (Atlanta, GA), 2010.

Beowulf and Grendel, illustrated by Graham Howells, Franklin Watts (London, England), 2009.

Contributor to books, including *Orchard Book of Ghost Stories,* Orchard Books, 2005.

Author's works have been translated into Albanian, Arabic, Bengali, Bulgarian, Chinese, Farsi, French, German, Greek, Gujarati, Hindi, Italian, Japanese, Korean, Kurdish, Malayalam, Nepali, Panjabi, Polish, Portuguese, Romanian, Russian, Somali, Spanish, Tagalog, Tamil, Turkish, Urdu, Vietnamese, Welsh, and Yoruba.

"NAPPER" SERIES

Napper Goes for Goal, illustrated by Barrie Mitchell, Puffin (London, England), 1981.

Napper Strikes Again, illustrated by Barrie Mitchell, Puffin (London, England), 1981.

Napper's Golden Goals, illustrated by Barrie Mitchell, Puffin (London, England), 1984.

Napper's Luck, illustrated by Richard Berridge, Puffin (London, England), 1993.

Napper's Big Match, illustrated by Richard Berridge, Puffin (London, England), 1993.

Napper Super-Sub, illustrated by Richard Berridge, Puffin (London, England), 1993.

"MYSTERY SQUAD" SERIES; ILLUSTRATED BY TERRY MCKENNA

The Mystery Squad and the Dead Man's Message, Blackie & Son (London, England), 1984.

The Mystery Squad and the Whistling Teeth, Blackie & Son (London, England), 1984.

The Mystery Squad and Mr. Midnight, Blackie & Son (London, England), 1984.

The Mystery Squad and the Artful Dodger, Blackie & Son (London, England), 1984.

The Mystery Squad and the Creeping Castle, Blackie & Son (London, England), 1985.

The Mystery Squad and the Gemini Job, Blackie & Son (London, England), 1985.

The Mystery Squad and the Candid Camera, Blackie & Son (London, England), 1985.

The Mystery Squad and Cannonball Kid, Blackie & Son (London, England), 1986.

The Mystery Squad and the Robot's Revenge, Blackie & Son (London, England), 1986.

"HARRIET" SERIES; ILLUSTRATED BY MARK BURGESS

Harriet and the Crocodiles, Abelard (London, England), 1982, Little, Brown (Boston, MA), 1984.

Harriet and the Haunted School, Abelard (London, England), 1984, Little, Brown (Boston, MA), 1986.

Harriet and the Robot, Abelard (London, England), 1985, Little, Brown (Boston, MA), 1987.

Harriet and the Flying Teachers, Blackie & Son (London, England), 1987.

"LITTLE DRACULA" SERIES; ILLUSTRATED BY JOSEPH WRIGHT

Little Dracula's Christmas, Viking Penguin (London, England), 1986.

Little Dracula's First Bite, Viking Penguin (London, England), 1986.

Little Dracula at the Seaside, Walker Books (London, England), 1987, Candlewick Press (Cambridge, MA), 1992.

Little Dracula Goes to School, Walker Books (London, England), 1987, Candlewick Press (Cambridge, MA), 1992.

Little Dracula at the Seashore, Candlewick Press (Cambridge, MA), 1992.

"SHAKESPEARE RETOLD" SERIES; ILLUSTRATED BY ALAN MARKS

The Tempest, Franklin Watts (London, England), 2008.

Macbeth, Franklin Watts (London, England), 2008.

Romeo and Juliet, Franklin Watts (London, England), 2008.

Richard III, Franklin Watts (London, England), 2008.

A Midsummer Night's Dream, Franklin Watts (London, England), 2009.

"SINBAD" SERIES; ILLUSTRATED BY O'KIF

Sinbad and the Diamond Valley, Franklin Watts (London, England), 2009.

Sinbad and the Whale, Franklin Watts (London, England), 2009.

Sinbad and the Ogres, Franklin Watts (London, England), 2009.

Sinbad and the Monkeys, Franklin Watts (London, England), 2009.

FOR YOUNG ADULTS; UNDER PSEUDONYM CATHERINE SEFTON

In a Blue Velvet Dress: Almost a Ghost Story, illustrated by Gareth Floyd, Faber (London, England), 1972, published as *In a Blue Velvet Dress,* illustrated by Eros Keith, Harper (New York, NY), 1973, published under name Martin Waddell as *The Ghost in the Blue Velvet Dress,* Walker Books (London, England), 2001.

The Sleepers on the Hill, Faber (London, England), 1973.

The Back House Ghosts, Faber (London, England), 1974, published as *The Haunting of Ellen: A Story of Suspense,* Harper (New York, NY), 1975, published under name Martin Waddell, Walker Books (London, England), 2001.

The Ghost and Bertie Boggin, illustrated by Jill Bennett, Faber (London, England), 1980.

Emer's Ghost, Hamish Hamilton (London, England), 1981.

The Finn Gang, illustrated by Sally Holmes, Hamish Hamilton (London, England), 1981.

The Emma Dilemma, illustrated by Jill Bennett, Faber (London, England), 1982.

A Puff of Smoke, illustrated by Thelma Lambert, Hamish Hamilton (London, England), 1982.

Island of the Strangers, Hamish Hamilton (London, England), 1983, Harcourt (San Diego, CA), 1985.

It's My Gang, illustrated by Catherine Bradbury, Hamish Hamilton (London, England), 1984.

The Blue Misty Monsters, illustrated by Elaine McGregor Turney, Faber (London, England), 1985.

The Ghost Girl, Hamish Hamilton (London, England), 1985.

The Ghost Ship, illustrated by Martin Ursell, Hamish Hamilton (London, England), 1985.

Flying Sam, illustrated by Margaret Chamberlain, Hamish Hamilton (London, England), 1986.

Shadows on the Lake, Hamish Hamilton (London, England), 1987.

Bertie Boggin and the Ghost Again!, Faber (London, England), 1988.

The Day the Smells Went Wrong, illustrated by John Rogan, Hamish Hamilton (London, England), 1988.

The Haunted Schoolbag, illustrated by Caroline Crossland, Hamish Hamilton (London, England), 1989.

The Boggart in the Barrel, illustrated by Maureen Bradley, Hamish Hamilton (London, England), 1991.

Horace the Ghost, illustrated by Caroline Crossland, Hamish Hamilton (London, England), 1991.

Along a Lonely Road, Puffin (London, England), 1993.

The Ghosts of the Cobweb and the Skully Bones Mystery, Hamish Hamilton (London, England), 1993.

The Ghosts of the Cobweb Street and the Circus Star, illustrated by Jean Baylis, Hamish Hamilton (London, England), 1993.

The Cast-Off, Hamish Hamilton (London, England), 1993.

The Ghosts of the Cobweb and the TV Battle, Hamish Hamilton (London, England), 1994.

The Ghosts of the Cobweb, Puffin (London, England), 1994.

"IRISH POLITICAL" NOVEL TRILOGY; UNDER PSEUDONYM CATHERINE SEFTON

Starry Night, Hamish Hamilton (London, England), 1986, published under name Martin Waddell, Walker Books (London, England), 2001.

Frankie's Story, Hamish Hamilton (London, England), 1988, published under name Martin Waddell, Walker Books (London, England), 2001.

The Beat of the Drum, Hamish Hamilton (London, England), 1989, published under name Martin Waddell, Walker Books (London, England), 2001.

ADULT FICTION

Otley, Stein & Day (Briarcliff Manor, NY), 1966.

Otley Pursued, Stein & Day (Briarcliff Manor, NY), 1967.

Otley Forever, Stein & Day (Briarcliff Manor, NY), 1968.

Come Back When I'm Sober, Hodder & Stoughton (London, England), 1969.

Otley Victorious, Stein & Day (Briarcliff Manor, NY), 1969.

A Little Bit British: Being the Diary of an Ulsterman, August Tom Stacey, 1969.

Adaptations

Otley was adapted for a motion picture starring Romy Schneider and Tom Courtenay, Columbia, 1969; *In a Blue Velvet Dress* was adapted for "Jackanory" reading, BBC-TV, 1974; *The Sleepers on the Hill* was adapted as a television serial by BBC-TV, 1976; *Fred the Angel* was broadcast on BBC-TV; *Island of the Strangers* was broadcast on Thames TV.

Sidelights

Winner of numerous honors for his writing, among them the 2004 Hans Christian Andersen Award, Irish author Martin Waddell has worked in numerous genres: mysteries, picture books, slapstick comedies, football stories, and ghost stories for children as well as adult novels and emotionally charged young-adult dramas under the pseudonym Catherine Sefton. Characteristic of Waddell's writing is a strong "hook," a tantalizing turn of plot that encourages readers to keep turning pages to discover the "what-happened-then" of his story. Although his list of books numbers in the hundreds, Waddell is perhaps known most widely for the picture book *Farmer Duck,* which has been translated into dozens of languages and published throughout the world.

Waddell's gentle bedtime story in **Night Night, Cuddly Bear** *is brought to life in Penny Dale's evocative illustrations.* (Illustration copyright © 2000 by Penny Dale. Reproduced by permission of Candlewick Press, Somerville, MA, on behalf of Walker Books, London.)

Born in Belfast, in 1941, during a bombing raid on that Irish city, Waddell came into a family with a long ancestry in County Down. Part of this ancestry includes the writers the Waddell clan has produced, four of whom were authors of note. Waddell, like other urban children, was evacuated to the countryside during the bombings of World War II. At the close of the war, he and his family returned to Belfast, but his parents soon divorced and from age eleven Waddell was raised in County Down by his single mother. Leaving school at age fifteen, he worked for a time for a local newspaper, then tried his hand—or foot—at professional soccer. When that came to nothing, Waddell found himself living in England and needing to make a living. He turned to the tradition of his ancestors and took up writing.

"Why writing?" he asked himself in *SAAS.* "I suppose the answer is that writing had always come easily to me. I had never had to work at it at school; it was something I knew I could do. That goes back to story, and reading. My love of story, of being told stories and being read to, had transferred to a love of books."

After six years of working at the craft, Waddell had a stack of unpublished novels. He also had an agent, Jonathan Clowes, who believed in his abilities and it was Clowes who introduced Waddell to the work of Len Deighton, the spy novelist. Shortly thereafter, in 1966, Waddell produced *Otley,* a satirical spy-thriller. A movie adaptation, plus subsequent adult novels about Otley, provided the financial security that enabled Waddell to return to Ireland and buy a house in Donaghadee, a quiet seaside town. In 1969 he married and took his career on an entirely different course by writing his first book for children. That book was *In a Blue Velvet Dress,* a Victorian ghost story that M. Hobbs, writing in *Junior Bookshelf,* also described as being narrated with "most endearing and effective humor." "The lyrical novels weren't even publishable," he recalled of this time in *SAAS.* "The thrillers were hopelessly padded to make the length, but *In a Blue Velvet* at 25,000 words was full of fun and adventure and emotion. I had got it right, at last!"

Waddell published *In a Blue Velvet* under a pen name because his own was associated with comedies and thrillers. He came up with Catherine Sefton, a name composed of his grandmother's maiden name and the Christian name of Catherine, which he had always liked. *In a Blue Velvet Dress* was dramatized by the BBC, and a second Catherine Sefton book, *The Sleepers on the Hill,* an Irish mystery, was also dramatized by the BBC.

Waddell and his wife had their first two children and his career seemed to be in high gear by mid-1972, when he was nearly killed in a bomb blast in a local church. For the next six years he was unable to write, suffering a mental and emotional block. During this period Waddell moved back to his original village of Newcastle; his wife went back to teaching to help with finances, and their third son was born during this time, too. The

Catherine Sefton novel *The Back House Ghosts,* a combination of ghost story and daily adventures of a group of young people, was the only work to emerge from this time. It is a "story that is full of excitement and humor," remarked Sylvia Mogg in *Children's Book Review.*

In 1978 the ability to tell stories returned and in a flurry waddell wrote children's books of all genres. There were two Catherine Sefton books for young adults, *The Ghost and Bertie Boggin* and *Emer's Ghost,* the latter set in Northern Ireland and praised by many critics. For example, *Times Literary Supplement* contributor Ann Evans called it "a beautifully wrought story" and described Waddell as "a writer of rare order." Under his own name, Waddell also began his "Napper" series of soccer books in which he uses his own history as a goalkeeper to tell stories that bring the game and the characters to life. In this same period he wrote his first picture book, *The Great Green Mouse Disaster,* a "magnificent wordless saga," according to George Hunt in *Books for Keeps,* in which a group of mice invade a hotel, wreaking havoc from floor to floor.

While the pseudonymous Catherine Sefton kept "her" ghost stories and more emotionally charged books for young adults flowing, Waddell continued producing fun-oriented books in his "Napper" and "Mystery Squad" series as well as his "Harriet" stories (which relate the comic adventures of an accident-prone child) and "Little Dracula" books about a young vampire and his family. Additionally, he began to produce picture books for which he has become increasingly known and which he takes seriously despite their light themes. "Books for beginners should be clearly and brightly written with vivid characterization and exciting or amusing situations piling one on top of the other," Waddell commented in *SAAS.* "Add to this the need to use words and images which are freshly minted, not recycled, and the [very short text] becomes a daunting challenge."

Waddell's picture books included *Going West, The Park in the Dark, Farmer Duck, Sam Vole and His Brothers, Can't You Sleep, Little Bear?,* and *Captain Small Pig. Going West* is an unsentimental depiction of a family's move west by wagon train. "It is a story of high adventure . . . ," wrote Colin Greenland in the *Times Literary Supplement,* "but also elemental, bare, summoning the reader's own emotional responses." With *Can't You Sleep, Little Bear?,* Waddell and illustrator Barbara Firth "created a classic picture book," according to Keith Barker in *School Library Journal.* Another of Waddell's nighttime books also drew critical acclaim. "Here is a picture of childhood which is beautiful and true and is also accessible," Marcus Crouch noted in a *Junior Bookshelf* review of *The Park in the Dark.* In *Farmer Duck* Waddell fashions a picture book resonant of George Orwell's *Animal Farm,* but "with a sharp edge to its wit," according to Crouch in another *Junior Bookshelf* review. About the same title, a critic in *Publishers Weekly* observed, "Waddell's uncomplicated story gently encourages readers to recognize and fight

Waddell and artist Barbara Firth team up to create a picture-book classic in **Can't You Sleep Little Bear?** (Illustration copyright © 1988 by Barbara Firth. Reproduced by permission of the publisher Candlewick Press, Somerville, MA on behalf of Walker Books, London.)

injustice." In *Sam Vole and His Brothers* Waddell "pleasantly presents the subtle shades of emotions among siblings," in the words of Judith Gloyer, writing in *School Library Journal.*

During the 1990s Waddell concentrated almost wholly on picture books, expanding his ever-popular "Little Bear" books, illustrated by Firth, and adding the endearingly titled *Sailor Bear* and *Small Bear Lost* as well as a jumble of other books featuring animals from frogs to mice to ducks to rabbits and kittens. In *Let's Go Home, Little Bear,* the wee one is frightened on the way home, fearful of the scary noises he hears in the woods. "They're back!" declared a reviewer for *Publishers Weekly,* in reviewing this new "Little Bear" collaboration. "Little Bear and Big Bear, arguably the most winning ursine specimens since Paddington and Pooh, return to print in a thoroughly delectable sequel." *You and Me, Little Bear* continues the adventures in a "warm tale of togetherness," according to a contributor for *Publishers Weekly,* the critic going on to note that Waddell and Firth "are a match made in heaven." *Good Job, Little Bear!* presents a "paean to familial love and security," according to *Horn Book* reviewer Ellen Fader, while in *Sleep Tight, Little Bear* the young hero finds a new home in a cave of his own until nighttime comes. In *Booklist* April Judge called *You and Me, Little Bear* a "charming combination of words and pictures" that will "captivate old and new bear friends," while Lauralyn Persson predicted in her *School Library Journal* review of *Sleep Tight, Little Bear* that young children will relate to the "tension between independence and protection" that makes Waddell's story "a stellar example of its kind."

Working with illustrators Virginia Miller and Virginia Austin, respectively, Waddell has created other bear books, including *Sailor Bear* and *Small Bear Lost,* both which relate the adventures of a very plucky stuffed bear. A contributor for *Publishers Weekly* dubbed *Sailor Bear* a "classic, comforting bedtime story," while *Booklist* critic Carolyn Phelan called *Small Bear Lost* a "simple, satisfying story for preschoolers." More bears take on the role of toddler stand-in in *Night Night, Cuddly Bear* and *Snow Bear,* the latter a tale illustrated by Sarah Fox-Davies.

With *What Use Is a Moose?* Waddell moves away from ursine matters, introducing a character that "is arguably

the goofiest and most endearing moose to come down the pike since Bullwinkle," according to a reviewer for *Publishers Weekly.* A feline family is presented in *Who Do You Love?,* a "story that almost melts with geniality," according to a contributor for *Kirkus Reviews,* while a mouse takes center stage in the "Mimi" books. Reviewing *Mimi and the Picnic* in *Booklist,* Phelan noted that "Waddell's use of repetition and internal rhyme give his writing a lilting quality that storytellers will appreciate and young children will savor."

Tom Rabbit is set on an English farm and tells of a little boy and his wonderful stuffed rabbit. Phelan dubbed this picture book "winsome" in her *Booklist* review, adding that Waddell's "beguiling little adventure [is] written with simplicity, brevity, and a fine-tuned sensitivity to the emotional lives of small children." *A Kitten Called Moonlight,* a rescue adventure tale, is a "glowing picture book," according to *Booklist* critic Hazel Rochman, while *Webster J. Duck* is a "heartwarming

Waddell takes readers to the northern climes in his picture book Sailor Bear, *featuring artwork Virginia Austin.* (Illustration copyright © 1992 by Virginia Austin. Reproduced by permission of Candlewick Press, Somerville, MA, on behalf of Walker Books, London.)

tale," according to a *Publishers Weekly* contributor, describing Waddell's story of a plucky duck who sets off to search for the mother he never saw. A pig, goat, and turkey round out the animal cast of *Captain Small Pig,* a multigenerational story illustrated by Susan Varley in which tolerance and friendship are reinforced during a day of boating. "This book pleases at every level," asserted *Booklist* critic Ilene Cooper, praising *Captain Small Pig* for "the simplicity of its concept, the ease of its words, and [the illustrator's] . . . mix of wit and whimsy." "Readers may recognize their own guardians' temperaments in the older characters," commented a *Publishers Weekly* contributor, and Waddell's story allows young children to share the ups and downs of a young child's "perfect day."

Although most of his stories feature animal characters, Waddell casts humans in several of his picture books. In *Rosie's Babies* four-year-old Rosie continues to ask her mother questions, vying for attention, as Mother takes care of her newborn infant. A reviewer for *Publishers Weekly* wrote that Waddell "perfectly captures the nuances of a child's conversation with her mother in this disarming story." In *The Hollyhock Wall* Mary's rock garden comes alive and she plays in it with her friend Tom. The next day, the garden appears inanimate, leaving Mary puzzled until she discovers that her grandmother has a garden similar to hers, with the real Tom in it waiting to play. A critic for *Kirkus Reviews* noted of *The Hollyhock Wall* that Waddell "toys with the boundaries between real life and imaginary realms in this convoluted fantasy," while *Booklist* critic Ilene Cooper called the picture book "eminently appealing."

In *The Adventures of Pete and Mary Kate* a grandmother tries to get a little boy to play with a doll, but her request is met largely with disgust until the doll actually begins to talk. Michael Kirby, reviewing the book in *School Librarian,* called *The Adventures of Pete and Mary Kate* a "gem of a book." Waddell presents the adventures of a toddler visiting a farm in *John Joe and the Big Hen,* a "beautiful and accessible book," as a reviewer for *Books for Keeps* described it, while an Irish legend is the basis for *Boneless and the Tinker.* Part of a series of scary stories in which Waddell's text is given added spookiness by James Mayhew's art, *Boneless and the Tinker* is "filed with the rhythmic music of an oral tale," according to London *Times* contributor Amanda Craig.

Waddell has also published works for older readers, including *Tango's Baby, The Life and Loves of Zoe T. Curley,* and *The Kidnapping of Suzie Q.* In the first novel, Brian Tangello does all he can to keep his girlfriend and their baby. A British teenager often on the wrong side of the law, Brian is not bad so much as she is misguided. A friend of Tango's narrates this "funky story with wry humor and wonderful sketches," according to *Booklist* writer Anne O'Malley.

A novel written in the form of diary entries, *The Life and Loves of Zoe T. Curley* "offers the fantasies of a young teenager about the possibility of falling in love with a boy," according to Michael Glover in the *New Statesman.* This "funny and precocious" faux autobiography, as Glover described it, deals with Zoe's family as well as her feelings of insecurity about herself. Included in the family menagerie are Zoe's very unsuccessful father and his attempts at writing and cartooning, and her two oafish brothers, whom she dubs Creep and Ob-Noxious. Reviewing *The Life and Loves of Zoe T. Curley* in *School Librarian,* Cecilia J. Hynes-Higman called it a "most enjoyable lively book," adding that although the book was created by a man, "the character of Zoe is utterly 'female adolescent.'"

The Kidnapping of Suzie Q is a thriller dealing with a teen who is taken hostage during a grocery store robbery. A reviewer for *Publishers Weekly* predicted of this novel that the "smart, breezy writing, jaunty heroine and tense setting should keep readers on the hook."

"I believe in writing very carefully for children, because they become much more involved in the small details of character than the average reader," Waddell once commented. "I do not suggest that children should be written down to, but that they should be written *for;* and this means rewards, ghosts, football, fantasy, treats, adventures, relationships. . . . I believe that children's stories should be directed first and foremost to their interests, and that they should be quick, clear, emotionally strong, and verbally bright."

Biographical and Critical Sources

PERIODICALS

Booklist, January 1, 1986, Ilene Cooper, review of *Island of the Strangers,* p. 687; December 15, 1995, Anne O'Malley, review of *Tango's Baby,* p. 698; September 15, 1996, Carolyn Phelan, *Small Bear Lost,* p. 251; October 1, 1996, April Judge, review of *You and Me, Little Bear,* p. 360; April 15, 1998, Carolyn Phelan, review of *Mimi and the Picnic,* pp. 1454-1455; June 1, 1999, p. 1845; August, 1999, Ilene Cooper, review of *The Hollyhock Wall,* p. 2067; March 1, 2001, Carolyn Phelan, review of *Tom Rabbit,* p. 1289; April 1, 2001, Hazel Rochman, review of *A Kitten Called Moonlight,* p. 1480; November 15, 2001, Connie Fletcher, review of *Webster J. Duck,* p. 584; December 15, 2002, John Peters, review of *Snow Bears,* p. 769; June 1, 2004, Abby Nolan, review of *Tiny's Big Adventure,* p. 1749; December 1, 2004, Terry Glover, review of *Room for a Little One: A Christmas Tale,* p. 663; February 1, 2005, Ilene Cooper, review of *It's Quacking Time!,* p. 966; February 15, 2010, Ilene Cooper, review of *Captain Small Pig,* p. 76.

Books for Keeps, September, 1989, George Hunt, review of *The Great Green Mouse Disaster,* p. 9; September, 1997, review of *John Joe and the Big Hen,* p. 21.

Children's Book Review, spring, 1975, Sylvia Mogg, review of *The Back House Ghosts,* pp. 22-23.

Guardian (London, England), June 5, 2004, Julia Eccleshare, review of *Tiny's Big Adventure,* p. 33; April 2, 2005, Julia Eccleshare, review of *Sleep Tight, Little*

Bear, p. 33; October 27, 2007, Julia Eccleshare, review of *The Orchard Book of Goblins, Ghouls, and Ghosts and Other Magical Stories*, p. 20.

Horn Book, March-April, 1999, Ellen Fader, review of *Good Job, Little Bear!*, p. 203; March-April, 2003, Kitty Flynn, review of *Hi, Harry!*, p. 207; July-August, 2004, Joanna Rudge Long, review of *Tiny's Bit Adventure*, p. 443; January-February, 2006, Susan Dove Lempke, review of *Sleep Tight, Little Bear*, p. 72.

Independent (London, England), March 23, 2005, Joey Canessa, interview with Waddell, p. 5.

Junior Bookshelf, November, 1972, M. Hobbs, review of *In a Blue Velvet Dress*, p. 2036; April, 1989, Marcus Crouch, review of *The Park in the Dark*, pp. 64-65; December, 1991, Marcus Crouch, review of *Farmer Duck*, p. 246; April, 1992, D.A. Young, review of *Along the Lonely Road*, p. 79.

Kirkus Reviews, March 15, 1999, review of *Who Do You Love?*, p. 458; June 1, 1999, review of *The Hollyhock Wall*, p. 890; August 1, 2001, review of *Webster J. Duck*, p. 1134; March 15, 2003, review of *Hi, Harry! The Moving Story of How One Slow Tortoise Slowly Made a Friend*, p. 480; October 15, 2005, review of *Sleep Tight, Little Bear*, p. 1148; July 15, 2009, review of *The Super Hungry Dinosaur*.

New Statesman, December 5, 1997, Michael Glover, review of *The Life and Loves of Zoe T. Curley*, p. 66.

New York Times Book Review, May 15, 2004, Karla Kuskin, review of *Tiny's Big Adventure*, p. 18.

Observer (London, England), March 27, 2005, Kate Kellaway, review of *Sleep Tight, Little Bear*, p. 16.

Publishers Weekly, January 20, 1992, review of *Farmer Duck*, p. 64; March 22, 1993, review of *Let's Go Home, Little Bear*, p. 78; January 22, 1996, review of *Sailor Bear*, p. 74; June 10, 1996, review of *The Kidnapping of Suzie Q*, p. 101; July 1, 1996, review of *What Use Is a Moose?*, p. 60; July 8, 1996, review of *You and Me, Little Bear*, p. 83; February 22, 1999, review of *Rosie's Babies*, p. 93; June 18, 2001, review of *Webster J. Duck*, p. 80; December 23, 2002, review of *Snow Bears*, p. 68; September 27, 2004, review of *Room for a Little One*, p. 61; February 14, 2005, review of *It's Quacking Time!*, p. 75; September 7, 2009, review of *The Super Hungry Dinosaur*, p. 43; February 15, 2010, review of *Captain Small Pig*, p. 129.

School Librarian, September, 1983, Pauline Thomas, review of *Island of the Strangers*, pp. 272-275; August, 1997, Cecilia J. Hynes-Higman, review of *The Life and Loves of Zoe T. Curley*, pp. 161-162; summer, 1998, Michael Kirby, review of *The Adventures of Pete and Mary Kate*, p. 90.

School Library Journal, May, 1989, Keith Barker, review of *Can't You Sleep, Little Bear?*, p. 56; January, 1993, Judith Gloyer, review of *Sam Vole and His Brothers*, p. 86; July, 2001, Gay Lynn Van Vleck, review of *Webster J. Duck*, p. 90; July, 2004, Genevieve Gallagher, review of *Tiny's Big Adventure*, p. 89; April, 2005, Joy Fleishhacker, review of *It's Quacking Time!*, p. 114; December, 2005, Lauralyn Persson, review of *Sleep Tight, Little Bear*, p. 122; September, 2009, Marge Loch-Wouters, review of *The Super Hungry Dinosaur*, p. 136; March, 2010, Susan Weitz, review of *Captain Small Pig*, p. 134.

Times (London, England), June 17, 2006, Amanda Craig, review of *Boneless and the Tinker*, p. 18.

Times Educational Supplement, May 5, 1989, Robert Leeson, review of *The Beat of the Drum*, p. B7.

Times Literary Supplement, November 20, 1981, Ann Evans, review of *Emer's Ghost*, p. 1359; February 10, 1984, Colin Greenland, review of *Going West*, p. 150.*

ONLINE

Walker Books Web site, http://www.walker.co.uk/ (August 12, 2011), "Martin Waddell."*

*   *   *

WALKER, Steve

Personal

Born in New York, NY. *Education:* School of Visual Arts, B.F.A. (cartooning illustration), 2005.

Addresses

Home—Philadelphia, PA.

Career

Illustrator. Worked as a photo pre-press technician; Art Students League, New York, NY, teacher of sequential art, beginning 2008.

Illustrator

Jared Axelrod, *The Battle of Blood and Ink*, Tor (New York, NY), 2011.

Illustrator of comic series "Fables of the Flying City," written by Jared Axelrod.

"SONS OF LIBERTY" GRAPHIC NOVEL SERIES

Alexander and Joseph Lagos *The Sons of Liberty*, colors by Oren Kramek, Random House Children's Books (New York, NY), 2010.

Alexander and Joseph Lagos *Death and Taxes*, colors by Oren Kramek, Random House Children's Books (New York, NY), 2011.

Biographical and Critical Sources

PERIODICALS

Booklist, June 1, 2010, Jesse Karp, review of *The Sons of Liberty*, p. 70.

Kirkus Reviews, April 15, 2010, review of *The Sons of Liberty*.

Library Journal, March 15, 2011, Martha Cornog, review of *Death and Taxes*, p. 104.

Publishers Weekly, May 3, 2010, review of *The Sons of Liberty*, p. 55.

School Library Journal, July, 2010, Douglas P. Davey, review of *The Sons of Liberty*, p. 106.

Voice of Youth Advocates, August, 2010, Kat Kan, review of *The Sons of Liberty,* p. 238.

ONLINE

Sons of Liberty Web site, http://thesonsoflibertybook.com/ (June 12, 2011).
Steve Walker Web log, http://stevejwalkerstudio.blogspot. com (July 15, 2011).*

* * *

WALLENFELS, Stephen

Personal
Born in NH; father a school psychologist; married; children: a son. *Education:* International University, B.S. (physical education). *Hobbies and other interests:* Racquet sports, hiking, reading, cooking, movies.

Addresses
Home—Richland, WA.

Career
Writer. Presenter at schools.

Awards, Honors
CYBILS Award finalist, 2010, and Cooperative Children's Book Council Choice selection, 2011, both for *POD.*

Writings

POD, Namelos (South Hampton, NH), 2009.

Author's work has been translated into French and German.

Sidelights
Born in New Hampshire but now making his home in Washington State, Stephen Wallenfels was inspired to write his first novel, *POD,* after he envisioned an intriguing science-fiction premise that was too multilayered to be contained within a short story. Wallenfels was interested in sports as well as in writing while growing up, but he put writing on the back burner in favor of athletics. While attending a California college on a tennis scholarship and a plan to major in physical education, he worked creative writing courses into his schedule whenever he had the chance; years later, he tapped this training in writing his first novel. Praising *POD* in *Booklist,* Courtney Jones called Wallenfels' debut "solid, straightforward sci-fi," something of "a rarity in these times when vampires and zombies reign unchecked."

In *POD* Planet Earth is under laser attack by aliens that are working to eradicate humans from the planet, Wallenfels plays out this scenario from the point of view of two teens from different locations. Fifteen-year-old Josh lives with his dad in a small town in western Washington when the smoky black, orb-shaped spacecraft appear in the sky, while twelve-year-old Megs is on her own and holed up in an L.A. parking structure when the invasion begins. Josh and his father find their relationship fracturing under the stress of their situation, as food becomes scarce and death seems imminent. For Megs, the desire to locate her mother helps her persevere, even in the face of violence as the city's residents increasingly abandon any vestige of civility during the twenty-eight-day siege. The future that Wallenfels evokes in *POD* "is hauntingly contemporary and familiar," noted *Bulletin of the Center for Children's Book* contributor April Spisak, and a *Publishers Weekly* contributor praised the "tense" novel as "an intense [depiction] . . . of humanity's reaction to an alien invaion." Both tales feature "a compelling story arc," according to *Horn Book* contributor Jonathan Hunt, "and while they only obliquely intersect, they [depict] . . . the human race in survival mode."

Biographical and Critical Sources

PERIODICALS

Booklist, May 15, 2010, Courtney Jones, review of *POD,* p. 50.
Bulletin of the Center for Children's Books, May, 2010, April Spisak, review of *POD,* p. 405.
Horn Book, July-August, 2010, Jonathan Hunt, review of *POD,* p. 125.
Kirkus Reviews, March 1, 2010, review of *POD.*
Publishers Weekly, March 8, 2010, review of *POD,* p. 57.

ONLINE

Stephen Wallenfels Home Page, http://site.stephenwallen fels.com (August 12, 2011).
Young-Adult Writers and Readers in Washington State Web site, http://www.ya-wa.com/ (August 12, 2011), "Stephen Wallenfels."*

* * *

WARNER, Marsha

Personal
Female.

Addresses
Home—New York, NY.

Career
Writer.

Writings

"GREEK" NOVEL SERIES; BASED ON THE TELEVISION PROGRAM

Double Date, Harlequin Teen (Don Mills, Ontario, Canada), 2010.
Best Frenemies, Harlequin Teen (Don Mills, Ontario, Canada), 2010.

Biographical and Critical Sources

PERIODICALS

Kirkus Reviews, April 15, 2010, review of *Double Date*.

ONLINE

Harlequin Web site, http://www.eharlequin.com/ (August 19, 2011), "Marsha Warner."*

*   *   *

WIGHT, Eric 1974-

Personal

Born November 15, 1974, in Philadelphia, PA; married; children: Ethan, Abbie. *Education:* Attended Carnegie Mellon University; School of Visual Arts, degree (animation).

Addresses

Home—Eastern PA.

Career

Author, illustrator, animator, and comics artist. Formerly worked as an amusement-park caricaturist, window painter, and video store clerk. Television work includes (artist) *The OC;* (creator) *Atomic County;* and (comic creator) *Six Feet Under.* Animator for ten years, with clients including Walt Disney, Cartoon Network, and Warner Bros.

Awards, Honors

(With others) Harvey Award for Best Anthology, and Eisner Award for Best Anthology, both c. 2004, both for *Escapist;* Russ Manning Award for Most Promising Newcomer, 2004; Great Graphic Novel for Teens selection, Young Adult Library Services Association/ American Library Association, 2008, for *My Dead Girlfriend.*

Writings

SELF-ILLUSTRATED

My Dead Girlfriend, TokyoPop (Los Angeles, CA) 2007.

Sword of Fools, Simon & Schuster Books for Young Readers (New York, NY), 2011.

SELF-ILLUSTRATED; "FRANKIE PICKLE" CHAPTER-BOOK SERIES

Frankie Pickle and the Closet of Doom, Simon & Schuster Books for Young Readers (New York, NY), 2009.
Frankie Pickle and the Pine Run 3000, Simon & Schuster Books for Young Readers (New York, NY), 2010.
Frankie Pickle and the Mathematical Menace, Simon & Schuster Books for Young Readers (New York, NY), 2011.
Frankie Pickle and the Land of the Lost Recess, Simon & Schuster Books for Young Readers (New York, NY), 2011.
Frankie Pickle and the Invasion of the Polka Dots, Simon & Schuster Books for Young Readers (New York, NY), 2012.

ILLUSTRATOR

(With others) Michael Chabon and others, *Escapist* (comics anthology; based on *The Amazing Adventures of Kavalier and Clay* by Chabon), Dark Horse Comics (Milwaukie, OR), 2004.

Contributor to comic-book series, including *Buffy the Vampire Slayer, The Goon, Hellboy, The Legion, Justice League of America,* and *Spike vs. Dracula.*

Sidelights

Eric Wight loved D.C. adventure comics while growing up, and he honed his artistic talent by creating his own comic strips. Eventually trained as an animator, Wight worked as a development artist for Warner Brothers, helping to create new animated characters for television. His move to author and artist came by creating art for comic-book series such as *The Legion* and *Justice League of America,* and then contributing illustrations to *Escapist,* the graphic-novel adaptation of Michael Chabon's popular novel *The Adventures of Kavalier and Clay.* Now Wight has even more young fans as the author/illustrator of *Frankie Pickle and the Closet of Doom* and its sequels, as well as of the teen manga *My Dead Girlfriend.*

Noting that the character Frankie Pickle is based on his own childhood and the games he played with friends, Wight explained to an interviewer for *Graphic Novel Reporter* online that Frankie "is a typical kid with an anything but typical imagination. Sometimes it leads him on adventures. More often it gets him into trouble. But the important thing is that he always figures out a way to set things right by using a little creativity." Although Frankie was originally intended to be an animated character for the Cartoon Network, Wight decided to re-craft him for the graphic-novel format. The lack of beginning chapter books geared for boy readers became apparent to Wight while he was raising his son, and *Frankie Pickle and the Closet of Doom* was the result.

Eric Wight entertains young graphic-novel fans with the antics of his engaging young hero in **Frankie Pickle and the Closet of Doom.** (Illustration copyright © 2009 by Eric Wight. Reproduced by permission of Simon & Schuster Books for Young Readers, an imprint of Simon & Schuster Publishing Division.)

In *Frankie Pickle and the Closet of Doom* the titular Frankie (his name is short for Franklin Lorenzo Piccolini) lives in another world—not literally, of course, but in his vivid imagination, where the fourth grader can transform his settings and himself to make everyday life an adventure. His mother has given up on nagging her son about cleaning his bedroom, but even Frankie has his tolerance for filth. Slowly the clutter piles higher and higher, until that fateful day when Frankie imagines himself a prison inmate and sets to the task handed down as his punishment. The "closet of doom" in his messy room ultimately yields a quantity of horrors, including a discarded and inedible sandwich that morphs into a monstrous creature in the boy's vivid fantasy world. "Hilarious twists of language are matched with a wicked sense of fun in the illustrations," asserted a *Kirkus Reviews* writer, the critic predicting that Wight's humorous chapter book will likely appeal to fans of Dav Pilkey's irreverent "Captain Underpants" saga. Noting that the author/illustrator's "comic illustrations [in *Frankie Pickle and the Closet of Doom*] brim with action and wit," a *Publishers Weekly* critic added that the young narrator is "funny without being smart alecky" and the story's "rib-tickling irony" makes the graphic novel "a strong start for the series."

Frankie's adventures continue in *Frankie Pickle and the Pine Run 3000, Frankie Pickle and the Mathematical Menace, Frankie Pickle and the Land of the Lost Recess,* and *Frankie Pickle and the Invasion of the Polka Dots* as the imaginative boy uncovers other adventures lurking in the mundane. In *Frankie Pickle and the Mathematical Menace* an unsolvable math problems on Frankie's math quiz literally turn monstrous. Transported to Arithmecca, the boy must team up with his parents and best friend Kenny and wield a sharp pencil in order to fight his way out of the monster-ridden tangle of thorny and incomprehensible equations. A chance to shine in his Possum Scouts pack sparks Frankie's imagination in *Frankie Pickle and the Pine Run 3000,* when he sets about creating the super speedy model car that will allow him to advance to a higher scout level, and in *Frankie Pickle and the Land of the Lost Recess* a trip to a natural-history museum leaves the preteen with a passion for everything prehistoric. Energized by Wight's upbeat storytelling, the "simple black and white line art [in *Frankie Pickle and the Pine Run 3000*] keeps the momentum of adventure moving forward and readers entertained," according to a *Publishers Weekly* critic.

In addition to his books for elementary-grade readers, Wight is also the author/illustrator of *My Dead Girlfriend,* a manga that focuses on a teenager who knows that his demise is near. However, for Finney Bleak, death may not actually be the end: after their various untimely and dramatic ends, each of his family members has returned in spectral form. School is not much more life-affirming: in fact, at Mephisto Prep, Finney's classmates run the horror-story gamut, ranging from vampires to werewolves and ghouls. As a normal teen, Finney is definitely an oddball, but he still manages to attract the affection of the beautiful Jenny Wraith. When he first meets Jenny at a carnival, the sparks immediately fly, but their relationship strikes a wall when Finney realizes that she is also a ghost. His loneliness and love for Jenny pushes him to the brink, where death may be the best solution in Wight's quirky and entertaining work. High-energy artwork, which a *Publishers Weekly* critic dubbed "poppy," enhances a "fast-paced story" that the critic asserted "will appeal to teenage readers." In *Kliatt* George Galuschak was even more enthusiastic, describing Wight's illustrations "highly original—blocky and cartoony and weirdly gothic." *My Dead Girlfriend,* Galuschak added, is "especially recommended for teens who like their horror with a light touch."

Biographical and Critical Sources

PERIODICALS

Booklist, February 1, 2010, Francisca Goldsmith, review of *Frankie Pickle and the Pine Run 3000,* p. 42.

Kirkus Reviews, April 15, 2009, review of *Frankie Pickle and the Closet of Doom;* January 15, 2010, review of *Frankie Pickle and the Pine Run 3000;* June 1, 2011, review of *Frankie Pickle and the Mathematical Menace.*

Kliatt, March, 2007, George Glauschak, review of *My Dead Girlfriend,* p. 30.

Publishers Weekly, January 29, 2007, review of *My Dead Girlfriend,* p. 49; May 18, 2009, review of *Frankie Pickle and the Closet of Doom,* p. 55; January 4, 2010, review of *Frankie Pickle and the Pine Run 3000,* p. 49.

School Library Journal, July, 2009, Lisa Egly Lehmuller, review of *Frankie Pickle and the Closet of Doom,* p. 69; February, 2010, Carrie Rogers, review of *Frankie Pickle and the Pine Run 3000,* p. 97.

ONLINE

Eric Wight Home Page, http://about.me/ericwight (August 15, 2011).

Graphic Novel Reporter Online, http://www.graphicnovel reporter.com/ (August 1, 2010), John Hogan, interview with Wight.

Simon & Schuster Web site, http://authors.simonand schuster.com/ (August 1, 2010), "Eric Wight."*

* * *

WRIGHT, Simeon 1942-

Personal

Born October, 1942, in Doddsville, MS; son of Moses and Elizabeth Wright (a farmer and sharecropper); married Annie Cole, June 12, 1971. *Religion:* Christian.

Addresses

Home—La Grange, IL. *E-mail*—1955@simeonwright speaks.com.

Career

Author and speaker. Worked as a pipe fitter, beginning c. 1964; retired.

Writings

(With Herb Boyd) *Simeon's Story: An Eyewitness Account of the Kidnapping of Emmett Till,* Lawrence Hill Books (Chicago, IL), 2010.

Sidelights

Simeon Wright chronicles the intersection between his own life and history in *Simeon's Story: An Eyewitness Account of the Kidnapping of Emmett Till,* a memoir coauthored by Herb Boyd. The cousin of Till, the victim of a tragic kidnapping and lynching that became a

Simeon Wright (Reproduced by permission.)

touchstone of the civil rights movement due to its violence and injustice, Wright wrote the book as part of his ongoing effort to help new generations of Americans understand what life was like for people of color living in the South during the early twentieth century. In *Simeon's Story* Wright also highlights the bravery of those who, despite reasonable fears of violent reprisal, bravely spoke up at Till's murder trial and beyond in their search for justice. "Hopefully, this book will be around as a record of what took place in Mississippi in 1955," Wright told Christopher Benson in an interview for *Chicago* magazine.

Wright was born in 1942, one of eleven children to farmer Moses Wright and his second wife, Margaret. After graduating from high school, Simeon would support his family by working as a pipe fitter. However, he was twelve years old and about to enter the fifth grade at the all-colored school in Money, Mississippi in late August of 1955, when his Chicago-born cousin Emmett Till arrived for a visit with the Wright family. A bit of a jokester, Till was known as "Bobo" by family and friends, and his northern upbringing made him unfamiliar with the behavior expected of blacks in the Jim Crow south, where whites were given preferential treatment. In his memoir Wright recalls the fateful Saturday night when he joined Bobo, his brother, and several other boys on a trip to a downtown convenience store. Bobo's whistle at the store's white owner, Carolyn Bryant, had tragic consequences: later that night Bryant's husband and brother in law invaded the Wright house and abducted Till, not even bothering to hide their identity. The fourteen-year-old Chicagoan was discovered the next day in the Tallahatchie River, shot and his body brutalized almost beyond recognition. Although Till's murderers were tried (and later confessed), they were found not guilty by an all-white jury who spent only minutes arriving at a verdict. The 100,000 people who attended Till's funeral in his native Chicago helped start the momentum that sparked the chain of resistance that helped solidify the civil rights movement.

In *Simeon's Story* Wright sets the stage for Till's tragic murder by describing what life was life for him, a typical young black boy growing up in Mississippi under Jim Crow laws. He also recounts the experiences told to him by friends and family members, including memories of terrifying nighttime "rides" by the local Ku Klux Klan, and he paints with vivid detail what it was like in the summer, during ten-hour workdays, picking cotton on his father's farm. Extending his story beyond Till's trial, Wright also recounts his family's move north to Chicago months after the trial, and his father's determined effort to work with the NAACP to condemn the Till verdict as a miscarriage of justice.

Calling *Simeon's Story* a "powerful firsthand account" in which great pains were taken to correct the historical record, Daniel Kraus added in *Booklist* that Wright's "ground-level insights into the character of 14-year-old Bobo . . . are invaluable." The "strong characterization" of Till in *Simeon's Story* "makes this a compelling read," asserted a *Kirkus Reviews* wrier, and in *School Library Journal* Kelly McGorray concluded that "Wright's story is chilling, and his honest account will hook readers from the beginning."

Biographical and Critical Sources

PERIODICALS

Booklist, February 1, 2010, Daniel Kraus, review of *Simeon's Story: An Eyewitness Account of the Kidnapping of Emmett Till,* p. 54.
Chicago, January, 2010, Christopher Benson, "Eyewitness Account: Emmett Till's Cousin Simeon Wright Seeks to Set the Record Straight."
Kirkus Reviews, December 15, 2009, review of *Simeon's Story.*
School Library Journal, February, 2010, Kelly McGorray, review of *Simeon's Story,* p. 135.
Smithsonian, November, 2009, Abby Callard, interview with Wright, p. 26.

ONLINE

Simeon Wright Home Page, http://simeonwrightspeaks.com (June 12, 2011).*

*   *   *

YEE, Ying S.
See LEE, Y.S.

*   *   *

YELCHIN, Eugene 1956-

Personal

Born 1956, in Leningrad, USSR (now St. Petersburg, Russia); immigrated to United States, 1983; mother a dance teacher; married Mary Kuryla (a writer); children: Isaac, Ezra. *Education:* Leningrad Institute of Theatre Arts, degree (set design); University of Southern California, master's degree (film production). *Religion:* Jewish.

Addresses

Home—Topanga, CA. *Agent*—Steven Malk, Writers House, 7660 Fay Ave., No. 338H, La Jolla, CA 92037. *E-mail*—eugeneyelchin@gmail.com.

Career

Illustrator, fine-art painter, and filmmaker. Set and costume designer for Soviet theatre until 1983; *Boston Globe,* Boston, MA, editorial illustrator, beginning 1983; storyboard artist, beginning mid-1980s; director of television commercials, beginning 1990s. Character designer for animated film *Rango,* 2011. *Exhibitions:* Paintings exhibited in museums and galleries throughout Europe and the United States, including solo exhibitions at Roy G. Biv Gallery, Palm Springs, CA, 1995; Umerov Gallery, Minneapolis, MN, 1995; Cypress College Gallery, Cypress, CA, 1996; Diane Nelson Fine Art, Laguna Beach, CA, 1997; Jan Baum Gallery, Los Angeles, CA, 2002, 2005; Mizel Art Center, Denver, CO, 2006; and Hillel USC, Los Angeles, 2007.

Member

Society of Children's Book Writers and Illustrators, Directors Guild of America.

Awards, Honors

Tomi DePaola Illustration Award, Society of Children's Book Writers and Illustrators, 2006; National Jewish Book Award, 2010, for *The Rooster Prince of Breslov.*

Writings

ILLUSTRATOR

Breaking Stalin's Nose, Henry Holt (New York, NY), 2011.

ILLUSTRATOR

Gary Clemente, *Cosom Gets an Ear,* Modern Signs Press (Los Alamitos, CA), 1994.
Karen Beaumont, *Who Ate All the Cookie Dough?,* Henry Holt (New York, NY), 2008.
Musharraf Ali Farooqui, *The Cobbler's Holiday; or, Why Ants Don't Have Shoes,* Roaring Book Press (New York, NY), 2008.
Ann Hodgman, *The House of a Million Pets,* Henry Holt (New York, NY), 2008.
(And coauthor with wife Mary Kuryla-Yelchin as The Ghost Society) *Ghost Files: The Haunting Truth,* HarperCollins (New York, NY), 2008.

(And coauthor with Mary Kuryla) *Heart of a Snowman,* HarperCollins (New York, NY), 2009.

Candace Fleming, *Seven Hungry Babies,* Atheneum Books for Young Readers (New York, NY), 2010.

Ann Redisch Stampler, *The Rooster Prince of Breslov,* Clarion Books (New York, NY), 2010.

Lee Wardlaw, *Won-Ton: A Cat Tale Told in Haiku,* Henry Holt (New York, NY), 2010.

Mary Kuryla, *The Next Door Bear,* Harper (New York, NY), 2011.

Barbara Joosse, *Dog Parade,* Houghton Mifflin Harcourt (Boston, MA), 2011.

Contributor of illustrations to periodicals and newspapers.

Sidelights

Born in the former USSR, Eugene Yelchin worked in Russian theatre before trading life under communism for a fresh start in the United States. In addition to winning respect for his work in advertising art and film— he designed the first polar-bear advertisements used by Coca Cola—Yelchin has become a widely exhibited fine-art painter. He has also found an outlet for his creativity in children's picture books, where his work appears alongside stories by Candace Fleming, Ann Hodgman, Lee Wardlaw, Ann Redisch Stampler, Barbara Joosse, and his own wife, author Mary Kuryla. In 2011 Yelchin also added "author" to his list of credits with a self-illustrated story that draws on his memories of growing up in the USSR: *Breaking Stalin's Nose.*

Eugene Yechin's illustration projects include Candace Fleming's engaging, toddler-friendly story in **Seven Hungry Babies.** (Illustration copyright © 2010 by Eugene Yelchin. Reproduced by permission of Atheneum Books for Young Readers, an imprint of Simon & Schuster Publishing Division.)

In Karen Beaumont's *Who Ate All the Cookie Dough?,* a lift-the-flap book that was also one of Yelchin's first illustration projects, a kangaroo searches for a cookie-dough thief. In bringing to life Beaumont's humorous tale, he creates what *School Library Journal* contributor Marge Loch-Wouters described as "stylized gouache illustrations" that feature the artist's characteristic "light, humorous touch." "The amusing illustrations of popular animals and the jaunty rhythm and rhyme will make this a favorite," concluded a *Kirkus Reviews* writer of the same book.

Yelchin revisions several unusual folktales in his artwork for Musharraf Ali Farooqui's Persian folktale retelling *The Cobbler's Holiday; or, Why Ants Don't Wear Shoes* and Stampler's *The Rooster Prince of Breslov,* the letter which updates a traditional Yiddish story. Farooqui's "dainty, droll fable" is enlivened with "a modish Jazz Age aesthetic" that includes what a *Publishers Weekly* critic described as "flappers and dandies sport-[ing] ritzy top hats and beaded caps." In *Kirkus Reviews* a critic concluded that Yelchin's use of "shifting perspectives and placement add . . . to the fun" of Farooqui's tale. Stampler's story, which focuses on a monarch who trades the pressures of leadership for life as a farmyard rooster, also benefits from what *School Library Journal* contributor Rachel Kamin described as "imaginative, graphite and gouache illustrations" that capture the energy of the author's "witty retelling." Praising *The Rooster Prince of Breslov* as "a venerable . . . tale with a message for our time," *Horn Book* reviewer Joanna Rudge Long added that the artist captures the wry humor in Stampler's text. Yelchin underlines the story's subtlety and humor with expressively exaggerated poses and apt caricatures rendered in minimal line and vivid gouache," the critic added.

Hodgman's *The House of a Million Pets* is a memoir of the author's experiences sharing her rural New England home with a menagerie of critters over many years. Described by *New York Times Book Review* contributor J.D. Biersdorfer as "part autobiography, part pet-care guide," *The House of a Million Pets* benefits from "Yelchin's black-and-white illustrations [which] add a note of whimsy." Featuring everything from cats and dogs to bunnies, voles, canaries, a prairie dog, and dozens of pygmy mice, the artist's "realistic, expressive animal drawings" help make the book "a natural for reading aloud," according to *Booklist* critic Debbie Carton. In *School Library Journal* Patricia Manning predicted that Yelchin's "small, soft black-and-white illustrations" are "certain to prompt pet-craving urges" in young readers, while a *Kirkus Reviews* critic dubbed the art for *The House of a Million Pets* "absolutely charming."

Described by Loch-Wouters as a "bouncy, onomatopoeic tale," Fleming's *Seven Hungry Babies* finds a mother bird busy finding food for her hungry young nestlings. Yelchin's use of "unexpected perspectives" and clean tones of blue, yellow, and red help make the book "perfect for group storytimes," according to Wouters, while a *Kirkus Reviews* writer noted the effective combination of the artist's "gouache illustrations" and Fleming's "perfectly pitched" text. A feline is the focus of *Won Ton: A Cat Told in Haiku,* and here Wardlaw's "Japanese haiku theme . . . is carried through with elements and backgrounds lifted from old woodblock prints," according to a *Publishers Weekly* critic.

Biographical and Critical Sources

PERIODICALS

Booklist, September 1, 2007, Debbie Carton, review of *The House of a Million Pets,* p. 110; January 1, 2010, Daniel Kraus, review of *Seven Hungry Babies,* p. 98.

Bulletin of the Center for Children's Books, November, 2007, Deborah Stevenson, review of *The House of a Million Pets,* p. 125.

Denver Westworld, September, 2006, Michael Paglia, "Eugene Yelchin: A Thousand Casualties."

Horn Book, January-February, 2008, Tanya D. Auger, review of *The House of a Million Pets,* p. 111; September-October, 2010, Joanna Rudge Long, review of *The Rooster Prince of Breslov,* p. 103.

Kirkus Reviews, August 1, 2007, review of *The House of a Million Pets;* May 1, 2008, review of *Who Ate All the Cookie Dough?;* August 15, 2008, review of *The Cob-* *bler's Holiday; or, Why Ants Don't Wear Shoes;* October 15, 2009, review of *Heart of a Snowman;* February 15, 2010, review of *Seven Hungry Babies.*

New York Times Book Review, October 14, 2007, J.D. Biersdorfer, review of *The House of a Million Pets,* p. 21.

Orange County Weekly, November, 1997, Rebecca Schoenkopf, "Shroud of Yelchin: Russian Artist Is a Mystery."

Publishers Weekly, September 3, 2007, review of *The House of a Million Pets,* p. 59; September 15, 2008, review of *The Cobbler's Holiday,* p. 66; October 26, 2009, review of *Heart of a Snowman,* p. 56; December 6, 2010, review of *Won Ton: A Cat Tale Told in Haiku,* p. 47.

School Library Journal, December, 2007, Patricia Manning, review of *The House of a Million Pets,* p. 152; July, 2008, Marge Loch-Wouters, review of *Who Ate All the Cookie Dough?,* p. 66; September, 2008, Mary Jean Smith, review of *The Cobbler's Holiday,* p. 145; October, 2009, Maureen Wade, review of *Heart of a Snowman,* p. 84; February, 2010, Marge Loch-Wouters, review of *Seven Hungry Babies,* p. 82; October, 2010, Rachel Kamin, review of *The Rooster Prince of Breslov,* p. 104.

ONLINE

Eugene Yelchin Home Page, http://www.eugeneyelchin. com (July 15, 2011).

Writers House Web site, http://www.writershouseart.com/ (July 15, 2011), "Eugene Yelchin."